Library of Congress Cataloguing in Publication Data
When the Rain Returns:
Toward Justice and Reconciliation in Palestine and Israel
Prepared by an International Quaker Working Party
on Israel and Palestine

Working Party Members: Kathy Bergen, Tony Bing (Co-clerk),
Max Carter, Helena Cobban, Jim Fine (Co-clerk), Deborah Gerner,
Stevie Krayer, Richard McCutcheon, Emily Mnisi, Jim Matlack,
Ron Mock, Hilda Silverman, Zoharah Simmons, Jean Zaru

Published by the American Friends Service Committee

**American Friends
Service Committee**

ISBN: 0-910082-48-0

Acronyms

AFSC	American Friends Service Committee
CMEP	Churches for Middle East Peace
CPT	Christian Peacemaker Teams
EAPPI	Ecumenical Accompaniment Program in Palestine and Israel
E.U.	European Union
FMEP	Foundation for Middle East Peace
FPT	Friends Peace Teams
GCMHP	Gaza Community Mental Health Program
ICC	International Criminal Court
ICG	International Crisis Group
IDF	Israeli Defense Forces
ILA	Israel Lands Authority
IQWP	International Quaker Working Party
ISM	International Solidarity Movement
J.A.	Jewish Agency
JNF	Jewish National Fund
NGO	Non-governmental organization
OPT	Occupied Palestinian Territories
P.A.	Palestinian Authority
PASSIA	Palestinian Academic Society for the Study of International Affairs
PCR	Palestinian Center for Rapprochement between People
PIPA	Program on International Public Attitudes
PLC	Palestinian Legislative Council
PLO	Palestinian Liberation Organization
U.N.	United Nations
UNGA	United Nations General Assembly
UNLU	Unified National Leadership of the Uprising
UNSC	United Nations Security Council
UNRWA	United Nations Relief and Works Agency
UPMRC	Union of Palestinian Medical Relief Committees
U.S.	United States
WZO	World Zionist Organization
YWCA	Young Women's Christian Association

When the
Rain Returns

Toward Justice and Reconciliation

in Palestine and Israel

Prepared by an
International Quaker Working Party
on Israel and Palestine

Published by

**American Friends
Service Committee**

Table of Contents

APPENDICES

Maps and Charts throughout the text

Foreword

Honoring all men is reaching God in every man.
—George Fox, Epistle 53

[Peace work is] an effort of one generation to see that
the next generation does not go through bloodshed.
—Shimon Peres, speaking at the Fourth World Summit
of Nobel Peace Laureates, Rome, November 2003

We have shown [in the Geneva Accords] that it is not necessary
that in order to fulfill my aspirations, I must destroy yours.
Instead, we show that in order to fulfill my aspirations
they must be reconciled with yours.
—Yasser Abed Rabbo, Former Minister of Information,
Palestinian Authority, December 3, 2003

Its authors and the American Friends Service Committee offer *When the Rain Returns: Toward Justice and Reconciliation in Palestine and Israel* as an aid to reflection and discussion about one of the most difficult problems in the world today, a conflict which has spanned six decades and been the source of at least six regional wars and countless acts of bloodshed. Though it speaks as clearly and simply as the circumstances allow, *When the Rain Returns* is necessarily a complex book. How can any sincere attempt to engage, understand, and respond to the Israeli-Palestine conflict not be complex?

At its most basic level, the book reports on a three-week trip through the region in June 2002, undertaken by fourteen concerned women and men, some already highly knowledgeable, experienced, and well-read in the history of Israel and Palestine and others bringing fresh eyes to the subject. Here they record what they heard and saw as they engaged nearly a hundred stakeholders in the conflict, among them Jewish Israelis in Israel and settlers in the occupied/disputed territories; Palestinian-Israeli citizens, Palestinian residents in Gaza and the West Bank, and Palestinian refugees living in the surrounding countries. They bring us the voices of leaders from Jewish, Christian, and Muslim communities; of peace and human rights activists on both sides of the conflict; of scholars, political leaders, diplomats, and military leaders in Israel and Palestine, Egypt, Syria, Lebanon, and Jordan. The authors also bring us the fruits of wide reading in the literature of the conflict. In recommending works in their bibliography, the authors write that calling a work "useful" does not mean that they agree with it but "that we believe it expresses a perspective that needs to be considered." Their list of recommended readings and useful websites is extensive.

The book is demanding on a reader, then, because its purpose is to present with integrity a number of passionate, engaged, sometimes self-justifying, apparently irreconcilable narratives, many of them predicated as Hanan Ashrawi says, on "...the denial or distortion of the narrative of the other...." The reader may be baffled by the contradictions, brought to tears by the suffering and anger which these narratives recount. That is a strength of the book. In *Some Fruits of Solitude*, William Penn wrote, "It is but too common for some to say both are to blame, which is a base neutrality. Others will cry, they are both alike; thereby involving the injured with the guilty...." The authors have tried to record and assess what they heard, neither resorting to such an indifferent, *base neutrality* nor confusing the injured with those who injure them, in order to hide behind a false even-handedness. They speak tenderly, bear poignant witness to the suffering on all sides of the conflict, and offer a Quaker perspective on the Israel-Palestine conflict deeply rooted in four key principles. Put briefly, these principles hold that:

1] All persons are of equal humanity and are entitled, as individuals, to human rights.

2] The rights of all people who have a direct stake in the situation should be respected and each of these direct stakeholders given an equal voice in the process of determining the outcome to this conflict.

3] Only mutual respect can lead to long-term security; no human community can assure its own security by imposing a state of insecurity on others.

4] Violence always leads to more violence; creative nonviolent ways do exist that allow the parties to this conflict to work together to bring about a fair, stable, and hope-filled outcome.

When the Rain Returns examines the most difficult questions through the lens of these principles. For example, can negotiating the "final phase" issues continue to be postponed? Or should the future status of Jerusalem as an "open city" and shared capital of two independent states, or a *corpus separatum* internationally administered, be addressed immediately? Do Israel's policies on the settlements, on fence- and road-building in the West Bank, render a non-dependent, politically and economically viable Palestinian state impossible? How can Israel remain both a democratic and a Jewish state? Is there any hope for nonviolent resolutions of the Israel-Palestine conflict?

The authors not only raise such questions, they offer their own considered judgments on what will advance a just peace in the conflict. They work scrupulously to be accurate and balanced in their own witness and take their stand with those *on all sides* who are for peace, for all those who suffer the consequences of this conflict deserve better than an evasive "base neutrality." *When the Rain Returns* also exemplifies some further words of William Penn: "They have a right to censure that have a heart to help. The rest is cruelty, not justice." For in even their most stringent criticisms of the parties in this conflict, these authors always have a heart to help.

Time does not stand still while a book goes to press, and peace is always a work in progress, so even the latest book on the Palestine-Israel conflict can only be a part of the long conversation. By the time these words are in print, new events will have occurred, and readers will need to assess for themselves such questions as the long-term impact of the unofficial "Geneva Accords," or what will result from continued Palestinian, Israeli, and international opposition to the building of the fence. But we are convinced that the spiritual and political wisdom of the four principles enunciated here will stand the test of new events and throw light on how to go forward.

An Emperor said of the Roman Legions that they created a desert and called it peace. The authors of this report have traveled through such a human-created desert, and they, as well as staff of the American Friends Service Committee who worked with them, have lived with writing about it for nearly twenty months. It has taken a great measure of intellectual and spiritual energy to keep faith with the stories they have heard, the contending visions of a solution to the Palestine-Israel conflict. Out of their experience they call on us to imagine creating a different landscape, one where peace will refresh and restore like the rain and justice will flow like a river. With gratitude for their work and vision, the American Friends Service Committee commends *When the Rain Returns* as useful for engaging the issues and advancing the discussion for people concerned to help bring a just peace to Israel and Palestine.

Paul A. Lacey, Chair
Board of Directors
American Friends Service Committee

3/11/04

Acknowledgements

We would like to acknowledge the work of the following persons and groups who made this document possible:

Helping the International Quaker Working Party with arranging meetings in the Middle East were: in Jordan, West Bank, Gaza, and Israel: Lilian Peters (AFSC), David Jackman (AFSC), Tareq al-Bakri (AFSC), and Suzanne Hammad (AFSC); in Lebanon: Saoud al-Mawla; in Syria, Mahat Khoury and Ibrahim Hamidi; in Egypt, Chris and Karen Anderson (Mennonite Central Committee).

We appreciate the time Quakers and friends of Quakers spent reading the document and sending us their reactions to it. These readers include: Bill Cousins, Don Peretz, David Neuhaus, Ian Lustick, Thomas Ricks, Jim Satterwhite, Jonathan Kuttab, Paul Hopkins, Samia Khoury, Ann Hardt, Ann Stever, Nadia Hijab, Richard Preston, Leila Barclay, Susan Schaefer Davis,Tippy and Calvin Schwabe, and Allan Solomonow.

We thank Carol Huang, Rachael Kamel, and Karen Cromley for helping to prepare the manuscript for publication. We thank the people close to us in our lives for supporting us, and our work on this project, for many long months.

Finally, we would like to thank all the monthly and yearly meetings of the Religious Society of Friends (Quakers) who offered us spiritual and financial support as we made our journey and wrote about our experiences.

A Note on the Text

- We have tried to adopt common transliterations for Arabic and Hebrew words used in this text.

- We have used English spelling and usage as known in the United States, with apologies to readers from other countries.

- On many occasions we use direct quotes to report on what we were told. These quotations are taken as honestly and directly as possible from meticulous notes taken during most of our encounters by one group member. However, several other group members were also taking close notes during our meetings, and where necessary these notes have been drawn on as supplementary sources.

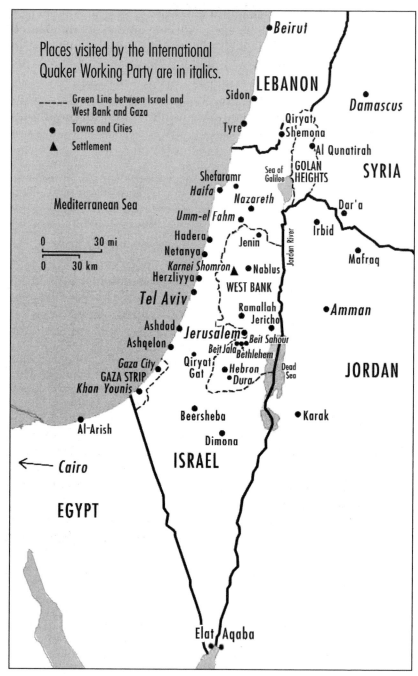

Places visited by the International
Quaker Working Party are in italics.

‐ ‐ ‐ ‐ ‐ Green Line between Israel and
West Bank and Gaza
● Towns and Cities
▲ Settlement

Israel, West Bank, Gaza and surrounding countries.

Preface

Our International Quaker Working Party on the Israel-Palestine Conflict (IQWP) traveled to the Middle East in June 2002, out of a concern for the suffering being experienced by our brothers and sisters of that part of the world. While there, we began and ended each day with a period of silent worship. Speaking out of the silence, we would share with one another our reactions to what we were experiencing, and we often asked ourselves what we should do with what we were seeing and hearing—how we might move beyond silence to words, and beyond words to action.

Then, in the months after we returned to our homes around the world, we continued to labor together over how best to describe the situation we had experienced so that we might help move as many other people as possible to take actions to help build a just and lasting peace between Palestinians and Israelis. That process of post-trip deliberation delayed the production of this report, but we feel that it enriched (or, to use a Quaker term, *seasoned*) its content considerably. In the meantime, to our sorrow, the situation in Israel/Palestine deteriorated in some ways from what we had seen in June 2002. Nonetheless, our impressions and experiences have remained generally valid.

When we visited the Holy Land[1] that June, it often seemed full of emptiness and silence. We stood at the Erez checkpoint between the Gaza Strip and Israel and saw only vast, bare expanses of concrete where, some years earlier, transit roads and lengthy pedestrian passage-ways were filled with a bustle of Palestinians crossing to jobs inside Israel from which they were now banned. Even the Israeli soldiers deployed at Erez seemed not to be fully present there. They appeared to us only as disembodied voices speaking through narrow slats in fortified pillboxes.

In Hebron, in the south of the West Bank region,[2] we walked

---

1 Many of us feel uncomfortable with the notion that any one portion of Planet Earth is more sacred than another. However, the term "Holy Land" is one that is easy to use and easily understood throughout much of the world. We use it in this report synonymously with the terms "Israel/Palestine" and "Palestine/Israel," and we understand all three terms to refer to the area between the Mediterranean and the Jordan River that was designated as the "Palestine" that was ruled until 1947 by Britain under a mandate from the League of Nations.

2 The West Bank is an area of 5,860 square kilometers of territory lying just west of the Jordan River, a fact that gives it this name. Many Israeli-nationalist hardliners, and the Israeli government, use the phrase "Judea and Samaria" to delineate this same region.

through nearly deserted downtown markets that gave the impression of a city without a living center. As our bus sped along newly-built "bypass" roads in the West Bank these rapid, intercity highways often seemed quite empty. (Palestinian vehicles were forbidden to use them. Indeed, these vehicles were trapped inside hundreds of the area's Palestinian villages and towns by massive, Israeli-built mounds of dirt and stone.) In one part of Jerusalem, we sat with an Israeli friend who broke off giving a highly articulate presentation about the political situation to sit in silent grief at the recent murder of a friend's daughter at the hands of a suicide bomber. In Tel Aviv, we drove along streets of once-bustling shops and sidewalk cafés that stood nearly deserted in the late afternoon as the Israelis who would normally be frequenting them stayed home from fear that any public place might be the target for the next suicide bomber. In countries neighboring Palestine/Israel, we looked into the eyes of Palestinians who had lived through a multi-decade exile from the homeland they loved: they talked with us about their plight, and described their sense of a world that continued to turn a deaf ear to their cries for justice.

Amidst all the suffering that we witnessed, we met scores of people whose outlook and actions were marked by kindness, resourcefulness, and a continued commitment to building a decent, hope-filled peace in their part of the world. But in both the Palestinian and Israeli communities, many of the peace-and-justice activists we met with told us that the failure of the diplomatic efforts of the 1990s had sometimes brought them to the brink of despair.

It had been with a good deal of humility that, in Spring 2002, fourteen of us responded to an invitation from the American Friends Service Committee (AFSC) that an international group of Quakers should visit the Middle East to see what the Religious Society of Friends (Quakers) might be called to do at this time of suffering for Israelis and Palestinians. We were not clear what we might be able to contribute in terms of relieving the suffering of these two peoples, but we felt we should make a witness to our faith that hope is a reality even in the bleakest situations. In our own lifetimes we have witnessed the power of nonviolence in achieving positive transformations of a number of conflicts—in Chile, the Philippines, Eastern Europe, the Baltic states, South Africa, and elsewhere—that at times seemed just as intractable as that between Israelis and Palestinians. Those examples strengthened our faith that even in this latter troubled relationship fear and distrust can one day be overcome, and the relationship transformed into one of respectful coexistence and even active cooperation.

We tried to prepare ourselves thoroughly and prayerfully for our journey, but even so we were shocked by the numerous manifestations of injustice and violence that we encountered. When we arrived in Jerusalem, the city's people were still reeling from the events of the preceding day, when Palestinian bombers detonated two bombs in Jewish-populated parts of the city, killing 19 Israelis. Three nights later, during street battles in Nablus, Israeli soldiers fired a tank-shell that killed an elderly Palestinian man and two children. Everywhere we went in Gaza and the West Bank, we saw Israeli soldiers—many of them impressionable teenagers—as they worked to impose a harsh regime of military rule on the 2.9 million Palestinians living in the occupied territories. As we pursued the routines of daily life inside Israel, we experienced the burden that the omnipresent sense of dread and the country's heightened internal security measures were placing upon the lives of Israel's people, too.

As a result of what we experienced on our visit, we concluded that unproductive silence was not an option for us. Too many people in our world in the past hundred years have perished because no one spoke out. In lifting up the voices of those Palestinians and Israelis who work against imposing odds for justice and reconciliation, we hope to help fashion a new discourse about peace in the Middle East: one that speaks of love not hate, of reconciliation not revenge, of hope not despair.

While we have come to unity about the document overall, we vary in how strongly each of us supports some of the specific ideas, words, or phrases used in it. We have endeavored to make the process of writing it, as well as the trip itself, spirit-led in the best tradition of Quaker thought and social action.

We dedicate it to all those past and present who have continued to affirm life in the midst of the death and destruction that have held sway in the Holy Land for far too long.

Kathy Bergen	Tony Bing	Max Carter
Helena Cobban	Jim Fine	Deborah Gerner
Stevie Krayer	Rick McCutcheon	Emily Mnisi
Jim Matlack	Ron Mock	Hilda Silverman
Zoharah Simmons	Jean Zaru	

*Via Dolorosa**

These days, when I lower my pitcher
into the well, I draw forth
only salt water. I don't see how
our thirst is going to be quenched.

Yet I believe the deepest wellspring
remains uncontaminated. This at least
I can do for you, sister,
since I still have tears

While you have wept your eyes
to a dry desolation: weep
on your behalf till the rain
returns and fills the riverbed.

Stevie Krayer

---

* Stevie Krayer, a member of our group who is a Welsh
Quaker of Jewish heritage, wrote this poem shortly after
our trip and dedicated it to Jean Zaru, a Palestinian
Quaker who was also a member of the group.

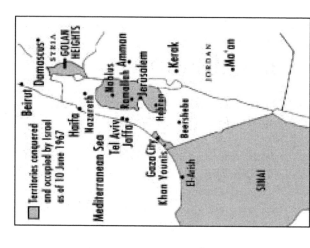

Palestine during the British Mandate, 1917–1947.

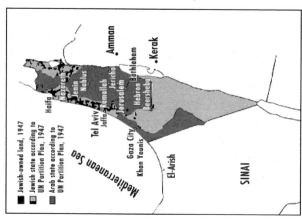

The United Nations Partition Plan for Palestine, 1947, showing proposed Jewish and Arab states; and Jewish-owned land as of 1947. Jerusalem proposed to be ruled as a corpus separatum.

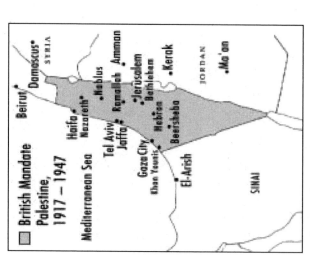

Israel and the territories occupied during the June War, 1967.

Maps adapted from PASSIA

[1]

Introduction

I hope you will address the causes of the crisis, not just the symptoms.
—Marouf el-Bakhit, Jordanian Foreign Ministry, 2002

[T]ruth is rather unpalatable at times. Sometimes it is harder to speak the truth
than to lose control, lash out and call upon others to do the same. But he who
knows the truth, the truth that alone can help us, is compelled to speak out,
no matter whether a whole people is listening or only a few individuals.
—Martin Buber, 1945

In June of 2002, a group of fourteen individuals traveled to Israel/Palestine and to neighboring countries to learn at firsthand about the grievous situation in which Israelis and Palestinians then found themselves. We are those travelers, and this is a report on our visit, and on our subsequent deliberations over what we had experienced together. Eleven of us are Quakers from different parts of the world, including one who is a Quaker of Jewish origin. Three of us—one a Muslim, one a Mennonite, the other a secular Jew—are individuals who have worked for many years with Quaker organizations. One of us, a Palestinian Quaker, is a direct party to the situation in Palestine/Israel. The rest of us are not as directly involved, though some of us have a long history of personal engagement with the region. Like millions of other women and men from around the world, however, all of us have felt a strong and loving concern for the well-being of the peoples of this troubled land. Throughout our engagement with this project, we have been informed and inspired by the traditional Quaker testimonies on equality, simplicity, truthfulness, and peace, as expressed in the quest for justice, nonviolence, and an end to militarism.

We fully understand that the conflict between Israelis and Palestinians, a struggle over land, identity, and political control, has been going on for many decades and represents today one of the most difficult dilemmas facing the international community. The long-drawn-out hostility between Palestinians and Israelis has

1

directly or indirectly spawned half a dozen regional wars in the past six decades. It has provided a pretext for increased militarization throughout the region, including the development of nuclear weapons. It has led, finally, to the ending or severe blighting of the lives of millions of people—most of them civilians—as a result of violent actions undertaken by both states and non-state actors.

In this context, it is not easy to discern how justice is to be served and a state of peace achieved between two groups of people each struggling to realize its national identity, national institutions, and right to self-determination within the same small territory. But we want to unite with the words of two very thoughtful, committed social activists from the region. The first is Jeff Halper, a Jewish Israeli peace activist who said,

> I do not locate myself on either of those [Israeli or Palestinian] 'sides'. For me, ... 'sides' means something different altogether. I am on the 'side' of Israelis and Palestinians who seek a just peace that addresses Palestinian rights of self-determination as well as Israeli concerns of security and regional integration. I am on the 'side' that stands for equality, human rights, democracy, peaceful co-existence and regional economic development.[3]

The second of these visionary activists is Hanan Ashrawi, a Palestinian teacher and community leader who has said,

> Neither side can lay claim to a monopoly of pain and suffering, in the same way as it cannot claim exclusivity of narrative and legitimacy... The denial or distortion of the narrative of the other has served as a convenient vehicle for the dehumanization of the adversary and hence as a justification for all forms of violations and atrocities... Historical records must be reconciled, whether in the recognition of the horror of the Holocaust and all its horrendous implications, or in the historical victimization of the Palestinian people and their dual tragedy of dispossession and exile, on the one hand, and oppression and occupation on the other.[4]

By the time of our trip, the two peoples of the Holy Land—the Palestinians and the Israelis—had been locked for 21 months already in a protracted process of deadly violence called the second, or Al-Aqsa, *intifada*.[5] To most of the world, the main features of

---

3 Jeff Halper, speaking at the European Union, Brussels, June 2002.

4 Hanan Ashrawi's acceptance speech on the award of the Sydney (Australia) Peace Prize, November 6, 2003.

5 *Intifada* is the Arabic word for "uprising" (literally, "shaking off"). The Palestinians' first *intifada* ran from 1987 through 1993. The second *intifada*, sometimes called the *Al-Aqsa Intifada* after the name of the central place of Muslim worship in Jerusalem, started in September 2000.

the second *intifada* were the use by hardline Palestinian activists of suicide bomb attacks against Israeli civilians and soldiers, and the use by Israeli security forces of such tactics as firing live ammunition into crowds of unarmed demonstrators, demolishing the homes of families and associates of terror suspects, undertaking extra-judicial killings of suspected Palestinian militants, imprisoning thousands of Palestinians—many of whom never saw the inside of a courtroom—and imposing strict movement controls and lengthy round-the-clock lockdowns on whole communities of Palestinians in the West Bank and Gaza.

Between the beginning of the second *intifada* in September 2000 and our visit in June 2002, this protracted wave of violence had led to the deaths of 1,399 Palestinians (including 234 minors under the age of 18) at the hands of Israelis, and 470 Israelis (including 58 minors) at the hands of Palestinians.[6] The violence continued during our visit, and throughout our preparation of this report. One major purpose of our visit was to learn more about the roots of this violence, and the prospects for ending it, than could be learned from most of the global media.

By June 2002, it was clear that the Oslo peace process, which had held out some hope throughout most of the 1990s that the Palestinian-Israeli conflict might soon be ended, had led only to a dead-end of distrust and severe disillusionment. No other similarly hopeful peace effort seemed to be in sight. While we were in the Middle East, U.S. President George W. Bush did make one significant speech in which he outlined a vision of a two-state outcome, with the Palestinians gaining the right to create their own independent state.[7] In the months that followed, however, the Bush Administration did little to realize that vision. In June 2003, Bush took a step toward reengagement in Palestinian-Israeli diplomacy when he revived his administration's interest in a "Roadmap" for Israeli-Palestinian peace, which had been crafted with three other outside powers in the latter months of 2002. But at this writing, the results of the Roadmap still look very slim.

---

6 Figures totaled from the "Monthly Statistics" tables on the website of B'tselem, the Israeli Information Center for Human Rights in the Occupied Territories at <http://www.btselem.org/English/Statistics/Al_Aqsa_Fatalities_Tables.asp>. The total number of violence-related deaths was higher. This page on B'tselem's site indicates the circumstances in which other such deaths occurred.

7 See chapter 9 below.

The experiences we had on our visit provided an informative snapshot of the situation in the Palestinian areas and Israel and its effect on the people living there—indeed, as we noted above, in some ways the situation worsened over the months that followed. (Not even the momentous events in Iraq, where in March 2003 Bush launched a broad military assault that toppled President Saddam Hussein from power and left the U.S.-dominated coalition with its own burdensome military occupation to administer, affected the situation in Israel/Palestine very much.) We hope, therefore, that our account can help build the kind of informed public understanding of this situation that will be necessary as faith groups, other civil society actors, and governments around the world all ponder how to give constructive help to the effort to build a just, sustainable, and hope-filled peace between these two peoples.

Our group convened first in **Jordan,** a country that has a long (and sometimes troubled) history of involvement with the Palestinian issue, and that is host to around two million Palestinian refugees. Jordan has had a peace treaty with Israel since 1994. We spent a few days there meeting with Jordanian and United Nations (U.N.) officials, as well as representatives of Jordanian, Palestinian, and international civil society groups. We visited a large refugee camp near the capital, Amman, that hosted scores of thousands of Palestinian refugees, many of whom have been in exile from their homeland since as long ago as 1948.

After a few days in Jordan, we fanned out in small groups to three other Arab countries that have been strongly affected by the Palestinian-Israeli conflict. Some of us went to **Lebanon,** which hosts some 430,000 displaced Palestinians.[8] Others went to **Syria,** host to a slightly greater number of displaced Palestinians. The remainder went to **Egypt,** the most powerful and populous of the Arab states bordering Israel. Egypt, which has had a peace treaty with Israel since 1979, currently hosts around 40,000 Palestinian refugees. In each of these places, we spent a few days meeting with people from the local community to hear their views of the Israeli-Palestinian conflict and their vision for resolving it. In addition, those of us who traveled to Lebanon and Syria held in-depth dis-

---

8 In this context, the terms "Palestinian refugees" and "displaced Palestinians" are interchangeable.

cussions with Palestinian refugees living in those countries.

We reconvened in Amman and traveled in cars westward to the Jordan River, where we crossed the King Hussein (or "Allenby") Bridge into the Israeli-occupied West Bank. We spent the next two weeks in Palestine and Israel, staying together as a group as much as we could. We were based mainly in Jerusalem, but we had overnight stays in Gaza and Haifa and undertook numerous daytrips outside Jerusalem, going sometimes to the West Bank, sometimes to Israel, and sometimes to both on a single day. In our time in the region we had substantive discussions with more than 90 people altogether, most of them Palestinians or Israelis.[9]

We soon realized that it was the Palestinian member of our group, Jean Zaru, the presiding clerk of Ramallah Friends Meeting in the West Bank, who was having the hardest time of any of us in undertaking the planned itinerary. So long as we were in Israel or the occupied territories, Jean was officially restricted from traveling anywhere outside her home city, Ramallah. For her even to be in East Jerusalem, a part of the Israeli-occupied West Bank that is ten miles from her home and with which she has many close ties, was technically illegal, given the stringent movement controls that the Israeli authorities were maintaining on the Palestinians of the occupied territories. The rest of us were able to travel around much of Israel, the West Bank, and Gaza, and to cross both the "green line," which marks the pre-1967 boundary between Israel and the West Bank, and the heavily barricaded frontier between Israel and Gaza, while suffering only minor delays and inconvenience. Jean, whose long-time family home is in this land, was completely forbidden from being in any of these places, or indeed anywhere else outside the fence that encircled Ramallah.[10]

Our intention was to visit quietly and sympathetically with as many people in both national communities, and spanning as broad a range of age, occupation, life experience, and political views, as we could. We wanted to express as best we could,

---

9 See Appendix B for a list of the people whom we met.

10 Some weeks before the planned trip, AFSC applied to the Israeli military authorities for permission for Jean to travel with the group, and AFSC staff members then made repeated follow-up contacts with the Israeli military to support this request. But permission was never granted.

through our presence, our words, and our careful listening, our compassion for the many forms of suffering both peoples were living through. We hoped to learn from our Israeli, Palestinian, and other Arab friends how they themselves saw the situation, and to discern from them and with them where the possibilities for a successful escape from the violence and oppression, and the building of a just and hopeful peace, might lie. We had also hoped to visit and worship with our Quaker brothers and sisters in the West Bank city of Ramallah—but because of the complete "closure" the Israeli military authorities maintained on the city this last, apparently simple, goal was not to be fulfilled.

Our journeying was informed by the 140-year history of international Quaker concern for, and activism in, Palestine/Israel. In the 1860s, New England Quakers established a school for girls in Ramallah. Over the generations this endeavor grew into a thriving, two-campus school that today provides a Quaker-based primary and secondary education to more than 900 students of both sexes. Around the school community, a gathering of Palestinian Quakers grew up, which has continued to this day to uphold the traditional Quaker testimonies in the midst of this troubled land.

In 1948, as Quaker aid workers in Europe were winding down programs they had run for Jewish and other residents of the vast "displaced persons" camps that were then scattered throughout that continent, AFSC was asked by the U.N. to organize relief services for the 200,000 Palestinians who—having fled or been expelled from their homes in the areas that became the state of Israel—ended up living as refugees in the Gaza Strip. AFSC (which was also the main sponsor of our fact-finding mission) continued to be the main outside provider of relief services to Gaza's refugee population for the next eighteen months, after which the newly-created United Nations Relief and Works Agency for Palestinian refugees (UNRWA) took over the work.

The concern of international Quaker bodies for the well-being of Israelis and Palestinians continued. AFSC and other Quaker organizations have undertaken numerous service projects in both national communities, along with various efforts at Quaker-style, quiet relationship building between leaders or citizen activists from both "sides" of the conflict.[11] In 1969, an AFSC team led by

---

11 See Appendix D for a chronology of international Quaker work in the region.

Earlham College President Landrum C. Bolling produced a land-mark study, *Search for Peace in the Middle East*. It urged the establishment of a Palestinian state in the West Bank and Gaza, two parts of historic Palestine that came under Israeli military occupation during the Arab-Israeli war of June 1967. Thirteen years later, in 1982, AFSC sponsored a follow-up study by Everett Mendelsohn titled *A Compassionate Peace: A Future for Israel, Palestine, and the Middle East*. A third document, *Principles for a Just and Lasting Peace between Palestinians and Israelis*, was adopted by the AFSC Board of Directors in 1999.[12] These previous undertakings informed the orientation of our working party a great deal.

In addition to our concern for all the people—Israeli and Palestinian—who currently reside in the Holy Land, Quakers have always maintained a strong concern for the situation of those Palestinians who in the Arab-Israeli wars of 1948 and 1967 fled or were expelled from their homes in order to seek temporary refuge elsewhere—and have not yet been allowed to return. Those refugees and their descendants now number more than five million. As we saw during our visits with Palestinian refugees living in Lebanon, Syria, and Jordan, many of even the youngest children in these diaspora communities retain a vivid attachment to the land of their forebears; and all the diaspora Palestinians with whom we met asserted their right to be allowed to return to their homeland. We believe that that assertion, which is based on rights enunciated in numerous U.N. resolutions as well as the Universal Declaration of Human Rights, must be heard and given due consideration.

This report builds on the foundation provided by the whole body of earlier Quaker work with the Palestinian and Israeli communities. We were also inspired in our travels by the example of the mid-18th century North American Quaker John Woolman, a tireless and spiritled activist against warfare, slavery, and other forms of institutionalized violence. In June 1763, as the colonists of English origin in Pennsylvania and New Jersey were becoming agitated by a fear of attacks from apparently hostile French and Native-American communities to the north and west, Woolman set out from his home in New Jersey in order to meet with Indians in central Pennsylvania. In his journal, he described his motivation for undertaking this journey in these terms: "Love was the first

---

12 See Appendix E.

motion, and then a concern arose to spend some time with the Indians, that I might feel and understand their life and the spirit they live in."[13] As we traveled, we sought both to feel and to understand the lives of those with whom we met.

We recognize that, being outsiders, most members of our group were fortunate in that after having a brief exposure—however indirect and vicarious—to some of the tribulations experienced on a daily basis by Palestinians and Israelis, we were able to "escape" back to our more-or-less secure homes elsewhere. So we feel a strong burden of responsibility to try to share with others, through this report, some of what we saw, felt, and learned in our journeying. We are aware, too, that the task of bearing witness to the situation in the occupied territories has frequently been a hard one, as the Israeli government has placed tough controls on the entry of outsiders into those areas (as well as on the movements of local residents). These measures make it harder still for accurate, timely news about developments in the occupied territories to reach the outside world.

In many ways, this is not an optimistic report. But amidst the pain, fear, and suffering that we encountered we were also inspired by the enormous reserves of resilience, grace, and good humor that we found among people in both national communities who were living in conditions of extreme and chronic stress. We were energized by the opportunity we had to meet numerous remarkable individuals who continued to work against often daunting odds for peace, justice, and the healing of relationships at all levels. We note that nearly all of these activists yearned for an outcome in which these two peoples, whose lives are now so deeply intermeshed via multiple layers of violence, fear, control, and resistance, could find a way to engage more positively with each other, and to share the land that they both love. One version of this vision—whereby the Palestinians would establish their own state in the West Bank and Gaza, which would live in peaceful coexistence with the already-existing Israeli state—was articulated in *Search for Peace in the Middle East*, the prescient Quaker report of 1969, and has been reaffirmed by numerous Quaker documents since then.

---

13 John Woolman, *The Journal and Major Essays of John Woolman*, edited by Phillips P. Moulton (Richmond, Indiana: Friends United Press, 1971), p. 127.

However, even as we visited the Holy Land, the Israeli government that had maintained a military occupation over Gaza and the West Bank since 1967 continued to act in ways that severely undercut the ability of the Palestinians to establish a viable state of their own in those areas. Since 1967, successive Israeli governments have worked hard at implanting Jewish-Israeli citizens into new "Jewish only" settlements in the occupied areas, nearly all of them in the West Bank (including East Jerusalem). That settlement project continued with few interruptions, even during the years that followed the conclusion of the Oslo Accords in 1993. By the end of 2002 the total number of settlers in the occupied Palestinian territories, including East Jerusalem, was around 400,000. (The number of Palestinian residents of these areas was more than three million.) To support the settlement project, large amounts of Israeli government funds—including international-aid dollars sent by the U.S. government—have been poured into building entire settler-only communities, linked by a web of settler-only, multi-lane highways. By the time of our visit to the region, these highways, from which all Palestinian traffic was banned, had cut the West Bank into more than sixty tiny cantons, and Gaza into three larger, but still separate, chunks.

This entire settlement project has repeatedly been deemed illegal under the Fourth Geneva Convention, which states unequivocally that when any country's military is running an occupation of someone else's land, "The Occupying Power shall not deport or transfer parts of its own civilian population into the territory it occupies."[14] But the fact of the project's success to date has made the goal of effecting a complete Israeli withdrawal from the occupied territories seem much harder to attain. By late 2002, increasing numbers of Palestinians were saying that if the Israeli authorities would not undertake any withdrawal from the occupied areas that was sufficiently extensive to provide Palestinians with the territorial base for a viable independent state, but instead remained intent on maintaining control over sizeable parts of the occupied areas—then perhaps the Palestinians would have to change their demand from a Palestinian state alongside Israel to that of full civil and political rights for Palestinians within a single, binational state.

---

14 Article 49 of the Fourth Geneva Convention.
Full text available from the International Committee for the Red Cross at
<http://www.icrc.org/ihl.nsf/7c4d08d9b287a42141256739003e636b/6756482d86146898c
125641e004aa3c5?OpenDocument>.

Nearly all the Jewish Israelis with whom we spoke were firm in rejecting that latter vision. Some judged it would render impossible the traditional Zionist goal of establishing Israel as a state that is both democratic and Jewish, while others expressed the fear that it would play into the hands of those territorial maximalists in Israel who have sought to annex the occupied territories without granting any meaningful rights to their indigenous Palestinian residents. The goal of establishing a single binational state is, as we indicate in chapters 7 and 8 below, a difficult one to attain.

It seems to us that either a "two-state" outcome or a "one-state" outcome to this conflict is still conceivable. But based on our many conversations—with our interlocutors during the trip, and with each other—we could not discern which of these outcomes might be preferable, or indeed which might still be possible. In a very real sense, the shape of the final outcome is a matter for the direct parties to this conflict to decide upon—though outsiders should certainly work to ensure that the terms of any such deliberation are equitable and balanced, and do not merely reflect the current huge disparities of power between the parties.

We are clear, however, that occupation by a foreign military force—a situation which under international law is envisaged as obtaining only for a short length of time between conclusion of a ceasefire and conclusion of a more far-reaching peace agreement—is an inherently anti-democratic form of government. When prolonged for any length of time, military rule constitutes a major infringement of the rights of the people under its power. Israel's occupation of the Gaza Strip and the West Bank is maintained primarily through force of arms. It is in no way either reliant on the consent of the three million Palestinian residents of those territories or answerable to their democratic control. For more than 36 years now, the continuing fact of Israel's occupation of Gaza and the West Bank has subjected the Palestinians of these areas to rule by a foreign government's army, which has ruled through long strings of military edicts backed up by a secretive system of military courts. In addition, Israel has committed further massive abuses of its responsibilities as an occupying power by seizing control of extensive tracts of Palestinian land for the exclusive benefit of Israeli settlers as well as by appropriating a considerable portion of the West Bank's groundwater for the preferential benefit of Israeli citizens both in Israel proper and in the settlements.

Israel's occupation of the West Bank and Gaza has continued for far too long already and has inflicted considerable physical and spiritual damage both on the occupied people and on their occupiers. **It is evident to us that before it inflicts any more harm, the occupation must be brought to a speedy end.**

In addition to the urgent need to end the occupation, the truth of the following four principles was underlined by what we experienced on our journey:

1) All persons are of equal humanity and are entitled, as individuals, to fundamental human rights.

2) The principle that the rights of all of the people who have a direct stake in the situation in the Holy Land should be respected and each of these direct stakeholders given an equal voice in the process of determining the outcome to this conflict. We understand that these direct stakeholders are: (a) all Israeli citizens (who include Jewish Israelis, Israelis of Palestinian ethnicity, and some other smaller groups of Israeli citizens); (b) all Palestinian residents of the occupied territories; and (c) all the Palestinian refugees. The interests of these persons should be considered primary.

3) The principle that only mutual respect can lead to long-term security, and that no human community can for long assure its own security by imposing a state of insecurity on its neighbors.

4) The principle that violence always leads to more violence, that creative nonviolent ways that allow the parties to this conflict to work together to bring about a fair, stable, and hope-filled outcome do exist, and that these ways should actively be sought and pursued.

Far from creating security or a basis for peace, Israel's continuing occupation of the West Bank and Gaza has brought insecurity and suffering to both Israelis and Palestinians. The Israeli and Palestinian use of violence has only increased the suffering. A nonviolent, compassionate approach by both sides, supported by constructive international action, can achieve both justice and peaceful, productive relations. As Quakers, and friends of Quakers, we want to join with the words of our sister Katherine Whitlock who—in a different context—proclaimed: "The call to love and justice is a joyous call to resistance and transformation. We are called to resist

11

unjust beliefs, structures, and practices in ourselves, our communities, and our society. We are called to transform by example the corrupt ethic of dominance and supremacy that declares some categories of people superior or subordinate to others."[15]

We lay this report before you, our readers, and we invite you to join with us and our Israeli and Palestinian friends in discerning and following the paths that all of us, wherever we are, can take to respond to this call "to love and justice."

---

15 Katherine Whitlock, *In a Time of Broken Bones: A Call to Dialogue on Hate Violence and the Limitations of Hate Crimes Legislation* (Philadelphia: American Friends Service Committee, August, 2001), p. 4.

Part One

———

The Voices
We Heard

[2]

Life and Violence
in the Holy Land

For all our powerful and strong army, we are afraid.
If you find an Israeli who says he is not afraid, don't believe him.
— Gadi Golan, Israeli Foreign Ministry, 2002

I feel like a stranger in my own land.
The whole country has become like a giant prison.
— Jean Zaru, Palestinian Quaker, 2002

We arrived in the Middle East at a time of turmoil for Palestinians and Israelis. Ever since the second *intifada* started in September 2000, both peoples had been held in the grip of deadly violence. The rate of killing was particularly shocking during the three months immediately before our arrival. During March, April, and May 2002, a total of 195 Israelis—18 of them minors—were killed by Palestinians, and 540 Palestinians— 59 of them minors—were killed by Israelis.[16]

Most of the Israeli casualties at that time were being inflicted by Palestinian "suicide bombers"—men or women who would strap explosives onto their bodies and seek to detonate them at a place where they would cause the maximum number of Israeli casualties. In some testimonies, suicide bombers or their helpers explained that their prime intention was that these casualties should be Israeli security personnel. But these testimonies also stated that if such a target proved hard to find, then the bomber would instead carry out the detonation in a place thickly peopled with Israeli civilians. Buses, night-clubs, and cafés were among the locations they chose. Among the 195 Israelis killed in those three months, 127 were civilians and 68 were security personnel.

On the Palestinian side, most of the fatalities and other casualties

---

16 B'tselem figures, totaled from <http://www.btselem.org/English/Statistics/Al_ Aqsa_Fatalities_Tables.asp>. Other reliable sources of casualty figures are, for Palestinian casualties, the Palestinian Red Crescent Society, <www.palestinercs.org>, and for Israeli casualties, the Israeli Ministry of Foreign Affairs, <www.mfa.gov.il>.

had been inflicted by the Israeli security forces. These killings included the deliberate assassinations of a number of Palestinians accused by Israel authorities of having organized suicide bombings or other forms of anti-Israeli violence—though the evidence for these accusations was never examined in any legal proceeding. In undertaking these extra-judicial killings, the Israeli hit squads frequently also killed bystanders, including children. Other Palestinian deaths resulted from the Israeli forces' use against unarmed demonstrators of weapons of a lethality that human rights groups judged to be clearly excessive, as well as from these forces' exchanges of fire with armed Palestinians. On many of these occasions, the heavily armed Israeli security forces seemed to act with reckless disregard for the lives of Palestinian civilians. In addition to the above total of Palestinians who were killed through the direct actions of Israelis, uncounted scores of Palestinians met untimely and avoidable deaths by being restricted from traveling through the Israeli army checkpoints spread through the occupied territories—for example, for appointments to receive treatment for chronic medical conditions or problem pregnancies.

This violence inflicted considerable pain and suffering on both communities. As we reached Palestine/Israel, we mourned the life of each one of the individuals who had been killed by an act of direct or indirect violence. We knew that the bereaved families would continue to bear a heavy burden of grief for many years to come, and that uncounted thousands of other individuals had been left wounded—many of them seriously—by the attacks that had killed their neighbors and friends. During our visit we gained a vivid appreciation of the degree to which the generalized sense of fear, and the resulting psychic traumatization, were blighting the lives and spirits of all Palestinians and Israelis. We also learned that the security measures being undertaken by Israeli authorities were placing a heavy burden on the Palestinians, and to some extent also on the Israelis themselves. All of these experiences enabled us to see the violence inherent in the occupation itself— that is, in the attempt by one people's government to dominate another people against its will.

On each side, we discovered that the reaction of many individuals to the general sense of being trapped in a situation of great suffering and fear was to urge even greater violence, "in response to" or "in retaliation for" violence from the other side. As people of faith who hold that all human life is sacred—that "there is that of God in everyone," as Quakers say—we cannot help but consider that this desire for revenge or domination is itself a symptom of a deep spiritual crisis that cries out for a compassionate and healing-based response. We say this even though we recognize that there is a significant difference between the kind of instrumental violence that is used with the aim of maintaining an unjust status quo, and that which seeks to end it.

Early in our trip we heard at first hand about the growing divide between Israelis and Palestinians. On our second morning in Jerusalem, Israeli peace activist Gila Svirsky came to the East Jerusalem Young Women's Christian Association (YWCA), where we were staying. With a somber expression, she told us that the general mood among her compatriots was one of "more anger, more hatred of Palestinians, more people agreeing with the view that 'most Palestinians are terrorists.'" She said, "Part of what's happening here is a hardening of hearts—on all sides."

The next day, we heard a similarly disquieting assessment from the Palestinian side. Meeting us in his East Jerusalem office, Mahdi Abdel-Hadi, the head of the Palestinian Academic Society for the Study of International Affairs (PASSIA), told us, "The Palestinians today are living a catastrophe, and the Israelis, a nightmare. The Palestinian catastrophe affects our land, our society, and our economy. And for the Israelis—the Zionist dream has still not been realized, even more than fifty years after the establishment of the State of Israel. Where is the haven they longed for?"

Even Israeli government officials expressed similar sentiments. At the Ministry of Foreign Affairs, a tree-shaded compound in West Jerusalem, Gadi Golan, the head of the ministry's Bureau of Religious Affairs, told us with apparent candor, "Like most Israelis, I'm confused." He said, "Both sides are in a cycle of violence. But it will lead us nowhere. ... Apart from the small numbers of Israelis of the far right and the far left who 'know' exactly what to do, the majority don't know what to do." He, too, described his country's current situation as "a nightmare."

> "For all our powerful and strong army," Golan said, "we are afraid. If you find an Israeli who says he is not afraid, don't believe him. If someone belongs to the far right and says that all the Arabs [Palestinians] have to be sent away, it's because that person is afraid. ... Around us, there are so many millions of Arabs! When we look at our environment, we have reason to be afraid. ... Because we can't protect ourselves."

Referring to the Palestinians' principal demand, that Israel withdraw completely from the two areas it had occupied in 1967, the West Bank and the Gaza Strip, Golan said, "Even if we returned to the pre-1967 borders, I'm not sure we'd have peace." He said that in order for any diplomacy to move forward, the Palestinian leader, Yasser Arafat, would have to resolve his problems with the Palestinian extremists, and that "the Israeli government has to resolve the problems with our extremists."

One person we spoke with who had a particularly clear-eyed view of the ongoing violence was Azmi Bishara. He is a Palestinian citizen of Israel and an elected member of Israel's Knesset (Parliament), but he has also spent a lot of time in the West Bank, where he taught philosophy at Bir Zeit University for many years. "There is a Palestinian claim that the suicide bombers 'broke' the security theory of Israeli Prime Minister Ariel Sharon," Bishara said. "That's true. But who said this is a theoretical debate? Politically, the use of suicide bombs has backfired." Throughout the history of the encounter between Palestinians and Israelis, he noted, "Killing civilians unites Israeli society; killing soldiers splits it. In the latter case, people in Israel blame the Israeli government for their losses, since soldiers represent policies. But civilians represent society."

Within Israeli society, the suicide bombers have frequently had a devastating—and quite indiscriminate—impact. The people they have killed have been young and old; women and men; Jewish and Palestinian citizens of Israel, and some foreigners; people on the political right and the political left. Naomi Chazan, a staunchly pro-peace parliamentarian who at the time was the deputy speaker of the Knesset, shared with us the anguish she felt when a longtime supporter of her party, the peace-oriented Meretz Party, lost a daughter to a recent bombing. "And then, with the recent bomb in the bus in Gilo," Chazan added after a pause, "my own daughter was only five minutes away from being killed by it. ... Anyone who can act normally under these circumstances deserves a medal."

At the time of our visit, Palestinian society was also reeling from recent and continuing violence inflicted by Israeli security forces. While we were in Jerusalem, the Israeli government started to send their military to reoccupy most of the areas of the West Bank that an earlier Israeli government had handed over to

Palestinian Authority (P.A.) control under agreements concluded subsequent to the 1993 Oslo Accords. From 1995 through early 2002, the P.A. had exercised all local government functions, including local security functions, in nine heavily populated Palestinian cities in the West Bank and much of the Gaza Strip.[17] But three months before our visit, in late March 2002, Prime Minister Ariel Sharon ordered the military to undertake an action called Operation Defensive Shield, which sent Israeli troops to reoccupy most of those West Bank cities. (A few weeks after Defensive Shield, the troops were pulled out of the cities—though only, it turned out, temporarily.) During Defensive Shield, the Israeli military units inflicted considerable damage on the residents and civilian infrastructure of the targeted cities.

One of the cities affected most during Defensive Shield was Jenin, where the Palestinian refugee camp abutting the city was the scene of some particularly abusive actions by Israeli troops. The number of Palestinians killed in Jenin, and the question of whether they were combatants or civilians, was hotly contested. But Amnesty International, which did the most thorough analysis of these questions, later reported that "in Jenin refugee camp and Jenin city, more than half of the fifty-four Palestinians who died ... between 3 and 17 April appear not to have been involved in the fighting. Among those killed were seven women, four children, and six men over fifty-five. Six had been crushed in houses."[18]

We heard from a senior international aid worker about the inspection visit she had made to Jenin refugee camp shortly after the Israeli authorities finally allowed her and some colleagues from various relief organizations to enter the area. "A football field-sized piece of the camp had been destroyed, and all the shelters within it totally flattened," she said. She added:

> What we heard from surviving residents was what you often hear about Israel's frequent practice of demolishing Palestinian homes. Either people in the homes had not been warned, or they had not been warned clearly, or they had not been warned in time to remove any of their belongings.

---

17 The Palestinian-populated cities handed over to the P.A. in the mid-1990s did not include East Jerusalem, which historically had been the Palestinians' metropolitan hub in the West Bank. A significant portion of downtown Hebron was also never handed over to the P.A.

18 Index# MDE 15/154/2002 (Amnesty International: November 4, 2002). Available on Amnesty website <web.amnesty.org>. At least twenty-three Israeli soldiers also lost their lives during the April 2002 fighting in the Jenin refugee camp.

At the beginning of this *intifada,* if someone shot at the Israeli soldiers from one house, the soldiers would destroy that house and those around it. Then that type of action escalated. ... In Jenin, the soldiers pulled a U.N. vehicle out of the clinic there and wantonly flattened it. Inside the clinic, they even shot up the baby scale and the washing machine.

Another aid worker told us that during Defensive Shield, the Israeli troops who had entered Ramallah had also engaged in acts of seemingly deep hatred. "In the offices of the General Union of Disabled Palestinians they destroyed every wheelchair they could find," she said. "In the [Palestinian] Ministry of Culture, there were signs of defecation and urination everywhere. And one day in Ramallah, the solders gathered nine Palestinian ambulances, corralled them for six days so the Palestinians couldn't use them— and then flattened them with their tanks."

Such were some of the acts that Palestinians had experienced in the weeks before our visit. Then, in early June 2002, the Israeli government declared it would soon undertake a new, and quite possibly much longer, reoccupation of the Palestinian cities. That fact would have a huge impact on the lives of the Palestinians. It also made it harder for us to realize our plan of visiting various parts of the occupied territories.

Traveling Around the Occupied Territories

Our group planned to travel around Israel and the West Bank in a bus chartered in East Jerusalem. In Israel the standard color for vehicle license tags is yellow: Israeli citizens, whether they reside in Israel proper or in settlements in the occupied territories, have yellow tags on their vehicles. Palestinian vehicle owners who live in East Jerusalem have also—since Israel effectively annexed that portion of the city in 1967—been issued yellow tags for their vehicles. Our bus therefore had yellow, Israeli tags. By contrast, Palestinian vehicle owners who are residents of other parts of the occupied territories are issued with blue, green, or white license tags. By the time we were in Palestine/ Israel, vehicles with the non-yellow (Palestinian) tags had been banned for many months from the network of "Israelis only" highways that Israel built in the West Bank and Gaza in the late 1990s. As we were driven around the beautiful, ancient hills of the West Bank we were keenly aware that most of the West Bank's two million Palestinian residents were being totally denied the freedom to engage in vehicular travel, since they lacked the all-important yellow tags.

Wherever we went on the West Bank's inter-area road network, the only other vehicles we saw were those bearing yellow tags. Most of these were traveling either to or from the region's numerous Jewish-only settlements. As we drove past access roads leading to Palestinian cities, towns, or villages, we saw that every one of them had been made impassable by the Israeli military. At each such junction, the military had either thrown up a pair of eight-feet-high dirt barricades or dug deep trenches across the access road. Any Palestinians who wanted to leave their home communities to go to school, work, or a family event elsewhere had to scramble over or around these obstacles on foot. In addition, several of the Palestinian cities seemed to be totally encircled with high fences that were topped with razor-wire. Passage through the few gates in these fences was kept under the close control of Israeli soldiers in heavily fortified checkpoints.

Under these circumstances, which had been in place for many months already and would continue for many months after our visit, the territory's Palestinians had no hope of sustaining a normal economic or social life.

On our first trip out of Jerusalem, we drove to Hebron, a large, ancient city whose central place of worship is considered the final resting place of the Prophet Abraham and is viewed as very holy by both Muslims and Jews. (Adherents of both religions claim Abraham as a very important ancestor.) Hebron's downtown area contains a small but militant population of Jewish settlers alongside its large Palestinian population. As our bus neared the city, it became clear that the driver could only hope to enter by driving through the Jewish settlement of Kiryat Arba, which abuts Hebron to the east. The security guards at Kiryat Arba's fortified entry point refused our bus entry for a long time on the grounds that our driver was an ethnic Arab. Only when the driver explained that two of his passengers were Jewish and wanted to visit the Jewish holy places in Hebron did the guards let us proceed.

Once inside Hebron, we found that the extensive and once bustling downtown market area had become nearly a ghost town. In the mid-1990s, when all other Palestinian cities (except East Jerusalem) were handed over to Palestinian control, the central swathe of downtown Hebron was still kept under Israeli control. As that regime continued, zealots from the Israeli settler movement used many means to wrest as much physical control over the downtown area as they could from its longtime Palestinian residents and shopkeepers. Those means seemed clearly to have included widespread intimidation of local Palestinians. In arcade after arcade of the stone-built market area, we saw that many Palestinian-owned shops had been closed with metal shutters that were spray-painted with racist slogans like "Death to the Arabs!" in large Hebrew letters. In some places, new and sizeable Jewish institutions like schools or colleges had been built right on top of the Palestinian shops. A few Palestinian shop owners hung on. But most of their customers had been scared away by the climate of intimidation of which the shop owners told us. A Hebron-based representative of the Christian Peacemaker Teams (CPT), a nonviolent protection force, told us that such intimidation has often involved the looting or spoiling of goods from Palestinian stores and market-stalls by miscreants from the settler community—who seemed, she said, to act with impunity.

The stone-arched alleyways of Hebron's central market were nearly empty. Civilian settler men with guns strode confidently around the whole downtown area. On one street corner, we saw a squad of five or six Israeli soldiers questioning a Palestinian youth and, as a matter of seeming routine, making him stand spread-eagled against a wall and kicking his shins sharply to spread his legs further. When some members of our group started photographing this activity, the soldiers threatened our bus driver that they would break his arms if he did not stop us from doing so.

The Palestinian Friend who was a part of our group, Jean Zaru, later expressed the anguish she felt on this visit. She recalled that in earlier years her family, like Palestinian families from many parts of the West Bank, used to travel to Hebron to buy the locally grown produce and locally manufactured wares then available in its markets. Hebronites, she recalled, made the best shoes and grew the best grapes and eggplants in the West Bank. But now— "I feel like a stranger in my own land," she said. "The whole country has become like a giant prison."

After leaving Hebron, we traveled to the nearby agricultural town of Dura to meet with writer and local resident Khaled Amayreh. To make this visit, we had to leave our bus on the highway and join the stream of local people climbing over the dirt barricades that blocked the town from the highway. Once over, we hailed green-tagged local taxis from among those lined up on the other side of the barricades for use around the town.

Amayreh welcomed us into his house with coffee, tea, and cold drinks as he told us of the privations his community had suffered over recent years. "We have an acute shortage of water here," he said. "The Israelis," he continued,

> control the taps for water, and sometimes they cut it off for six months at a time. They find ways to send Israeli produce into our town, but we cannot ship our produce out. So they create a captive market here. It's classic colonialism. And meanwhile, we cannot even send our agricultural products to Hebron! Now, we are prisoners: surrounded, entrapped. Women are forced to give birth at home, because they can't reach the hospitals. Some babies die because of this. This curfew is lethal, as well as hateful.

A couple of days later, we took another bus trip out of Jerusalem. This time we traveled around part of the central West Bank with Michael Warschawski, a Jewish Israeli and a veteran anti-settlement activist. The steep hills around the Palestinian village of Hizma, northeast of Jerusalem, were scorched dry, and the few remaining clumps of the previous spring's grass had been bleached to a crisp by the heat of the massive blonde-colored rocks. On a hilltop east of the village, we saw a large yellow sign that read "Almon." But Almon itself, an Israeli settlement, was nowhere in sight. "True, the settlement's houses are a few kilometers away," Warschawski explained. "But now, for planning purposes, the perimeter of the settlement has been extended up to here. As you can see, this sign is telling Palestinians in the village right beneath it that all the land between them and the houses of Almon now belongs to Almon."

On another hill, he stopped our bus at an isolated gas station staffed by a bored private-sector security guard cradling a chunky machine pistol. "Here we are at what's called the Psagot gas station," Warschawski said. He added:

> Of course, despite the name, we are quite far from the settlement of Psagot, which is over that crest. Then, if you look down the hill from here, you'll see the layout for a future industrial park. So now we have a Jewish-Israeli axis of control that—to protect these facilities—will require a road leading to the next settlement. Voilà! You see how they've diced through the Palestinian land once again—and this time without putting in even a single additional settler! It's like the Japanese game of Go. The aim is to cut off and encircle the other side. And so far, the settlement project is winning hands down.

At a third stop, we stood on a hill near Jerusalem looking at the arid hills to our north and east. The hills we were looking at were all crowned with solid blocks of red-roofed houses. This was Ma'ale Adumim, the massive settlement to the east of Jerusalem that almost cuts right across the Palestinian West Bank at its thinner central waist. Warschawski explained that the administrative boundaries of Ma'ale Adumim had recently been pushed out to rub up against all surrounding Palestinian towns and villages, just as we had seen with Almon. In the process, Ma'ale Adumim had simply taken control of the grazing grounds formerly used by the semi-nomadic community of Palestinian herders called the Arab al-Jahalin (also known as the Jahalin Bedouin.) The Jahalin people's traditional form of shelter, breezy goat-hair tents, had been removed from the land, and the people relocated in an area also used today as the Jerusalem municipal garbage dump. These people's only form of shelter was now windowless shipping containers that someone had provided for the purpose. Roads leading to the scrubby hillside on which these makeshift container/homes perched were marked with many signs giving clear warning—in Hebrew but not in Arabic—that the entire area was toxic.

In the Gaza Strip, we found this same process of aggrandizement of the Israeli settlers' domain also underway. The Gaza Strip is a finger of land, about 25 miles long and five-to-six miles wide, that lies sandwiched between southern Israel and the southeast corner of the Mediterranean Sea. The small southern end of the Strip borders on Egypt. Whereas the West Bank is high, hilly, and dry—and even in summer, the night air is often breezy—the Gaza Strip just sits and swelters all summer long in the torpid moisture from the sea.

Along the entire length of the Strip's border with Israel, the Israelis some years ago built a substantial fence topped by overlapping coils of razor wire. Access for Palestinians through this barrier is limited to a small number of crossing-points. We entered through the Erez crossing, the main access-point at the north end of the Strip. Here, once again, we had to leave our bus on the Israeli side of the crossing. We carried our bags over to the grandiosely named "internationals" section of the border post for passport checks and an interrogation. Then, after being cleared for passage by the Israeli border guards there, we had to take our bags along the quarter-mile concrete roadway to the "Palestinian" end of the crossing. To our left lay the warren of fenced-in enclosures and passageways along which more than 100,000 Palestinian laborers used to be herded daily, in the long-gone days when large numbers of them were "allowed" to perform menial labor inside Israel. Now, those enclosures were silent. Fewer than 500 of Gaza's 1.1 million Palestinians were permitted to work inside Israel at the time of our visit.

We stayed overnight in Gaza City. The next morning, we took a bus trip north and east, traveling through the massive Jabaliya refugee camp (which has a registered population of 101,600 Palestinian refugees) to the northern edge of the town of Beit Lehia. This Palestinian community's carefully irrigated fields of eggplant and tomato butt up against the boundaries of two Israeli settlements, Elei Sinai and Nisanit. As our bus came to the last few houses before the town's fields began, residents of the houses waved to our driver to halt. Looking ahead, we saw an Israeli tank perched atop a nearby sand dune with its gun pointing down toward us. Under the protection of the tank, Israeli armored bulldozers were at work near the base of the dune, ripping the crops out of a swathe of the Palestinian fields.

We saw evidence of similar destruction in the other parts of Gaza. For example, near the settlement of Netzarim, southwest of Gaza City, we saw a number of large, flat fields where all the crops had been uprooted. They were bordered by the stumps of Palestinian trees that the Israelis had recently sawn down, and rubble from recently demolished Palestinian homes.

The Israeli authorities claim they need to establish a broad "no-man's-land" around the areas where the settlers live in order to provide a clear line of sight for security people trying to defend the settlements from Palestinian infiltrators. The effect, in the dense overcrowding of the Gaza Strip, is to reduce even further the amount of land available to the Palestinians for farming or for residence. Raji Sourani, the Director of the Gaza City-based Palestinian Center for Human Rights, told us that under the Oslo-derived negotiations of the mid-1990s, 58 percent of the Strip's surface area, containing its entire Palestinian population of 1.1 million souls, was handed over to the P.A.'s control. The Israeli settlers in the Strip number around four thousand. For their protection, under the Oslo process, the Israeli security forces were allowed—pending a final-status agreement—to stay in control of the remaining 42 percent of the Strip. Now—for the further benefit of the four thousand settlers—the 58 percent of the land into which the Strip's Palestinians had already been squeezed was being further eaten into.

While we were in Gaza, matters were not standing still in the West Bank. There, the Israeli commanders were once again sending their tanks, armored bulldozers, and other armored vehicles back into the heart of all the area's cities except Jericho, as they had previously announced they would. As a result of these new military operations, our plans to visit Ramallah, Bethlehem, and Jenin repeatedly had to be revised. Each morning, we would call a humanitarian-aid coordinating center to learn whether our group would have a chance of getting into any of these cities that day. Finally, toward the end of our stay, we learned that Bethlehem was supposed to be "open" that day.

In the days before Israeli barriers and checkpoints barred the way, the trip from East Jerusalem to Bethlehem was an easy 15-minute drive, depending on the traffic. On the day we tried to go there we found, as we expected, that there was an Israeli checkpoint controlling the most direct route into Bethlehem. We stopped our van not far from it, and an AFSC staff person walked ahead to ask the soldiers if the checkpoint might be opening soon. As we waited for her to return, tanks, armored personnel carriers, and other military vehicles maneuvered around us on the dusty road, gears grinding. The staff person returned to say the checkpoint would remain closed. She described the soldiers staffing the checkpoint as "very nervous." Our van then circled around the area's rocky hills to the back of the neighboring Palestinian town, Beit Jala, from where we had a hope of walking in. We talked to the driver of an Israeli tank who was guarding this road. He told us in English that it would be "very dangerous" for us to go into the town, but said the checkpoint should be open for foot traffic until around 2:00 or 3:00 p.m. Leaving the van behind, we once again joined the local townspeople who were walking carefully around the large, staggered concrete barricades, using this chance to bring in groceries, medicines, and other necessities for their families. Then, as we had at Dura, we found local cabs lined up inside the barriers, and hired two or three of them to take us to our destination, the Bethlehem office of the Applied Research

Institute of Jerusalem (ARIJ), where we met with ARIJ's executive director, the veteran nonviolence activist Jad Isaac.

Isaac spelled out to us that the expansion of the Israeli settlements in the occupied territories had proceeded at its fastest pace ever over the preceding five years. This development was considerably aided, he said, by the U.S.-financed construction of a new settler-only road network and lubricated by the sizeable subsidies that successive Israeli governments gave to Jewish Israelis willing to live in the settlements. "Yes, there is a master plan for the settlements," he stressed. "It is conscious and premeditated. And even the so-called 'illegal outposts' established by some settlers relate to the overall plan." Reviewing the figures for settlement construction, Isaac said that Israeli Prime Minister Yitzhak Rabin (1992-95) had slowed the expansion of settlements somewhat. But then, he said, Binyamin Netanyahu, who was prime minister from 1996 through 1999, "went crazy with settlements. And Ehud Barak, who followed him, kept up the pace. Since Barak's short tenure as prime minister, Sharon has pushed even harder for the settlements. The result has been vast, cumulative seizures of land from the Palestinians.... And most of this expansion has taken place in the last five years."

In the Bethlehem district, Israel's land expropriations were having devastating effects on the local residents. "The new road the Israelis are building will encircle Bethlehem," Isaac said. "There will be no open space left for us. ... We will never find land to build houses for our young people. They are putting a new road further into Bethlehem, too, and taking more of our land in the Jerusalem district. Around us, there is the big road, and two fences, and two trenches—altogether, an ecological disaster. Then, they have cut the Bethlehem area into three parts, forcing us to live with a population density of 3,720 people per square kilometer. It would only be 250 per square kilometer if we had access to all our land."

At one point Isaac stood up, looked through the window of his office, and said, "I was standing here and I watched them uprooting all the trees. You must remember that I watched those trees grow—each and every one of them. ... I feel like I don't have anything more to live for. I can only say that there is a need for Bethlehem to offer a hopeful future for its young people.

"The Palestinians must have a viable and sustainable state," he stressed. He spoke of the particular pain that the Bethlehemites feel at the rigid separation the Israelis have imposed between them and their neighbors (and, often, close relatives) in nearby Jerusalem.

> Bethlehem has so many close ties to Jerusalem! Back in 1947, when the U.N. drew up its Partition Plan for Palestine, Jerusalem was supposed to be administered separately from both the envisaged Jewish state and the envisaged Palestinian state. It was to have been a *corpus separatum* [a separately ruled jurisdiction]. The first Mayor of the *corpus separatum* was supposed to be a Philadelphia Quaker, Harold Evans. And under that plan, Bethlehem was supposed to be part of the *corpus separatum!* But now, we have been totally cut off from Jerusalem.

Isaac, who is a Palestinian Christian, spoke of his sadness that Israel's restrictions had already led to a wave of departures by younger members of the city's historic Christian population. "Why don't the Christians of the world react when they see a conspiracy to dismember our city?" he asked. "When the number of local Christians diminishes, we lose the 'living stones' of our faith here. Why do Christians elsewhere let this happen?"[19]

We had also wanted to visit Jenin, the site of the atrocities of the preceding April, and Ramallah, a historically Christian city in the West Bank to which Quakers have had ties for 135 years. Reaching Jenin always looked like a tough proposition—and especially so, after the Sharon government launched its new offensive back into the Palestinian cities. Ramallah, however, lies much closer to Jerusalem than Jenin: our group continued to try to get into Ramallah, right down to our very last day in Jerusalem. Early on that last morning we left the East Jerusalem YWCA—in the company of Landrum Bolling, the veteran Quaker peace activist who was the principal author of the 1969 Quaker document, *Search for Peace in the Middle East*—and made one last try to reach Ramallah. We took one set of cabs to the Ram checkpoint on the Jerusalem perimeter, walked across that checkpoint, and took a second set to the checkpoint at Kalandia that controls movement in and out of Ramallah. Jean Zaru had made her way into the city a few days before, but only with great difficulty. On this Sunday morning, she

---

19 After our visit to Bethlehem, one member of our group wrote of the experience, "The poverty is so pervasive—as people mostly can't work under the circumstances. The persistence and desperation of the street hawkers were so great that though most members of our group had spent time in third world countries, this experience was still a particularly intense and difficult one for us."

and other Ramallah Quakers were waiting for us inside the city where they had planned a schedule for us that included a Quaker worship session and some time to visit with local people.

At the checkpoint outside Ramallah, we found long lines of vehicles and pedestrians waiting patiently for the passage to open up. Our friends inside the city reported by cell phone that Israeli army loudspeaker trucks had been touring the streets announcing that the curfew was on again for the day, and that any residents seen on the streets would be shot. We waited outside the city for a while, then returned to the Ram checkpoint to wait a little longer, in case the Israelis should change their minds. While we waited, we bought tea and coffee from a nearby shop and sat outside enjoying the fellowship of the many other people waiting to go through. Finally, we were disappointed to learn that Ramallah would remain under lockdown all day and we would be unable to proceed with our visit.

A couple of evenings earlier, we had been able to receive a little news from the city and from the community around the large Friends School there, when principal Colin South and his spouse, Kathy, came by the YWCA on their way to England for their summer leave. Colin and Kathy spoke about the stress inflicted on the people of Ramallah by the very long curfews to which they had been subjected. "There is continuous pressure," Colin said. "Back in April, there were invasive house searches and arrests. Now, the soldiers have been blowing up a number of houses. Tanks roam around the streets all day. Some of the Israeli soldiers are just kids, really, and they race their tanks up and down. They batter down people's doors at night. The experience for the young children in the city has been terrifying, ever since October 2000."

He reported that despite all the difficulties of the 2001-2002 school year, the school had been able to keep instructional programs more or less on track for the 950 students, though he worried that there might still be timing problems for the formal exam to leave school, the tawjihi, that all Palestinian students need to take. The school had been badly affected by the general economic collapse in Ramallah, he said. "With all the curfews, there is no possibility of work. So the parents run out of money, and then, we don't know. The worst thing, for everyone, is the uncertainty, the total inability to plan."

Here is one last vignette from our travels around the occupied territories. Early one overcast morning our trusty Jerusalem bus driver picked us up from the YWCA, drove down through the rocky hills of the West Bank into Israel proper, then headed north to a prearranged rendezvous at a gas station. There, we climbed into the armored Volvo bus with bulletproof windows that we had hired for the occasion at the suggestion of our host for the morning, Sondra Baras, a Jewish Israeli. Baras is a settler activist who directs the Israel office of an international, pro-settler group of Christian Zionists called Christian Friends of Israeli Communities. She lives in the settlement of Karnei Shomron, in the hills between Qalqiliya and Nablus in the northern West Bank.

"We have suffered also," Baras told us as we visited with her in her office inside the settlement.

> We have lost members of our community to terror here. Last August, a friend was driving with her family on the same road you came in on. She, her husband, and one of their daughters were all shot. She was killed. The other two ended up paralyzed. And they have two other kids who now also need to be cared for. We care for each other in all circumstances. Then, in February, there was a suicide bomber who blew himself up in our shopping area. Several teenagers were killed and others injured.

> I am pessimistic. There is no end in view. The whole western world must face up to the problem of terrorism everywhere. We are a microcosm of that. We can't negotiate!

She led us on a short tour of the settlement, which consists of three distinct neighborhoods, each perched on its own hilltop. Karnei Shomron's six thousand residents have their own schools, and seven synagogues serve different segments of the community. "Everyone builds their own house," Baras said. "We lease the land from the state." She explained that the settlement was first established in the mid-1980s by new immigrants from the United States. Those pioneers included Baras herself, who grew up in Ohio and migrated here in 1984. (On the wall in her office we saw her graduation certificates from Barnard College in New York, and from Columbia University Law School.)

Over the years, Karnei Shomron has gained many amenities. As we drove around, we went along tree-lined streets; and we saw colorful public gardens, a stoutly-fenced schoolyard, a shopping center, and—here, in the parched West Bank—a swimming-pool.

"As a Jew, I believe this is the Biblical land of the Jews that was promised to Abraham," Baras told us. "God finds a way to fulfill his promises, and we should respond." She described the 1967 war, during which Israel took over the West Bank, as "a miracle." "We did not seek this war, but we see a miracle in Israel's victory. ... 'Karnei Shomron' means 'the horns of Samaria.' This is the land that was promised us by God."

Of her Palestinian neighbors, she said, "We have not done one ounce of reprisals. We should act fiercely against those who harbor terrorists. ... We should bomb whole neighborhoods. ... Only massive force, firmly applied, will quell them. We can do no less. Otherwise we will be attacked."

She seemed adamant in her opposition to the establishment of any Palestinian state in the West Bank (which she referred to as "Western Israel"[20]). "The Palestinian state could be in Jordan, or in the Sinai," she concluded.

---

20 This is a term used by some Israeli territorial maximalists. It refers to the ideas that the "Land of Israel" includes not just the land between the Mediterranean and Jordan River, but also much of the territory of modern Jordan, to the east. These territorial maximalists believe that by giving up a claim to "Eastern Israel," that is, present-day Jordan, the Israelis have already shown their willingness to be flexible.

[3]
Voices from the Eye of the Storm

The situation on the ground is very ghoulish and transcends reality.
I cannot convey the persecution. It is an affront to civilization.
— Khaled Amayreh, Palestinian journalist, 2002

The price of peace is the end of occupation.
— Beate Zilversmidt, Israeli peace activist, 2002

Politics and Fear

"It would be disastrous," a top international aid official stressed to us, "if the world saw this as a humanitarian crisis rather than a political crisis. In that case, we'd start going down the same slippery slope we went down in Afghanistan in the 1990s, where the political issues did not get addressed. While of course we have to draw attention to the humanitarian issues, we should keep the political reality of the occupation as central. Don't let the Palestinians be seen just as 'charity cases'. This is a man-made disaster."

Our visit to Palestine/Israel gave us a number of vivid snapshots of the Israeli occupation of the West Bank and Gaza, which by the time of our visit had been continuing for more than thirty-five years. These snapshots were accompanied by scores of in-depth conversations with officials, peace activists, human rights advocates, and many others on the "front lines" of the turmoil in Israel and Palestine. We arrived at a significant moment in this protracted confrontation. During our visit, Sharon's government was sending the Israeli military back into the Palestinian cities of the West Bank for what the Palestinians called the "second reoccupation" of the cities. (The "first reoccupation" had been Operation Defensive Shield, in March and April of 2002. The original and continuing occupation had been in place since 1967.) The second reoccupation would prove both long-lived and very harmful to the Palestinians. It also imposed mounting costs, in

33

both blood and treasure, on Israeli society. Those costs helped persuade the Labor Party to pull out of Sharon's governing coalition in October 2002, an action that forced Sharon to call an election earlier than he might otherwise have chosen. As it happened, he won the election, held in late January 2003, and thus emerged politically strengthened by the whole affair. But within weeks of his re-election he was still forced by the dynamics of the situation to cautiously enter peace talks with the Palestinians.[21]

Despite its scale, the second reoccupation of June 2002—like many of the Israeli leaders' previous attempts to resolve the Palestinian issue through force—failed to bring either peace or security to Israel's citizens. During our visit to the region, it was evident that intense frustration had been building up for some time in many sectors of Israeli society, over the fact that there was seemingly no forceful strategy that the government could employ to quell the Palestinians and bring security and peace to Israel. Given the right circumstances, this sense of frustration might provide enough momentum to swing Israeli public attitudes back in favor of the country's peace movement. But while we were in Israel, public attitudes there seemed volatile, contradictory, and bellicose. On our first Friday in Jerusalem, some of us joined the midtown vigil that the pro-peace organization Women in Black has held in cities throughout Israel every Friday for many years. The vigil participants, most of whom were Jewish-Israeli women, were confronted by a hostile group of counter-demonstrators who shouted epithets like: "traitor!" "you belong in Auschwitz or Treblinka!" or "no more Arabs, no more terror!" One distraught elderly Jewish man held up a full-color poster of photos of Israelis killed in terror attacks and screamed repeatedly in Hebrew that those murders were the fault of people like the Women in Black. Another counter-demonstrator held a hand-lettered sign that read simply "Destroy Refugee Camps."

Israeli peace activist Gila Svirsky[22] had told us in a meeting we

---

21 On May 26, 2003, as he made this move, Sharon told leaders of his Likud party that Israel could not continue indefinitely to maintain its "occupation" over the Palestinians of the West Bank and Gaza. His use of this term was highly significant because supporters of the settlement project have always tried to avoid using it. (See <http://www.cbsnews.com/stories/2003/05/26/world/main555555.shtml>.)

22 In 2002 AFSC nominated Svirsky and one of the organizations she works with—Women in Black—for the Nobel Peace Prize. (AFSC had been joint winner of the prize in 1947, along with the British Friends Service Council.)

had with her just a few hours earlier that "the general mood in Israel is one of more anger and more hatred of Palestinians. More people here are prepared simply to say that all Palestinians are terrorists." She recalled that on one recent evening, she had been trying to get to sleep "but at a time when I knew that a mother and child were being threatened by death in a hostage situation in the West Bank. I cried some, but then I tried to get back to sleep. In the morning, the mother and her children were killed. I cried again. Our own hearts have been hardened by the repeated violence. And this is happening on all sides."

Svirsky, a leader of the Coalition of Women for a Just Peace, said that self-censorship had been growing in Israel—as had outward censorship about what was happening to the Palestinians. "So the Israelis just don't know what's happening to the Palestinians. They know the number of Palestinians killed is greater than the number of Israelis. But it still doesn't add up to a real picture of the degree of Palestinian suffering." She noted that a large number of Jewish Israelis supported the government's recently implemented plan to build a high, fortified fence to separate the northern West Bank from Israel proper. The implications of this support disturbed her: "A fence means, 'I am in despair about a political settlement. ... I don't want to *see* those people any more. ... I don't want to negotiate.'

"Two-thirds of Israelis support Sharon's attitudes," she said. "They are engaged in a frenzy of revenge. And yet, at the same time, 60 percent of Jewish Israelis say they want to see all or most of the settlements dismantled. ... These people really want to see the end of the occupation. They say, 'why send my son to protect the crazy settlers?'" (Under Israel's burdensome system of conscription, all Jewish and Druze males are required to do 36 months of compulsory service at age 18, and unmarried women to do 24 months. Muslim and Christian citizens are not required to serve. Neither are men undertaking Jewish religious training.[23])

Svirsky said that the main factor that propelled Sharon's election victory in 2001 was fear. "It all comes from fear. Fear pushes all the buttons from our historical memory as Jews. Every bomb

---

23 Information from The International Institute for Strategic Studies, *The Military Balance 2002-2003* (London: IISS, 2002), p.107. The Druze are members of a small religious denomination that broke off from Shi'ite Islam in the eleventh century CE. It has adherents in Israel, Syria, and Lebanon.

inside Israel sends an additional one hundred votes to the right."

Like many of the Israeli peace activists with whom we spoke, Svirsky expressed particular anger with former Prime Minister Ehud Barak. Barak, the leader of the Labor Party, had been elected in 1999 on a clearly pro-peace platform. But the diplomacy he conducted once in office was not sure-footed: he made decisions— on timing, and on the content of his diplomacy with the Palestinians and the government of Syria that all resulted in very damaging failures[24]. In addition, as a newcomer to politics, he proved a poor player in Israel's rambunctious internal democracy. Those weaknesses also paved the way for Sharon's victory at the polls in February 2001. "Barak did more to hurt the peace process than any other Israeli politician," Svirsky told us. "His spin on what had happened at the end of the negotiations—that Arafat 'was offered the moon and turned it down,' and that 'Arafat is therefore not a partner for peace'—this was all a most important factor in bringing the swing votes behind Sharon. This Barak spin, and the Palestinian bombings inside Israel are the two greatest causes for the present move toward extremism on the Israeli side."

Uri Avnery is a decades-long organizer in the Israeli peace-and-justice movement, and currently one of the leaders of a grouping called Gush Shalom—the Peace Bloc. We traveled to the busy coastal city of Tel Aviv to meet with him and three other members of the Gush Shalom leadership. We had to meet them at an "undisclosed location"—they had received so many death threats from Israeli extremists that they were forced to move their office, and no longer listed its address publicly.

"The vast majority of Israelis believe there is no partner for peace," Avnery told us. He explained that after the failure of the "make-or-break" summit meeting that Barak had held with Arafat (and U.S. President Bill Clinton) at the U.S. presidential retreat in Camp David in July 2000, Barak claimed he had made a very "generous offer" to Arafat but the Palestinian leader had turned it down. "This was the lie that Barak put out, and it's now being spread by all the Israeli media, and is believed by 95 percent of Israelis," Avnery said. He recalled that when Barak was first elected, in 1999, "We danced in Rabin Square [in Tel Aviv], we were so happy! But it turned out Barak was deeply disturbed. ... Maybe

---

24 Barak's diplomacy is described more fully in chapter 4.

he intended all along to sabotage the peace process. Either that, or he didn't know anything at all about the Palestinians."

Avnery and his colleagues described in detail the seeming contradiction in Israeli attitudes to which Svirsky had alluded, whereby a majority of Israelis expressed support for a large-scale withdrawal from the occupied territories and the dismantling of many settlements, while another majority (even stronger than the first) expressed support for Sharon's tough posture toward the Palestinians. "Why did the Israeli public become so angry after the start of this *intifada*?" Gush Shalom activist Beate Zilversmidt asked rhetorically. "Because they understood that—as Gush Shalom has always said—the price for peace is just as high as we said it was: a total withdrawal from the West Bank, and not a negotiation over dividing the West Bank. They are angry because they see that they can't push the Palestinians around. The current wave of anger and racism that is sweeping Israel, I see as stemming from frustration at finally seeing these truths."

Despite the many pressures of the situation at that time, Zilversmidt's colleague (and spouse) Adam Keller remained sanguine over the long-term prospects for reconciliation: "We have one thousand times the reasons to hate the Germans than we have to hate the Palestinians. So if you look at the reconciliation we have been able to reach with the Germans, then I am hopeful over the long term about reconciling with the Palestinians."

It was the short term that, to most of these Gush Shalom activists, seemed more worrisome. "I am always optimistic over the long run," Avnery told us. "But I'm very pessimistic in the short run. We are at the very beginning of a war of attrition. I don't remember a period like this since 1948. The Israeli government is using all the means at its disposal. It aims to get rid of Yasser Arafat and the Palestinian Authority, and to end the cohesion of the Palestinian people."

Many pro-peace Israelis and Palestinians told us they feared a repeat of the events of 1948. For most Israelis, 1948 is identified as the historic year in which, following two thousand years of Jewish exile and persecution, a Jewish state was established in the Middle East. Most Palestinians, by contrast, remember 1948 as the year of the *nakba* ("catastrophe"), a tragic event in which the establishment of the Jewish state brought about the exile and dispersal of four-fifths of the Palestinians who lived in the area that became Israel and the expropriation of these refugees' lands and properties. Although many members of the Israeli peace movement have expressed sympathy for the pain that the events of 1948 caused their Palestinian neighbors, relatively few of them would be prepared to offer the Palestinians whole-scale restitution of the actual landed property that they "lost" that year. But none of these activists would like to see a similar train of events take place again, whether in the West Bank or Gaza or (as some Israeli hard-liners advocate) against Israel's remaining Palestinian Arab population.

During our visit to his home in the West Bank town of Dura, Palestinian journalist Khaled Amayreh talked about some of the fears felt by people in his encircled community: "I can't even convey the torment, the anguish, suffering, and sense of persecution that we live with." He recalled that Britain's Lord Gilmour, on a recent visit to the West Bank, had described the situation as "an affront to humanity." Some people, Amayreh noted, had compared Israel's actions against the Palestinians with the Nazi treatment of the Jews in Europe. "There is some exaggeration in this," he said, "but the issue is, should the international community wait until the situation becomes exactly the same as that?[25] No! People can be killed in other ways than in gas chambers. The Palestinian population centers have already been reduced to huge detention camps in which people are already dying from a number of otherwise preventable causes. And people are feeling so closed in."

He noted the rise in open discussion inside Israel over the preceding months of the possibility of what the Israelis refer to as "transfer," that is, a mass deportation of Palestinians from the occupied territories, or even from inside Israel. He said that on the same day we were meeting with him in Dura, the rightwing Israeli Moledet ("Homeland") Party was holding a conference in Jerusalem with the slogan of "Transfer Now"— with Ariel Sharon as one of the featured speakers.[26] Amayreh said that many influential people in Israel were working hard to try to drive the

---

25 We are conscious that some readers may find these comments offensive. After much reflection, however, we decided to include them in our report because they do reflect one strand of thought among Palestinians.

26 For more information about this party, including clear explanations of its support for "transfer," see its English-language website <http://www.moledet.org.il/english/public.html>.

Palestinians out of the occupied areas, in one way or another. "But we will not go. ... There would be no 'transfer' without genocide.

"Transfer will not solve the problem, anyway," he continued. "It would complicate it. It would condemn the whole region to another hundred years of turbulence. If Israel deports three million Palestinians to Jordan, the Hashemite Kingdom there will fall. ... Also, if the Israelis are hell-bent on transferring me, then I would try to reciprocate."

We asked him how he would describe, and try to deal with, the many deep fears we had heard Israelis express to us about their security. He replied:

> Some of the fears they talk about are genuine. But there are also some psychotic fears, stemming perhaps from their experience during the Holocaust. I don't know how the Palestinians can treat those ones. But the genuine fears that they have, that stem from the suicide bombing, those ones we do need to address. ...

> But this fear and terror exists on both sides, you know. We have so many Palestinian kids who have fears of the Apache helicopters, or of the terror of the checkpoints! But all this terror on both sides is only a symptom of the conflict. The conflict itself is the malady, and the fears are the symptom. We need to address, and resolve, the root causes of the conflict. The danger is that, over time, the fears/symptoms themselves can then become causes for future conflicts.

We found many in Israel, too, who were worried that the continuation of the conflict was strengthening the forces of extremism in their own society. In Tel Aviv, anti-militarism activist Ruth Hiller told us she was concerned at the manifestations of racism that seemed to pervade much of Israeli society. "Even the play staged at my kids' school contained so many racist 'jokes,'" she said. "I'm afraid we're raising a generation of fascists. The situation here is desperate. ... We're feeling fear and desperation. I am fearful for the Palestinians—and I'm also fearful for the kind of country we may turn out to be."

Also taking part in that meeting was Tanya Reinhart, an outspoken advocate of equality and justice who teaches linguistics at Tel Aviv University. We asked Reinhart if she felt the conditions in Israeli society were permitting advocates of transfer to increase their influence. "Yes," she replied, "transfer could certainly happen. For example, if there's a big regional war." She described the policies already being undertaken by her government as constituting "a slow suffocation of the Palestinians. ... Gaza is already a prison. Now the government is making the same situation in the cities of the West Bank. It means a collapse of their economy and their society."

Reinhart had long been a vocal critic of the Oslo process, arguing that Oslo did not do nearly enough to end Israel's occupation of the West Bank and Gaza or to meet the Palestinians' basic needs. "Oslo produced a series of Bantustans for the Palestinians," she said, referring to the highly dependent "homelands" that the white minority regime in South Africa tried to establish for the country's black citizens in the 1970s. "What the Sharon government is doing now is much worse. Can you call it prisons? Or ghettos? What can you call it? No, they are not extermination camps; we should not exaggerate. There is one simple solution, though: if the Israelis want all that land, then they should take it all and give all the people there their full rights. ... But no, they want the land without the people."

On the same topic of "transfer," anti-settlement activist Michael Warschawski told us:

> Sharon is not crazy. He has a very coherent plan and has pursued it since the 1970s. He is not simply engaging in blind violence without reason.... Like every military officer, Sharon has a 'Big Plan' and a 'Small Plan' to fall back on if the Big Plan proves unrealizable. The Big Plan is to operationalize the longtime Likud slogan that "Jordan is Palestine." It is based on large-scale 'transfer' of Palestinians from the West Bank to the East Bank [of the Jordan], that is, on ethnic cleansing. Then, Sharon can continue to build the demography of the Jewish state in the West Bank.

> To do this, though, he would need a big war in the region that could help to hide his actions. But he can't provoke this war alone.

In Warschawski's view, Sharon's 'Small Plan' would consist of recognizing a Palestinian state inside the areas where the Palestinians had exercised some local control under the Oslo plan. "Sharon would have no problem calling that a Palestinian state— or an empire, or a kingdom. But in reality, it would have no control over resources or over its borders, and there would be no contiguity between its six or eight or ten different parts."

In his office in Haifa University's airy campus atop Mount Carmel, psychology professor Dr. Benjamin Bet-Hallahmi gave an analysis of the mental condition of many of his fellow Jewish Israelis, twenty-one months into the second *intifada*:

Many Israelis have a self-image that says, 'We came here peacefully and the Palestinians attacked us.' They ask, 'What have we done to deserve these attacks?' ... But I see Zionism as a last vestige of colonialism in the world, and the events of the last two years have broken up the coloniz- ers' fantasies. Zionism has to face the stark reality that its actions have not been cost-free for other people, and that there will be no end to the resistance of those others.

This is depressing for all Israelis. It leads to worry, fear, and anxiety for the future.

Bet-Hallahmi saw Israelis becoming "more paranoid, more fearful." He suggested that "there is a basic insecurity over how we justify what we do to the Palestinians. Israelis become so vocifer- ous against any criticisms precisely because they are so uneasy in their conscience. This self-image is crucial; there are many decent, thoughtful Israelis who are living in complete denial of what their government is doing on the West Bank and in the Gaza Strip—a denial that is, it seems, essential to their mental health."

International Law and Blueprints for Peace

When we were in Gaza, human rights advocate Raji Sourani also expressed great pessimism. "I believe the worst is yet to come," he told us. "I see black and bloody days ahead."

He argued forcefully that Palestinians had two main needs: an end to the occupation and the implementation of international humanitarian law. "If you take away the protections we're sup- posed to have under international humanitarian law, then you take away the credibility within Palestinian society of all the human rights organizations, the peace activists, and the people working to build a healthy civil society here. If you defeat international humanitarian law, you defeat the *crème de la crème* of the human experience since World War II. You defeat all the forces of human- ism, and you bring in more Taliban activists!"

Sourani was speaking to us in the long conference room of the organization he heads, the Palestinian Center for Human Rights (PCHR), which was founded in the mid-1980s. Lining the walls of the room were numerous boxes containing detailed reports of the many very serious human rights violations that Israel has commit- ted in Gaza and the West Bank during its lengthy occupation— and also of the many rights violations committed by the Palestinian Authority during its much shorter life. In September 2002, PCHR was awarded the Bruno Kreisky Prize for Outstanding Achievements in the Area of Human Rights. (Israeli journalist Amira Hass was a co-recipient.) In 1991, Sourani personally was awarded the Robert F. Kennedy Human Rights Award.

As we left his office, Sourani handed us the latest of the "Weekly Reports" that PCHR compiles. In terms of killings, it had not been a "bad" week. But in other ways it had. The report started, "This week, Israeli occupying forces ... invaded and encroached into Palestinian areas such as Nablus, Jenin, Tulkarm, Qalqilya, Hebron, and Rafah. This week, four Palestinian civilians, including a child, were killed by Israeli occupying forces..."[27]

Moshe Ma'oz was someone we met who seemed at some level to have an idea of how this situation could be ended. Ma'oz is an Israeli and a much-published scholar of Arab affairs who directs the Harry S. Truman Institute for the Advancement of Peace at the Hebrew University of Jerusalem. He told us, "I was born in this country, and fought in five of its wars—in each of which I was promoted."

He told us that, in his view, a "blueprint" for peace had now been established, with its shape delineated by four significant steps toward an agreement. These were:

- The Camp David talks of July 2000,

- A compromise peace proposal put forward by U.S. President Clinton in December 2000,

- The results of Israeli-Palestinian negotiations held in Taba, Egypt, in January 2001,

- A peace proposal put forward by Saudi Arabia's Crown Prince Abdullah and adopted by a summit meeting of all Arab leaders in March 2002.[28]

---

27 This report (for the week 30 May – 5 June, 2002) is available through the "Reports" button at this section of PCHR's excellently organized website: <http://www.pchrgaza.org/pchr_doc.htm>. The site contains considerable amounts of very useful information on the human rights situation in the occupied territories. Check the "Fact Sheets", "PCHR Documents", and "Theme Packages" sections of the site.

28 This initiative proposed that if Israel would withdraw fully from the lands occupied in 1967 and allow a just resolution for the Palestinian refugees, then the Arab states would establish "normal peaceful relations" with Israel. Most international leaders including U.S. President Bush welcomed it, but rapidly escalating violence in Israel/Palestine soon swamped its significance.

"The Saudi initiative was a breakthrough," Ma'oz stressed. "And between those four formulas I have mentioned, we now have a blueprint for peace. But how many more people will have to die before we get there?" He said he thought that people on both sides were not thinking rationally. "They are acting out of emotion only—frustration, despair, and anger."

He decried the absence of visionary leadership on both the Palestinian and the Israeli sides and criticized an argument common among Israelis, that they cannot make peace with the Palestinians until Palestinians show that they actually like them. "It's not about love!" he said. "There is no 'love' in the politics of the Middle East. But there is a strong interest in peace." People in conflicts, he noted, "always tend to speak of their own victimization. But there are victims on both sides. Here, people bring up irrelevant things like the Holocaust. ... Unfortunately, most Israelis don't even see what's happening to the Palestinians." Many Israelis, he said, "don't even think of Palestinians as human, but as somehow less than human. Except when the Palestinians do suicide bombings. That, paradoxically, is when they start to get some respect." In general, though, he said, "People don't have any sympathy left—on either side of the line."

We asked him what he thought could be done about the situation. His answer was simply, "To pray!" Like many other supporters of peace with whom we met, he described himself as "on the verge of despair."

The Strategic Analysts

The Jaffee Center for Strategic Studies was founded at Tel Aviv University in the mid-1970s as an independent research institution that could "see over the horizon" of Israel's current security concerns and warn of threats to come. When our bus reached the security gate at the well-guarded perimeter of the university campus, the guards had to call up to the Jaffee Center to confirm our appointment before we were allowed to proceed to our meeting there.

We were warmly received in the Center's conference room overlooking the heart of the campus. Yossi Alpher is a senior researcher at the Center who over the years has conducted a number of path-breaking studies of the Palestinian issue. For example, in 1989, two years into the Palestinians' first *intifada* in the occupied territories, Alpher coordinated a group of Israeli strategic experts who studied their country's options in the occupied Palestinian territories. He was the lead author of the report that resulted, *The West Bank and Gaza: Israel's Options for Peace.*[29] In recent years he has worked with Palestinian community activist (and more recently, Minister of Labor) Ghassan al-Khateeb to co-edit a Palestinian-Israeli website called "Bitter Lemons" that carries a lively but respectful dialogue over current affairs.[30] Alpher told us,

> Israelis are totally preoccupied in the short term by the threat from suicide bombings—and this is so even though the numbers killed in suicide bombings are less than those killed in traffic accidents. This preoccupation leads to support for any policy which will separate "them" from "us." Hence the forty percent of support you find expressed for transfer. But hence, too, the large support you find for a withdrawal from most of the territories, plus the dismantlement of the settlements.

He indicated that the kind of withdrawal he would advocate would be nowhere near a total pullback to the pre-1967 line, but would involve border modifications that would keep most of the West Bank's 400,000 settlers on the Israeli side of the line. He said that under the formula he proposed only some 50,000-70,000 settlers would have to be evacuated. Around 5,000 of these were, he estimated, people whom it would be "very difficult" to evacuate. "We should have offered compensation to the settlers to help them to come back inside Israel, back at the beginning of the peace process," he said, echoing an idea that was voiced in the early 1990s but never implemented. "We didn't do that. Instead, we continued to view the settlers as a bargaining chip."[31] In other words, the Israeli negotiators had hoped that the presence, and perhaps even the increasing number, of the settlers would continue to strengthen their hand in the post-Oslo negotiations with the

---

29 The Jaffee Center Study Group, *The West Bank and Gaza: Israel's Options for Peace* (Tel Aviv: Tel Aviv University, 1989.) This book, and a short companion volume, *Israel, the West Bank and Gaza: Toward a Solution*, included some of the earliest attempts by Israeli security experts to explore the scenario of creating an independent Palestinian state in West Bank and Gaza.

30 <www.bitterlemons.org>.

31 In 2002, the U.S.-based organization Jewish Alliance for Justice and Peace (Brit Tzedek v'Shalom) launched a campaign to persuade the U.S. and other governments to start offering financial incentives to the settlers to return "home" to Israel. See <www.btvshalom.org>.

Palestinians. But instead, the political weight of the settlers formed an increasingly burdensome impediment to progress in the talks.

Back in the early days of the Oslo process, Alpher concluded, "people used to look at the peace process as a grand reconciliation. But now, it is looked at more as a very messy divorce."

Shai Feldman, the director of the Jaffee Center, echoed this theme. "The only sound basis for a settlement now is a total divorce," he told us. "As in any divorce, that means dissolving all the 'joint bank accounts'. So we cannot keep on having 140 settlements inside the occupied territories." Inside Israel, he said, "There is massive support for this kind of divorce. The most important thing for Israelis is the demographic factor, and the implications of the area's demography for preserving the Jewish character of the Israeli state."

He predicted that the continued focus of Israel's voters on this goal would generate continuing pressure for a unilateral Israeli withdrawal from most of the occupied territories.

> But I don't see how a unilateral withdrawal can avoid leading to a disaster. The first issue is, if we really mean that we seek disengagement from the Palestinians, then any real disengagement would mean dismantling 80 percent of the settlements, holding 20 percent of the settlers.[32] But if there is a willingness on our part to do this, then why do it unilaterally? Why not embed it in a total resolution of the conflict? ... A unilateral disengagement doesn't even start to address other issues like the rights of the refugees, or the Temple Mount question in Jerusalem.[33] Also, with a unilateral withdrawal, Israel would have sent the message that it is withdrawing under fire. That undermines the credibility of our broader posture of deterrence.[34]

He was dismissive, too, of the idea that the security fence being built inside the northern West Bank could ensure the safety of

---

32 This formulation indicates that Feldman envisaged the dismantling of mainly small, sparsely populated settlements and the annexation to Israel of the much larger ones that between them house 80 percent of the settlers. It was not clear whether he was proposing any evacuations of settlers from East Jerusalem, or even whether he included these Israelis among the "settlers" whose numbers he was discussing. See chapter 5.

33 The Temple Mount is a site in Jerusalem considered to be extremely holy by many observant Jews. But it is also co-located with a site venerated by observant Muslims. For more on this topic, see chapter 5.

34 For more discussion of the issue of the "credibility" of Israel's deterrence, see chapter 10.

Israelis. "The fence is a tactic, not a strategy," he said. "It will have only a limited impact."

We asked Feldman what he, a respected expert on strategic affairs, could recommend as a strategy for ending the problem of the suicide bombings. "I don't have a purely military recommendation," he said. "Our military leaders have always said it has to be a joint military and political solution to deal with this problem. This is not a confrontation between two armies, after all, but one between two societies."

The Deputy Speaker

When Naomi Chazan spoke with us, she had just rushed to the East Jerusalem YWCA from meetings she was holding at the Knesset in her role as its deputy speaker. "The situation is deteriorating," she told us right away. A political scientist by training, she described the situation since late 2000 as having settled into "a dreadful routine" marked by three main features:

> The first is the cruelty of the violence employed—with no excuses for any side. It has been unspeakable on both sides ... The suicide bombers are violating human rights at a very basic level, and the people carrying them out against civilians are committing crimes against humanity. But to use F-16s against civilians, or attack helicopters, or to cut off food and medicine to whole communities—these are also gross violations. ... So now, on both sides, we have deep societal traumas. People are scared and jittery and jumpy; and they do things they would normally consider unacceptable.

"Then, too, the policy on both sides has become emotion-driven," she asserted, "based on the misplaced idea that there is a military solution. This idea is misplaced on both sides. And even if it's true that more Israelis now are prepared to see the establishment of a Palestinian state, still they don't want the Palestinians to win it by force."

She identified the second main feature of the "dreadful routine" as "the total breakdown of trust on both sides." She recalled that she had been meeting with representatives of the PLO in various places around the world since 1980.[35] "We spent all that time

---

35 Until the early 1990s, it was illegal for Israelis to meet with PLO representatives anywhere in the world. Those who did so, like Chazan or Uri Avnery, risked criminal prosecution. (One of Chazan's early meetings with a PLO representative had been organized by Everett Mendelsohn of AFSC.)

building up trust. But the last twenty-one months have shattered that," she said. "This breakdown of trust has brought out the absolute worst in both peoples! Racist and fascist utterances have become commonplace. In the Knesset, what I have to listen to is sometimes so anti-Arab it makes you weep. What is said about Arabs in the Knesset I could not accept to be said about Jews. But also what I read on some Palestinian websites is grossly anti-Semitic and not just anti-Israeli. ... It's making us all ugly."

A third feature was, she said, that "there are two narratives that don't meet. It's a conversation of the deaf, but also of the dead—because if you don't hear, you eventually die. The two narratives force everyone to take sides, because if you accept the Palestinian narrative, it becomes almost obligatory to reject the Israeli narrative, and vice versa." She noted that this lack of communication had made the possibility of finding a resolution more remote. "But for myself, I would reframe the issue as you're either for peace or you're part of the problem."

She issued an impassioned appeal for international engagement. "The objective is clear," she said. "We need some combination of the Clinton proposal, what was discussed at Taba, and the Saudi plan. ... But what's been totally lacking in the last sixteen months has been a diplomatic channel that will help us get there." She said that international intervention was now urgently needed.

"The situation is desperate now," she said. "But it can get worse."

Some Palestinian Christian Thinkers

Naim Ateek is a canon in the Anglican church who is director of Sabeel, the Palestinian Center for Liberation Theology. (*Sabeel* is the Arabic word for "way.") We spoke with Ateek and some of his Sabeel colleagues in the organization's headquarters in a beautiful, stone-vaulted traditional Arab house in East Jerusalem.

Ateek expressed quiet frustration that the Palestinians' concerns—including those of the ten percent of Palestinians who are Christians—seemed to be heard so little in the United States. "We totally despair of the U.S. Congress," he said. Despite the many forces he saw as lined up in the U.S. against the Palestinians, he still expressed hope that the U.S. could become a force for peace. "The U.S. is really capable of helping us decisively, if they choose to do so."

He identified another potential source for peace as lying inside Israeli society itself. Just the preceding week, he said, some people from Sabeel had held a meeting with some Israeli peace activists, with both sides trying to rebuild links of cooperation that had been strained almost to the breaking point since the beginning of the *intifada*.

Sabeel board member Samia Khoury described a third potential source of help, "We should not give up on the U.N.—it is the right and legitimate place to address these issues. How can we put pressure on the U.N. not to lose its independence, which we see as having been hijacked by the U.S.?" Regarding the continuing call for democratic reform in Palestinian institutions, Khoury said, "I don't know if we Palestinians are unable to transform the situation, or unwilling." She recalled that after the end of the siege the Israelis had imposed in April 2002 around Arafat's headquarters, "We thought Arafat would say he could no longer cooperate with the Israelis and the Americans, who had treated him so badly, and that he would step down. Palestinians who had tried to bring about political change inside their own community had largely given up their efforts in despair."

"Anyway," she added, "the first job is to end the occupation. We need to get the nightmare of the occupation off our backs!" She noted sadly that "the Palestinians had tried to fight for democracy inside our movement for ten years or more, and the U.S. had always refused to help us in that. But now they have made such an issue of seeking to oust Mr. Arafat that if we dare to ask for reform any more we'll just look like collaborators."

On a different note, Khoury, a veteran educator, said, "I was so glad to see the end of the school year that just finished. Every day, we would worry so about the safety of our children going to and from school. ... This occupation is killing us all."

The discussion turned to the issue of reconciliation and forgiveness. One Sabeel board member discussed the traditional Palestinian and Arab conflict-resolution mechanism known as *sulha* and commented,

> Reconciliation involves a fundamental repair to human lives, especially of those who suffered. Before there can be forgiveness, there should be a recognition of the harm that has been done. Forgiveness is a gift from God, and it is the outcome of righteousness, right relationships.

We Palestinians need to be able to exercise forgiveness toward the Israelis for the harm they have done us. We need to be able to do that for our own sanity, and for our spiritual growth, not to be triumphalistic about it. But that forgiveness comes after recognition of the wrong that has been done.

Naim Ateek expressed a similar view. "The sequence we work on is 'justice first.' Justice will then lead to peace, and peace to reconciliation and forgiveness. By justice, we mean the end of the occupation. And this indeed would be a form of justice with mercy, since even with the ending of the occupation we would still have to give up many of our other longstanding claims against Israel."

Samia Khoury said she still sometimes has dreams of the relationships that existed between the different communities in Palestine before 1948. "We all got on so well together then. We had Jewish neighbors from that time who, after the West Bank was occupied in 1967, came to look us up and see how we were doing. But now, our children and grandchildren know the Israelis only as soldiers."

Two Societies in Pain

By the time of our visit to Israel/Palestine, it was evident that the closures, curfews, and other measures taken by the Israeli security forces throughout the preceding years were inflicting a serious, continuing humanitarian crisis on the three million Palestinians of the occupied territories. Meanwhile, inside Israel, the general crisis of insecurity caused by the Palestinian suicide bombers was imposing a heavy social and economic burden on Israelis. The broad counter-insurgency campaign that the Israeli authorities continued to wage against the Palestinians was also imposing its own costs on Israeli society. For example, whenever we traveled through West Jerusalem or other Israeli cities we saw numerous young people in uniform on the streets, on their way to or from postings ordered under the mandatory 36 months of full-time service required of most 18-year-old Jewish Israeli men, or the 24 months of service required of most young Jewish Israeli women. Regular reserve duty for these Israelis continues until age 41 for men, and until age 24 or marriage for women. Such a conscription system places a heavy burden on a nation, both socially and economically.

However, while the economic cost to Israelis of the security crisis amounted to some percentage points of reduction in the country's gross domestic product, causing a generally depressing economic climate there, for the Palestinians of the occupied territories the cost of the crisis amounted to a broad destruction of Palestinian national infrastructure, institutions, livelihoods, and civil society—in short, to the pauperization of much of the Palestinian society within the occupied territories.

When we met with human rights activist Raji Sourani he told us that 81 percent of Gaza's Palestinian residents were living under the poverty line, and 61 percent were unemployed.[36] Speaking of those 55 percent of the Palestinians in the occupied territories whose families are refugees from the area that became Israel in 1948, one official from an international aid agency told us, "Before the intifada, we had six percent of our registered refugees who were listed as 'special hardship cases.' Now that figure has jumped to 60 percent. We have taken on the feeding of 127,500 families in Gaza, and 98,000 families in the West Bank. Multiply that by five for the number of individuals involved."[37] This official said the main problem that all aid agencies faced was that of safe humanitarian access: that is, getting relief shipments through the numerous Israeli roadblocks and checkpoints in the occupied territories, in a timely fashion.

This official and other aid workers described the complicated measures the Israeli authorities had imposed on those attempting to move relief shipments through the checkpoints. It was called "back-to-back." Since no vehicles were allowed to pass through the checkpoints, aid organizations had to rent separate fleets of trucks to operate within each inter-checkpoint zone; at each checkpoint, the trucks had to be offloaded by hand, and the goods inspected, before the goods were carried across the checkpoint—still by hand—to the trucks waiting on the other side. This made the delivery of aid shipments not only extremely expensive but also very unpredictable since, as we discovered during our travels, the checkpoints could be opened or closed with little notice. "In the West Bank, it is almost impossible to know where or how to get through," the aid official told us. "And in Gaza, they have only been letting in one-third of the Strip's daily flour requirement."

---

36 Sourani's comment on this was: "It looks as though the Israelis are trying to push us, through economic pressure, to leave."

37 Up-to-date information on the humanitarian situation in the occupied territories is available from the U.N. Humanitarian Information Center for the Occupied Palestinian Territories at <www.reliefweb.int/hic-opt>.

A January 2003 report from the Union of Palestinian Medical Relief Committees (UPMRC) cited the roadblocks as also contributing to a drastic deterioration of Palestinian health conditions. The report stated that since September 2001, 83 Palestinians had died at checkpoints while awaiting access to necessary medical care such as kidney dialysis or emergency coronary care, and 36 babies had been born at checkpoints while their mothers waited to pass. The report quoted a study that found that in the six preceding weeks 33 percent of Palestinians in the West Bank and Gaza requiring emergency care, 44 percent of dialysis patients, and 46 percent of chemotherapy patients had been blocked at checkpoints from reaching vital medical facilities. It quoted Union president Mustafa Barghouthi as saying, "It is the first time that an entire people has been prevented from using their roads for a period of almost two years. The effects on the health situation are catastrophic."[38]

The steps the Israeli authorities were taking in the occupied territories were inflicting considerable damage not only on the Palestinians' physical well-being but also on their mental health. In the Gaza City headquarters of the Gaza Community Mental Health Program (GCMHP), clinical psychologist Dr. Ahmed Abu Tawahina told us that he and his colleagues worked on the assumption that, because of the stress imposed on them by the closures, repeated Israeli attacks, and general sense of insecurity, "one hundred percent of the Palestinians have a psychological problem. That includes even our own professionals here, who feel the powerlessness of professionals who are unable to solve people's problems. Like, when a person comes in here who is suicidal because he can no longer provide for his family. We can't 'treat' the underlying cause of that problem."

We met Abu Tawahina and his colleague Husam al-Nounou in a meeting-room in the clinic whose walls were covered with diagrams illustrating intervention methods for cases of depression or trauma. Nounou explained how the GCMHP carried out its work:

> Our organization started in 1990, as a Palestinian non-governmental organization. We have held thousands of community meetings with different groups over the years. In this region, there's often a huge stigma attached to the idea of mental health problems. People think it might be a hereditary madness or a sign of demonic possession. What we try to do

---

38 The UPMRC press release of January 8, 2003, is available at <www.upmrc.org/content/publications/publications_b.html>.

is reassure people that the kinds of mental health disorders they see are the normal responses of people who are facing abnormally stressful circumstances.... We stress that it's the situation that's abnormal....We have community-based educational programs. We're trying to teach people how to deal with the continuing stress.

Clinician Abu Tawahina spoke a little about mental health professionals who had come to Gaza from richer, more secure societies and started talking about the condition that American psychiatrists call "post-traumatic stress disorder." "What do they mean, 'post'-traumatic?" he asked rhetorically. "'Post' is not our issue here!"

Nounou recalled with nostalgia the wave of hope that had swept through the Palestinian communities back in 1991, when for the first time in half a century a Palestinian delegation was allowed to participate in an Arab-Israeli peace gathering. That was the Middle East peace conference convened in Madrid by U.S. President George H. W. Bush. The much-loved Gaza City physician Dr. Haidar Abdel-Shafi led the Palestinian delegation there. "You saw the Palestinian reaction to Madrid," Nounou said. "There was widespread excitement and hope! We saw a message of peace. For us, we thought this meant the end of the occupation. ... Instead of which, we ended up with the desperate situation that you see."

He said that he and his colleagues were convinced that health and dignity were among the most fundamental human rights. "We believe that there is a correlation between mental health and human rights. Nobody can talk about achieving healthy psyches under occupation."

In March 2003, Save the Children-Sweden and Save the Children-UK published a study about the lives of Palestinian children growing up under prolonged in-home curfews and community closures. As part of the study, children were encouraged to talk and write about their expectations for their future. The report stated that "this was a challenging exercise, especially for boys. They needed a lot of clarification and it is clear that many have difficulty viewing the future. Some in fact even left their paper blank."[39] The Israeli journalist Amira Hass reported in 2003 that when an educational counselor who had been meeting regularly

---

39 *Growing Up Under Curfew: Safeguarding the Basic Rights of Palestinian Children* (Save the Children—Sweden and Save the Children—UK, March 2003), p. 14. The full text of this report is available at <www.savethechildren.org.uk/development/ reg_pub/Curfew.pdf>.

with children in the refugee camp in Kalandia, in East Jerusalem, asked the children how they saw themselves in 20 years, they replied, "buried."[40]

While Palestinian society was reeling from the economic and psychosocial costs of the violence, and from the despair engendered by the collapse of previous hopes for peace, some similar phenomena were visible inside Israeli society, too. "The economy is a shambles," Moshe Ma'oz from Hebrew University told us. "We have real fears of an economic collapse as serious as the recent one in Argentina." Shortly before our visit, the Israeli government had ordered sizable cutbacks in the benefits allowed to Israeli families under the country's traditionally generous social-welfare schemes.[41] Later in 2002, as already noted, the country's continuing budget woes helped persuade the Labor Party to withdraw from the Sharon-led ruling coalition.

Haifa University professor Benjamin Bet-Hallahmi shared Ma'oz's sense of the seriousness of Israel's economic downturn. "The university work force is in near revolt over their pay scales," he said. "People say there might be another *intifada,* launched by the workers here on the campus!"

Bet-Hallahmi is a social psychologist. He judged that, in addition to paying a heavy economic cost for the continuation of the violence, Israelis had also been paying a heavy psychosocial cost. "Israelis have been traumatized by the Palestinian bombs," he noted, adding:

> You have to understand that Israel has made huge advances in the technology of our weapons systems. We can send nuclear warheads to any place we want to, anywhere in the world.[42] But still, we fear to ride the buses at home, or to go to the grocery store!

Mental illness among Palestinians resulting from an oppressive occupa-

---

40 Amira Hass, "What the fatality statistics tell us," in *Ha'aretz,* September 9, 2003.

41 These cuts applied most harshly to families of which neither parent was an armed forces veteran. The cuts thus hit hardest against Israeli families of Palestinian ethnicity, ultra-Orthodox Jewish families, and families headed by single mothers, since these are the groups for which military service is not mandatory.

42 The usually authoritative, London-based International Institute for Strategic Studies assesses that Israel "is widely believed to have nuclear capability with up to 100 warheads." Delivery means could include aircraft or missiles with a range of up to 2,000 kilometers. Israel's air force has 237 F-16 fighter planes, advanced early-warning planes, and drones in its fleet. *The Military Balance 2001-2002* (London: Oxford University Press, 2002), pp. 135-36.

tion finds its counterpart in a growing number of nervous breakdowns among Israeli soldiers who have felt their own consciences violated by acts they performed while on duty in Gaza and the West Bank.

Suffering, and a Way out of It

During our visit to Palestine/Israel we were pained to see at firsthand the suffering that acts of violence and of forceful repression had inflicted, and continued to inflict, on the lives of the nine million of our fellow humans who live between the Jordan River and the Mediterranean Sea. The physical damage—to scores of thousands of human bodies, to homes, to community facilities, and the lives of individuals and communities—was bad enough. But we clearly discerned that the violence was inflicting deep wounds on human dignity, human psyches, and human souls, too. Among the many other symptoms of this spiritual wounding that we witnessed at firsthand, or were told about, we were troubled by the apparent blunting of the ability of many Palestinians and Israelis to recognize the full and equal humanity of members of the other community, and the readiness of increasing numbers of Israelis and Palestinians to undertake or condone acts of violence against members of the other community that in normal times would be considered deeply abhorrent. This spiritual wounding has thus helped to keep the cycle of violence turning in the land where Jesus of Nazareth first proclaimed his message of nonviolence, peace, and universal love.

As people who are in the main not directly involved, we hesitate to put forward our views on specific details of the "best" political outcome. We do note, though, that among the thirteen million people who are directly involved—who include around four million Palestinians forced to live in exile from their homeland as well as the nine million people who now live in Israel/Palestine—a strong majority have called urgently for an immediate end to Israel's military occupation of the West Bank and Gaza, with or without some form of internationally supervised transition. And a clear majority of these people—including many Jewish Israelis and virtually all Palestinians—seemed to support the call for urgent and effective international intervention that would bring the violence, the occupation, and the continuing assault on people's fundamental rights to an end.

What is important now, we believe, is to proclaim once again the deep-seated belief in human equality that lies at the heart of our hopes for building a better, more peaceful world; to listen with compassionate attention to the voices of all Israelis and all Palestinians—whether these voices express pain, fear, anger, compassion, or inspiration; and to find ways to work with all these women and men to end not only all acts of cruelty and violence but also all the social and political structures of cruelty and violence that have been maintained in Israel/Palestine for far too long.

Part Two

*Dimensions
of the Crisis*

Israeli settlements (in italics) in the West Bank and Gaza Strip,
2004. Circles show relative population of settlements. Inset (not to
scale) shows Israeli settlements as dots in the Gaza Strip. Palestinian
towns and cities are shown only for location, not for population.
Adapted from Foundation for Middle East Peace

[4]

Occupation, Settlements, and Peace Talks

[S]ince the Six Day War, we are as close to the Palestinians as a jailer is to the prisoner handcuffed to him. A jailer cuffing his wrist to that of a prisoner for an hour or two is a matter of routine. But a jailer who cuffs himself to his prisoner for 36 years is himself no longer a free man. The occupation has also robbed us of our freedom.
—Amos Oz, 2003

Peace can only last where human rights are respected, where the people are fed, and where individuals and nations are free.
—The Dalai Lama, 1989

Behind the Visible Violence

As people of faith who are convinced that violence cannot solve human problems, we found it particularly sad to encounter so many Palestinians and Israelis who felt themselves so deeply trapped in an ever-turning cycle of tit-for-tat violence. But we also discerned two other significant things about this apparent "cycle" of violence: firstly, it was highly asymmetrical, and secondly, it was not the only process of violence involved in the encounter between these two peoples.

Regarding the asymmetry of the physical violence, we noted that on the one side the vast majority of the killings of Palestinians were carried out by members of organized security forces under the control of a powerful, well-armed, elected government, while on the other side the majority of the killings of Israelis were carried out by non-state actors, including armed paramilitary units and individuals—and that nearly all of these acts of violence were denounced by the elected Palestinian leadership.

Regarding the existence of other, perhaps less easily visible forms of violence, we saw that the occupation, a highly anti-democratic regime of foreign military rule that has abused the rights of the Palestinians of the occupied areas at every turn and has been maintained over these three million people only by the application of massive force, was itself a human-made structure of great violence. We also saw that behind the cover provided by the occupation, Israeli authorities were escalating their pursuit of the fundamentally colonial project of expropriating Palestinian land and other natural resources for the exclusive benefit of Israeli settlers.

We noted that a high proportion of the Israeli security personnel actually running the occupation were conscripts. Indeed, while some of the soldiers whom we encountered doing this job seemed to take pleasure in throwing their weight around, others seemed not to relish the duties assigned to them. In Hebron, we saw both kinds of soldiers. At one spot in the city, as previously noted, we saw a squad of soldiers hitting and harassing a Palestinian youth. Elsewhere in the city, by contrast, three soldiers who stopped us at a checkpoint talked quite readily once we had broken the ice: they told us how eager they were to finish their distasteful duty and return home.

By June 2002, more than 450 Israeli reserve officers had signed a declaration that they would refuse to serve in the occupied territories since they judged that the major aim of the deployment there of the Israeli Defense Force (IDF) was to preserve the settlements. Their declaration read, in part:

- We, who sensed how the commands issued to us in the Territories, destroy all the values we had absorbed while growing up in this country...
- We, who know that the Territories are not Israel, and that all settlements are bound to be evacuated in the end.
- We hereby declare that we shall not continue to fight this War of the Settlements.
- We shall not continue to fight beyond the 1967 borders in order to dominate, expel, starve, and humiliate an entire people.
- We hereby declare that we shall continue serving in the Israel Defense Forces in any mission that serves Israel's defense.
- **The missions of occupation and oppression do not serve this purpose—and we shall take no part in them.**[43]

---

43 (Emphasis in the original text.) The full text of the declaration and updated information about its signers can been found at <http://www.seruv.org.il/defaulteng.asp>. For more information about Israel's military refusal movement, see chapter 10 below. By late 2003, the numbers of the Israeli "refusers" had grown even greater, and they included members of the most elite units such as the air force and the 'Sayeret Mitkal' commando units.

We agree with these courageous Israeli reserve officers that the main purpose of the operations by the Israeli Defense Force (IDF) in the West Bank seems to have become one of protecting (and indeed, expanding) the settlement project, and that these operations have inflicted quite unacceptable harm on the Palestinians. We feel it is necessary to underline the colonial nature of the settlement project, and to recognize that the interaction between this colonial project and its anti-colonial opponents forms an essential component of, and backdrop to, all the violence that the two nations have experienced over the past 36 years.

Israeli government spokesmen have frequently claimed that the actions the IDF has undertaken in the occupied territories are part of a "counter-terror" campaign, and many Israelis and friends of Israel worldwide seem sincerely to believe this is the case. So, too, do many Israeli soldiers. For example, in May 2002, two North American members of our group had been able to undertake quick, earlier visits to Ramallah. When one of them reached the main checkpoint leading into the city, she greeted the two soldiers there cordially and started a friendly conversation. "What is it exactly you're doing here?" she asked. "Stopping the terrorists from bringing bombs into Israel," one soldier said confidently, as his buddy nodded agreement. When she pointed out that this particular checkpoint was controlling passage from Israel into Ramallah rather than vice versa, they seemed at a loss as to how to respond.

What we all saw the IDF doing in the occupied territories seemed to involve something different, and far more troubling, than a counter-terror campaign. In the latter type of an undertaking, after all, the principal strategy needs to be one of winning allies in the fight against the perpetrators of violence, in order to isolate those malefactors and bring them to justice. But Ariel Sharon's government did not appear to have any interest at all in winning allies on the Palestinian side by, for example, giving a fair hearing to the concerns of Palestinian moderates, or making serious efforts to alleviate the suffering of the general Palestinian population. One of the most revealing signs of Sharon's true intentions toward the Palestinians seemed to us to be the numerous bombings he carried out against Palestinian leadership locations and police stations: these actions considerably weakened the Palestinian leadership's ability to act against the terrorists in their community.

"This is not an anti-terror operation that Sharon is undertaking," anti-settlement activist Michael Warschawski stressed to us. "That would require quite opposite tactics to those that Sharon is using.... It is a 'pacification' operation, such as has frequently been used by colonial powers throughout history.... Sharon's decision to destroy the Palestinian leadership is not accidental. This has been seen before in colonial history. It is totally unoriginal. But it won't work. The will of the Palestinians is not about to be broken."

Further evidence to back up Warschawski's claim that the IDF's actions in the West Bank and Gaza had more to do with "breaking the will" of the Palestinians than with ending the conditions in which terrorism flourishes comes from none other than the man who in late summer 2002 was appointed the IDF's new chief of staff, Lieutenant General Moshe Ya'alon. In an interview with the Israeli daily *Ha'aretz* shortly after he took up his new job, Ya'alon provided an apparently candid description of the goals of the IDF's operations in Gaza and the West Bank. He described Israel's confrontation with the Palestinians as one "between two societies that are competing for territory and, to a certain degree, for existence. I don't think that there is an existential threat to the Palestinian society. There is an existential threat to us. In other words, there is asymmetry here, but it is reversed: everyone thinks we are Goliath and they are David, but I maintain that it is the opposite."

Asked how he defined "victory," Ya'alon said, "I defined it from the beginning of the confrontation: the very deep internalization by the Palestinians that terrorism and violence will not defeat us, will not make us fold. If that deep internalization does not exist at the end of the confrontation, we will have a strategic problem with an existential threat to Israel. If that [lesson] is not burned into the Palestinian and Arab consciousness, there will be no end to their demands of us."

Ya'alon also told the *Ha'aretz* interviewer a little about his experience of having grown up near Haifa as the child of a mother who survived the Holocaust. He said, "I see myself as a Jew, an Israeli, a humanist, a liberal, a democrat, and a seeker of peace and security. But I know that I am facing a cruel reality and that I have to defend myself. In the face of cancer, one has to defend oneself."[44]

---

44 Ari Shavit, "The enemy within," *Ha'aretz*, August 29, 2002. Ya'alon seemed unaware of the ironies involved in his cancer analogy: cancer frequently responds to treatment by mutating into more virulent forms; chemotherapy does great harm to healthy cells and often causes new cancers.

We tended to agree with Warschawski's description of the Israeli campaign in the occupied territories as being, in good part, mainly a "pacification" operation, one whose aim was to break the Palestinians' will to resist. Ya'alon's words seemed to support this conclusion. We agreed, too, with the view expressed by a high-ranking diplomat stationed in Gaza, who told us, "We see the Israeli government as hell-bent on the settlement program, and as wanting to keep the Palestinians subjugated to that end.... It is our view that most of this 'war' is actually a war in defense of the settlements."

So how important was continued pursuit of the settlement project to the Sharon government? From his seat in the Israeli Foreign Ministry, Gadi Golan described the Israelis' disagreement with the Palestinians over the settlements as merely "a misunderstanding." We had asked him about the impact of the settlements on the Palestinians. He replied, "No doubt it's a misunderstanding. Because I don't doubt but that when there are negotiations, the settlements will be discussed. It's true, the majority of Israelis don't want us to hang onto the settlements forever. But we always said we needed to hang onto them as a bargaining chip in any negotiations. I guess that we misunderstood the impact of the settlements on the Palestinians."[45] He assured us that, in his view, the settlements issue, "will not hold up a solution."

We noted, however, that though Golan was speaking as a high-level employee of the Israeli government, his views on this matter did not seem to be shared by Sharon and the rest of the right-wing grouping that then dominated the government's actual decision-making. Shortly before our visit, Sharon had publicly declared that the tiny settlement of Netzarim, in the heart of the Gaza Strip, was, "as dear to me as Tel Aviv." In October 2002, he reaffirmed his strong support for the settlement project when he refused Labor leader Benjamin Ben-Eliezer's request that the government reduce the amount allocated to provide incentives for potential settlers, in order to prevent further social welfare cuts. Sharon showed that he was prepared to see Labor pull out of the governing coalition, and government fall, rather than cut back on the subsidies offered to the settlers. For Sharon and his allies, the colonial project of maintaining and even expanding the settlements seemed to be anything but a mere "misunderstanding."

---

45 The Jaffee Center's Yossi Alpher had spoken of earlier Israeli negotiators having viewed the settlements as a "bargaining chip". See chapter 3.

Settlements and International Law

As we noted in chapter 1 above, international law states unequivocally that a country that for whatever reason finds itself running a military occupation of someone else's land—something that can happen during wars—is absolutely barred from moving members of its own civilian population into the occupied areas. Back in 1949, acting in the somber knowledge of the kinds of actions that Germany and Japan had taken in the preceding decade, representatives of governments from around the world gathered in Geneva, Switzerland, to re-codify many long-standing laws of war into the four "Geneva Conventions," which form a major portion of international humanitarian law. Crucially, Article 49 of the Fourth Geneva Convention states in its last sentence: "The Occupying Power shall not deport or transfer parts of its own civilian population into the territory it occupies." (Other portions of the laws of war, including Article 53 of the Fourth Geneva Convention and Article 23 of the 1907 Hague Regulations, also directly outlaw key aspects of the settlement project.)

Under international law, military occupation is considered a temporary state of affairs that lasts only the few months or years that it takes for the warring parties to conclude a peace agreement delineating the terms under which the occupying power will withdraw its forces. Then, the occupying country must withdraw and return sovereign control to the owners of the land. For example, in 1991, after U.S. and allied military units had forced Iraq's troops out of Kuwait they pushed further forward and ended up controlling some Iraqi territory; but they withdrew from it within weeks.[46] In the case of the Allied occupations of Germany and Japan after World War II, it took some years to reach peace agreements. Still, in neither of these latter cases did the victorious Allies ever imagine they could simply move parts of their own civilian population into the occupied lands. And even in the extremely challenging cases of Germany and Japan, the occupations were formally brought to an end in less than a decade.

By the time our group arrived in Palestine/Israel, Israel's occupation of the West Bank, the Gaza Strip, and the Syrian Golan area

---

46 The occupation that ensued from the March 2003 U.S. military action against Iraq did not end quickly, and rapidly became very problematic for both Iraqis and Americans.

(to the north) had lasted for 35 years. And throughout that period, starting back in 1967, successive Israeli governments from both major parties, Labor and the Likud, had systematically been moving parts of Israel's civilian population into the occupied territories. Many of Israel's early settlements in the occupied areas had a quasi-military nature. Since an occupying power is allowed under international law to station troops inside the lands it occupies, this made it easier for the Israeli governments of those years to avoid confrontations with governments concerned about possible transgressions of international law. Over the years, however, the pretense that the new settlements had any important defensive purpose was left behind.

Since 1967, all Israeli governments, whether led by the Labor Party or the Likud Party, have challenged the basic premise that the West Bank and the Gaza Strip in fact constituted "occupied territories." They have based their argument on the claim that "the rightful owner of these territories is still an unresolved question," noting that neither Jordan (which exercised sovereignty over the West Bank between 1949 and 1967) nor Egypt (which administered the Gaza Strip between 1948 and 1967) had any rightful claim to those lands. Therefore, they argued, the exact disposition of sovereignty over these areas remained unclear, and rather than constituting "occupied territories," these lands could best be described as "disputed territories." Building on the view that the West Bank and Gaza are not technically "occupied territories," successive Israeli governments have claimed that they have the right to settle members of their own population in them.[47]

In pursuing these policies, however, Israeli governments have generally avoided annexing the occupied territories outright. The exceptions to this were a dramatically expanded East Jerusalem and the Golan Heights (Syrian territory conquered in 1967). Both these places have been the subject of Israeli legislation that unilaterally extended Israeli's jurisdiction over them. Israeli officials have tried to argue that such moves stopped short of outright annexation, though they have been hard-pressed to spell out what the difference is. Crucially, in both those places, Israel considers that its law is sovereign, and it has not only offered Israeli citizen-

---

47 Some supporters of Israel have also claimed that since Israel captured these lands during a defensive war, it can do as it pleases in them. International law provides no basis for this argument.

ship to their residents but also, on occasion, vigorously pressured them to accept it. In both places, the vast majority of the residents have resisted these pressures.[48]

If Israel had annexed all of the occupied territories, then as the democracy that it claims to be, it would have been under pressure to allow the territories' Palestinian residents to exercise full and equal political rights within the thus-expanded Israel. This would have considerably diluted Israel's Jewish character, and would have threatened to bring the country's Jewish majority to an end within a (possibly small) number of years. Therefore, rather than annex the territories, successive Israeli governments kept the exact juridical status of these lands in an uneasy limbo. Meanwhile, the settlement project continued, fueled by ever-increasing government subsidies to settlers and the promise that inside their settlements (and in widening swathes around them) they would be subject only to Israel's law.

In contrast to the Israeli government position that the West Bank and the Gaza Strip are not "occupied territories" under international law, we agree with the U.N., U.S., and nearly all other governments around the world who consider these lands to be occupied territories. We note, too, that the U.N. spoke authoritatively about the sovereignty of the two areas through the 1947 resolution that divided Mandate Palestine into a Palestinian Jewish state and a Palestinian Arab state. The Palestinian Arab state mapped out in that resolution contained all of Gaza and the West Bank, except for parts in and around East Jerusalem, which would form part of the Jerusalem *corpus separatum.* Indeed, in addition to Gaza and the West Bank, it also contained additional large tracts of land that were seized by the Israelis in 1948 and incorporated into the State of Israel.

Back in 1947, the Palestinian Arabs rejected the U.N.'s partition resolution—a policy choice that may have seemed logical in an era of worldwide decolonization, when self-determination was the norm. In addition, the fact that Jews made up around one-third of the population of Mandate Palestine and owned only seven percent of the land, yet were awarded 54 percent of the land under the resolution, made it seem extremely inequitable to the Palestinian Arabs. Over the decades that followed 1947, most

---

48 For more discussion of Jerusalem, see chapter 5.

Palestinians did come to accept the logic of the partition resolution, though not the exact lines it prescribed—which paradoxically would have given them much more land than they were claiming from the 1970s on. However, the fact that the Palestinians rejected partition in 1947 by no means undermines the standing of this resolution in international law—any more than Israel's rejection of numerous U.N. resolutions since then undercuts their standing, either.

We are strongly convinced that the fact of that 1947 U.N. ruling, taken in conjunction with the clearly expressed preference of these territories' indigenous people, means that the claim of the Palestinian Arabs to exercise their own sovereign rule over the West Bank and Gaza—with some possibility of a special arrangement for Jerusalem—is a compelling one. Certainly, there is no provision of international law that would allow Israel somehow to have acquired these territories solely through force of arms. Successive U.N. resolutions on the Arab-Israeli issue have clearly and repeatedly reaffirmed the "inadmissibility of the acquisition of territory by force."

On our journey, we heard and we think we clearly understood the articulation by Sondra Baras and other settlers whom we met of the strong attachment and sense of ownership they feel, as Jews, to areas within the West Bank that they sincerely believed had been promised by God to their forebears in Biblical times. We must conclude, however, that claims based on such promises from God cannot constitute a determining argument in today's world. Do all Christians have a valid claim to settle and live in Rome, Byzantium, or Jerusalem, if they consider those places particularly sacred? Do all Buddhists have a valid claim to settle and live at the place of the Buddha's enlightenment in Bodh Gaya, India, or all Muslims in Mecca, Medina, or Jerusalem? No, for to recognize the validity of such claims would be to invite chaos and endless conflict. We are deeply skeptical of appeals to religious dogma that are used to bolster claims to land and resources.

A claim to be able to visit places of religious significance and to engage there in rituals associated with sacred pilgrimage is one matter. A claim to settle, reside forever, and rule over these places is quite different. We therefore urge the men and women in the Israeli settler movement and the Israeli government to be open to exploring ways in which they and all other Jews can express their attachment to these spots on the planet and to the sacred Jewish sites therein in ways—such as visits, pilgrimages, or the creation of cultural institutions—that can be implemented in cooperation with the land's indigenous population rather than in contravention of their rights and in total disregard of their equally deep attachment to it.

The Palestinian National Movement and the Peace Process

For some three decades now the response of most of the world's eight million Palestinians to Israel's pursuit of its colonial project in the West Bank and Gaza has been to demand a full Israeli withdrawal from those territories and the establishment therein of an independent Palestinian state. This Palestinian demand has not always been clearly articulated or intelligently pursued. The main Palestinian national organization, the Palestinian Liberation Organization (PLO), emerged in the 1950s and 1960s mainly in the refugee camps of the Palestinian diaspora. In its early years the PLO's program was dominated not by the demand for an independent Palestinian state in Gaza and the West Bank but by the refugees' very basic demand that they be allowed to return to the homes they had left inside what had become the State of Israel.[49]

Throughout the period 1967-1974, as Israel consolidated its occupation of the West Bank and Gaza, the PLO was still calling for the total overthrow of Israel as a Jewish state and its replacement by a "secular democratic state" in the whole of British-mandate Palestine. From the way PLO leaders described this state, it seemed clear that none of the Jews who had arrived in Israel since 1948—or perhaps, since much earlier than that—would be allowed to stay in this state, which would be a definitely Arab-cultured state with no special provisions for its Hebrew-speaking citizens. Then, in a significant policy shift in 1974, the PLO started to espouse the creation of a (state-like) "Palestinian national authority" in any part of Mandate-era Palestine that would be evacuated by Israel, which was taken to mean the West Bank and Gaza. At that time, however, Jordan still claimed to speak on behalf of the Palestinians. That claim, which Jordan continued to pursue

49 Palestinian claims regarding a "right of return" to properties they fled from (or were forced to leave) in 1948 are discussed more fully in chapters 6 and 9 below.

until 1988, competed with the PLO's claim to represent the Palestinians and further muddied the diplomatic waters for the PLO and its supporters.

The PLO's main roots lay in a number of precursor Palestinian guerrilla groups, including one headed by Yasser Arafat called "Fatah," which remains in existence until now. After Israel occupied the West Bank and Gaza in 1967, guerrilla units from Fatah and other PLO-affiliated groups mounted a short guerrilla struggle from inside the West Bank before the IDF managed to expel them to Jordan a few months later. The guerrillas regrouped in Jordan and for three years maintained their most important bases there. But their influence there grew so rapidly that Jordan's King Hussein felt threatened. In 1970-71 the Jordanian army took harsh actions to expel all the PLO units from there, too. They regrouped once again in Lebanon, where they soon became entangled in that country's deadly civil war.

In 1982, Ariel Sharon, then the defense minister in a right-leaning Israeli government, led a large-scale campaign against the PLO forces in Lebanon. After a punishing ten weeks of fighting, much of it in still-populated residential areas of the capital, Beirut, Sharon forced Arafat to take all the PLO fighters out of the city. They went into an uncertain period of exile in Tunisia, much further away from their homeland. The PLO forces left Beirut in August 1982. The next month, the Israeli government directly reneged on a promise it had made to the U.S. that its troops would not enter the parts of the city evacuated by the Palestinians. In September, Israeli officers coordinated an operation in which Lebanese militiamen allied to Israel entered the now-defenseless Palestinian refugee camps of Sabra and Shatila in the Beirut suburbs and massacred many hundreds of unarmed Palestinians in both places. An Israeli commission of inquiry into the event found that, as defense minister, Sharon bore significant responsibility for the massacres and recommended that he not be allowed to occupy high office in Israel again.

Inside Gaza and the West Bank, meanwhile, the Palestinians who lived in those areas had clung for some years after 1967 to the hope that some force from outside—whether the armies or the diplomats of the Arab states, the intervention of a concerned and compassionate world community, or the exile-based PLO—might soon lift from them the burden of foreign military occupation. By the mid-1980s, however, it had become very clear to them that they were not about to see any "liberation" from outside. They would need to take their fate into their own hands. In late 1987 they launched a broad popular uprising that, they hoped, could persuade Israel to end its occupation and allow the establishment of an independent Palestinian state in the West Bank and Gaza.

That first *intifada* lasted from 1987 through 1993. It was a predominantly nonviolent, citizen-based mass movement, though on many occasions groups of young Palestinians would throw stones at Israeli soldiers or settlers in the occupied territories. The Israelis tried to crush the first *intifada* using a combination of brute force and other means of massive repression, such as curfews, detention without trial, destruction of property, and the outright suppression of even nonviolent resistance activities. One 1988 pronouncement from Yitzhak Rabin, a Labor Party stalwart who was defense minister in a coalition government, called explicitly on Israeli soldiers to "break the bones" of Palestinian youths accused of throwing stones.

On the Palestinian side, the eruption of the *intifada* gave the Palestinians' national leadership, the PLO, a basis of new self-confidence from which it was able to launch some new political initiatives. In late 1988, the PLO's broader decision-making body, the Palestinian National Council (PNC), adopted a resolution that formally accepted the U.N.'s 1947 partition resolution and declared the establishment of a State of Palestine. Little was done to give concrete content to the newly declared "state"; but Arafat built on the political base that the PNC resolution had established and made a historic public declaration in Geneva in which he announced the PLO's recognition of the State of Israel and its renunciation of any further use of terrorism.

In January 1989, the U.S. administration responded to these moves, announcing that it was ready to open mid-level talks with the PLO. Those talks continued, in Tunisia, until May 1990. That month, guerrillas belonging to a pro-Iraqi faction represented in the PLO leadership undertook an attack against Israel from the sea, using a rubber dinghy. The Israeli navy intercepted the assailants before they reached the shore. Israel and the U.S. then demanded that Arafat expel the faction that had organized the attack from the PLO. When he refused, the U.S. suspended the dialogue with the PLO.

The U.S. had nearly always been an important ally for Israel, while throughout most of the life of the PLO Washington had refused to have any overt contacts with it. So the short-lived dialogue of 1989-90 was significant, though it led to no immediate broader breakthrough in the quest for peace.

In 1991, in the context of the continuation of the first *intifada* and Washington's recent military success in Iraq, U.S. President George H. W. Bush launched a serious effort to broker an Israeli-Palestinian peace. He convened the Arab-Israeli peace conference in Madrid referred to earlier and insisted that the Israeli government attend that forum alongside a Palestinian delegation. However, the U.S. did not force the Israelis to swallow too much of a challenge all at once: the Palestinian team headed by Gaza physician Dr. Haidar Abdel-Shafei was officially present at the conference not on its own account but as part of a "joint Jordanian-Palestinian delegation." And even after Madrid, the U.S. continued to deal only with Palestinians who, like Abdel-Shafei, were not openly identified with the PLO, which was still strongly reviled by the Israeli authorities.

In 1991, the Israeli government was still in the hands of the strongly pro-settler Likud Party. In elections the following year, the Labor Party, led by Rabin, won handily.[50] Rabin moved from being defense minister in a Likud-led coalition to being prime minister.

Rabin's first few months in office continued to be marked by the tough approach toward Palestinians that he had taken as defense minister. By spring 1993, however, he became increasingly aware that a purely military response could not quell the challenge posed by the Palestinians' continuing *intifada*. He started lending his weight to some secret contacts Foreign Minister Shimon Peres had been maintaining with the PLO, through Norwegian intermediaries, in Norway's capital, Oslo. Within months, the Israeli and Palestinian negotiators had reached an agreement and were ready to go public. In an attempt to bring the U.S. on board, they allowed President Bill Clinton to host the sign-

---

50 The Bush administration (discreetly) helped steer Israelis toward Rabin by making clear that an extra U.S. $10 billion in loan guarantees that Israel wanted, in order to help it absorb a predicted influx of one million new immigrants from the former Soviet Union, could not be used to build housing in the occupied territories—which was where Prime Minister Yitzhak Shamir wanted to build much of it.

ing ceremony of the "Oslo Accords" on the White House lawn. It was there, on September 13, 1993, that Rabin and Arafat exchanged a historic handshake—the first one ever between Israeli and Palestinian national leaders.

Given the importance of the Oslo Accords and their legacy in subsequent stages of the conflict, the next section will examine the agreement and its consequences in some detail.

The Oslo Accords and What Followed

The Oslo Accords consisted of a number of documents. In one, the PLO expressed its formal recognition of the State of Israel. In another, Israel recognized the PLO as the representative of the Palestinian people. Beyond an exchange of recognition, the two parties signed a complex set of interim agreements whereby, among other things:

- Both parties forswore the use of further violence in their conflict;

- Israel agreed to undertake a series of three phased withdrawals from the occupied territories over a period of five years;

- In early 1994, the PLO leadership would end its lengthy exile and return to the occupied territories, where it would establish a "Palestinian Authority" (P.A.);

- In 1996, elections would be held throughout the occupied territories for the P.A. leadership, and for another new body, a "Palestinian Legislative Council;"[51] and

- The P.A. would take over all civil functions of governance over the Palestinians of the occupied areas (but not the settlers), as well as security functions within the cities of the West Bank, and most of Gaza.

At the insistence of the Israeli side, the Oslo Accords notably did not spell out the shape of the final-status agreement that would follow the five-year interim period. The two sides agreed instead that no later than early 1996, they would start to negotiate

---

51 Israel and the U.S. set the ground rules under which these elections were to occur, which made it hard to accept their later claim that Arafat—who was duly elected as P.A. leader in 1996—was an illegitimate leader. Significantly, under these ground rules, only those Palestinians then residing inside the West Bank and Gaza were allowed to vote. The larger number of Palestinians still exiled outside the historic homeland were excluded from the vote.

the terms of the final agreement, so that it could go into implementation immediately after the interim phase had been completed, in May 1999. The parties agreed that the matters to be discussed in the final-status talks would include: the final disposition of Israeli settlements and settlers; demarcation of the line of the final borders between Israel and the Palestinian entity; a final resolution of the Palestinian refugee issue; the status of Jerusalem; and water issues. In a notable lacuna, the Oslo Accords did not spell out what would happen if no final-status agreement had been reached by 1999. But Israeli government lawyers pointed out at the time of the Oslo signing that (under the same international law that in other respects they continued to reject!) Israel would retain its broad rights as an occupying power throughout the territories, even after concluding a partial transfer of policing functions to the projected Palestinian authority.

Under the Oslo Accords, the PLO leaders agreed that Israel's many existing settlements could stay in place during the interim period. Israel's leaders agreed not to build new settlements but insisted that the accords still allowed for the "natural growth" of existing settlements. The PLO agreed that Israel could construct "bypass roads," to allow the settlers to travel more safely to and from their homes during the interim phase. But as matters turned out—and as we saw clearly on our travels—these roads became a major factor that radically transformed the human geography of the West Bank in the settlers' favor. The roads provided excellent communications between the settlements, while they cut the Palestinian cities off from one another.

Regarding the size of the settler population, so long as Rabin was still alive he did slow—though not end—this population's growth. But after Likud returned to power in Israel in 1996, the implantation of settlers was once again accelerated (as Jad Isaac pointed out to us when we visited with him in Bethlehem.) Likud's Prime Minister from 1996 to 1999, Binyamin Netanyahu, and his settler allies claimed that they were abiding by the letter of the Oslo Accords by not building any "new" settlements. But they built numerous well-serviced clusters of new housing, and then claimed that these were merely "new neighborhoods" of some of the existing settlements—though often they were very far away. From 1993 to 1998, the five-year period during which Israeli occupation was supposed to reach the stage of implementation of the final status agreement, the number of settlers in Gaza and the West Bank (excluding East Jerusalem) rose from 120,000 to 180,000.[52] In East Jerusalem, between 1992 and 1996, the number of settlers rose from 124,000 to 160,000.[53]

The Oslo process left a mixed legacy to both Palestinians and Israelis. For the Israelis, Oslo represented a significant diplomatic breakthrough that ushered in an era of unparalleled prosperity for the Jewish state. Once Israel had established relations with the Palestinians, numerous countries in East Asia, Africa, and Eastern Europe that had previously expressed their disapproval of its treatment of the Palestinians by participating in formal or informal boycotts against it rapidly lifted those boycotts and established active diplomatic and economic ties. Vast new markets for Israeli exports—including significant quantities of arms exports—opened up almost overnight in Japan, China, and elsewhere in East Asia and the rest of the world. Most of the Israeli troops who prior to Oslo had been kept busy maintaining the vast apparatus of control over the Palestinians could now, under the new security arrangements with the P.A., be demobilized or sent to training in hi-tech units of the army or air force. Israel rode the crest of the international dot-com boom and achieved a standard of living equivalent to that of many West European nations.

On the downside for Israel, the security arrangements, under which the P.A. agreed to clamp down on Palestinian militants and prevent them from taking action against Israeli targets were not nearly as effective as had been hoped. Israelis still suffered inter-mittent security crises. In early 1996, for example, four Palestinian terror bombs rocked the city centers of Jerusalem and Tel Aviv; and there were continuing concerns that Yasser Arafat was not doing enough, as Israelis expressed it, "to rein in" armed Palestinian militants.

On the Palestinian side, the evacuation of Israel's security forces from much of Gaza, and from the Palestinian cities of the West Bank, brought huge relief to the residents of many of those areas. (By the time of the evacuation from Gaza, the population

---

52 Approximate figures from the Foundation for Middle East Peace (FMEP) are available at <http://www.fmep.org/charts/chart9905_2.gif>.

53 Approximate figures from the FMEP are available at <http://www.fmep.org/reports/sr9905.html#chart1>.

there had lived under a twelve-hour in-house lockdown every night for six years.) Palestinians were happy, too, that they could start to build national institutions like a health ministry, an education ministry, a port and airport in Gaza—and a representative democracy. In January 1996, 79.9 percent of registered Palestinian electors went to polling-stations throughout the occupied territories and cast their votes for president *(ra'is)*, a position that Yasser Arafat won by a landslide, and for 88 members of a new Palestinian Legislative Council.

For the Palestinians, however, the downside of the post-Oslo years was proportionately greater than it was for the Israelis. In the years after Oslo, the much-promised economic boom never happened for the Palestinians. By most measures, their standard of living continued to decline throughout the 1990s. This decline was attributed—by the World Bank and others—primarily to Israel's practice of imposing strict closures around portions of the West Bank or Gaza in response to perceived security threats; to its reluctance to open the borders to Palestinian laborers seeking work in Israel; and to the debilitating effects on the agriculture and transport sectors of the construction of the new, settler-only roads and the continued expansion of the settlements. In addition, throughout the post-Oslo period, just as for the quarter-century of Israeli occupation that had preceded Oslo, Israel continued to maintain tight controls and high tariffs on all imports of Palestinian products into Israel, while treating the occupied territories as a captive market onto which they could dump Israeli-made products at will. Early in the post-Oslo years, Palestinian inexperience in financial management was also an obstacle; but intensive help from international institutions and the integration of skilled financial managers from the Palestinian diaspora gradually reduced the size of this impediment.

The negative outcomes for the Palestinians in those years can be traced to a number of factors. Of prime importance was the inequitable nature of the Oslo Accords themselves. The PLO team that negotiated at Oslo was doing so in secret—out of the sight of all but a handful of Palestinians—and in the context of a highly unfavorable power imbalance. At Israel's insistence, the Palestinians were not allowed to bring into the negotiation any "external" actor or set of ground-rules that might help to balance the role played behind the scenes there by the U.S., which continued to provide significant financial, military, and political support to Israel throughout the negotiations. In 1993, Arafat was politically weak and desperate to regain his and the PLO's political relevance; so he grabbed at the opportunity the Oslo talks provided. It is also possible that, as some people close to him have suggested, he believed that Oslo's interim period was unimportant and hoped to strike a much better deal for his people in the all-important final status talks. Since he had not been physically present in the occupied territories since 1967, it is possible he did not grasp the immensity of the impact that interim steps such as the road-building provision would have on the status quo.

Because of the power imbalance at Oslo, the Palestinian side was forced, to a large degree, to throw its fate into the hands of the Israeli leadership and hope for its sheer goodwill to steer the process constructively forward. Rabin turned out to be the Palestinians' most effective partner for peace, having apparently undergone a significant personal transformation—from calling on Israeli soldiers to "break bones" in 1988, to leading his nation in an unprecedented and visionary direction five years later. Then, just two years after the Oslo Accords were signed, a Jewish-Israeli extremist angered by Rabin's stated readiness to withdraw from the occupied territories assassinated him at the end of a peace rally in Tel Aviv.

After Rabin was killed, his longtime partner in the Labor leadership, Shimon Peres, followed him into the prime minister's office. Peres, however, was not nearly as effective a national leader as Rabin had been; and in the 1996 Israeli elections, he and Labor were swept out of office in a very close, but definitive, election. Likud returned to power, led this time by Binyamin Netanyahu. Netanyahu and his party had earlier voted against the Oslo Accords when they were presented to the Israeli parliament. Throughout the three years that he was in office, he cooperated only reluctantly and minimally with the steps he was required to take under it. He (and his successor) delayed time after time and ultimately never made the third of the troop withdrawals that Israel had promised. As a result, the Palestinian-controlled areas of the West Bank remained non-contiguous fragments on the map.

The Netanyahu government imposed more and more debilitating closures around Palestinian cities. One major goal of the closures—which Rabin had started and then Netanyahu accelerated—was to cut East Jerusalem off from its natural hinterland in the West Bank, and to reduce or even end its role as the central metropolis of the Palestinian West Bank. Instead of being situated in Jerusalem, the centers of Palestinian governance on the West Bank were located in Ramallah, a Palestinian city a few miles to the north. Some portions of Gaza City saw a modest real estate boom as thousands of Palestinians who had worked with the PLO in exile came back to Gaza to work in the P.A. and some scores of Palestinian exiles—now successful businesspeople—returned to investigate possible investment opportunities in their homeland. But early in the post-Oslo years their hopes and plans were frustrated and largely extinguished by the harshness of Israeli occupation—e.g., endless checkpoints, restrictions, and mounting instability. For example, no longer could Gazans seeking work simply sneak across the border to work on construction sites or plantations inside Israel, as they had before. The era of prosperity and well-being that the Palestinians had hoped would grow out of the Oslo process never came to most Palestinians in Gaza or the West Bank.

Human rights activist Raji Sourani described the legacy of the Oslo Accords for the Palestinians to us as "sad and bad." Under the timetable laid out in the accords, the interim phase was supposed to end, and implementation of the final status agreement begin, in May 1999. Instead, Sourani said, "by May 4, 1999, it was clear that the harvest of the Oslo Accords was the total economic and social strangulation of the Palestinian territories, and the creation here of a de facto Bantustan."

Meanwhile, under both Netanyahu and his successor, Ehud Barak, the settlement project—including the construction of settler-only residential areas, public amenities, and highways—continued apace.

Throughout the 1990s, Israeli opinion showed itself to be highly volatile on the central issue of relations with the Palestinians. In 1992, Israelis voted for a Labor Party perceived as being pro-peace. In 1996, they voted for the Likud Party largely because it was considered tough on Palestinians. (The latter election was highly influenced by a wave of Palestinian suicide bombings in preceding weeks.) In 1999, after Netanyahu showed that his toughness did not solve their continuing security problems, Israelis voted for a new Labor leader, Ehud Barak.

Like Rabin, Barak had been a highly decorated military officer. Also like Rabin, he ran for office on a pro-peace platform. But Ehud Barak had few of the political skills that Yitzhak Rabin had honed over his long career in politics. Almost immediately after coming into office in the summer of 1999, he started to lose the coalition allies that any Israeli prime minister needs to survive in Israel's complex system of parliamentary democracy. He also stalled, fatally, before engaging in any serious peacemaking with the Palestinians. He delayed an entire year—a long time in Israeli politics—before he "suddenly" decided in June 2000 that he needed to win a final-status agreement from Arafat in double-quick time.

Barak easily persuaded U.S. President Bill Clinton to join this plan. The Palestinian leader was more reluctant. From Arafat's viewpoint, Barak's refusal to undertake the third of the interim withdrawals required under Oslo and the apparently strong support Barak had given the Israeli settlers seemed like signs of questionable intentions on Barak's behalf. But Clinton persevered and convened what was billed as a "make-or-break" summit at his presidential retreat, Camp David, in late July 2000, just a few weeks after Barak had proposed it. Clinton and Barak announced that their goal was the speedy conclusion of the long-delayed final-status agreement with the Palestinians.

The summit failed. None of the participants had prepared enough for it. With a U.S. election looming close—an election, moreover, in which his wife was running for a seat in the Senate— Bill Clinton was unwilling to push any specifically U.S. peace plan, but rather contented himself with trying to "sell" Barak's plan to a skeptical Arafat. After some days' work, the summit broke up without reaching an agreement, and the myth of Barak's "generous offer"—as referred to, scathingly, by Uri Avnery (see chapter 3)— was born.[54]

The fact that the summit was held at such short notice, with so little preparation, and then failed, considerably weakened people's hopes of negotiating an end to the conflict. After the very public failure of Camp David, Barak's political standing in Israel fell even

---

[54] In August 2001, Robert Malley, who was Special Assistant to President Clinton for Arab-Israeli Affairs and a member of the U.S. peace team at the Camp David summit, and Hussein Agha, a longtime advisor to Arafat, published their account of what transpired at Camp David and subsequent rounds of diplomacy in *The New York Review of Books*. The article is available at <http://www.vopj.org/issues6.htm>.

further as Israeli voters and Knesset members once again swung away from the peace camp. On the Palestinian side, many activists in the occupied territories who had long criticized the way Arafat had handled Camp David began to challenge his authority more openly after it failed.

A New Intifada, and Complications in Diplomacy

In late September 2000, the feelings of unease on the Palestinian side came to a head when the Palestinians' old nemesis from the confrontation in Lebanon in 1982, Ariel Sharon, announced his intention of visiting the traditional site of Herod's Temple, which is co-located with the Muslim holy site—the *Haram al-Sharif* ("Noble Sanctuary")—that lies above the Western Wall in the heart of historic Jerusalem. Barak acceded to Sharon's plan, and arranged for a 1,000-person security detail to accompany him. For many Palestinians, this "invasion" of one of Islam's holiest sites was the last straw. Palestinian youths from throughout the occupied territories took to the streets and threw stones as rowdily as their elder brothers had done the first *intifada*, a decade before. Barak ordered the Israeli military to reply with live ammunition, some of it fired onto crowded streets from helicopter gunships. Thus began the second *intifada*. By the end of 2000, 272 Palestinians had been killed by the Israeli forces; 82 of those killed were minors.[55]

This time around, unlike during the first *intifada*, the Palestinian community had some police and gendarmerie forces of its own. The Palestinian commanders knew quite well that in any forceful confrontation with the Israeli military, the Israelis would easily outgun them. But on some occasions, when they felt themselves under threat, individual units did fire at the Israelis. In addition, the Islamic Jihad organization, an armed paramilitary faction, undertook three suicide bombings between October and December 2000. By the end of that year, a total of nineteen Israeli soldiers and eighteen Israeli civilians had been killed by Palestinians. The level of pain, suffering, and fear was thus high on both sides, and the events of those months provided an initial momentum to trigger the cycle of inter-communal violence that would keep it turning until well after our visit in June 2002.

---

55 Casualty figures in this and next paragraph are available at <www.btselem.org>.

One speedy casualty of the violence of the new *intifada* was Barak's government. In December 2000 he lost a no-confidence vote in the Knesset and was forced to call an election for the premiership for early February 2001.[56] It was significant, however, that despite his increasingly precarious political situation at home, he still tried to make progress in the negotiations with the Palestinians. It was significant, too, that despite the strong political challenges that Arafat faced from many in his own community, he also remained committed to the pursuit of the negotiations. In January 2001, negotiators representing the two leaders met for intensive peace talks in Taba, Egypt. There, the two teams considerably narrowed gaps that they had been unable to bridge at Camp David—and they did this on a broad range of final-status issues, including even Jerusalem and refugees.

Despite this progress, on January 27—with the clock ticking toward Israel's February 6 election—the two sides agreed to adjourn. They issued a statement that said:

> The Taba talks were unprecedented in their positive atmosphere and expression of mutual willingness to meet the national, security and existential needs of each side.

> Given the circumstances and time constraints, it proved impossible to reach understandings on all issues, despite the substantial progress that was achieved in each of the issues discussed.

> The sides declare that they have never been closer to reaching an agreement and it is thus our shared belief that the remaining gaps could be bridged with the resumption of negotiations following the Israeli elections....[57]

The following day, Barak called the Israeli team back from Taba to Israel, in a last-ditch effort to save his nose-diving reelection campaign.

On the crucial issue of settlements, the negotiators at Taba had agreed that Israel would evacuate all settlements in the Gaza Strip.

---

56 Israel's voting law had been changed in 1992 to allow separate votes for the prime minister and the Knesset. The February 2001 vote was the only vote ever held solely for prime minister. After that election, the law was changed back to its earlier provision that elections would be held only for the Knesset, with the prime minister—usually the head of the largest party in the Knesset—being whoever could form a majority coalition in order to govern.

57 The full text is available through the Israeli Foreign Ministry website at <http://www.mfa.gov.il/mfa/go.asp?MFAH0j7o0>.

They also produced different maps of the West Bank, to discuss how to modify the pre-1967 boundary so that Israel could extend its sovereignty to a limited number of consolidated settlement blocs. According to an "agreed account" of the negotiations produced by special envoy Miguel Moratinos of the European Union (E.U.):

> The Israeli maps were principally based on a demographic concept of settlements blocs that would incorporate approximately 80 percent of the settlers. The Israeli side sketched a map presenting a 6 percent annexation... The Palestinian illustrative map presented 3.1 percent in the context of a land swap [that is, an exchange of some land inside pre-1967 Israel for some inside the West Bank]. Both sides accepted the principle of land swap but the proportionality of the swap remained under discussion.[58]

Because of the stormy domestic political dynamic that had held both societies in its grip for the four months since the second *intifada* had begun, the Taba talks came far too late, and probably had little chance of success. (Another factor in their failure was the fact that January was the month of the presidential turnover in Washington. There was literally no one from the U.S. who had any mandate to help the Taba talks succeed.) Nine days after pulling his negotiators home from Taba, Barak lost his bid for reelection. Israel's new prime minister proved to be the latest in a long line of Likud Party leaders: Ariel Sharon.

Sharon came into office declaring firmly that—in line with his election promises—he would not negotiate with the Palestinians until after the complete cessation of all Palestinian violence, and he stressed that he and he alone would be the one to determine when this precondition had been met. He received considerable support for this position from the man who became U.S. president in January 2001, George W. Bush. Bush entered the White House with little knowledge of the Middle East. Above all, he seemed determined to differentiate his policies in this region from those of Bill Clinton. Where Clinton engaged closely in Israeli-Palestinian diplomacy and had tried hard to build good relations with both

---

58 The full text of the Moratinos document, as published in *Ha'aretz* in February 2002 is available at <http://www.haaretzdaily.com/hasen/pages/ShArt.jhtml?itemNo= 130196&contrassID=2&subContrassID=5&sbSubContrassID=0&listSrc=Y>. It has been published in paper as an Appendix to International Crisis Group, *Middle East Endgame II: How a Comprehensive Israeli-Palestinian Peace Would Look* (Amman, Washington, and Brussels: ICG, July 2002).

Palestinians and Israelis, the new president avoided an active role. Bush's near-total disengagement from the peace process allowed Sharon to deal with the Palestinians virtually as he saw fit, even after the Israeli leader escalated Israel's use of (U.S.-supplied) fighter planes and helicopters to attack Palestinian targets in areas packed with civilians, and of deliberate, extrajudicial killings of Palestinian activists. Bush may have overlooked or even condoned Sharon's tactics because after the September 2001 terrorist attacks on the World Trade Center and Pentagon, he adopted some similar tactics in his own "war against terror," though fortunately, crowd control using attack helicopters never became a routine U.S. tactic.

In late March 2002, Sharon added a further precondition to the one he had proclaimed a year earlier. Now, a mere cessation of Palestinian violence would not be enough to allow peace talks to resume. Henceforth, he said, he would not negotiate so long as Arafat remained in power. (That declaration was made in conjunction with Sharon's first campaign to send troops back into the Palestinian cities of the West Bank.) For a while, it was not clear if Bush would support Sharon in this new toughening of his stance. Then on June 24, 2002, in a major policy speech on the Israeli-Palestinian issue, Bush signaled the strong backing he was willing to give Sharon when he said, "Peace requires a new and different Palestinian leadership, so that a Palestinian state can be born. I call on the Palestinian people to elect new leaders, leaders not compromised by terror."[59]

We watched Bush's delivery of this speech on television when our group was in Gaza. We welcomed his articulation of support for the goal of a Palestinian state, but we thought that the fact that he had now joined Sharon in insisting on Palestinian "regime change" as a precondition for negotiations constituted quite unacceptable interference in the Palestinians' internal affairs. It also erected a significant new hurdle in an already difficult peace process. Most Palestinians firmly rejected the notion that either Israel or the U.S. could summarily override the choice they themselves had made when they elected Arafat as their leader in the election of 1996, which had been backed by the U.S. itself. It was true that many Palestinians had their own strong criticisms of

---

59 See the text of Bush's speech of June 24, 2002, at <www.whitehouse.gov>.

aspects of Arafat's rule. These Palestinians had long been eager to build more checks and balances to his sometimes capriciously exercised influence, and to make him more accountable in all respects—including in the crucial area of peace diplomacy—to the Palestinian grassroots. But they certainly did not feel that their national leaders should serve at the whim of either Sharon or Bush! For their part, neither Bush nor Sharon seemed eager to support the Palestinians' own internally generated movement for political reform.

Later in 2002, in the context of trying to build international support for his planned confrontation with Iraq's Saddam Hussein, Bush coordinated with the E.U., Russia, and the U.N. in crafting a joint diplomatic initiative known officially as "A perform-ance-based roadmap to a permanent two-state solution to the Israeli-Palestinian conflict." The Bush administration's three part-ners in the "Quartet" that sponsored the Roadmap did not share his view that progress would only be possible in the negotiations if the Palestinians produced a new leader. However, Bush's officials stuck to their position, and in early March 2003 the Palestinian Legislative Council (PLC) voted to approve the creation of the new post of "prime minister" in the P.A. leadership. (Arafat's position remained that of *ra'is*—president.) On March 19, just a few hours before the U.S. launched its long-threatened invasion of Iraq, Mahmoud Abbas accepted an invitation from Arafat to take up the new post and to form a new Palestinian cabinet. Abbas was a 45-year ally of Arafat's in the leadership of the largest Palestinian fac-tion, Fatah. He was also a well-known moderate who had under-taken much path-breaking work in exploring options for peace, especially in coordination with veteran Israeli Labor politician Yossi Beilin.

Abbas's assumption of his post allowed Bush—once the first big phase of the war against Iraq had finished—to start a new engagement in peace diplomacy, which he did on the basis of the Roadmap (see chapter 9). However, the Roadmap represented a noticeable step backwards from the place the negotiations had reached in late 2000 and at Taba in that (like the Oslo accords ten years earlier) it notably failed to give any details of the shape of the final outcome it aimed for—save for the fact that there should be a "Palestinian state" of undefined powers and uncertain borders created alongside Israel. On all of the other substantive, final-status issues in this relationship, the Roadmap remained silent. On the issue of settlements, however, it did state that in Phase I, operative immediately, the government of Israel should immediately dismantle settlement outposts erected since March 2001 and freeze all ongoing settlement activity including that connected with claimed "natural growth" of settlements. [60]

Some Positive Legacies from Oslo and Taba

There is no doubt that, for many in both the Israeli and Palestinian communities, the brave experiments of Madrid and Oslo ended very badly. For many in Israel, the experience of those years seemed to have proved the truth of propositions like, "You can't make a deal with the Palestinians: they just still want to destroy Israel," "Barak offered them nearly all they wanted, and still they said no!" or, "There's no one we can even talk to on the Palestinian side: Yasser Arafat is quite untrustworthy."

For many Palestinians, meanwhile, their experience in the post-Oslo years also seemed to have proved the mirror image of the negative lessons learned by many Israelis. For these Palestinians, the post-Oslo legacy "proved" such truths as, "The Israelis never intended to deal with us honestly at Oslo: look how they kept on taking our land for settlements," "They will never treat us as equals," or, "The only thing that Israelis seem to understand is the language of force." Certainly, during our visit, we heard many times from our friends in the Palestinian and Israeli peace camps that these were the kinds of negative judgments that they had to deal with every day as they worked with people in their own communities.

The disappointment and disillusionment engendered by the failure of the post-Oslo diplomacy gave rise to a tragic legacy of alienation and despair. (We explore this more deeply in chapter 10.) But the record of those same years can also be viewed as having left at least two considerable grounds for optimism.

First, it is important to remember and reconnect with the broad waves of optimism, relief, hope, and goodwill that greeted the convening of the Madrid conference in October 1991, and the announcement and signing of the Oslo Accords in September 1993. Despite everything that subsequently went badly in that

---

60 The text of the Roadmap is available at <http://www.state.gov/r/pa/prs/ps/2003/20062.htm>.

diplomacy, those were two quite transformative moments that showed both the strength of the yearning for peace inside both communities, and the ability of individuals at every level of society to undergo deep and consequential personal transformation in a pro-peace direction.

We need to acknowledge that on occasion after occasion throughout these years, people in many walks of life expressed their longing for peace and their willingness to undertake the hard work necessary to reach it. Among these supporters of a negotiated resolution, many men with significant security responsibilities inside each society came out with strong public declarations to the effect that they saw no way to bring about their people's goals using military means alone. On the Israeli side, Prime Minister Yitzhak Rabin was only the most prominent of the Israelis who made this argument to their people, and worked hard to urge them to support sincere engagement in negotiations. Numerous other former leaders of the Israeli military—including Ehud Barak, Benjamin Ben-Eliezer, and Amram Mitzna—echoed Rabin's words.

On the Palestinian side, Yasser Arafat and many other people with high security responsibilities in the P.A. and the PLO continued to seek a negotiated outcome and to speak out clearly against the violence used by some Palestinian individuals and factions. The Israeli and U.S. governments tried to diminish the importance of the condemnations that Arafat repeatedly voiced of the Palestinian groups that continued to carry out suicide bombings and other acts of anti-civilian violence, and they criticized him vociferously for not taking more forceful actions to counter the armed Palestinian factions. But those criticisms seemed disingenuous since the Israeli forces themselves had attacked, bombed, and destroyed the headquarters and most of the field offices of the P.A. security forces, a campaign that radically undercut Arafat's ability to take effective actions to control the security situation inside the occupied territories. Arafat's key 1993 decision in favor of negotiations and against violence was supported by nearly all the rest of the historic leadership of the Palestinian movement, including men who for decades had been leaders of Palestinian guerrilla units. The post-Oslo years showed that in a situation of hope and optimism, such transformations of attitudes, from wariness and distrust to a burgeoning of trust and hope, can and do multiply.

Second, we need to hang on to the fact of the considerable progress that was made—admittedly only at the very last minute, in the contacts that were held after the collapse of the Camp David talks—toward filling in the details of what a sustainable two-state solution between Israelis and Palestinians might look like. The outline that the two sides were working with in Taba was neither completed nor by any means perfect. It was, in any event, officially "taken off the table" by Sharon. But whenever the world is ready for a serious reengagement in peace diplomacy aiming at a two-state solution, then the points of increasing agreement reached at Taba stand ready to show everyone, in considerably more detail than anything that was available at the time of the Oslo talks, what the outline of such a solution might look like.

In the two chapters that follow, we will look in more detail at two of the crucial "final-status" issues that the negotiators at Taba were dealing with—Jerusalem and the Palestinian refugees. We will start to examine whether the record of Taba indicates that on these two issues, a sustainable negotiated outcome is still possible that is based on the two-state template that was used by the negotiators there.

Table 1:
Population Figures of Palestinians and Israelis
(all figures for 2000, in thousands)

	Israelis	Of which, Jewish Israelis	Palestinians	Of which, registered refugees[a]
Israel (within pre-1967 borders, but including settlers on Golan)	5,809.5[b]	4,743.2[c]	1,066.3[d]	0
West Bank, incl. E. Jerusalem	373.0[e]	373.0	2,011.9[f]	591.1
Gaza Strip	6.7[g]	6.7	1,138.1	837.8
Jordan			1,849.7[h]	1,609.6
Syria			472.5	387.6
Lebanon			433.3	380.1
Other countries			986.0	0
TOTAL	6,189.2[i]	5,122.9[j]	7,957.8	3,806.1

NOTES FOR POPULATION CHART

a Figures in this column are the "official" UNRWA figures for registered refugees, at <http://www.un.org/unrwa/publications/pdf/uif-dec00.pdf.>. The total number of Palestinian refugees with outstanding claims against Israel is much higher since in order to register with UNRWA, refugees must live in a country or area where UNRWA offers relief services, and either be, or be descended from, a refugee who in 1948 was indigent enough to qualify for those services.

b This figure is derived from that for Total Israelis (bottom of column), by subtracting the figures for Israelis in West Bank (including East Jerusalem) and in Gaza, which are separately derived. It includes about 15,700 Israeli settlers on the Golan. (Golan figure, from <http://www.fmep.org/database/golan.html>.)

c This figure has been derived from that for Total of Jewish Israelis by subtracting the numbers of Israelis living in the West Bank and Gaza.

d The Israeli Bureau of Statistics gives an average of 1,166.3 thousand "Arabs" in Israel in 2000, at <www.cbs.gov.il/sidrnge.cgi?sid=3709&stid=1&tid=2>. 100,000 has been subtracted from this figure, representing the Palestinians of East Jerusalem who are not Israeli citizens, and who are counted in this table under the category of Palestinians resident in the West Bank.

e Total of Israeli settlers in East Jerusalem in 2000 estimated at 180.0 thousand by Geoffrey Aronson, Assistant Director of the Foundation for Middle East Peace, Washington DC. Figure for the rest of the West Bank (193.0 thousand) from FMEP website, at <http://www.fmep.org/database/westbank.html>.

f This figure and the one below it, from the Palestinian Central Bureau of Statistics at <www.pcbs.org/English/populati/dem97_03/table_04.htm>.

g FMEP website at <http://www.fmep.org/database/gaza.html>.

h This figure, and the three below it, are all from the website of the Palestinian Refugee Center of London, UK, <www.prc.org.uk/English>. These figures are derived from those provided at the button "Where are they today?"

i The Israeli Bureau of Statistics gives an average total of 6,289.2 thousand Israelis in 2000, at <www.cbs.gov.il/sidrnge.cgi?sid=3706&stid=1&tid=2>. 100,000 has been subtracted from this figure, representing the Palestinians of East Jerusalem. They are not Israeli citizens, and they have been counted separately as Palestinians resident in the West Bank (figures for that total from the Palestinian Central Bureau of Statistics.).

j The Israeli Bureau of Statistics gives this figure for "Jews and others" among the Israeli population, as distinct from their category of "Arabs" in the population. See <www.cbs.gov.il/sidrnge.cgi?sid=3705&stid=1&tid=2>. "Jews and others" includes Russian immigrants whose Jewishness is either unproclaimed by the individuals concerned or contested by the Rabbinic authorities.

Jerusalem 1948–1967

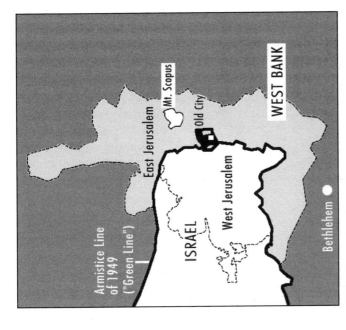

Jerusalem city limits unilaterally expanded by Israel, June 28, 1967; Israeli law extended, July 30, 1980.

Jerusalem city limits, 1947

Motsa

Deir Yasin

Ein Karim

Al Maliha

Sharafat

Lifta

Shu'fat

Jerusalem

Al Isawiya

Et Tur

Al Azzariya

Abu Dis

Silwan

Sur Bahir

Umm Tuba

Beit Safafa

Ramat Rahel

Beit Sahour

Beit Jala

Bethlehem

Corpus Separatum under 1947 U.N. Partition Plan

Jerusalem during the British Mandate in 1947 showing the Palestinian villages around the center of the city. Many of these were destroyed after 1948 to make room for the building of West Jerusalem.

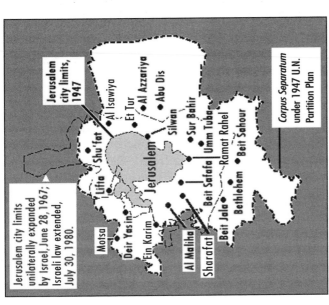

Armistice Line of 1949 ("Green Line")

ISRAEL

West Jerusalem

East Jerusalem

Mt. Scopus

Old City

WEST BANK

Bethlehem

West Jerusalem and East Jerusalem as occupied in 1967.

Maps adapted from Foundation for Middle East Peace

89

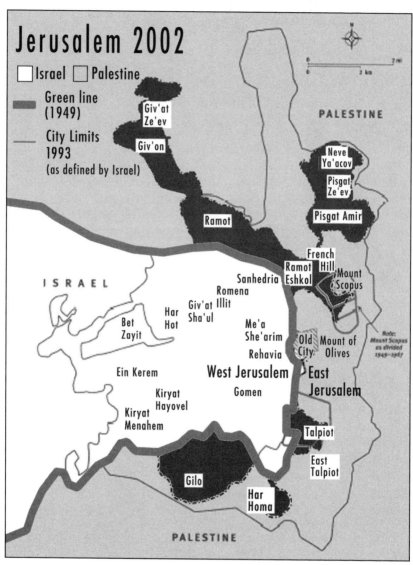

Greater Jerusalem showing West and East Jerusalem, including the Israeli settlements (black type in white boxes) built in East Jerusalem since 1967.

Adapted from Foundation for Middle East Peace

[5]

Views of Jerusalem

Jerusalem should be the capital of the world, an open city.
— Moshe Ma'oz, Hebrew University, Jerusalem, 2002

Is there a Palestine without Jerusalem? Is there an Israel without Jerusalem?
What would Judaism be without Jerusalem? Or Christianity? Or Islam?
— Mahdi Abdel-Hadi, PASSIA, Jeruslaem, 2002

On our first evening in Jerusalem, after we left a dinner meeting with Jonathan Kuttab, some of us returned to the YWCA by a route that took us by the vast stone walls of the Old City of Jerusalem. We then walked along Salah al-Din Street, which in decades past used to stay open late, the buzzing commercial heart of Palestinian East Jerusalem. Now, though, very few stores were open. Many looked as though they had been padlocked shut for weeks or even years; trash blew unimpeded along the nearly empty sidewalks. Our route through the windy, late-evening streets of this hill-spanning city took us past the large, well-fenced buildings that—in the heart of occupied East Jerusalem—house Israel's Ministry of Justice. We passed the heavy concrete barriers that had recently been erected to block access to Orient House, a historic Palestinian home that used to be the hub of Palestinian political and cultural activity in East Jerusalem. We walked down the hill past the small ancient mosque of Sheikh Jarrah; from there we saw dimly outlined on the brow of the hill ahead of us the bulky national headquarters of Israel's Border Police.

Closer at hand, in a side street near the fine, four-story YWCA building in which we were staying, we saw some makeshift tarpaulin-covered structures in which people appeared to be living. The shelters were built right on the street. Two men sat on sofas placed outside one of them, with a naked light bulb hanging behind their heads. The men were watching a couple of small boys who played on scooters in the nearly empty, ill-lit street.

We approached and greeted them. They greeted us cautiously. We inquired about their situation. They pointed to a sturdy stone house right across the street. "That is our house," one of them told us, adding that they had title deeds that proved that the house had been in their family for 150 years. But in the late 1960s, they said—that is, in the early days of Israel's occupation of East Jerusalem—some Jewish people had filed a counterclaim to this same property, backing it with ownership papers that, the men claimed, had evidently been forged. For thirty years, the case had moved slowly through the Israeli courts without reaching any resolution. The men said that the case still had not reached legal resolution when, a few weeks before our visit, they and their families received an abrupt eviction order.

"They came at 11:30 p.m., with police, border guards, and mounted police," one of them said. "They even had a water cannon. There was no way we could resist being evicted. So we decided at the very least to stay near our home by building these tents." Two families were living there in this way, including, as they reported, seven children.

"Our Palestinian people suffer in Jenin, we suffer in Nablus—but we also suffer in Jerusalem," said one of our hosts.

A Much Loved, Much Longed-For City

Throughout their long history of dispersion, throughout all the sufferings that beset the Jewish people, their poems and prayers recalled their attachment to Jerusalem. "Let my right hand be struck from me, if I should forget thee, oh Jerusalem," they prayed during two millennia. At the end of the special ritual meal, the seder, that Jewish families around the world eat on Passover, they drink a toast and say, "L'shanah ha'ba b'Yerushalayim"—Next year in Jerusalem! A small community of Jewish believers remained continuously present in Jerusalem even while most Jews were scattered in their diaspora. From the late nineteenth century on, and as the city came under British control after World War I, the city's Jewish community began to grow in size.

In 1947-48, during the Arab-Jewish fighting that surrounded the creation of the modern state of Israel, the Jewish irregular forces made determined efforts to bring and keep Jerusalem under their control. The Arab forces, which at first comprised only local, Palestinian irregulars but which later also included Jordanian regular army units that had been sent to reinforce

them, also fought to keep their hold on the city. Both those campaigns directly challenged the U.N.'s 1947 Partition Plan for
Palestine, since the U.N. negotiators—precisely because they
understood that both Jews and Arabs have a deep attachment to
the city—had planned to keep the whole area of a "Greater
Jerusalem" outside both the Palestinian Jewish state (Israel) and
the Palestinian Arab state mandated by their plan. Instead, the
U.N. had decreed, Greater Jerusalem should be ruled as an internationally administered *corpus separatum*. (The U.N. even, as noted
earlier, named Philadelphia Quaker Harold Evans as the city's first
international administrator.)

In the end, in 1948, Zionist forces were unable to keep hold of
Jerusalem's historic, walled Old City. But they did keep an important foothold in the newer urban areas that abut the Old City to
the west. West Jerusalem then became incorporated into the new
State of Israel—along with a small, isolated enclave to the northeast of the Old City, where Hebrew University sits atop Mount
Scopus. The rest of Jerusalem, comprising the Old City and extensive suburbs to its north, east, and south, were kept under the control of the Jordanian army. In 1949, Jordan tried to annex the
whole of the West Bank, including East Jerusalem. Few states recognized the legitimacy of that annexation, but Jordan remained in
physical control of East Jerusalem until 1967.

During and immediately after the fighting of 1947-48, both
sides engaged in near-total ethnic cleansing, leaving West
Jerusalem nearly empty of its Palestinians and East Jerusalem,
including the Old City, empty of Jews. Approximately sixty thousand Palestinian residents fled or were expelled from West
Jerusalem and the villages surrounding it that came under Israeli
control, while around two thousand Jewish residents fled or were
expelled from the Old City.[61] In addition, during and after the
fighting, both sides made significant changes to the physical structures of the areas that they controlled. As Israeli researcher
Raphael Israeli has noted, "the destruction by the Jordanians of
the Jewish Quarter [of the Old City] ... went a long way to de-
Judaize much of the millennia-old Jewish holdings in East

---

61 Michael Dumper, *The Politics of Jerusalem since 1967* (New York: Columbia University
Press, 1997), p. 65.

Jerusalem, just as the [Israeli] takeover of abandoned Arab neighborhoods in West Jerusalem ... led to their de-Arabization."[62]

Over the nineteen years that followed, the young Israeli state invested heavily in building up West Jerusalem. It constructed there the gracefully airy Israeli Knesset building, the Israel Museum, and many other establishments of key importance to the new state. But the Old City still sat tantalizingly just across the U.N.-guarded armistice line. Jordanian-controlled East Jerusalem meanwhile continued in its centuries' long role as the metropolitan center for the entire West Bank.

During the Arab-Israeli war of 1967, Israel's forces easily and quickly gained control of East Jerusalem. In her home in the settlement of Karnei Shomron, Sondra Baras had explained to us how she and many of her Jewish friends judged it "a miracle" when the West Bank—which she called "Judea and Samaria"— came for the first time under Israel's control. Central to this miracle, for many secular as well as observant Jews, was Israel's capture of the Old City of Jerusalem and the whole, extremely beautiful, urban area around it.

We recognize that many Jewish people—inside and outside Israel—have a deep attachment to this city, which is the site of both temples central to Judaism in biblical times. It is equally important, however, to recognize that the city's Palestinian daughters and sons have kept their own deep attachment to it, which has endured whether or not they have been able to stay in their ancestral city. The city of Jerusalem is holy to Muslims and Christians, as well as Jews—and it is holy to these believers not only in Israel/Palestine, but around the world.

At the level of national and ethnic politics, attachment to "Yerushalayim" is central to the identity of most Jewish Israelis *as Israelis*. Similarly, for Palestinian Arabs everywhere, their attachment to "Al-Quds" (the Holy City), as Jerusalem is known in Arabic, is central to their identity as Palestinians. In refugee shelters, and in the homes and workplaces of Palestinians throughout the world, photographs or other representations of the glittering golden shell of the mosque known as the Dome of the Rock in the Old City are given pride of place.

---

62 Raphael Israeli, *Jerusalem Divided; The Armistice Regime 1947-1967* (London and Portland, OR: Frank Cass, 2002), p. 24. Israeli's account (*ibid.*, p. 21) of the "evacuations" of the respective populations is also interesting.

For Christian believers in the Palestinian community and worldwide, Jerusalem is seen as the location of some of Jesus' teachings, and most importantly of his crucifixion and subsequent resurrection from the dead. Bethlehem, just six miles south of the Old City, was the traditional site of Jesus' birth. Jesus, his disciples, and their first converts had all been, by birth, Palestinian Jews. Palestine's indigenous Christian population claims its descent from those very earliest believers. Many of them are members of local Orthodox congregations that have existed since the days of Jesus. The most revered Christian site in Jerusalem is the extensive and architecturally complex Church of the Holy Sepulcher, in the heart of the Old City.

In the Middle Ages—after Christianity had spread from its Palestinian birthplace to Europe—Jerusalem became a strategic "prize" that attracted the bellicose attentions of the Western European crusaders (though their campaigns, significantly, were opposed by most of the local Christians[63]). Throughout the past two millennia, Christian denominations from all parts of the world have built churches and pilgrimage hostels in and around Jerusalem and Bethlehem, as well as in the city of Nazareth, which lies inside Israel.

Muslim believers, for their part, consider Jerusalem to be the place from which the prophet Mohammed departed on the mysterious "night journey" that took him on a brief visit to heaven shortly after the entire text of the Qur'an had been divinely revealed to him. In Mohammed's era, the seventh century CE, Jerusalem was linked by many overland trade routes to the great trading cities of the Arabian interior. Along those routes, the beliefs and folklore of Jewish and Christian traders traveled easily among Jerusalem, Damascus, the coastal cities of the Mediterranean, and as far south as Yemen. Before Mohammed received the word of God, he had worked as a trader in a company owned by his first wife. He may have already traveled to Jerusalem in that role. But certainly, working in the cross-desert trade as he did, he would have heard the stories of his Jewish and Christian contemporaries about that beloved city. And, of course, many of the stories from Jewish and Christian sacred texts—including those about Jerusalem—resurfaced, still clearly recognizable, in the Qur'an.

---

63 The crusaders were the most ruthless conquerors in the recorded history of Jerusalem. They slaughtered the city's indigenous residents quite indiscriminately: Jews, Muslims, and local Christians.

The Muslim faith was incubated in Mohammed's home cities of Mecca and Medina, in today's Saudi Arabia. In 638 CE, the Muslim armies captured Jerusalem from its (Christian) Byzantine ruler. Some of the Christian families that lived in and around the city at that time converted to Islam; others did not. Muslims honored Jews and Christians as fellow "people of the Book" and gave those who remained in the area the right to worship in their traditional manner.[64]

From many vantage points the skyline of Jerusalem is still, today, dominated by the glowing, ornate dome of the place of Muslim worship called the Dome of the Rock. That structure was built by the city's early Muslims over the rock from which the Prophet had left on his night journey. Close by the Dome of the Rock is a more austere, black-roofed structure, the al-Aqsa ("farthest") Mosque, which is judged by Muslims to be one of their religion's three holiest places, the others being Mecca and Medina.

The Dome of the Rock and Al-Aqsa Mosque are located on the broad, stone-paved plaza of Haram al-Sharif, which contains a number of other structures, some groves of trees, wide open-air courtyards, and places of ablution where Muslim congregants undertake the ritual washing required before they pray. The Haram is a walled enclosure, with several gates, some of which are reserved for the Muslim faithful. It occupies about one-sixth of the entire Old City, sitting atop a high ridge at the Old City's eastern edge. From the eastern side of the Haram a visitor can look out over the city walls and the Vale of Kidron to the vast Jewish cemetery built on stone terraces that climb up the Mount of Olives.

For Jewish believers the site of the Haram is also the Temple Mount, the location of the First and Second Temples, which represented the essential core of Jewish religious practice until they were destroyed. For many generations—except during the 19-year period when Jordan ruled the Old City—pious Jews have made their way to the southern portion of the massive wall that buttresses the western side of the Temple's foundation (which is also the foundation of the Haram), in order to express their deep

---

64 When Muslims first conquered the city, the local Byzantine Patriarch, Sophronius, handed the city's keys over to the Muslims' highest leader, the Caliph Umar Ibn al-Khattab, and invited Umar to pray in the Church of the Holy Sepulcher with him. Umar declined, fearing it might establish a precedent of Muslim takeovers of churches. He established instead a separate place of prayer for Muslims next to the church.

and prayerful lamentation over the destruction of the First and Second Temples. This portion of the Western Wall is known internationally as the Wailing Wall. In today's Israel, it is known simply as *ha-Kotel* (the Wall).

The location of two places of such intense religious attachment as the Haram and the Kotel in the same site adds a heavy overlay of religious significance to secular political tensions over who controls the city, and especially this much-contested spot at the heart of it.

"Why is Jerusalem so important?" Mahdi Abdel-Hadi of PASSIA asked rhetorically, when he met with us. "Is there a Palestine without Jerusalem? Is there an Israel without Jerusalem?" Abdel-Hadi, a Muslim, told us of an explanation that some Palestinian Muslims give for the holiness of the city: "People may ask why Mohammed traveled to Jerusalem after he received his revelation in Mecca. The answer to this, according to our folklore, is that God can reach you wherever you are; but if you want to reach him, then the easiest place to do that from is Jerusalem." Many observant Jewish people believe the same.

Decades of Israeli Occupation

One of the first things the Israelis did, after they conquered the Old City in 1967, was to demolish all the buildings in a wide area in front of the Kotel, creating a broad, paved plaza there that is used for many ceremonies big and small, from bar mitzvah visits to military graduation exercises. Today, Jewish people from around the world come to the Kotel to pray. Some spend long hours *davening* (praying) in front of the Kotel, and oftentimes they will tuck little pieces of paper bearing their most heartfelt prayers between the huge stone blocks at its foot. One part of the worship area at the Kotel is set aside for female worshippers. (Clashes have occasionally arisen when Jewish women have sought to pray in the "men's section.")

According to Palestinian records, the buildings demolished to make way for the plaza at the Kotel included 135 homes, the ancient Buraq and Afdali mosques, and a Sufi zawiya (place of pilgrimage). Approximately 650 people were reportedly evicted from the area without warning.[65]

---

65 Dumper, *The Politics of Jerusalem since 1967*, p.162.

The creation of the plaza at the Kotel was just one early step in a broad campaign to "judaize" the environment of occupied East Jerusalem—a campaign that has been pursued with zeal by every Israeli government since 1967. (Although this terminology is seldom employed outside of Israel, the project of "judaizing" Jerusalem and other parts of Israel/Palestine is a key element of Israeli political discourse.) On June 28, 1967, the Knesset passed the law that unilaterally "extended Israeli jurisdiction" to the area that had formed the Jordanian municipality of East Jerusalem.[66] From that date onward successive Israeli governments treated East Jerusalem as if it were under their sovereignty and spoke proudly of their "reunification" of the city. The Knesset also considerably expanded the municipal boundaries. The new boundaries were traced on the map in a way that carefully included the Kalandia airstrip to the north of the city, and as much other usable but uninhabited land as possible, while excluding as many as possible of the concentrations of Palestinian population that had grown up around the east, north, and south of the city. According to the Israeli human rights group, B'tselem, "Of the 70 square kilometers annexed to Jerusalem following the Six Day War, 23.5 kilometers, or slightly more than a third, was expropriated [by the Israeli government].... The majority of the expropriated land was privately owned by Arabs."[67] The 60,000 or so Palestinians whose homes fell within the new municipal boundary were offered Israeli citizenship. But few of them took up this offer. They reasoned that to do so would signal a degree of consent to the annexation that they preferred to withhold. Besides, they and the rest of the West Bank's Palestinians remained confident that Israel's occupation of East Jerusalem would not last very long.

Almost immediately after the occupation started, the Israeli government started pouring massive resources into building Jewish-only settlements throughout East Jerusalem. Some of these, like French Hill, East Talpiot, and Ramot Eshkol, were large, entirely new complexes that were constructed in some of the newly expropriated areas outside the Old City. Inside the Old City, meanwhile, the government pursued a plan to re-establish the Jewish character of the city's historic "Jewish Quarter," moving back into it some

---

66 See chapter 4.

67 B'tselem, *A Policy of Discrimination: Land Expropriation, Planning, and Building in East Jerusalem* (Jerusalem: B'tselem, May 1995), pp. 55-56.

of the families that had fled in 1948 and building large housing complexes and institutions for religious studies. Later, throughout occupied East Jerusalem, came additional housing complexes and "national" institutions like the government ministries and other administrative establishments that we saw during our visit.

As the Israeli population of East Jerusalem started to grow, the municipal authorities imposed tight restrictions on the ability of the city's Palestinian community even to undertake normal urban functions, let alone pursue any meaningful urban growth. The East Jerusalem Municipality was dissolved by fiat. The East Jerusalem Electric Company was forced to hand over operations to an Israeli electric company. Gradually all other traces of Palestinian community control were similarly ended—with the sole exception of the Muslim and Christian religious bodies that were allowed to retain their customary control over their respective holy places. (At the entrances to the Haram, the Jewish religious authorities posted notices informing Jewish believers that precisely because the site is so extremely holy to Jews, they should not enter it. These notices—which were still there during our visit—helped to avoid a lot of inter-communal friction trouble that might otherwise have occurred at the Haram over the years.[68] But they did not prevent Ariel Sharon from insisting on visiting the Haram in late September 2000.)

By the mid-1990s, the number of Israeli settlers living in East Jerusalem had come to equal the number of Palestinians, with each population then listed at around 150,000. For the Palestinians, that figure apparently counted the number of Palestinians who carried the special Jerusalem ID cards issued to the city's Palestinians after they refused the offer of Israeli citizenship. In reality, however, many of the Palestinians carrying those cards had moved out of the city over the years, relocating either to neighboring areas like Abu Dis or al-'Azzariyeh (Bethany), or even moving further afield to pursue work or study opportunities in Arab countries, Europe, or the United States. Some had left Jerusalem to join spouses in Gaza or the West Bank who were

---

68 Numerous times since 1967, Jewish or other pro-Israeli fanatics have undertaken very provocative acts against Muslim facilities in the Haram. One lengthy description of these, compiled by members of an extremist, fundamentalist group that seeks to build Judaism's "Third Temple" on that spot, can be found at <http://www.templemount.org/tempprep.html>.

denied residency in Jerusalem. In Jerusalem—as in Bethlehem—the out-migration of indigenous Palestinians was often prompted by the lack of opportunity locally, and by the stifling living conditions imposed on them inside the city. In 1993, the average housing density for Jerusalem's Jewish residents was 1.1 persons per room. For the city's Palestinians, it was twice that. Whatever the reasons for the out-migration, one Palestinian census taken in the late 1990s counted the Palestinians of East Jerusalem at only 85,000.[69]

In 1995, less than two years after the signing of the Oslo Accord, an inter-ministerial committee of the Rabin government proposed a new plan that significantly enlarged the area of the "Metropolitan Jerusalem" whose control the government now apparently sought to safeguard. (It did this even as the post-Oslo diplomacy proceeded.) The new scheme would incorporate a vast new portion of the West Bank into "Greater Jerusalem" for planning purposes even though—like much of the land taken into the city's boundaries in 1967—this area had never historically been part of Jerusalem. There were several indications that with this latest move, the authorities were seeking to exclude this vast additional piece of West Bank land, along with the rest of East Jerusalem, from any territorial compromise that might be part of a final peace agreement. As had happened with the 1967 enlargement, once again the lines were drawn to exclude heavily Palestinian-populated areas like Bethlehem or Ramallah. But this time, unlike in 1967, there were already many Jewish settlements located just outside the existing municipal area. They were brought into Greater Jerusalem under the plan, which also proposed ambitious new projects for their further enlargement. The settlements brought into this new Greater Jerusalem included many of those we saw during the bus tour we took with Israeli anti-settlement activist Michael Warschawski, including Ma'ale Adumim (where residents had evicted the Palestinian herding community and left them on the Jerusalem municipal garbage dump), Almon, and others.

The 1995 enlargement sent a finger of Israeli control eastward, to include not only the many different "neighborhoods" of Ma'ale Adumim, but also the settlement of Mizpe Jericho to its east. This finger took the claimed city boundary two-thirds of the way to

69 B'tselem, *A Policy of Discrimination*, p. 2; and *Report on Israeli Settlement in the Occupied Territories* 9.2 (March-April 1999), p. 8.

the Jordan River, which is the eastern boundary of the entire West Bank. If this whole area stays in Israel's hands, it will almost cut the West Bank into two. Throughout the late 1990s, it was these settlements included in the new planning area of Greater Jerusalem that saw the heaviest degree of Israeli investment.

We talked with anti-settlement activist Michael Warschawski in the West Jerusalem office of the Alternative Information Center, of which he is one of the leaders. He told us that, whereas in the rest of the West Bank, the goal of the settlement project as pursued by Sharon and his allies over the years has been primarily geographic —that is, seeking to obtain control over as much territory as possible—in and around East Jerusalem, the primary goal has been demographic. "In 1967, the Jewish population of the 'reunified' city was 78 percent," he said. "The goal of Israeli governments has always been to keep the Palestinian population beneath one-third. That has not been easy, because the Palestinian birthrate has been so high."

He explained some of the tactics the inter-ministerial committee on Jerusalem has pursued over the years. These included a deliberate use of planning mechanisms to stifle the growth of Palestinian neighborhoods and the simultaneous investment of huge government resources to build Jewish-only settlements in and around the city. Inside the city's few ethnically mixed neighborhoods, he noted, the discrimination is evident. In the Ras al-Amoud district, for example, Palestinian property owners are allowed to build only four-story structures and have to secure their own financing for them. But Jewish owners in the same neighborhood are allowed to build eight-story structures—for which, moreover, they receive hefty government loans and subsidies. Another tactic he described was the building of a huge "barrier wall" of Jewish settlements that could cut off the Palestinians of East Jerusalem, demographically, from the rest of the West Bank. "It is a human wall of settlers," he said. His words were borne out by what we witnessed as we drove around the city: vast fortress-like structures that dominated every ridgeline and spread down hillsides to surround, engulf, and cut off Palestinian farms and villages below.

Throughout the 1990s, in addition, activist settler organizations stepped up their efforts to gain control of properties in the heart of the Palestinian-peopled districts of Jerusalem. They did this in a number of ways, such as by using middlemen to buy properties from Palestinian families who had been reduced to penury by the high Israeli taxes and the low economic and job prospects, or by claiming they had found deeds to properties previously owned by Jewish families, even though sometimes—as in the case of those who had evicted the family we met outside the YWCA— these claims may have been fraudulent. Although the Israeli courts have always approved documented claims by pre-1948 Jewish property owners wishing to return to properties in East Jerusalem from which their families had fled that year, these same courts have refused even to consider the cases of Palestinian property owners who sought to return to properties in West Jerusalem from which their families had fled in 1948.

The establishment of small, Jewish-Israeli "bridgeheads" in the heart of the city's Palestinian-populated districts has occurred both inside the walled Old City and in the less ancient urban areas of East Jerusalem. For many centuries prior to 1948, the Old City had been divided according to traditional norms of Middle Eastern city planning, into recognized zones controlled by the city's different communities. In Jerusalem, there was a Jewish Quarter, a Muslim Quarter, a Christian Quarter, and an Armenian Quarter. Starting in the late 1980s, activist settler organizations started acquiring properties deep inside the Muslim, Christian, and Armenian Quarters. One of these activists was Sharon himself, who in late 1987—less than a week after the outbreak of the first Palestinian *intifada*—bought an apartment in the heart of the Muslim Quarter to use as a second home. His presence there required heavy security arrangements, which considerably disrupted the lives and assailed the dignity of Palestinian families living nearby. His argument was that a Jew should be able to live anywhere in Eretz Israel (the claimed "Land of Israel.") He notably did not extend the same right to Palestinians.

Wherever settler activists have established bridgeheads in the city, they have brought disruption and fear to the Palestinians. Less than a hundred yards away from where we found the evicted Palestinian families living on the street near the YWCA, some settlers had established a small bridgehead of six or seven apartments that seemed intermingled with apartments in which Palestinians were still living. A small group of us decided to visit with these settlers. Here, as in many places we went, we found the settlers being guarded by a young man from a private Israeli security company. The firm, he told us, had been hired by the Israeli government to provide these services. He sat in a small booth with his machine-pistol at the ready, guarding a small grassy knoll with the settlers' apartments grouped around it. He gave us permission to proceed with our visit.

Our first stop was at the door of a single-story stone structure in which four or five men and a couple of boys were sitting around computers, with some of them apparently studying Torah. We had hoped to speak with them, but they paid us little heed. Then, we greeted a young woman in the long skirt and distinctive headwear of an ultra-orthodox Jewish woman, who was carrying a baby to her home nearby. She graciously invited us in and gave us water while we chatted with her. She and her husband had lived there only about four months, she told us. Conditions inside the two rooms of the tiny apartment were simple. It seemed to have been made out of the vaulted undercroft of an old stone building. Palestinian Arabs lived upstairs, and all around, our host told us. She claimed that the apartment had belonged to a Jewish family before 1948, "so we are just coming back." (She did not, however, claim any blood relationship to those previous owners.) She said that she was particularly worried about her husband: he had been involved in the most recent call-up of army reservists and was serving in Gaza.

We found this visit very disturbing. We could not help but be touched by the generosity of the young mother, by her willingness to share her story with us, and by the loving care that she lavished on her baby daughter. Of course we expressed our heartfelt thanks to her for her hospitality and openness with us, as well as our sincere hopes for the welfare of her husband in the risky task to which he had been assigned. At the same time, it was evident to us that her presence there, and that of the rest of the activist settlers in the nearby apartments, had been accomplished only through the use and threat of superior force, in clear contravention of international law, and certainly not through any process of consultation with their Palestinian neighbors, the indigenous Palestinians. Moreover, there was no reciprocity at any level of the encounter between the two communities. Attractive though all the official rhetoric about the "reunification" of the previously-divided city may seem at first glance, it was evident to us that—in the case of this tiny settlement, as in all aspects of the city's life—this reunification had been achieved only through the wholesale suppression of the rights of the city's Palestinian community.

We were glad that some of us were able to connect at a human level with this mother in the tiny bridgehead settlement. However, we feel that the course she and her husband chose in joining the settlement is terribly misguided, based as it is on a tragic blindness to the rights, interests, and essential humanity of their Palestinian neighbors.

Isolating East Jerusalem and Its Leaders

In addition to the "demographic" assault inflicted on the Palestinians of East Jerusalem by the implantation of Jewish-only settlements over the past thirty-five years, these Palestinians have also, throughout the 1990s, faced determined efforts by the Israeli administration to sever as many as possible of the connections that have historically linked them to the Palestinians of the rest of the West Bank.

During the early years of the first *intifada* (that is, beginning in 1987), East Jerusalem rapidly emerged as an important meeting point for Palestinians from throughout the occupied areas. In those days, it was still relatively easy for West Bank Palestinians to reach the city, and it was not too hard for people from Gaza to travel there. Moreover, once the networks of community activists who coordinated and sustained that *intifada* had sent their representatives to Jerusalem for their periodic planning meetings, it was far easier for them to issue public declarations or meet with diplomats or media representatives from around the world in Jerusalem than it would have been anywhere else in the occupied territories. In this respect, the fact that Israeli law applied in East Jerusalem gave a degree of protection for their freedom of association and freedom of the press that their compatriots living elsewhere in the occupied territories did not enjoy, subject as those others continued to be to the military orders that controlled most aspects of their lives.

In the late 1980s and early 1990s, East Jerusalem personalities like Hanan Ashrawi and Faisal Husseini became well known in the international media as eloquent spokespeople for the Palestinians. In the rounds of diplomacy leading up to, and following, the 1991 Madrid peace conference, U.S. Secretary of State James Baker and other diplomats met with Ashrawi or Husseini in Jerusalem and in the U.S. State Department, in Washington.

This development caused evident discomfort to Israel's then-prime minister, Yitzhak Shamir. The prominence of these East Jerusalem Palestinians threatened to undermine all the efforts Israel had made over the years to render unrealizable the long-standing Palestinian claim to East Jerusalem. In 1992, the Israelis introduced a significant new policy that imposed a tight "movement control" regime on all roads leading between East Jerusalem and the rest of the West Bank. This regime continued to allow easy passage both ways for cars bearing the yellow, Israeli license plates, but it tightly restricted the ability of people driving West Bank vehicles to enter East Jerusalem. These controls were retained, and even in some respects tightened, after the Oslo Accords were concluded. Thus, throughout the 1990s, it became harder and harder for West Bank Palestinians to travel to jobs, schools, hospitals, professional appointments, or cultural or political gatherings in East Jerusalem.

Speaking of the effects these new movement controls had on the East Jerusalem Palestinians, Warschawski said, "It was like cutting the heart from the body of the West Bank. So then the body dies—or else you make a new heart, like Ramallah."

Indeed, when the new Palestinian Authority (P.A.) mandated by the 1993 Oslo Accords came into being, it had no choice but to establish its West Bank headquarters in Ramallah rather than in Jerusalem. Successive Israeli administrations worked hard to continue to ensure that the P.A. would have no administrative responsibilities at all inside East Jerusalem. In January 1996, the Israeli government even tried to prevent the East Jerusalem Palestinians from voting in the elections that the P.A. held that month. The U.S. government, to its credit, insisted that these Palestinians could not be thus disenfranchised. But the Israelis still refused to allow the election organizers to have Palestinian ballot-boxes inside East Jerusalem; instead, the East Jerusalem voters placed their ballots inside special "postal" containers, which were then taken "through the mails" to be counted in Ramallah.

Under pressure from the many western countries that had long had consular (though not embassy-level) representation in Jerusalem, the Israelis for some years allowed the Palestinians to continue operating Orient House, the graceful old house in the Sheikh Jarrah neighborhood that acted as a *de facto* center for Palestinian political activities in East Jerusalem. Running the activities of Orient House was Faisal Husseini, the gentle and visionary leader of the East Jerusalem Palestinian community. (Husseini's father, Abdul-Qader al-Husseini, had been a historic political and military leader for the Palestinians; he was killed in the fighting of 1948.) Faisal Husseini did not have a position in the P.A., but he was a member of the Executive Committee of the PLO, the broader Palestinian organization, where he had a special responsibility for Jerusalem affairs. In that capacity he participated in many joint gatherings and projects with pro-peace Israelis, and in high-level diplomatic encounters with representatives of many governments, as noted above. He died in May 2001 during a visit to Kuwait. A few weeks after his death, the Israelis closed down his beloved Orient House. It was still closed in June 2002, when we visited the city.

Husseini's job of representing the interests of Jerusalemites on the PLO Executive Committee was briefly taken over by Sari Nuseibeh, the president of Al-Quds University. We had a very informative talk with Nuseibeh while we were in Jerusalem, as described in chapter 8 below. A few weeks after our visit, the Israeli police moved into the university office where we had met Nuseibeh, confiscating numerous records before they closed down that office, too. (A few weeks later, they allowed it to reopen, but only on the condition that Nuseibeh use it solely for university business and not attempt to carry out political work there.[70])

From Occupation to a City at Peace?

Successive Israeli governments have worked hard since 1967 to promulgate the claim that Israel's takeover of East Jerusalem resulted in the total, laudable, and above all irreversible reunification of the Holy City. That effort has been pursued at many different levels, including the use of the language in which Israeli leaders have encouraged their people and others to think about the city. Thus while many Jewish Israelis are prepared to enter into heated discussions over the fate of the settlements in the rest of the occupied territories—pro or con—at least they do explicitly

---

70 Nuseibeh was "released" by P.A./PLO head Arafat from his job of representing the Palestinians in Jerusalem at around that time. Arafat took that step in apparent response to some comments Nuseibeh had made about giving up the Palestinian refugees' right of return.

use the term "settlements" on most of those occasions. With regard to the settlements of East Jerusalem, however, it became natural for most Israelis—and many of Israel's supporters elsewhere—not to use that term at all, but rather, to describe the Israelis-only housing complexes built on expropriated land there as "neighborhoods" or "suburbs," terms that tend to make them sound less intrusive, more organic, and more generally acceptable. It frequently happens, therefore, that even some people in Israel's pro-peace camp who say they would be prepared to see the evacuation of "all or most of the settlements" turn out, on closer inspection, not to be referring to the settlements of East Jerusalem at all.

It seems clear, too, that in the mid-1990s, as it started spreading (and acting on) the concept of a Greater Jerusalem, the Israeli administration was hoping that the settlements included within that expanded boundary could soon also benefit from being thought of as "neighborhoods" rather than "settlements."

In reality, the much-vaunted reunification of Jerusalem did not result in any reunification where it really counts—at the human level. Israel's control over East Jerusalem brought no grand rapprochement among members of the city's richly diverse historical communities of Jews, Muslims, Christians, Armenians, and others. Instead, it resulted in the imposition of a highly discriminatory regime on all the city's non-Jewish residents. That discrimination was manifested in many realms of life. We have discussed above the strong discrimination embedded in the design and implementation of city planning codes. Regarding the provision of municipal services, the many journeys we took in and around the city showed us clearly that while in West Jerusalem and the settlements and other Jewish-populated parts of East Jerusalem there are well-paved streets with sidewalks, good street lighting, parks, efficient trash collection, public libraries, and a whole range of other municipal services, these services seemed to be provided only poorly, if at all, in the mainly Palestinian areas. Three Israeli writers who are intimately familiar with the policies successive mayors have pursued towards the city's Palestinian residents have written: "Most Israelis would be surprised to know that in the city they call their capital, just a few dozen yards from the holiest spot for Jews worldwide, the Western Wall, there are Arab neighborhoods where human waste literally pours into the streets. Some Arab neighborhoods do not have trash pickup, and debris just piles up in abandoned lots."[71] Regarding the access of residents to decent job opportunities, or to a justice system that would restore to them properties that had been evacuated under duress in 1948—in these areas, too, there has been clear discrimination.

Israel's post-1967 campaign unilaterally to incorporate East Jerusalem into its own body politic has not only led to a highly discriminatory social order in the city, it has also been in fundamental contravention of the provisions of international humanitarian law. As a result, neither the U.N., nor any major national government anywhere, nor any international organization has recognized the legitimacy of that annexation. (Only Micronesia, Costa Rica, and a couple of other small states have moved their embassies there.) For all major actors on the world scene, the status of East Jerusalem is exactly the same as that of all the rest of the West Bank: it is occupied territory. Therefore, despite all the tricks of rhetorical legerdemain that Israel has sought to deploy to try to convey the impression that East Jerusalem really is part of Israel, and that the "Jewish neighborhoods" there are not settlements, neither of these propositions is accepted by the international community.[72] (In a landmark study in 1995, B'tselem, Israel's premier human-rights organization, concluded that "East Jerusalem is occupied territory, [and] that its status is the same as that of the rest of the West Bank"; and that "such acts as the "expropriation of lands in East Jerusalem in order to establish Jewish neighborhoods," the establishment of these neighborhoods itself, and "the granting of financial benefits encouraging Jews to live there" all constituted violations of the Fourth Geneva Convention.[73])

Between the positions of international law rigorously applied and that of successive Israeli governments, a number of pro-peace activists from both national communities have over the years pur-

---

71 Amir Cheshin, Bill Hutman, and Avi Melamed, *Separate and Unequal: The Inside Story of Israeli Rule in East Jerusalem* (Cambridge, MA: Harvard University Press, 1999), p.124. Cheshin was the Jerusalem Mayor's advisor on Arab affairs, 1984-94, under Teddy Kollek and Ehud Olmert. Melamed was Mayor Olmert's advisor on Arab affairs, 1994-96.

72 The formal position of the U.S has until 2003 remained that East Jerusalem is occupied territory, and that its disposition should be the subject of negotiation along with that of the rest of the West Bank. But spokesmen for the administration have engaged in much complex obfuscation to avoid stating this clearly in public, given the pressures the administration has faced from a very pro-Israeli Congress to recognize Israel's annexation of East Jerusalem as legal and to move the U.S. Embassy from Tel Aviv to Jerusalem in recognition of that status.

73 B'tselem, *A Policy of Discrimination*, pp.11-12, 15, and 16.

sued numerous discussions to try to discover a "middle way" by which the demographic egg of East Jerusalem might be partially unscrambled and the rights of all of its communities—principally, the rights of its two national-political communities—as well as those of all of its individual citizens/residents might somehow be respected. As early as 1991, Naomi Chazan worked jointly with the Palestinian-American scholars Rashid Khalidi and Fuad Mughrabi on a study titled *Negotiating the Non-negotiable*, which explored possible ways to approach and resolve the thorny Jerusalem issue. One of the points Chazan stressed in her contribution was that consideration of the Jerusalem issue should certainly not be left to the end of any negotiating process on the grounds of its claimed complexity. Instead, she argued, the very complexity of this issue meant that exploration of possible outcomes should continue throughout the negotiating process and be incorporated as appropriate into the implementation steps along the way to a final settlement. Otherwise, she predicted, the injection of this issue at the very end of the negotiating process could prove explosive and destroy all the progress made until then.

Sadly, this dire prediction proved all too prescient. In the text of the 1993 Oslo Accords, Jerusalem had been one of the five specified topics on the peacemaking agenda on which negotiation was explicitly left until the final-status talks. Those talks did not even begin in earnest until the Camp David summit of July 2000—and then, just as Chazan had predicted, the Jerusalem issue proved one of the most explosive. In particular, reports that at the Camp David talks, Barak had insisted that Israel would not recognize Palestinians' sovereignty over the Haram, and that the Muslim *Waqf* (charitable foundation) might lose some of the functional control that it had exercised over the Haram area until then, provoked cries of indignation from throughout the Muslim world—including from the pro-U.S. governments of Egypt and Saudi Arabia.

Some of the ideas for Jerusalem's future governance that teams of (unofficial) Palestinian and Israeli researchers had brainstormed in the late 1980s and the 1990s were innovative and potentially productive. One of the most constructive was that the city be placed under the sovereignty neither of the Israelis nor of the Palestinians, but instead, of a new version of the *corpus separatum* decreed in the 1947 U.N. partition plan. Instead of coming under international control, most of these researchers agreed, this new *corpus separatum* might more appropriately come under joint Israeli-Palestinian control; and within it, the various Jewish and Palestinian neighborhoods could exercise a substantial degree of local control under some variant of a New York-style "borough" system. Since most of the research teams that produced such plans were made up of determinedly pro-peace members of the two national groups, they generally had no problem in proposing that the national capitals of both states should be located in the city. One helpful study, which took the form of a survey of a broad range of views on only the Israeli side of the conflict, emphasized that finding a workable solution for Jerusalem would involve the people of both national groups being willing to engage in compromise at three important levels: territorial, functional—and emotional.[74]

In early fall 2000, once the acrimony that had followed the breakup of the Camp David talks had cleared a little, Barak and Arafat resumed their final-status talks, as noted in chapter 4. At that point some of the approaches suggested in those earlier explorations reemerged at the official level. In particular, the "Moratinos document," which summarized the achievements of the Taba talks of January 2001, noted that the Israeli and Palestinian negotiating teams there "Both ... favored the idea of an Open City." The document said that both sides had "accepted in principle" a suggestion President Clinton had made the previous month, namely, that the future Palestinian state should have sovereignty over the city's Arab neighborhoods; and the Israeli state, over the Jewish neighborhoods. The document indicated that at Taba considerable, but by no means total, progress had been made toward resolving the complex issues around the Old City and the sacred sites of the "Historic Basin" area that abuts the Old City to the east. In addition, the document noted that there was apparent agreement that Jerusalem would be the seat of the capitals of both Israel and the future state of Palestine.[75]

In July 2002, a global international-affairs policy institute called the International Crisis Group (ICG) published its own suggestion of how the ideas explored at Taba might be pushed to a successful conclusion based on the two-state approach. The ICG's staff people consulted extensively with policymakers and independ-

---

74 Israel/Palestine Center for Research and Information, *The Future Status of Jerusalem— Possible Fields of Compromise* (Jerusalem: IPCRI, 1995).

75 "Moratinos document" (see note 58 above), pp. 33-34.

ent thinkers in both communities, and came up with two different formulae for how the Jerusalem question might be resolved in a two-state context. One was based on dividing the sovereignty in both the Old City and its environs, and in Greater Jerusalem. The other was based on having an "international protectorate" over the Old City and the adjacent areas, while having a division of sovereignty elsewhere in the city. The maps included as part of the ICG report underlined, if anything, how geographically complex (and therefore, how hard to make workable) any such outcome would be.[76]

A review of the negotiating record between July 2000 and January 2001 shows that the two sides still had significant gaps to close between them, on the Jerusalem issue as on settlements generally (and, as we shall see in the next chapter, on refugees). Nevertheless, in just those six months of the two sides' real engagement on final-status issues, they had traveled a significant distance toward unpacking the many complex dimensions and sensitivities around the Jerusalem issue and sketching out how it might, perhaps, be resolved in the context of a two-state solution. Jerusalem, this record strongly suggests, need not be the totally intractable stumbling block that it often has been supposed to be. When there is a return to serious peace negotiations on the Israeli-Palestinian issue in the near future, peace activists and people of good will from both national communities now have a lot of very constructive proposals to work with as they continue to explore ideas for the future of this vitally important city. Certainly, we invite and encourage all our readers to join in this exploration.

We would like to add two things to this process. First comes a restatement, with special regard to Jerusalem, of the principles enunciated in the first chapter; and second, the addition of a wider optic of optimism and vision that we encourage our readers to explore.

Regarding the four principles, it is worth restating, with regard to this most hotly contested of cities, the principles of human equality and nonviolence, with this latter principle necessarily involving a clear prohibition on imposing outcomes on other people through the use of force. In considering Jerusalem's future, the views of all those with a direct stake in the city's well-being must be fully and fairly consulted and the rights of all of them assured. Also with regard to Jerusalem, we wish to emphasize the

---

76 International Crisis Group, *Middle East Endgame II*, pp.11-13. The relevant maps are on pp. 25-27.

important principle that the primary stakeholders in the city's future must be recognized to be the city's people themselves— including its current residents (both Jewish and Palestinian), and those sons and daughters of its indigenous families who are currently prevented from living in Jerusalem or even entering it.

The access restrictions that Israel has imposed on native Jerusalemites who are refugees today cause considerable suffering and must be ended. But this is certainly the case, too, with the access restrictions placed on native Jerusalemites who now live just outside the hated roadblocks and often within clear view of the city of their birth. All these native sons and daughters of the city must be allowed full access to it—and beyond that, a full and equal voice in determining its future. Just as people in Bosnia who were living in forced exile from their home towns and cities were not deemed to have lost their voting rights therein on account of their forced migration to other areas, so too, the Palestinian Jerusalemites living elsewhere in the West Bank, or elsewhere around the world, cannot have lost their say simply because of an Israeli diktat. In any future deliberation over the long-term future of this city, ways must be found (as they were for the Bosnians) for them to share in the deliberation and in the final, electoral ratification of the outcome.

It is true that in the broader Israeli and Palestinian communities, as well as in the broader communities of Muslim, Christian, and Jewish believers worldwide, there is also considerable longing, concern, and affection for Jerusalem, as well as numerous, very concrete links to it. The existence of those broader interests in the city should not, however, obscure the fact that, like any other healthy city, Jerusalem should be regarded first and foremost as the city of its own residents, and only after that as a symbol of national sovereignty for both nations, or as the locus of religious longing or cultural identity for broader communities worldwide. Consider present-day Rome, which combines the functions of a healthy, livable city for its own people, a national capital, a host to the Vatican City (which has its own separate sovereignty), and a magnet for pilgrimage by Catholics from around the world. Or consider Brussels, which is a healthy, livable city for its bicultural residents, the national capital of Belgium, and host to the E.U. headquarters. Like those cities, or like bilingual and multicultural Montreal or numerous other multicultural, multi-functional cities around the world, Jerusalem will flourish in the long run only if it provides a hospitable, livable environment that meets the legitimate needs of all of its own inhabitants.

Finally, we want to introduce a wider optic and invite readers to join us in considering what Jerusalem could become if it were truly not only nominally the City of Peace but also, more fundamentally, a City *at* Peace.

Within the framework of a two-state solution, the only status for Jerusalem that makes any sense for us would be for it to be the national capital for both of the resulting states. Thus, most of the investment that Israel has put into making Jerusalem a well-developed modern city would be essentially safeguarded, though institutions like the Ministry of Justice and the Border Police headquarters would most likely have to be relocated westward from their current positions in East Jerusalem. Other Israeli national institutions—in the fields of the arts, entertainment, and business, as well as politics—could be located to a new and expanded Jerusalem at peace. But at the same time, the Palestinians would have to be allowed to establish their own national institutions there, covering all the same fields of human endeavor, and to recreate the city's long-time role as the central metropolitan hub for the whole of the Palestinian West Bank.

If this Jerusalem were an "open city" as well as the national capital of both states, we could think of it as a beacon of the engaged coexistence of, and interaction among, believers and leaders from all three of the Abrahamic faiths. Once Jerusalem is at peace, pilgrims from all three faiths will be flocking to it—why should they not engage in cooperative interaction in new interfaith institutions of study or social outreach that might be established there? In addition, Jerusalem might become as a center of bicultural publishing, translation, and general cultural interaction between the Hebrew-speaking and the Arabic-speaking worlds... Why not? What else might a Jerusalem at peace become?

At the time of our summer sojourn in the City, and in the months we have labored over this discussion, events did not seem to be traveling in that direction. During our visit we saw suffering, fear, intolerance, and anger in Jerusalem—as we did in the rest of the Holy Land. Nonetheless, we also saw a strong yearning for a better way, and we were deeply inspired by the dedication of the many Jerusalemites we met who were working to bring that way into being.

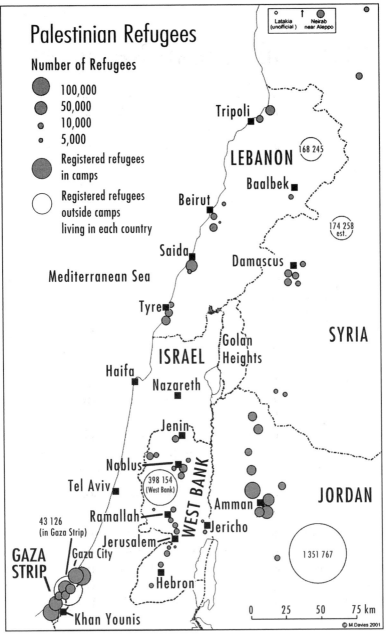

Palestinian Refugees

Number of Refugees

- 100,000
- 50,000
- 10,000
- 5,000

Registered refugees in camps

Registered refugees outside camps living in each country

Latakia (unofficial)   Neirab near Aleppo

Tripoli

LEBANON

168 245

Baalbek

Beirut

174 258 est.

Saida

Damascus

Mediterranean Sea

Tyre

Golan Heights

SYRIA

ISRAEL

Haifa

Nazareth

Jenin

Nablus

Tel Aviv

398 154 (West Bank)

WEST BANK

JORDAN

Ramallah

Amman

Jericho

43 126 (in Gaza Strip)

Jerusalem

GAZA STRIP

Gaza City

1 351 767

Hebron

0   25   50   75 km

© M.Davies 2001

Khan Younis

The 59 Palestinian refugee camps in the Middle East, showing the number of Palestinian refugees living in each camp, and the number of registered refugees living outside of the camps in each country in 2003.

Adapted from United Nations Relief and Works Agency

[6]
The Palestinian Refugees

*We have suffered a long time. It is enough. There will be no peace if the
two-thirds of Palestinians who live "outside" [of Palestine/Israel] have no rights.
There will be no security for Israel as long as there are refugees.*
— Woman camp leader, Ein el-Hilweh camp, Lebanon, 2002

*The practical solution to the problem will come about by agreement
based on just, fair, and practical considerations.*
— Gush Shalom, Israel, 2002

Visiting with Refugees in Jordan...

About a twenty-five minute drive northwest of Jordan's capital, Amman, the busy highway took some broad curves that swooped down from the ridgeline, and around several rapid folds in the sides of these steep golden hills. There was a place where a couple of pedestrian overpasses soared over the road. Our van slowed, and the scrub-covered limestone hillside gave way to a low-slung tangle of concrete cubes that looked like many third-world shantytowns. We turned into the heart of the tangle, and drove along a small, potholed street to a dusty square where unwieldy vans and small buses maneuvered into impossibly small spaces and street vendors competed noisily to sell nuts, towels, and an array of other goods to passengers passing through.

This was the Baqa'a refugee camp, home to more than 80,000 Palestinian refugees.

After we dismounted from the vans, our guide led us along a narrow street and up some bare stairs to a second-story office for the camp's administration. A genial older man in flowing robes and checkered *kaffiyeh* headscarf greeted us, served us with the always-offered beverages, and introduced himself as Sheikh Atta al-Wahidi, vice-chair of the Camp Committee. Speaking through an interpreter, he expressed appreciation to the Jordanians for having hosted the refuges for so long and so generously. "People here have suffered much," he continued. "They were compelled to leave their homes. I'm happy to speak to you, but we are full of pain and bitterness."

115

His tale of suffering spanned many decades. "I remember all the U.S. presidents going back to Harry Truman!" he said, referring to the president whose support in 1948 had helped the infant Jewish state to survive. "There have been so many promises made over the years to the Palestinians. But so little has been done."

He recalled that in 1952, U.S. Secretary of State John Foster Dulles claimed that the Palestinian refugee problem would die down as the older generation of refugees died. "But just the reverse has happened."

We asked Wahidi about his own family's story. They lived near Beersheba, he said, referring to a large town in the south of today's Israel. "In 1948, the Jewish forces were much stronger than the Arab forces, and well armed. They would come to Palestinian villages and would burn Palestinian towns, seeking to drive out the Palestinians. My family fled to Hebron, and then to Jericho. Then in the fighting of 1967, we were pushed out once again, into Jordan."

He had three sons, he told us. One was now a doctor, one worked with the Jordanian government's Department of Palestinian Affairs, and one was a contractor.

He told us emphatically that he did not approve of the attacks some Palestinian militants from the occupied territories had recently undertaken against Israeli civilians. "We are committed to early Islam, which forbids killing children and the elderly and the destruction of trees," he said. "We do not approve of terror attacks against any civilians. We seek no bloodshed or revenge. We want an oasis of peace and security for all peoples ... But we seek the right of return and the implementation of all U.N. resolutions. We don't want violence, but only the enforcement of international laws and resolutions."

After the meeting was finished, one of Wahidi's aides led us on a tour of part of the camp. We walked along narrow alleyways that threaded between the concrete shelters. Utility wires criss-crossed the sky above our heads. Our guide pointed out the high iron balconies of a three-story middle school along the way. Children darted around us in the alleys, and we passed purposeful-looking men who seemed, as late afternoon made way for early evening, to be returning home from work.

Our guide knocked on one large metal door set into a high

wall. A gaggle of small children opened the door a crack and then called for their mother, who let us in. A dozen of us filed into a small, ill-lit but high-ceilinged room that was, she told us, one of three in which the seven members of her family made their home. Pastel-covered bedrolls were stacked neatly on top of large painted armoires that seemed to hold all the family's other household goods. An image of the gleaming gold carapace of Jerusalem's Dome of the Rock hung on the wall.

Her husband joined us, and we asked the young parents about their views on the issue of return. "Never will I give up my right, even if they gave me a palace here!" the mother said, her eyes flashing in the gloom. After we all trooped back out of her door, she sent two of the children running out after us to make her point clearer. They carried a panel on which was embroidered a map of Mandate Palestine. "There! There!" they said excitedly, pulling at our sleeves to make sure we all saw what they were pointing at: a star embroidered right in the middle of today's Israel: "That's our village!"

... in Lebanon...

A few days later, some of us were in Lebanon, in the large refugee camps of Ein el-Hilweh, near Sidon, and Rashidieh, near Tyre, both cities that date back to biblical times. Lebanon hosts a dozen Palestinian refugee camps administered by the U.N. Relief and Works Agency (UNRWA), which has provided relief services to Palestinian refugees since 1950. In 2002, these camps were home to 217,000 of the 387,000 registered refugees in the country.[77]

Most of the refugees in Lebanon are from families that fled here in 1948 from the Galilee hills in the north of Mandate Palestine. Many of those who spoke with us in Ein el-Hilweh and Rashidieh were born in Lebanon. They told of the times when the only shelter they had was under tents; how over time they built sturdier shelters of corrugated zinc and mud bricks; and how it

---

77 UNRWA figures from June 30, 2003, accessed at <http://www.un.org/unrwa/publications/pdf/uif-june02.pdf>. UNRWA has its own definition of "registered refugees," which is described more fully below in footnote 80.

was not until the PLO took control in the camps in 1969 that they were able to build with concrete.[78]

The people we met in these camps had bitter memories of their treatment at the hands of the Lebanese authorities, of some of their Lebanese neighbors—and of the Israeli army. The Israelis invaded South Lebanon in 1982, and stayed in this part of the country for a further three years.[79] During the 1982 invasion, some 19,000 Palestinian and Lebanese people lost their lives—including many hundreds of residents of Rashidieh and Ein el-Hilweh. Afterward, as the Lebanese government and Lebanese political parties regained their grip on this region, the Palestinian refugees still felt very vulnerable. Many parties and factions in Lebanon's multifaceted citizenry have often shown great hostility to the Palestinian refugees living in their midst. And the refugees, being citizens of no state, have had no state anywhere that worked to protect their interests.

In Ein el-Hilweh, we met in the local headquarters of the General Union of Palestinian Women (GUPW) with some of the camps' GUPW leaders and male leaders. We started by briefly introducing ourselves and our mission. When it was Ramallah Friend Jean Zaru's turn to introduce herself she mentioned that her elder brother had been Hanna Mikhail, a prominent Palestinian liberation activist who in the early 1970s left his teaching career in the U.S. and traveled to Lebanon to help build the Palestinian movement there. Mikhail disappeared with eleven other Palestinian organizers in 1976 while traveling in a boat that was trying to evade the naval blockade that Israel maintained around Beirut in those days.

Our hosts were very excited to learn of the relationship. One of the GUPW leaders, Amneh Jibril, ran over to hug Jean, breaking into tears of emotion at this unexpected meeting with

---

78 Under its mandate from the U.N., UNRWA is responsible only for provision of relief services—including shelter, sanitation, education, and health services—inside the designated camp areas. Responsibility for security in the camps remains with the authority providing security in the surrounding locale, which is usually the state (or, in Gaza and the West Bank, the occupying power, Israel). In Lebanon, the PLO exercised security authority over most of the refugee camps from 1969 through 1982 under an agreement with the government. During those years, the government's previous restrictions on camp life were lifted.

79 Israel stayed in a broad area south and east of Tyre until 2000.

Mikhail's sister. She then ran to an outer office and called in some younger GUPW staff people to meet Jean. "This woman's brother," she declared, "was the first one to make women believe in themselves! What we remember him for was his quiet manner, and also the effective way he embodied his compassion and his values. He was a real leader!"

As the meeting settled down again, our hosts told us more about conditions for the 60,000-70,000 people living in their camp, which they described as "very crowded." The Lebanese state was enforcing tight restrictions on many aspects of the refugees' lives, they said. Refugees were not allowed to own land or real property in Lebanon. They had to pay high fees to attend state universities; work permits were difficult to obtain, and more than 70 professions were officially designated as "proscribed" for Palestinians. As a result, the unemployment rate topped 60 percent. In addition, as "foreigners" under Lebanese law, Palestinians were not eligible to take advantage of governmental health facilities or other social services. Not surprisingly, therefore, many of the Palestinians with whom we spoke were adamant about claiming their right to return to their families' ancestral land.

One of the GUPW women told us:

We don't want charity, we want justice! We want you to advocate for this. ... We Palestinians had a program of offering to live in peace with Israel—but we also want our rights. We have suffered a long time. It is enough. There will be no solution if the two-thirds of Palestinians who live "outside" [of Palestine/Israel] have no rights. There will be no security for Israel, as long as there are refugees.

She added, "If all the Palestinian refugees in Lebanon returned to their villages [in Israel], the population density would still be much less than in Gaza today. So what's the problem?"

Still in Ein el-Hilweh, we crowded into a room in a small community center and watched an energetic group of young people rehearsing for a performance of traditional Palestinian folk dancing—*debkeh*. The fifteen or so dancers ranged in age from around ten to late teens. A speaker system provided cheerful music that had a strong underbeat from traditional hand-drums. The girls wore black dresses enlivened with colorful embroidery and appliqués. Some dances were performed just by the girls; some, by the boys. In a couple of numbers, girls and boys danced together, stamping out the rhythms on the linoleum tile floor. One dance was a traditional harvest dance: the girls carried large baskets and swooped them low to the ground to mime the gathering of the grain. On the wall of the narrow room hung several pictures of Yasser Arafat, an enlargement of a recent news photo from an *intifada*-related confrontation in Gaza, and a picture of the skyline of Jerusalem, a city just 120 miles away that none of these young people—and possibly, none of their parents—had ever seen. Beneath the picture of Jerusalem was the Arabic inscription, "*al-awda hatman*"—"Return is inevitable."

In Rashidieh, we talked with Sultan Abul-Ainayn, a camp leader and staunch PLO loyalist. He spoke movingly about his many friends and comrades who had been killed in the struggle for Palestinian rights. He also told us about the tough conditions inside Rashidieh: among them, an unemployment rate of 65 percent and significant cutbacks in the medical care offered by UNRWA, the U.N. agency that has provided relief to the Palestinian refugees since 1950.

Asked about his preferences for a settlement of the refugee issue, Abu-Ainayn said he personally would prefer to go back to a Palestinian state (rather than to Israel). But he insisted that the Palestinians were still not ready simply to relinquish their right of return. "Who am I to relinquish the right of return of all Palestinians?" he said a number of times. He did, however, tell us that he thought most of the camp's residents would accept any decision the Arafat-led Palestinian Authority (P.A.) might make. "I believe that many of the people here would be satisfied to re-settle in the new Palestinian state, rather than in Israel," he said. "They would regard that as a true exercise of their right of return. ... We have to have a peace with sovereignty and dignity."

... in Syria ...

Khairia Kasmieh had had a long morning of administering exams in the Damascus University College of Letters, where she is chair of the History Department. But when three members of the working party knocked at her office door she greeted us warmly, lifted piles of books off chairs to make space for us to sit, and poured tasty herb tea for us from a large vacuum flask.

Kasmieh was born to a middle-class family in Haifa in the early 1940s. "Oh, I remember Haifa!" she told us fondly, before proceeding to talk about the "great pain and trauma" her family experienced when they joined the flight of Palestinians from that city in 1948. The family had fled first to Lebanon, traveling by car; and they lived for a while in cramped rented space in Tyre. Many other Haifa Palestinians had, she said, undergone a parallel flight in fishing boats. She and her siblings would see these other refugees over the months that followed, camping out—quite destitute—on the beaches around Tyre.

The Kasmiehs stayed only eight months in Lebanon before they joined relatives in the Syrian capital, Damascus. "We were in the last wave of refugees to enter Syria," she said. "Everywhere we went in those years, the authorities would drive us around like cattle—just because we were refugees." She recalled that for a number of years her parents could not afford to buy warm clothes to help her and her siblings brave the unaccustomed chill of Damascus winters. "All five of us were living off the salary my elder sister made as a schoolteacher. She died at forty-six, God rest her soul. She died young because she worked so hard all her life, to support us."

In Damascus, as in Tyre, the family found a cramped rental apartment to live in. Kasmieh said she realized that their family was much better off than were the totally pauperized Palestinians who lived in the refugee camps that dotted the area around Damascus. Moreover, she was able to study at the elite private school where her sister taught: "I was the only Palestinian student there."

She studied at Damascus University and embarked on what turned out to be a distinguished career as a historian, working mainly on Palestinian issues. She has taught at universities in the U.S., Lebanon, and Saudi Arabia. For some years in the 1970s, she was a researcher at the PLO-linked Palestine Research Center in Beirut, Lebanon. (She recalled with great sadness how, during Israel's 1982 occupation of Beirut, the center's collections of Palestinian historical documents were boxed up by Israeli soldiers and carried off to Israel. She also recalled the time back in the 1970s, when Israeli secret agents sent a letter bomb to center director Faiz Sayegh: when Sayegh opened it, his hand was blown off, but he survived.)

"Palestinians are more accepted here in Syria than they are in Lebanon," she said. "Here, there is no sectarian clash, as there is there. Here in Syria, the Palestinians use the special 'Palestinian refugee' ID cards issued by the government, and are not given citizenship by the government; but in all other respects their rights are equal with those of Syrians. They enter schools, colleges, and the job market on an equal footing with Syrians and have equal rights to social benefits."

She recalled that some years earlier—"in better times"—she had participated in a meeting in Europe, alongside several activists from the Israeli peace movement. "Now, we accept the State of Israel," she said. "But they have to recognize what a huge concession this is, that we give them 78 percent of the land of Mandate Palestine! ... My family home in Haifa is gone, forever. I know that."

She recalled that when the Oslo Accords were signed in 1993, many Palestinians from the refugee camps had been hopeful—they thought that at last the U.S. government would lend its weight to the search for a just resolution of the Palestinian issue. She, however, had always had some doubts. "The crucial mistake of Oslo was to ignore the Palestinian refugees. ... The only thing that made me happy about it was that my parents were not alive at the time to see Arafat taking part in that betrayal of their dreams of return."

Now, she said, all the hopes that other Palestinians had invested in Oslo had long ago been lost—"and my own doubts about it have been proven valid."

During part of her time with us, Kasmieh was joined by her colleague and compatriot Ahmed Berqawi, a voluble professor of philosophy, also in his late fifties, with a broad and engaging smile. He expressed views that were at some variance with hers. ("We debate these things all the time!" Kasmieh told us, smiling.)

"The Palestinians are stronger than the Israelis because they—we—have a larger Arab nation to support us," Berqawi said. "All the fences Israel builds cannot change this! It's just like all the false hopes people put throughout history into the building of city walls. History shows that walled cities have always been overcome. The Israeli state cannot be walled off from history."

Over the 40 minutes that followed we had a lively discussion with Berqawi on questions of violence and nonviolence in the Palestinian movement. He told us he favored an outcome "built on the political basis of coexistence—one in which we share the land in equality. Not by separation or occupation. Neither side should oppress the other! This outcome offers the best future for Israel." And in order to bring about this outcome, he judged that the actions of suicide bombers—which he termed "martyrdom actions"—were slowly proving to be effective.

We respectfully disagreed with this last judgment, a question that we will return to in more detail in chapter 10.

... and in the Occupied Territories

As our full group drove around the West Bank, we frequently passed close to some of the region's nineteen refugee camps. Soon after we crossed the King Hussein (Allenby) Bridge from Jordan to the West Bank, we passed close by the Aqabat Jabr camp, where UNRWA provides relief services to 5,000 registered refugees.[80] Near Bethlehem is Dheisheh camp, home to more than 10,000. On the road to Hebron is Arroub camp, home to 8,900. Two refugee camps are located within the Jerusalem municipal boundaries—Shu'fat (pop. 9,400), and Kalandia (pop. 8,900).

The refugee camps in the West Bank generally have a similar physical appearance to the concrete-cube shantytown "look" of the Baqa'a camp we visited in Jordan. Many are located near the West Bank's cities and larger towns. But by the time we visited it was clear that—unlike the Baqa'a camp—these camps were not linked to any functioning local economy. Instead, along with the cities and indigenous villages all around them, they were taking a harsh economic battering from the lengthy regime of closures and lockdowns imposed on the region since (and even before) September 2000.

We did not have the opportunity to visit any refugee camps in the West Bank on this trip, although several of us had done so in the past. Our main goal had been to visit Jenin camp (pop. 13,800), which in April 2002 had been the site of fierce battles between Israeli soldiers and Palestinian fighters. Those battles, as noted in chapter 2, left at least twenty-three Israeli soldiers and

---

80 UNRWA keeps excellent records, but these cover only the refugees who are "registered" with it. To qualify for UNRWA registration, a Palestinian must both (1) currently live in one of UNRWA's fields of operation, and (2) be either someone who during the original registration in 1950 met UNRWA's definition of indigence, or the patrilineal descendant of such a person. This definition excludes many Palestinian refugees. UNRWA's website spells out that "for the purposes of repatriation or compensation ... the term 'Palestine refugee' is used with a different, much less restrictive meaning as compared to UNRWA's need-based definition." See <http://www.un.org/unrwa/overview/qa.html#c>.

fifty-four Palestinians dead, with more than half of the Palestinian dead being civilians. On many mornings during our time in Jerusalem, we would tentatively plan to make the trip to Jenin, which is in the north of the West Bank; but a call to a coordinating center for aid workers would reveal that the whole Jenin area was once again "closed" for the day.

When we were in Gaza, however, we were able to make a quick, drive-through visit to Jabalia camp, easily the largest of any of the sixty camps operated by UNRWA, with a population of 101,600 refugees. Jabalia appeared to be a vast, sprawling warren of one-story concrete shelters interrupted by a number of taller mosques and a number of areas of (frequently unfinished) multi-story apartment buildings. Most of the parts of the camp we drove through seemed impossibly crowded: the little concrete "homes" were divided only by four-feet-wide alleys; most alleys had a recessed drain running down the center—and some of these drains seemed to have broken or non-existent covers, leaving many families living by open sewers.

At one point, the narrow street our bus was driving along opened out into a ramshackle market square where vendors sat listlessly near a tangle of open bed carts, waiting for customers to come and buy from the colorful mounds of tomatoes or eggplants they had brought in on the carts many hours earlier. The donkeys that had pulled the carts here munched quietly in one corner of the square.[81]

The vendors looked resigned to another bad day. Our guide told us that their prices were rock-bottom, since the closures meant they could not send their produce to markets in Israel, Egypt—or even to many other parts of the Strip itself. But even at prices of a few pennies per pound, very few camp residents could afford what would otherwise have been a healthful addition to their diet. (Our guide told us that many vendors ended up giving away their produce rather than having it rot away uneaten.)

In Gaza City, we had a very informative meeting with Karen Koning AbuZayd, the deputy commissioner-general of UNRWA,

81 Throughout the Strip, donkey carts had become an important means of transportation, for people as well as for goods. Before the first *intifada* there were many more cars in the Strip, but the punitive licensing requirements imposed by Israel after 1987 proved so cumbersome and expensive that many car owners sold their motorized vehicles and reverted to donkey carts.

whose central headquarters is located there. She talked a little about the range of conditions faced by Palestinian refugees in the five different "fields" where the organization operates camps. "You have seen how in Jordan, the refugees have the significant benefit of having citizenship in the host country," she said. "In Syria, they have a pretty good situation. Those in Lebanon are the worst off. Life is so bleak for refugees there! But since the *intifada* began, we have had to keep most of our attention on the condition of the refugees here in the West Bank and Gaza, because of the crisis right here. We are now feeding 127,500 families in Gaza and 98,000 families in the West Bank. Multiply that by five for the number of individuals."

AbuZayd spent most of her career working for a parallel refugee agency, the U.N. High Commission for Refugees. She told us that when she took up the position with UNRWA, shortly before the current *intifada* began, one central task she thought she would be pursuing would be to start planning for a durable, long-term solution to the Palestinian refugee problem. "But now, instead of doing that, most of my work is in very basic emergency response."

She expressed some concern with the lack of cooperation UNRWA received from the Israeli authorities. "Nowhere else in the world are U.N. vehicles, including ambulances, and U.N. diplomats subjected to the same treatment we get from the Israelis. I have been thirty-five years in this exact kind of work, working in some of the world's most violent places. But no one has ever been as intransigent a partner as Israel."[82]

A few days earlier, we had met with William Lee, the director of all of UNRWA's operations in Jordan. He expressed some frustration with a large-scale campaign that UNRWA's leaders were seeing mounted against their agency in some western countries, including the U.S., on the grounds that UNRWA was allegedly "harboring terrorists" in the refugee camps where it provided services. "But we have never, since the beginning of our mandate, had any authority for the security situation inside the refugee camps," he said. "For example, since Israel is the occupying power in the West Bank, it has responsibility for the security situation in the seven refugee camps in the West Bank. We have never had it.

---

82 For a lengthier exposition of AbuZayd's views, see, "Interview with UNRWA Deputy Commissioner-General Karen AbuZayd," in *Migration Information Source*, July 1, 2002, accessible at <http://www.migrationinformation.org/Feature/display.cfm?ID=30>.

Under our mandate we provide only relief services, not security. And yet, they repeat these false charges against us over and over again!" On the basis of these charges, Lee said, extremist groups linked to the Israeli settlers had mounted a campaign to cut off the U.S. government's funding to UNRWA, which made up about one-third of the agency's annual operating expenses of some $300 million. He urged us to speak out against what he described as the "slander campaign" against UNRWA.

The Long Evolution of the Refugee Issue

The Palestinian refugee problem was born in the thirteen months between the U.N.'s adoption of its Partition Plan for Palestine in November 1947 and the end of 1948. That period was marked by repeated outbreaks of fighting in which the forces of the emerging Israeli state engaged militarily, first with a network of Palestinian irregulars and then later—after the British Mandate came to an end, as planned, on May 15, 1948—with the hastily assembled armies that some of the Arab states sent to Palestine in a (largely unsuccessful) effort to help the indigenous population there.

During those months of fighting, somewhere between 600,000 and 900,000 Palestinian Arabs fled or were expelled from homes and properties inside the area that became the Israeli state, and a few thousand Jewish residents fled or were expelled from areas that remained under Arab control.

There has been much controversy over whether the Palestinian refugees fled voluntarily, or at the orders of Arab commanders—or whether they were expelled by the Zionist forces. In the 1980s and 1990s, historical scholarship by Jewish Israeli "new historians" has brought to light documentary evidence supporting longstanding Palestinian claims of expulsion. In one such work, Benny Morris cited a report prepared by the IDF's own Intelligence Section in summer 1948, which found that some 70 percent of the Palestinians who had left their homes prior to June 1, 1948, had done so as a result of, or in response to, actions by members of the Zionist fighting forces, while only some 5 percent of villages evacuated by that date had been emptied in response to requests from commanders of Arab fighting forces. (The pre-June exodus of Palestinians accounted for only about half of the total number of Palestinians who fled. No analogous report has been found that covers the June-December 1948 period.)[83]

What is incontestable is that after the cessation of the fighting, the new Israeli state did not allow any significant number of the refugees to return.[84] This remained true even though in December 1948 the U.N. General Assembly passed a resolution stating that "the refugees wishing to return to their homes and live at peace with their neighbors should be permitted to do so at the earliest practicable date, and that compensation should be paid for the property of those choosing not to return and for loss of or damage to property which ... should be made good by the Governments or authorities responsible." This was Resolution 194, which over the decades that followed became a touchstone for refugee claims that the U.N. had assured them of a "right of return."[85]

During many periods of conflict throughout history, people have fled their homes in the affected zones in large numbers, seeking what they hope is a temporary refuge in a place they judge to be safer. Just one year earlier, in 1947, the fighting that surrounded Britain's withdrawal from India was accompanied by a blood-soaked "population exchange" of millions of Muslims and Hindus between India and Pakistan; in 1945-46, some eight million ethnic Germans were summarily expelled from non-German lands in Eastern Europe. By 1948, however, the international community was moving decisively toward favoring repatriation of refugees (that is, a return to their original homes, or if they are uninhabitable, at least to their home communities) as the preferred outcome, once the conflicts that had forced their flight died down sufficiently to permit a safe return. Just one day before the passage of Resolution 194, the General Assembly adopted the Universal Declaration of Human Rights, whose Article 13 proclaims that "Everyone has the right to leave any country, including his own, and to return to his country." In numerous crises since 1948—right down to those in Bosnia, Kosovo, or Afghanistan in recent years—the major focus of the international community has been on the post-conflict repatriation of refugees, rather than their

---

83 Benny Morris, *1948 and after: Israel and the Palestinians* (Oxford and New York: Oxford University Press, 1994), pp. 88-90, 102.

84 The only exception to this was the small number of Palestinians allowed to return under a tightly limited "family reunification" scheme.

85 In 1948, the Arab states voted against Resolution 194 at the U.N. since they judged that its acceptance would imply granting recognition to the State of Israel.

resettlement, that is, their permanent absorption elsewhere.

In the years after 1948, the vast majority of Palestinian refugees have continued to cling to their goal of returning—one day—to their ancestral homes and properties inside Israel/ Palestine. Further, as noted in chapter 4 above, when Palestinian national liberation groups grew up in the 1950s and 1960s, they sank their first and deepest roots in the refugee communities of the Palestinian diaspora.

For their part, most of the Arab countries around Israel that ended up hosting large concentrations of refugees exhibited a strong resistance to any suggestion that the refugees might simply be resettled where they were. (Countries that host conflict-driven inflows of refugees are under no international obligation whatsoever to absorb them permanently. If that were the case, governments would be far more reluctant to offer even temporary refuge to those fleeing violence elsewhere.)

The Palestinian refugees' host countries adopted a variety of policies toward them. Jordan, which controlled the West Bank from 1948 through 1967, chose a broadly assimilative policy, offering passports and a version of Jordanian citizenship to all those refugees who ended up in the East Bank (Jordan proper) or the West Bank. Egypt, which controlled the Gaza Strip from 1948 through 1967, and Syria, both denied passports to the refugees whom they hosted; but both these countries gave the refugees access to education and jobs on a more or less equal footing with their own citizens. Lebanon offered citizenship to only a handful of refugees—mainly Palestinian Christians, so that they might boost the proportion of Christian voters in this country, which has suffered chronic divisions between Christians and Muslims. Meanwhile, during periods when the Lebanese state has been relatively strong, it has maintained very tough restrictions on access to education, housing, and jobs for refugees who were not Lebanese citizens.

Back in 1948, the worldwide trend may have been tipping toward repatriation rather than resettlement as the preferred goal for populations of refugees fleeing zones of conflict, but the leaders of the infant Israeli state steadfastly resisted all the entreaties made by the U.N., the U.S., and other governments that they allow a sizeable proportion, or all, of the exiled Palestinians to return to their homes. During the fighting of 1947-48, the Zionist forces had succeeded in gaining control of around 78 percent of Mandate Palestine—an area considerably larger than had been allotted to the Jewish state by the U.N. partition plan. Though 600,000 to 900,000 Palestinian residents had fled or been forced to flee from the Israeli-held area, some 250,000 remained; the Jewish population of the infant Israel was around 600,000. Any large-scale return of Palestinian refugees to their homes would have tipped the demographic balance of a state that had been designed to be explicitly Jewish. Therefore, rather than acceding to requests that they allow a return of the refugees to their homes, Israel's leaders urged the refugees' Arab host countries to absorb them instead.

Then, over the years that followed 1948, Israel and international Zionist organizations actively worked for the emigration of Mizrachi ("eastern") Jews from the many Arab countries where those communities had been part of the social fabric for millennia. More than half a million Mizrachi Jews left their countries and were ferried to Israel by international Zionist organizations.[86] Many were placed almost immediately in the homes and farms that the exiled Palestinians had left behind. Once that migration was underway, Israel's leaders urged that the Arab countries should simply accept the idea of this broad population exchange and resettle the Palestinians where they were. This proposal had a serious flaw: its proponents made no attempt to consult the Palestinians themselves on their preferences in this matter. In addition, the Arab states unanimously rejected it.

---

86 The exodus of Mizrachi Jews from their countries of origin was precipitated in part by anti-Jewish actions taken by the various Arab governments. At the same time, international Zionist organizations played a significant role in fomenting the atmosphere of threat that provoked the flight of Jews from, for example, Egypt and Iraq; these organizations then made the logistical arrangements necessary for the Mizrachim to move to Israel. The cross-border migrations of the Palestinians and the Mizrachim are thus not symmetrical. Nonetheless, this coercive process of migration represented a massive violation of human rights and resulted in the destruction of these ancient Jewish communities, which had endured for more than 2500 years.

Over the half-century that followed 1948, all the relevant populations increased considerably (see Table 2).

Table 2: Population Growth 1948 – 1998
(approximate figures)

	1948	1998
Jewish population of Israel	600,000	4,850,000
Palestinian population of Israel	250,000	950,000
Palestinian refugees	700,000	4,200,000

Two further wrinkles in the evolution of the refugee question are worth noting. First, in addition to leaving hundreds of thousands Palestinians outside the armistice lines (which have marked the de facto borders of the State of Israel), the fighting of 1947-48 left scores of thousands of displaced Palestinians within Israel. Over time, these internally displaced people, like all the Palestinians who had remained in home communities that were now inside Israel, were granted Israeli citizenship. But even though Israel granted these internally displaced Palestinians citizenship, they continued to bar them from returning to their original homes. By the time of our visit, the number of these internally displaced Palestinian Israelis was estimated at around 250,000.[87]

The other wrinkle was that during the fighting of 1967 that took Israeli forces into the West Bank and Gaza, scores of thousands of Palestinians from the West Bank fled across the river to the East Bank, that is, into Jordan proper. Many of those who took part in this flight had—like the camp elder we met in Baqa'a camp in Jordan—already been refugees before this displacement. This was the second exodus these families undertook under war conditions in less than twenty years.

The Human Costs of the Refugee Problem
As was noted previously, in Jewish-Israeli society there has always been a broad majority of opinion that has opposed any large-scale return of the refugees to anywhere inside Israel. In addition to this opposition to the physical return of the refugees

---

87 Data from the Association for the Defense of the Rights of Internally Displaced Persons in Israel <http://www.ittijah.org/member/interndisplaced.html>, accessed June 30, 2003.

and their descendants to their ancestral homeplaces inside Israel, there has often been a strong reluctance even to discuss any of the other types of claim that the refugees had against Israel—for example, any claim to compensation instead of return, as specifically allowed for in Resolution 194.

Just as we continue to urge Palestinians to listen to the fears and longings of the Jewish Israelis who are their neighbors, we also implore Jewish Israelis and their supporters around the world to open their hearts to an awareness of the many different kinds of harm that those Palestinians who live in exile from their homeland have suffered as a result of their 55-year-long exile.

How might we describe these human costs? One such listing might group them under headings like the following:

- *Displacement and family fragmentation:* The refugee families were uprooted from homes that were laden with meaning for them. These places were the locations of dense and familiar social support networks like mosques, churches, schools, extended families, and economic networks like markets, and sources of credit, or production inputs; they were the locus of folktales and a wealth of other aspects of the people's culture; and they were usually the sites of the ancestors' graves. In addition to being displaced from those locations, during and in the decades after their displacement, the refugee families were often widely scattered into a Palestinian diaspora whose fragmentation has, in nearly every Palestinian family, split sibling from sibling, or parent from child. This dispersion has made it impossible for most refugee families to organize even such "simple" but important observances as extended-family gatherings for weddings or funerals.

- *Dispossession:* Most of the Palestinians uprooted in 1948 were peasant farmers whose family wealth was vested mainly in their lands. Once they lost their lands and homes, their best hope for economic survival was to work for others; but such work was often hard, or impossible, to find. Wealthier Palestinians who found themselves in exile may have been able to export some portion of their wealth before 1947, and may have found more opportunities to generate income after 1948. They, too, however, have been denied all access to (and even any income from) the fixed assets they left behind. All the refugee families have thus suffered considerable and long-standing economic harm as a result of their displacement.

- *Statelessness and disfranchisement:* In the U.N.'s partition resolution of 1947, the Arab Palestinians were—like the Jewish Palestinians—offered a state of their own that could, among other things, protect them from the multiple vulnerabilities of statelessness. But the Arab Palestinians never got the state they were promised; and after the dissolving of the Mandate (which had given Palestinians some of the attributes of citizenship), many of the refugees found themselves actually stateless.[88] This condition disproportionately impacted those of modest means, since people with wealth and connections have generally, throughout history, been able to acquire some form of citizenship. Stateless people suffer a number of notable harms. A stateless person finds it extremely hard to cross national boundaries. (For Palestinians, whose family members are often scattered among a number of national jurisdictions, this imposes a particularly intimate harm.) Stateless persons have no government to represent their interests and are therefore extremely vulnerable to the caprice of the authorities in whichever jurisdiction they find themselves.[89] Stateless persons, by definition, have no hope of struggling through any established political means to affect the policies of "their" national leadership and are thus totally disfranchised.

- *Marginalization and humiliation:* The above kinds of harm that the refugees have labored under have contributed to a multi-faceted assault on their dignity as humans and to their continuing marginalization from the main locations of power in regional and international society. In addition, numerous Israeli spokespeople and their supporters have tried to question the very basis of the biographical narrative of these peoples' lives. These people have accused the Palestinians in general—but in particular, the Palestinian refugees—of having no valid rights to or claim on the land of Palestine/Israel but of being at best the descendants of migrant peoples who had spent only a short time in Palestine before 1948, or at worst, of being, all of

---

88 The exception to this was those who ended up in Jordan or the West Bank, who were granted Jordanian citizenship.

89 In recent years Palestinian communities in Kuwait, Lebanon, Iraq, and elsewhere have received sobering lessons in the vulnerabilities of statelessness.

them, merely "terrorists." The refugees have thus suffered a significant assault to their human dignity, their cultural and historical identity, and their understanding of the meaning of their lives.[90]

The Politics and Diplomacy of the Refugee Issue

The cause of the diaspora Palestinians has been a central one for the Palestinian national movement since the movement's rebirth in the 1950s. Even those Palestinians who have always lived in the West Bank or Gaza hold this cause dear, since every single Palestinian in the occupied territories has close family members who have been forced by the stifling conditions of 36-plus years of occupation to pursue studies or job opportunities in the diaspora and then lost their right to return to the occupied territories.

When the PLO leadership concluded the Oslo Accords with Israel in 1993, the initial purview of that agreement was the West Bank and Gaza, and the residents of those two portions of historic Palestine. As we noted earlier, when the elections for the P.A. and the Palestinian Legislative Council (PLC) were held, as mandated by the Oslo agreement, the franchise was extended only to those residents. And when the P.A. started issuing its own Palestinian "passports," these documents were likewise issued only to Gaza and West Bank residents. The stateless Palestinians residing in Syria, Lebanon, or elsewhere remained stateless and disfranchised.

However, the Palestinian negotiators at Oslo clearly viewed those accords as dealing only with an interim period of limited term. And they continued to insist that in the negotiations for the final-status agreement the claims of all the Palestinians—including those living outside the land of Mandate-era Palestine as well those residents in Gaza and the West Bank—would have to be on the agenda. At Oslo, the Israeli government explicitly agreed to that.

However, when we met with Israeli Foreign Ministry official Gadi Golan, he said that many Israelis had been surprised when, once the final-status talks mandated by Oslo eventually (and belatedly) got underway in the latter half of 2000, the Palestinian negotiators insisted that the rights of the diaspora refugees still needed

---

90 Some Palestinians have also denied important truths about Jewish historical narratives, including the Holocaust. There is however a significant difference: the Palestinians were not responsible for the Holocaust, while successive elected governments in Israel have continued to enact the policies that have maintained the Palestinians' exile and dispersion.

to be discussed. Indeed, he indicated that the insistence of the Palestinian leadership on raising the refugee issue at that point was seen by many Israelis as a sign of the Palestinian leaders' bad faith!

One possible cause for that misunderstanding may have been that Palestinian leaders have nearly always referred to the claims of the refugees solely in terms of their longstanding claim regarding the right of return. Any prospect of the actual, physical return of Palestinian refugees to the homes and properties they left or were forced to leave in 1948 is unacceptable to most Jewish Israelis. For example, when we talked with Shai Feldman, the Director of Tel Aviv's Jaffee Center, he described the right of return as, quite simply, "the deal-breaker." (And Feldman was someone who was still quietly proud of the role he had played as "one of the architects of Oslo.")

Feldman told us that it was precisely because he saw "no flexibility" from Yasser Arafat on the right of return issue that he had become convinced that Arafat needed to be replaced.[91] In the next breath, he made exactly the same diagnosis of the attitude of most Israelis toward the refugee issue—but this time with apparent approval. "The right of return is one issue on which there is no flexibility here," he said. "Look around you at our campus here, and its surroundings. This area, for us, is our neighborhood of Ramat Aviv. But in Arabic, this area was called Sheikh Mu'nis. ... No! A return to 1948 is just not on the table."

He argued that a just solution of the refugee problem would not be the same as full implementation of the right of return and suggested that the long-term settlement of refugees could take place in four different kinds of location: inside Israel, in the future Palestinian state, in the Arab states, and in other states. "Of course, we would need to negotiate ceilings for each of these options," he said. "We would also establish an international institution to administer disbursements of compensation. And the agreement should certainly have a paragraph that says that 'this solution implements Resolution 194 and ends all claims arising from the right of return'."[92]

---

91 At the Taba talks of January 2001, Arafat's negotiators did start to display some flexibility on the refugee issue. See below.

92 Feldman suggests an approach very similar to the one used by the negotiators at Taba. See below.

Other Jewish Israelis have expressed views on the refugee question that are much harsher than Feldman's. Writing in *The Washington Post* in June 2003, former Prime Minister Binyamin Netanyahu wrote that, "We insist ... that the Palestinians give up their claim to a 'right of return'—a euphemism for destroying the Jewish state by flooding it with millions of Palestinians."[93]

Many Israeli peace activists, by contrast, have struggled to think through the many moral issues involved in the refugee question. "Most Israelis think that the Palestinian refugees should have no right to enter Israel," Gila Svirsky, of the Coalition of Women for a Just Peace, acknowledged. But, she added,

> Most of the people on the Israeli left favor an outcome that might involve things like an acknowledgement of Israel's role in contributing to and perpetuating the refugee problem and some kind of acknowledgement of an abstract "right" of return. But only limited implementation of actual return—no mass return. We must find a way to make these acknowledgements while negotiating the implementation. This would help bridge the gaps with the Palestinians.

The focus that Svirsky placed on the importance, for the Palestinians, of Israel undertaking such "symbolic" actions as expressing some form of acknowledgment of the Palestinians' "right" of return, regardless of the actual steps taken to implement that right, seemed to be borne out by some conversations we had with Palestinian refugees. For example, one of the many thoughtful refugees with whom we spoke said, "Many Palestinian refugees say that Israel must at least express recognition of the right of return in some way, and recognize the wrong they caused us in 1948." But once that recognition has been adequately conveyed, then resolution of the actual issues facing the Palestinians might not, this person indicated, be very difficult to reach.[94]

---

93 Binyamin Netanyahu, "A limited Palestinian state," *The Washington Post,* June 20, 2003, p. A25. Four days later, the newspaper carried a clarification stating that Netanyahu disagreed with the editors' choice of the word "state" in the title they gave his article, and that the kind of self-governance entity he proposed for the Palestinians would not be a "state."

94 We note that even such symbolic actions would likely be highly controversial within Jewish-Israeli society. For example, the Jaffee Center's Yossi Alpher wrote to us, "The Palestinian demand that Israel recognize the right of return and admit guilt for the events of 1948 [is] understood to mean that we admit we were 'born in sin'." (See chapter 7.)

Exiled Palestinians and the Future

Relatively few Jewish Israelis have taken the step of trying to imagine what life must be like for Palestinians displaced from their ancestral homeland, stripped of their former possessions, and left scattered, stateless, and disfranchised. Nonetheless, the Palestinian refugees' claims will have to be discussed, and an agreement regarding every aspect of them concluded, if a durable solution to the Palestinian-Israeli conflict is to be found. Is there any reason to believe that this complex and sensitive issue can be resolved? Yes, for at least three reasons.

First, though the post-Oslo final status negotiations were late getting started, once they did get underway, the two sides showed during the talks they held in early 2001 in Taba, that they were capable of considerably narrowing the gap between them on this issue (as on the issue of Jerusalem) and went a good way toward sketching what the main elements of settling the refugee issue might look like in the context of a two-state solution. According to E.U. delegate Miguel Moratinos, both sides agreed at Taba that the refugee issue was central to the Israeli-Palestinian relationship and that "a comprehensive and just solution [to the refugee issue] is essential to creating a lasting and morally scrupulous peace." According to Moratinos's account, the Israeli side expressed its understanding that the Palestinians' desire to undertake "return" as per Resolution 194 should be implemented in the context of a five-pronged approach consisting of some mix of: (1) return to Israel; (2) return to a location within the portion of land currently inside Israel that Israel would cede to the Palestinian state in the context of reciprocal border adjustments; (3) repatriation to the Palestinian state; (4) resettlement in the present host country; and (5) relocation and resettlement elsewhere.

The Israeli side suggested a fifteen-year program for the return track and informally suggested that 25,000 refugees might return to Israel in the first three years of this program. Moratinos' account notably does not mention that the Palestinian side voiced any objection to this five-pronged approach. Both sides apparently agreed that in all these programs, refugees in Lebanon would, because of their particular vulnerability, be given priority. Moratinos noted that the Palestinians did not counter Israel's proposal regarding the numbers that might be accorded return to Israel. But apparently, time had run out on the negotiation before they could do so. He did report that both sides had agreed on the establishment of international mechanisms for funding the resolution of the refugee issue and that Israel would contribute to this international fund as "compensation for material losses, land, and assets expropriated." Significantly, too, both sides agreed that UNRWA "should be phased out" according to an agreed timetable —a clear indication that both saw the resolution of the refugee issue as one that would help end the conflict between them altogether.[95]

On this issue, therefore, as on settlements and Jerusalem, the two sides were still far from reaching agreement when the Israeli team pulled out of the talks at Taba. Nonetheless—regarding the refugee issue as much as those other issues—the record of Taba showed that once national-level negotiators from the two sides did engage seriously in discussing a key final-status issue, considerable progress could be made. The record of Taba indicated a considerable degree of flexibility and creative thinking on behalf of both national leaderships regarding refugees. That creativity will provide a resource for any negotiators in the future. It showed, crucially, that a mechanistic implementation of "return" is by no means the only option for resolving this issue.

A second reason for hope on this issue, which perhaps complements the first, is that we found on our visit considerable flexibility from some of the refugees we talked with regarding how they see a workable resolution of their claims. In other words, it is not only leaders closeted away in a resort hotel in Taba, Egypt, who can envision flexible and creative solutions to this issue: so, apparently, can many of the refugees themselves. From Sultan Abul-Ainayn, in Rashidieh camp in Lebanon, we heard that he judged that a resolution acceptable to many of the refugees in Lebanon might involve a return to the future Palestinian state rather than to their original homes and properties inside Israel. From a number of conversations with refugees, we also learned that there were significant symbolic gestures Israel could make—primarily at the level of according some formal recognition of the right of return—that would make it possible for many Palestinians to accept very flexible approaches to the actual exercise of that right.

---

95 All these details are from the text of the Moratinos document given in International Crisis Group, *Middle East Endgame II*, p.35.

We recognize, however, that despite these signs of some flexibility the question of the right of return continues to be an extremely contentious issue not just for many Jewish Israelis, but also for many—perhaps most—Palestinians. For example, in July 2003, Khalil Shikaki, the head of the Ramallah-based Palestinian Center for Policy and Survey Research, conducted a survey of refugee opinion that found that "just 10 percent" of Palestinian refugees living in the West Bank, Gaza, Jordan, and Lebanon would be interested in returning to their former homes inside Israel if given the chance. But when he released a first digest of these findings in Ramallah, he was met by dozens of furious refugees from among his neighbors who wrecked his office and pelted him with eggs. "This is a message for everyone not to tamper with our rights," one angry refugee was reported as saying.[96] A more temperate criticism came from Salman Abu Sitta, the president of the London-based Palestine Land Society, who wrote an article that accused Shikaki of having asked only leading questions in the survey and argued forcefully that, "Ethnic cleansing, that is expelling inhabitants from their homes, is a war crime." Abu Sitta concluded by referring to a recent event where 300 Palestinian refugee participants from 14 European countries had met to "affirm their right to return home." This gathering, he wrote, "refute[d] the assumption that the refugees only want shelter, food, and legal papers and willingly accept settlement elsewhere."[97]

Despite the evident sensitivity with which the right of return issue continues to be viewed by many or most Palestinians, we continue to believe that the flexibility we heard on this issue from a number of refugee Palestinians—at a time, moreover, when the continuation of the tensions inside the occupied territories was rubbing the feelings of all Palestinians very raw—was a mark of pragmatism and hope for the future that should not, however, be mistaken for weakness. The existence of this reserve of flexibility and creativity in the refugee communities leads almost directly to the third reason we have for having some hope the refugee issue can be resolved. This reason comes in the form of a not-so-modest

---

96 "10 percent of Palestinians would want to use right of return," in *Ha'aretz*, 13 July 2003. Shikaki's report is available at <http://www.pcpsr.org/survey/polls/2003/refugeesjune03.html>.

97 "Inalienable and sacred," by Salman Abu Sitta, in *Al-Ahram Weekly*, 14-20 August 2003. Available at <http://weekly.ahram.org.eg/2003/651/op11.htm>.

proposal, one that is in line with our strong belief that the refugees remain direct stakeholders in the well-being and future of the Holy Land, namely that as part of a search for a final agreement to the conflict, the diaspora Palestinians must be actively engaged and granted a voice in this process and their rights assured.

For too long now, the diaspora Palestinians (that is, those four million or so Palestinians who continued to be prevented from returning to any place in Israel or the occupied territories even after the implementation of the Oslo Accords) have been sidelined from any real decision-making power. The marginalizing of these people's political influence and even their political "voice" has been assiduously pursued by successive Israeli governments, and has been colluded in more recently by the U.S., by many governments around the world—and even on significant occasions in the 1990s by the PLO/P.A. leadership itself. When the diaspora Palestinians have been considered at all by participants in international diplomacy, nearly this entire portion of the Palestinian people has too frequently been viewed only as forming a large part of the "problem," but seldom as forming a real and potentially vigorous part of the solution. Unfortunately, treating the diaspora Palestinians as part of the problem has all too often become a self-fulfilling prophecy.

How might these and all the other Palestinian refugees be engaged in the problem-solving venture of making a real peace, and how might they be given a real voice in this process? In a real sense, this is a matter for the Palestinians, all Palestinians, to decide. But at a minimum, as any further steps are taken to "democratize" the Palestinian body politic, the enfranchisement and political organization of diaspora Palestinians—and especially of those who have no stable citizenship elsewhere—should be a top priority. As a concomitant to that enfranchisement, a truly representative Palestinian leadership should have the same power to protect the interests of those newly enfranchised Palestinians—even if they live outside Palestine—that other governments have to protect the interests of citizens living overseas. At this point in human history, it seems quite unconscionable for any group of persons to be kept in a position of statelessness, regardless of whatever else may be happening at the level of international diplomacy.

We are hopeful that as the Palestinian leadership and others start to take seriously the need to protect and advance the interests of all Palestinians, this leadership will find that the energies, skills, global contacts, and finances of the Palestinians living in exile can strengthen its ongoing campaign to secure Palestinian rights, and that the exiled Palestinians will not prove to be the huge stumbling block to diplomatic progress that negotiators have often considered them to be.

Palestinian-Jewish Relations Inside Israel

Equality is among the fundamental principles of the State of Israel.
Every authority in Israel, starting with the State of Israel, its institutions,
and employees, must treat various elements in the state equally.
— Aharon Barak, Chief Justice of Israel, 2000

I'm afraid the coming generation is being pushed into a place
where there seems to be no room for coexistence any more.
— Rana Bishara, Palestinian NGO Network, 2002

Umm el-Fahm

One Thursday toward the end of our trip, our bus took us out of the oleander-fringed campus of Haifa University and southeast along a road that in pre-*intifada* days led straight to the city of Jenin, twenty-eight miles away. The road took us through a mountain landscape whose steep slopes and rugged ridge lines were gilded by the rays of the departing sun. Then it emerged onto the Plain of Jezreel, where irrigated vegetable fields stretched into the distance.

There is a junction on the road at Megiddo, the site of the biblical Armageddon. Today, Megiddo is the site of a large prison whose high walls topped with razor wire rise forbiddingly, very close to the highway. In an earlier era, it was the British who were the jailers; in those days, the prison held independence activists from both the Jewish and Palestinian communities. These days, it's Israel's blue-and-white flag that waves from the prison watch-towers; and many thousands of accused activists for Palestinian independence have spent time inside in recent years.

We could see Jenin on a ridge ahead. But the city was "closed" again that day. We turned right and went to the Israeli city of Umm el-Fahm, home to some 40,000 Israeli citizens who are ethnic Palestinians—people (and the descendants of people) who stayed in their home community in 1948 when so many other Palestinians fled or were forced to flee.[98] In the city, we met with Mayor Suleiman Aghbariyeh, a compact, energetic man in his early forties.

He told us that back in 1948, the people of Umm el-Fahm had owned around 120,000 *dunums* of land. (A *dunum* is equal to 0.1 hectare or about 0.25 acre.)

> But the Israelis have taken so much land from us since then! Now we are down to 23,000 *dunums*. The Jewish areas around here grow and expand. They have space. We do not. And we certainly don't get the same infrastructure or budget for municipal expenses that Jewish towns get. Thirty-five percent of the homes here lack connection to a sewer system, and eighty-five percent lack full utility connections. There is discrimination here! It is because we are Arabs that we don't get services and funds.

Here, as just over the nearby Green Line that divides Israel proper from the occupied West Bank, access to land was a constant concern. Aghbariyeh told us:

> Here inside Israel, the density of our Palestinian Arab communities is so high. But look at the wide spaces that are given to the Jewish citizens— and the size of their homes! In Israel, ninety-four percent of the land is held by the state and is not available to the Arabs. But all this land originated as Arab land. It was owned by our families.

> So many of our people were pushed out in 1948, as refugees. The others are still here—but we have lost so much of our land. The Jewish Trust takes our land: it has much media attention, and always has a lot of funds. Meanwhile, the Islamic and Christian trusts have had many of their lands taken away.[99]

When the Israeli authorities took lands away from the local Islamic trust, he said, they told the city's people, "Allah is absent," and argued that therefore they felt entitled to seize the land under the same Absentee Land Law that was used to take control of the lands of the departed Palestinian refugees.

---

98   Just over one million of Israel's citizens are Palestinian Arabs indigenous to the land. The naming of this group is hotly contested. Most of them have expressed a preference to be described as Palestinian citizens of Israel. Most mainstream Jewish Israelis refer to them as Israeli Arabs.

99   The "Jewish Trust" Aghbariyeh was referring to was probably the Jewish National Fund, a supranational body that by special agreement with the Government of Israel helps to control much of the nation's land (see discussion below). The "Islamic and Christian trusts" are the *'awqaf'* religious trusts traditional in Muslim-dominated societies where frequently their properties, too, include holdings in real estate. *Awqaf* is the plural of *waqf.*

Aghbariyeh, by training a dentist, is associated with the northern branch of the Islamic Movement inside Israel. He told us that in its then-current crackdown on the civil liberties of Palestinian citizens the government was using many laws first enacted by the British when they ruled Palestine under the Mandate. Just a few months earlier, Aghbariyeh had moved up from being deputy mayor of Umm el-Fahm to being mayor, after his predecessor, Sheikh Raed Salah, resigned. (Salah, a charismatic leader in the Islamic Movement, said he wanted to spend more time on his religious studies.) Aghbariyeh said, "Now, they have placed a 'military order' on the Sheikh, to prevent him from traveling." He added:

> No accusation has been proved against him. And they imprison people without trial, using the provisions of 'administrative detention'. We have no recourse against this power, even though we are citizens. They closed the offices of the Islamic Society for Humanitarian Relief, which aids orphans and the needy in the West Bank and the Gaza Strip. The 'Emergency Orders' from the 1940s are used to abuse us and curtail us. They do it on racial grounds: acting against us as Arabs.

He recalled two large-scale confrontations the city's people had had with the Israeli security forces in recent years. The first was in September 1998, when Palestinian Israelis from around the region gathered in Umm el-Fahm to protest the IDF's takeover of a nearby area for use as a training-ground. "Five thousand soldiers attacked that protest," he recalled. "Six hundred people were injured that day. We cared for them right here, in the secondary school. Finally, the issue was defused when we got a new agreement with the government on use of that land."

Then, in early October 2000, just days after the second *intifada* broke out in the adjacent West Bank, ethnic Palestinians from throughout Israel organized a series of gatherings to express their solidarity with their compatriots across the Green Line—people who were, in many cases, close kin from whom they had been artificially separated by the lines drawn in 1948-1950—and to protest the lethality of Israel's response. Some of those demonstrations happened here, in Umm el-Fahm. And here, as in other towns, the Israeli police responded to the unarmed demonstrators with live fire. Three of the 13 Palestinian Israelis killed in those days lost their lives in Umm el-Fahm, Aghbariyeh told us, and a further 120 were injured.

He told us about the most recent threat the city's people faced:

the immense new security barrier that the Israeli government was planning to build just a few yards away from some of Umm el-Fahm's houses. He criticized the decision to construct the barrier in strong terms:

> The fence will take another one thousand *dunums* of land from Umm el-Fahm. It will prevent West Bankers from coming here to work or visit. It will keep them hungry and imprisoned, and keep us all apart.
>
> One thousand *dunums!* People will lose their privately-owned lands. We expect no compensation. And it'll block many roads in the area, too...
>
> It's purely a political move for the Israelis to build this fence. It's not for security reasons. Security will come from enacting justice for the Palestinians.

The Aghbariyeh clan is a big one in this part of Israel. A short while earlier we had met in a local medical clinic with Raja Aghbariyeh, the general secretary of the Abna' al-Balad ("Sons of the Country") movement, which espouses a secular nationalist viewpoint in the Palestinian community in Israel. Raja Aghbariyeh explained to us that Umm el-Fahm and the surrounding region—known as the "Triangle"—came under Israeli control not during the fighting of 1948 but in 1950, as part of an agreement between Jordan's King Abdullah and Israel's Prime Minister David Ben-Gurion. "They didn't ask our opinion," Raja Aghbariyeh noted dryly.

These days, he said, many Jewish Israelis had started to speak easily about "giving the Triangle back"—to the West Bank, from which it had been severed in 1950. (Indeed, diplomats have frequently identified the Triangle as one portion of present Israel that might, in the context of a two-state outcome, be handed to the Palestinian state in a swap for some of the areas of the West Bank heavily populated with settlers.)

"In the Knesset and places like that, they speak a lot about the 'demographic threat'," Raja Aghbariyeh said,

> and they express fears that the Arab Israelis' numbers will grow to two million by the year 2020. There are some who are eager to put us back over the line. They think they could get rid of the whole Triangle and get rid of 400,000 Arabs that way. ...
>
> But most of us reject this idea. We refuse to be 'exchanged' for settlers. The two situations are not equivalent! This is our land. These are our homes. We lived here originally. Our private land matters to us.
>
> Sure, we could be part of a Palestinian state. But not as part of such a land-swap.

He explained that he had worked for a two-state outcome for a long time.

> But now we seek a unified, democratic secular state [in the whole of Israel/Palestine]. It seems the best solution. It is our dream.

> Yes, we may have to settle for a two-state outcome. But if we gain that, then we Palestinians here would continue to be Israeli citizens, even though the laws are all against us. ... So we would have to continue to speak up for our own rights here, inside Israel—to be an assertive national minority, just like anywhere else in the world.

Nazareth

We did not, unfortunately, have time to visit the Biblical city of Nazareth, perched among the wooded hills of Galilee some fifteen miles north of Umm el-Fahm, but two residents of Nazareth came to meet with us in Jerusalem and brought us some flavor of the life led by the city's Palestinian residents. Azmi Bishara is an engaging man with a broad smile and an animated way of talking. As a highly visible, articulate member of the Knesset since 1996 and the head of a Palestinian Israeli political party called Balad ("Country"), he has attracted a lot of hostile attention from the state authorities and from anti-Arab members of the Jewish Israeli community.

Azmi Bishara is a Palestinian Christian. He came to visit us with Rana Bishara, the director of the Palestinian Non-Governmental Organization (NGO) Network who is also his wife. She made an eloquent plea for the violence between the two peoples of the Holy Land to be brought to an end. "I speak as a human being and a mother," she said.

> We are at such a critical stage! The violence is having a critical impact on the young. I'm afraid the coming generation is being pushed into a place where there seems to be no room for coexistence any more. Israeli society is ... pushing our children into a corner. What can redeem them?

> Why does the Israeli peace camp stay so muted on what is happening? Israel is becoming militarily obsessed. It seeks answers through the pure use of force. I feel that at the moral level, Israelis have already suffered the loss of their values, while we have had gross suffering in physical terms.

She shared her memories of what happened to their family during the October 2000 inter-communal clashes inside Israel:

> I was here in Jerusalem, and Azmi was in Nazareth. I was expecting to have a baby at any time. I was watching the t.v. as I saw the [Palestinian] movement start to become active in the 1948 lands [i.e., inside Israel]. I was calling Azmi all the time. On the television they had stories about

Palestinian Israelis being killed. Azmi was getting death threats.

Then one night, at two in the morning, someone called to tell me that settlers had gone to our house in Nazareth to burn it.

Luckily, Azmi used to change his place to sleep each night, and he was sleeping someplace else. But up to three hundred people attacked our house that night.[100]

Yes, that was scary. But it was just part of the daily abuse that Palestinians have to suffer.

We asked Azmi and Rana Bishara how they felt the future establishment of a Palestinian state in the West Bank and Gaza, alongside Israel, might affect the status of Palestinians who are citizens of Israel. Azmi Bishara replied,

That depends on the political context within which it happens. If it happens while the rightwing is still in control in Israel, then the establishment of a Palestinian state would just lead to more abuse against the "inside" Palestinians [that is, the Palestinians living inside Israel], and to pressures to have them leave and go over to the Palestinian state. But if we were to imagine the state created in a spirit of true peace and trust, then we could see our rights situation, as Palestinians inside Israel, actually improving.

We can't tell now which way it will go. We on the inside cannot and should not prescribe the details. But in general, we back the establishment of a Palestinian state and the Palestinians' right to self-determination.

He said he saw a direct link between the policies that different Israeli governments pursued in the occupied territories, and those they pursued toward the Palestinian Israelis. "Under Rabin, and in the early Oslo period, the Israelis were much more relaxed in their dealings with us, not so strained or tense as at present. Now, we see raw racism against all Arabs." He said he urged Palestinian Israelis to "be assertive, as Arabs who deserve rights."

He referred to the many actions the government had recently taken against Arab non-governmental organizations (NGOs) in Israel and to moves made against him personally by the government and its supporters in the Knesset. In November 2001, the Knesset took the unprecedented step of voting to strip one of its members—himself—of his parliamentary immunity. Just days after that vote, Attorney General Elyakim Rubenstein filed two indictments against him. The first charge was one of incitement, brought in connection with speeches he had made in June 2000,

---

100 For a Jewish Israeli's account of these events, see p. 159 below.

in Umm el-Fahm and then, a few days later, during a visit he made to Damascus, Syria. In both those speeches, he had expressed support for the right to resist Israel's occupation of the Palestinian territories and South Lebanon. "But I never said I supported armed struggle," he stressed to us.

The second charge related to a program he organized while he was in Syria, which enabled elderly Palestinian citizens of Israel to travel to Syria to visit relatives living there whom they had not seen since 1948.[101]

"They also charged me with not recognizing the Jewish state," he told us. "But on that one, the Supreme Court found in my favor. I merely say that the state should be a state for all its citizens."

He also told us of his fear that during Israel's next elections, the government would try to prevent him and his party from even running in the election. In the run-up to the election of January 2003, that prediction proved correct. But once again, the Supreme Court found in his favor; and in that election his party increased its representation in the Knesset from one Member of Knesset (MK) to three.

We asked Azmi Bishara why the Israeli peace movement seemed to be weakening.

> Everyone has been disappointed in them, including us! It has been a great disappointment to see what has happened to the so-called "left" inside Israel. The defense minister and foreign minister right now—under Sharon—are both from Labor.[102] As usually happens here when there's a national unity government, the progressive movement is paralyzed.

> The self-identified 'left' has declined from 24 percent to 9 percent. Israeli society has become so aligned with the war. But the war was started by Barak!

> Also, the suicide bombers have had a political impact, stoking resentment and fear on the Israeli side. After a bomb goes off, it's hard for the left to go out and demonstrate.

He spoke about the many threats that individuals and groups in the Jewish Israeli community had made against him, and the effect

---

101 On 1 April 2003, the Nazareth Magistrate Court dismissed this latter indictment. See http://www.adalah.org/eng/bishara.php.

102 Later in 2002, Labor left the ruling coalition, sparking Sharon's decision to move the 2003 election forward to January. (See chapter 4.)

those threats had had on him: "There have been two or three peace demonstrations in Tel Aviv that I helped to plan. But then, I can't take part in them, because if I walked in a demonstration I know I would be attacked. I can't walk in Jewish streets, or go through the airport. When I travel, I have to fly through Amman airport, because I am not safe in Ben Gurion airport. There is such a racist response to me! The venom and the fear just spill out."

Haifa

Before 1948, the deep-water port in Haifa was pivotal to the British Army's operations throughout the Middle East. By 1947-48, this beautiful, mountain-ringed city had a local population of around seventy thousand Arabs and seventy thousand Jews—and many thousands of British Empire soldiers. According to the Jewish-Israeli historian Benny Morris, during the early months of the 1947-48 fighting, "thousands of prosperous and middle-class Arab families fled the city. Tens of thousands more fled Haifa during and immediately after the Haganah [pre-state Jewish forces] conquest of the city's original Arab neighborhoods in April 1948."[103]

By July 1948, Morris wrote, only 3,500 of Haifa's original Arab (Palestinian) inhabitants remained. Most of those who remained were Christians. In a meticulously researched account, Morris explains how, in early July 1948, the authorities of the infant Israeli state proceeded to "concentrate"—their word—those Palestinians into two small city neighborhoods. Between July 2 and July 9, IDF troops trucked some 720 families from their homes outside the zones of concentration to accommodations that had been hastily prepared within them. One Israeli official cited by Morris wrote of conditions in the concentration zones: "The flats are filthy, like the streets. There is no water, no electricity, and there are no locks on the doors. There is no time to properly arrange the allocation of the flats." Once the relocation was finished, IDF engineering units demolished much of the housing and other properties evacuated by the relocated families.[104]

---

103   Benny Morris, *1948 and after: Israel and the Palestinians* (Oxford and New York: Oxford University Press, 1994), p 215. See chapter 6 for an account of our meeting with Khairia Kasmieh, one of those refugees.

104   Ibid., pp. 215-231, passim.

When we were in Haifa, we met with several Palestinian Israelis and one Jewish Israeli activist working for equal rights for all Israeli citizens.

For our first meeting, Suhad Bishara and Rina Rosenberg of a group called Adalah (the Legal Center for Arab Minority Rights in Israel) came to the Catholic convent in the heart of Haifa where we were staying. Rosenberg supplied numerous facts and figures to sketch the dimensions of the discrimination that Palestinian citizens of Israel faced.[105] She explained that Adalah—which is the Arabic word for "justice"—handles two main categories of cases: one in which it challenges national budgets to try to obtain proportional funding for programs benefiting the country's Arab minority and one in which it seeks to obtain additional funds to compensate for the effects of decades of past discrimination.

According to the most recent figures from Israel's Central Bureau of Statistics, in 2001, 1.2 million (18.8 percent) of the country's population of 6.4 million were described as Arabs.[106] Rosenberg told us that until recently the Ministry for Religious Affairs allocated only 2 percent of its $4 billion budget to the Christian, Muslim, and Druze religious bodies that serve the country's Palestinians. Adalah brought suit against the ministry in the Supreme Court, requesting that it ensure that budget allocations were proportionate. That lawsuit failed, but the judges who rejected it then advised Adalah that more narrowly focused suits might have a better chance of success. "Since then, Adalah did succeed in winning a case relating to the ministry's spending on cemeteries," Rosenberg said. "We checked the ministry's budget and found that none of its spending on cemeteries was going for non-Jewish cemeteries. But everybody dies! For that item, we won the court's recognition of the principle of proportional shares."

She said Adalah had also won a suit requiring that road signs on national routes display destination names not only in Hebrew but also in Arabic—the second of the country's two official lan-

---

105 Many such data can be accessed through Adalah's website: <www.adalah.org>.

106 These figures include the numbers for East Jerusalem and Golan, which were annexed by Israel in 1967 and 1981 respectively.

guages.[107] (She noted that in many of its cases including language rights and other "economic, social, and cultural rights," Adalah built on precedents established in Canadian courts that have done groundbreaking work in balancing the language rights of French, English, and indigenous-nation minorities with those of majorities in each respective jurisdiction.)

Rosenberg and Suhad Bishara both noted that much of Adalah's work focuses on land issues. But Rosenberg exclaimed at one point that, in addition, "There are so many laws that attack people's civil rights!" She listed some of them:

> The government has resumed its previous practice of imposing travel bans on suspects, and has issued indictments for such actions as holding up Palestinian flags or pictures of Sheikh Nasrallah [the leader of Hizbollah, a political party and associated militia, in Lebanon].

> All applications for citizenship or residency that are based on marriage are being held up—but only for applications from people in the occupied territories. This could break up many families.[108] And then, with the latest budget cuts, they plan to cut the child allowance by four percent for people who've served in the army—but by twenty-four percent for people who haven't, which includes nearly all Palestinian citizens.[109]

In Haifa, we also visited the headquarters of Ittijah, the Union of Arab Community Based Associations.[110] Here, representatives of a number of different groups gathered around a broad table in a busy central space to tell us about their work. One of the first to speak was Khalid al-Khalil, a veteran land-affairs activist. Khalil is a leader in a group dedicated to winning "recognition" for some forty Arab villages that had not yet won that status from the government. Only recognized villages are part of Israel's planning process, and only the residents of recognized villages are included in government plans for providing infrastructure and government services—like schools—to the country's citizens.

---

107 Details of these cases and many others in which Adalah has played a role can be found on the organization's website (see above).

108 Just over a year later, in July 2003, the Knesset passed a law explicitly barring applications for "family unification" for Palestinians from the occupied territories who were married to Israeli citizens. See <http://www.adalah.org/eng/famunif.php>.

109 This provision also affected ultra-Orthodox Jewish families, since most people from this community are also excused military service. These families, like Palestinian-Israeli families, are often very large.

110 Information about Ittijah and its affiliated organizations can be accessed at <www.ittijah.org>.

"In 1965, the Israelis made a master-plan for the whole country. But they didn't recognize these villages at that point," Khalil told us. "So suddenly, our villages and homes, some of which had been there for centuries, became 'illegal'. They tried to evict everyone into what they called 'concentrations'.... The word they use for that in Hebrew is *rikuz*." He estimated the number of people affected at around 100,000.

"Our association made a plan for the unrecognized villages," he explained. "We found all the necessary data and suggested a solution. We suggested that some of these villages should receive recognition as they were, and some could be attached as new 'neighborhoods' to existing towns or villages." In the 1990s, he said, the group won recognition for nine villages—though he told us they had still not been provided with construction permits or basic services. "The issue is not about planning only, but about policy," Khalil stressed. "The issue is land, as between the state and us, the indigenous residents."

He said that in the Negev region, in southern Israel, "The government put 135,000 Arabs into seven 'concentrations'. But any Jewish family that goes to the Negev is given five hundred *dunums*, free. As for us, we're not even allowed to rent land there to use."

"They have started even more since October 2000 to treat us as enemies," he concluded. "But this is the compromise we offer to them: we want to be treated as equal citizens."

We also heard from two articulate younger-generation members of Ittijah's own central staff: its director, Ameer Makhoul, and program director Sanaa Hammoud, a lawyer.

Hammoud told us that 60 percent of Arab children in Israel live under the poverty line. "From the beginning, the Israelis put us on the margins of their national life. And since October 2000, things have become even worse. ... There are lots of laws being discussed that would harm our interests a lot, and lots of agitation against the Arab leaders here, especially the Arab Members of Knesset."

During the present *intifada*, she said, Ittijah had started doing some media outreach work related to it:

> We have been working with the foreign media, the Arab media, and even the Israeli media, trying to get news out about what has been happening in the occupied territories.

In general, we've found the Israeli media very unresponsive. We called our campaign, "Don't say you didn't know!" We were getting information and telephone calls in real time from inside Jenin camp during the battles there, and we tried to pass it on to colleagues in the Israeli media. But Aviv Lavie from *Ha'aretz* admitted that they are not publishing everything they know.[111]

When Makhoul spoke, he described some of the problems he saw the broader Palestinian national movement as facing. "All the Palestinians around the world are victims of Israel," he said. "One of our main issues as Palestinians is our fragmentation. There is fragmentation between Palestinians who are citizens here, the residents of the occupied Palestinian territories, and the refugees outside. The Palestinian issue is not just what happened in 1967, but also 1948."

He said that after much planning, in 2001, representatives of Palestinian NGOs in Israel, the occupied territories, and Lebanon were finally able to get together—but they had to go to Cyprus to do so. "The only way I could meet Raji Sourani was by going to Cyprus!" he noted with amazement, referring to the human rights lawyer we had earlier met with in Gaza, less than 100 miles away. "We are trying to work as a unified movement," he added. "The P.A. [Palestinian Authority] accepted cutting us 'inside' Palestinians off from Palestinian issues because including our issues made their agenda with Oslo harder. But now, Oslo is ended! It is clear that all Palestinians are at risk—we have seen the attacks against Azmi Bishara, the threats against Palestinian NGOs.... And all this is done here inside Israel by military order, not by the courts."

We asked Makhoul whether the Palestinian Israeli organizations affiliated with Ittijah had cooperative relations with similar organizations in Jewish Israeli society. He replied:

> After October 2000, many of the leftist Israeli organizations were in shock. That was really a period of 'taking off masks'. Now, the present period has shown us that we have several allies—groups like Physicians for Human Rights or B'tselem.[112] So we continue to coordinate with them.

---

111   We had earlier heard the Jewish Israeli peace activist Gila Svirsky talking about the "self-censorship" that, she said, exists in the media regarding developments in the occupied territories.

112   Physicians for Human Rights—Israel has a good website at <http://www.phr.org.il>. B'tselem, the Israeli Information Center for Human Rights in the Occupied Territories, has a good site at <www.btselem.org>.

Now, we need to talk about protection—for us, as well as for the Palestinians in the occupied territories. Protection, not just solidarity...

You know, we used to use the word "apartheid" for what was going on here. But now, we feel that the Palestinians are facing a new *nakba*, just like the one of 1948. They're facing that prospect in the occupied territories—but we're also facing it here.

We feel and fear that everyone is against us. We can't feel any sense of justice in the world.

Israel as a State for Jewish People Everywhere

Modern Israel was founded as an explicitly Jewish state in 1948, that is, at a time when people and policymakers around the world were still reeling from having learned about the devastation that the Holocaust had wreaked on the Jews of Europe, and keenly aware of the degree to which the condition of statelessness to which Hitler had reduced so many European Jews had increased their vulnerability and isolation. Israel has always claimed not only to be a state for its existing Jewish residents but also to have a close, organic relationship with Jewish people from all parts of the world. Most specifically, one of its central self-proclaimed missions as a state has always been to provide a safe haven for Jews living under threat anywhere in the world; and it has indeed done much to provide such a haven.

These facts have had profound consequences for the 1.2 million citizens of the country who are not Jewish but belong instead to the country's indigenous Palestinian Arab population.

The relationship between the State of Israel and Jewish people internationally is embodied first and foremost in the country's Law of Return, which was passed in 1950 and is still in force. This law grants every Jewish person everywhere in the world the right to enter Israel as an *oleh* (a Jew immigrating to Israel) and immediately to become an Israeli citizen.[113] Israel's relationship with Jewish people living in the Diaspora is also embodied in a set of formal agreements between the state and an interlocking network of organizations that function both as international NGOs and as quasi-state agencies in Israel. These organizations include the World Zionist Organization (WZO), the Jewish Agency, and the Jewish National Fund (JNF). Their work is aimed almost exclu-

---

113 The Law of Return does specify a few exceptions, including people who though Jewish are deemed to pose a potential threat to public order.

sively at serving the interests of Jewish people in and en route to Israel. Many of them started their work long before Israel was established and have continued it in the decades since then. The leaderships of these organizations typically include people from diaspora Jewish communities alongside representatives of the State of Israel.

In 1952, the Knesset enacted a law designating the WZO as "the authorized agency which will continue to operate in the State of Israel for the development and settlement of the country, [and] the absorption of immigrants from the Diaspora." The JNF, a funding organization linked to WZO, spells out on its website that it is "the caretaker of the land of Israel, on behalf of its owners— Jewish People everywhere."[114]

Before 1948, a substantial portion of the land of Mandate Palestine had—in keeping with the still-operative Ottoman land laws—been designated "state land." After 1948, Israel not surprisingly claimed control over those lands. In addition, it created an agency called the Custodianship of Absentee Property through which it started to exercise control over the lands of the departed Palestinian refugees (as well as those of Palestinians who had remained inside Israel and were Israeli citizens, but had been displaced from their homes during the fighting[115]). In 1960, the Knesset passed legislation establishing the principle that state and JNF lands could not be sold, but would remain in perpetuity a possession of the State of Israel. A new agency, the Israel Lands Authority (ILA), was created to manage those lands, which comprise 93 percent of the territory inside the country's pre-1967 borders.[116] An informational note published by a respected Israeli real estate company describes the ban on any sale of these lands, and explains that, "The Israeli government and the Knesset adopted this principle, in the belief that maintaining national ownership of the land would facilitate the absorption of immigration ... and prevent the transfer of the land to undesirable parties."[117]

---

114 JNF webite, at <http://www.jnf.org/site/PageServer>.

115 In an Orwellian turn of phrase, these internally displaced Palestinians (whose situation was discussed in chapter 6) were designated by the Israeli authorities as "present absentees."

116 The international Jewish organizations described above, and the ILA, have also played a variety of roles in acquiring and administering land in the occupied territories, and in providing services to Jewish Israeli settlers there.

117 Accessed from the website of Capital Property Consultants, Jerusalem, Israel, <http://www.property.co.il/information/legal.htm >, on June 28, 2003.

This 93 percent of the country's land that is not available for private ownership can, however, be leased from the ILA under leases that typically run for 49 years. For years, most Palestinian Israelis simply assumed that they would not be granted such leases, but in 1994 a brave Palestinian family, the Qa'adans, decided to test that assumption. They applied for a permit to build a home in Katzir, a community sited on land leased from the ILA on which, until then, only Jewish families had been allowed to build homes. When their application to build in Katzir was turned down, the Qa'adans sued to have the decision reversed. The case took some years to make its way through Israeli courts, but in a landmark ruling in March 2000, the Supreme Court supported the Qa'adans' suit. Justice Aharon Barak, writing for the majority, stated, "Equality is among the fundamental principles of the State of Israel. Every authority in Israel, beginning with the State of Israel, its institutions, and employees, must treat the various elements in the state equally.... The state must honor and protect the fundamental right of every individual in the state to equal treatment."[118]

Despite the clear nature of that ruling, the Qa'adans had still not received their building permit three years later; and the hopes of many rights activists in Israel that Aharon Barak's decision might usher in an era of equality in the country remained unfulfilled.

Education and Identity

Another of the younger activists we met at the Ittijah headquarters was Ghadir Shafei, who works with a youth organization called Baladna ("Our Country"). In her short discussion with us she touched on another very challenging issue that—along with land—affects many of Israel's Palestinian citizens very deeply: identity. "Being Palestinians living in Israel we have a dual identity," she told us. "We're educated in Israeli society but we're not treated as equal citizens. We are labeled as a minority in Israel, not as a part of the Palestinian people. But since October 2000, our Palestinian identity has been strengthened."

The question of identity has been a complex one for Palestinian Israelis to negotiate. During the fighting of 1947-48 the Arabic-speaking Palestinians who stayed in what became Israel

---

118 This quotation, and more details of the case, are available from the website of the Association for Civil Rights in Israel (ACRI), accessible at: <http://www.acri.org.il/english-acri/engine/story.asp?id=100>

found their status transformed within a few short months from being members of the majority Arab community in Mandate Palestine to being members of a small and vulnerable minority within an assertively Jewish state. Until 1966, most of Israel's Palestinian citizens were subject to special military regulations that controlled their movement within the country and severely curtailed their rights to free expression and free association.

During that period, the new state was putting into operation an education system designed to build a proud, Hebrew-speaking, Jewish nation out of the hundreds of thousands of Jewish immigrants and refugees whom it was bringing into the country from all around the world. This effort proved notably successful. Building on the pioneering work of earlier generations of Zionists who had revived Hebrew as a modern spoken language, the Israeli state was able to re-acculturate nearly all the post-1948 immigrants into being participants in a vibrant, multi-faceted Hebrew-speaking culture.

The role of the state's indigenous Arabic-speaking population within that endeavor was less clear. Continuing a practice that had grown up under the British, Israel ran separate school systems for the state's Jewish and Arab children. (Indeed, for the Jewish children, it ran three different systems, ranging from an essentially secular system to an ultra-orthodox, strongly religion-based one.) From the beginning, it was evident that many deep-rooted inequalities existed between the funding of the Jewish and Arab school systems, as did significant asymmetries between the content of these systems. At the dawn of the 21st century, these inequities were still firmly in place.

Regarding inequalities in funding, a 2001 study published by Human Rights Watch (HRW) cited an Israeli government report that stated: "In 1991, the total investment in education per pupil in Arab municipalities was approximately one-third of the investment per pupil in Jewish municipalities."[119] The effects of this gross inequality are evident throughout the whole school system. For example, the state is required by law to provide free education to all children between the ages of three and seventeen; but in 1998-

---

119   Human Rights Watch, *Second Class: Discrimination against Palestinian Arab children in Israel's schools* (New York: Human Rights Watch, September 2001), p.47. Funding by the national government is only one of four sources of funding listed in the report.

99, only 22.5 percent of Arab three-year-olds and 33.5 percent of four-year-olds went to kindergarten, compared with 89.3 percent of Jewish three-year-olds and 92.9 percent of Jewish four-year-olds.

Regarding asymmetries of content, the HRW report explained that Arabic and Hebrew are both official languages of the state and Hebrew is a required subject in the Arabic schools in grades three through twelve, and also a required subject in the all-important *bagrut,* the school-leaving examination—but there was no reciprocal requirement for Arabic-language proficiency from learners in Hebrew-language schools.[120] The report noted that the Hebrew language curriculum for Arab students contained what many Palestinian parents, learners, and teachers complained was compulsory instruction in the Hebrew Bible and in Judaism.[121] While Hebrew language and even some Judaic studies were required for Palestinian Arab students, until recently, scant time was allowed in the Arabic schools' curriculum for any meaningful study of their community's own cultural roots or history. The report quoted a tenth grade girl as saying, "They taught us nothing on Palestinian history in elementary or junior high school. Yes, they taught us world history, and old Arab history, but not Palestinian history. I would like to learn more. I learn Palestinian history in a special program outside the school."[122]

Palestinian Israeli children coming up through this system had to contend with not only the consequences of the separate and unequal investment in their school system but also the extra burdens placed on them by the content of their schooling. For example, Hebrew and English are the only two languages that are required components for the *bagrut.* For students in Jewish high schools, this requires that they learn only one non-native language; but students in Arab high schools need to demonstrate proficiency in two non-native languages. To be admitted to a university, students must not only score well on the *bagrut* but also pass a separate psychometric exam that is designed in Hebrew and then, for the Arab-education students, rendered into Arabic in a translation that many teachers claim is of a quality poor enough to be seriously confusing for their students.

---

120 Ibid., p.152.

121 Ibid., pp.152-3.

122 Ibid., p.155.

By age 17, the results of these inequalities are evident. In 1998-99, 31.7 percent of Arab 17-year-olds had dropped out of school, compared with 10.4 percent of their Jewish counterparts. Nearly 45 percent of Arab applicants to university were rejected, compared with 16.7 percent of Jewish applicants. Of all the Israeli students who received their first degree that year, only 5.7 percent were Palestinian Israelis.[123] As Majid al-Haj, a Palestinian-Israeli professor of education at Haifa University described it in 2000, the Israeli education system provided "asymmetric education, one-sided multiculturalism, where Arab students are educated for control and Jewish students for ethnocentric rule."[124]

The HRW report noted that in 1999, the Ministry of Education published a new history curriculum for Arab high schools that for the first time included a unit on Palestinian history.[125] This was a landmark development, in view of the stubbornness with which successive national leaders in Israel since 1948 had continued to deny that there was any such collective entity as a "Palestinian people." We have already seen, in chapter 6, how over the decades that followed 1948, the official Israeli discourse tried to minimize the claims brought against Israel by Palestinian refugees by defining them only as undifferentiated "Arabs" and then urging them simply to resettle alongside their Arab "compatriots," in the host countries where they found themselves. This quashing of the idea of a Palestinian national identity—and one which had specific claims to rights over much of the land controlled by the Israel—came to a head in 1969 when Prime Minister Golda Meir famously declared, "It was not as though there was a Palestinian people ... and we came and threw them out and took their country away from them. They did not exist."[126]

The depth and long duration of the denial by Israeli leaders that the "Palestinian people" as such even existed started to erode in 1991, when Prime Minister Yitzhak Shamir sat down in Madrid with a joint Jordanian-Palestinian delegation that contained an

---

123 Ibid., pp. 174-5.

124 Quoted in HRW, op. cit., p. 158.

125 Ibid., p.156. The report noted that, "The new curriculum has not yet been fully implemented in Arab schools as textbooks are lacking."

126 Golda Meir, interviewed by *The Sunday Times* (London), 15 June 1969; as cited in David Hirst, *The Gun and the Olive Branch* (London: Faber and Faber, 1977), p. 264.

identifiably Palestinian component. It eroded even more after Prime Minister Yitzhak Rabin concluded the Oslo Accords with the PLO, an unabashedly Palestinian leadership organization. But even after Israel's leaders had come to recognize that the people whom they were ruling over in the West Bank and Gaza might appropriately be called "Palestinians," they still remained very reluctant to concede that around a million of their own indigenous citizens might also have a strong Palestinian component to their identity.

Indeed, official Israeli discourse has always strongly preferred either to refer to these people simply as "Israeli Arabs" or to break them down into supposed ethno-religious categories like "Christian," "Muslim," "Druze," and "Bedouin": anything, it some-times seemed, rather than admitting they might be Palestinian, though this has long been the identity to which the majority of Israel's Arabic-speaking citizens have laid claim. In this context, the introduction of "Palestinian history" into the 1999 curriculum truly was a breakthrough—even though for that decision, as for those on "recognizing" additional Palestinian Israeli villages or on housing equality, implementation still remained problematic.

Coexistence Inside Israel: Jewish Israeli Views

The anti-state and inter-communal riots that took place inside Israel in October 2000 were an important watershed for members of both the Palestinian Israeli and Jewish Israeli communities. We have seen above how Rana Bishara described her memories of those days. From the other side of the inter-communal divide, one Jewish Israeli woman has written of that time:

> The riots seemed, at the time, to be an integral part of the awful violence that had erupted in the territories ... At the same time, there was real fear that the surrounding Arab countries would rally round their Palestinian brethren and attack Israel ... It was very scary.

> The Israeli Arabs ceased their rioting only after thirteen Arabs had been killed by police forces in the north, twelve Israelis, and one Gazan.

> Quiet returned, but everything had changed. The feeling of betrayal we Jews felt was overwhelming. Israeli Arabs had violently sided with the Palestinians against the rest of us.[127]

---

127 "Not a fish (provincially speaking)" weblog, accessible at <http://www.imshin.blogspot.com/2003_08_31_imshin_archive.html#106250625333195134>.

A few weeks after the riots subsided, Ehud Barak's government decided that an authoritative Commission of Inquiry should be appointed to look into both the causes of the rioting and the decision-making by the government and police that had led to these killings at the hands of the police. Supreme Court President Aharon Barak was instructed to appoint the Commission, and he asked Supreme Court Justice Theodore Or to head it.[128]

Over the three years that followed, the Or Commission continued its work. Meanwhile, many Jewish Israelis were reflecting on some of the problems and tensions involved in their desire to have their state be both Jewish and democratic. When we met peace activist Gila Svirsky in 2002 she told us, "Israel should be a democratic country, the state of all its citizens." (This phrase is heard much more frequently from Palestinian Israelis than from Jewish Israelis.) Talking about the Israel she would like to see emerge from a two-state solution to the conflict, Svirsky said,

> It should be a state that embodies the best of Jewish values. It should be open as a haven to Jews in need. It should be 'a light unto the nations'. It's true, perhaps, that Israel was born in sin, in 1948—but it was also born from historical exigencies in those days.
>
> For me, my Zionism is about the character of Israel, and its status as a homeland for the Jews, as it has been for the Palestinians.
>
> I know 1948 was a disaster for the Palestinians. I am grateful that they allow us to stay here, and hope that they can make a go of running their own state on their 22 percent of the land.
>
> You know, all national liberation movements are nationalist and racist to some extent... I just hope we can take those nationalist feelings and channel them into rivalry in international soccer!

Strategic analyst Yossi Alpher, whom we had met at Tel Aviv University's Jaffee Center, expressed a notably different view of the Palestinian Israelis' demand that Israel become the state of all its citizens:

> In the context that has emerged after the collapse of peace talks, the Palestinian demand that Israel recognize the right of return and admit guilt for the events of 1948 (understood to mean that we admit we were 'born in sin'), thirty-three months of bloodshed, and the radicalization of

---

128 The commission's other two members were Professor Shimon Shamir, a historian of the Arab world who (like Or) is Jewish and who had previously served as ambassador to Egypt and Jordan, and Sahel Jarah, a Palestinian Israeli judge in the Nazareth District Court. In 2001, Jarah resigned for health reasons and was replaced by another Palestinian Israeli judge.

Israeli Arab rhetoric, 'a state of all its citizens' is seen by myself and most Israelis as, deliberately or not, part and parcel of a long-term Palestinian objective to 'Palestinize' Israel, to turn a two-state solution into a 'one and a half Palestinian states' solution...

If, prior to [the collapse of the Camp David talks of] July 2000 and its aftermath, it was possible to deal with the demand that Israel become a state of all its citizens as a legitimate post-Zionist initiative, today it is seen as an attempt to undermine Israel. Small wonder that the Jewish post-Zionist contingent has shrunk to almost nothing, as Israelis 'circle the wagons' on this key issue.[129]

He wrote us that he agreed with the assessment that Arab Israelis faced systematic discrimination, "and [they] have for the past fifty-five years." He added that he thought most Jewish Israelis were aware of this discrimination: "Certainly, the Jewish Israeli leadership is aware, and periodically pays lip service to the need to right the situation. ... A revolution is needed here, in terms of genuinely equal treatment if not affirmative action. Sadly, I don't see the Israeli Jewish politicians who will make it happen."

In early September 2003, the Or Commission presented its final report. The commissioners had done a seemingly thorough job of examining the immediate sequence of events around the riots—including the decision-making (or lack of it) that led Israeli police officers to use rubber-coated metal bullets and all-metal bullets against Palestinian Israeli demonstrators who were in the main armed only with slingshots, stones, and occasional Molotov cocktails[130]—as well as the issue of the longer-term lack of trust between Palestinian Israelis and the state authorities. The report seriously criticized Ehud Barak, who had been prime minister at the time, on a number of counts, including that he "did not fulfill his duty as prime minister during the events of October 2000, in that he did not demand the police or its commanders make concrete, complete and detailed reports as soon as possible regarding ... specific events in which citizens were killed or seriously injured."[131] It expressed serious criticism of Public Security Minister Shlomo

---

129 Alpher kindly sent us these comments in response to a specific set of written questions we sent him in July 2003, as we sought to more clearly understand Jewish Israeli views on this issue.

130 *Ha'aretz* has published an authorized, English-language version of the digest of the Commission's 831-page report. This information is from the portion published at <http://www.haaretz.com/hasen/objects/pages/PrintArticleEn.jhtml?itemNo=335594>.

131 Same URL as above, but at <... itemNo=335599>.

Ben-Ami, the police commissioner, and other high-ranking police officers, along with serious problems in the "culture" of much of the police force. It also criticized three leaders of the Palestinian Israeli community, including MK Azmi Bishara and Raed Salah, the former mayor of Umm el-Fahm. Regarding Bishara, the Commission wrote that it judged "proven" the allegation that in the period before October 2000 he was responsible "for the transmission of messages supporting violence as a means of achieving the goals of Israel's Arab sector."[132] (When we met with Bishara he assured us he had never advocated any use of violence against the Israeli government; and we have never seen any evidence that he has.)

The most notable findings of the Or Commission report were not, however, the parts that looked at the immediate situation in October 2000, but those that examined the historical background of the plight of Palestinian Israelis:

> The events, their unusual character and serious results were the consequence of deep-seated factors that created an explosive situation in the Israeli Arab population. The state and generations of its government failed in a lack of comprehensive and deep handling of the serious problems created by the existence of a large Arab minority inside the Jewish state.
>
> Government handling of the Arab sector has been primarily neglectful and discriminatory...
>
> As a result of this and other processes, serious distress prevailed in the Arab sector in various areas. Evidence of the distress included poverty, unemployment, a shortage of land, serious problems in the education system and substantially defective infrastructure. These all contributed to ongoing ferment that increased leading up to October 2000 and constituted a fundamental contribution to the outbreak of the events.
>
> Another cause was the ideological-political radicalization of the Arab sector...[133]

In its concluding section, the report noted that "The clashes and their aftermath led to reduced contact between the two societies and increased distrust and hostility." It then looked to the future in a way that we consider pushes forward the public discussion on this sensitive topic in a very helpful way:[134]

132 Same URL as above, but at <... itemNo=335602>.

133 Same URL as above, but at <... itemNo=335594>, section 3.

134 Note, however, Adalah's critique of the report, available at http://www.adalah.org/eng/pressreleases/pr.php?file=03_09_04. Adalah expressed the position that "Despite many reservations, the report is an important document and its recommendations should be implemented immediately."

The commission considered the need to strive ... to ensure the peaceful coexistence of Jews and Arabs in this country, thereby ensuring that events similar to those of October 2000 will not recur. It noted that Jews and Arabs living alongside one another is a fact of life, and the two sides have only one practical option for maintaining this way of life—coexistence with mutual respect. All other options, it was noted, are recipes for increased tension, heightened distress, and undermining of the order.

(55.) The commission stressed that coexistence presents challenges that are not easy for either side. It obliges each side to listen to the other, understand its sensitivities, and respect its basic rights. Arab citizens must bear in mind that Israel represents the realization of the yearnings of the Jewish people for a state of its own, the only state in which Jews are the majority, a state that is partly based on the principle of an ingathering of the Jewish exile, and that this is the essence of the existence of the state for its Jewish citizens. The Jewishness of the state is a constitutional given, which is partly reflected in the primary nature of the heritage of Israel and of the Hebrew language in its public life.

At the same time, the commission noted that the Jewish majority must bear in mind that the state is not only Jewish, but also democratic. As stated above, equality is one of the primary elements of the constitutional structure of the state, and the prohibition against discrimination applies to all citizens of the state. The majority must understand that the events that made the Arabs a minority in the state were for them a national catastrophe, and that their integration into the State of Israel was attended by painful sacrifices. The majority must respect their identity, culture, and language.[135]

Palestinian Israelis as a Bridge?

All the Arab citizens of Israel whom we met saw themselves as part of a distinct Palestinian people that also included the residents of the West Bank and Gaza as well as the Palestinians living in exile outside their homeland. They saw the inequalities and indignities they suffered by virtue of the second-class nature of their citizenship in Israel as paralleling the many harms suffered over the decades by their fellow Palestinians in the occupied territories and in the *ghurba* (in exile). Many of them seemed to recognize, however, that though their citizenship in Israel might be of inferior quality, nevertheless it provided them with some valuable political safeguards not enjoyed by Palestinians living elsewhere. (Compare, for example, the thorough nature of the inquiry launched by the Israeli government into the police shooting of

---

135 Same URL as Or Commission report URL above, but at <... itemNo=335610>, sections 54 and 55.

twelve Palestinian citizens of Israel—and one non-citizen from Gaza—with the government's general lack of interest in conducting serious inquiries into the shooting deaths of hundreds of Palestinian non-citizens just over the Green Line, in the occupied territories.) At the same time, the status of Israeli citizen enjoyed by these million-plus ethnic Palestinians gave them a valuable platform from which they could work both to provide aid to other Palestinians in need and, however slowly, to change Israel's policies toward those other Palestinians. But as the severity of the confrontations of October 2000 showed, the Palestinian Israelis would have to pursue all these efforts carefully, to avoid suffering extreme damage at the hands of the Israeli government and of Arabophobic zealots from the country's Jewish-majority population.

The existence of a sizeable and quietly assertive Palestinian Arab minority inside Israel's body politic presents members of the country's Jewish population with a particular set of challenges. Many Jewish Israelis take pride in what they see as their state's specifically Jewish and democratic values—though it should also be noted that a small but significant proportion of Jewish Israelis have told pollsters that they do *not* value democracy as a value very highly at all, and that Jewish Israelis disagree very strongly amongst themselves over exactly how it is that they want their state to be "Jewish."

It is true that all states, even democratic ones, follow discriminatory practices to some degree. For example, all states privilege the use of one or more "official" languages, and every state follows a particular, culturally determined calendar for weekly and yearly planning. These practices discriminate against people whose mother tongues are not recognized as "official," or whose native culture would prescribe differing weekly days of rest or annual holidays. Israel has nearly 20 percent of its current citizens (leaving aside for now the question of those exiled Palestinians who seek to return to it) who are by neither mother tongue, culture, nor aspiration members of the "Jewish people." Therefore, at the very least, if it is to live up to its claim to be a rights-respecting democracy it must find ways to renegotiate its relationship with its Palestinian citizens in a way that respects their economic, social, cultural, and political rights.

Beyond that, it is hard to see how any state that claims to be a rights-respecting democracy can accord more rights to non-citizens who reside and have stable citizenship elsewhere than it does to people who are citizens and who bear all the burdens and responsibilities of citizenship. Yet that is exactly what Israel does when it accords decision-making power over many state functions, including land-use decisions and the provision of many social and educational services, to organizations that are acting in the name of "the Jewish people everywhere" rather than that of all Israeli citizens. A Jewish family from Brooklyn, Melbourne, or Addis Ababa could have instantly won permission to build a house in Katzir. But the indigenous, citizenship-holding Qa'adan family could not do so. A Jewish person with stable citizenship in a western democracy could move to the country and, under its Law of Return, immediately secure residency and citizenship rights there. But Palestinians born in the country who fled or were forced out during one of its previous wars are prevented from returning to it or gaining citizenship in it—even if, in exile, they suffer from the extreme vulnerabilities of statelessness and impoverishment.

It sometimes seems hard to disentangle the problems and issues facing the Palestinian citizens of Israel from those of their kinfolk and larger community who are not citizens. But these issues are serious ones that need to be resolved if Israel is to live up to its claim to be a democracy.[136] We therefore urge Jewish Israelis that if—in the context of a two-state solution to their conflict with the Palestinians of the occupied territories—they want their state to be one that combines the best elements of being a majority-Jewish state with the basic prerequisites of a democracy, then they should consider sitting down with their fellow-citizens of Palestinian ethnicity to discuss:

- How best to ensure that the social, economic, cultural, and political rights of the country's Palestinian minority are fully respected.

- Actions that Israel can take to become truly egalitarian in its treatment of all its citizens, including:

  – Policies to ensure that the claims of current non-citizens (for example, for residency or naturalization) are addressed in a clearly nondiscriminatory way, and

  – Policies to ensure that relationships between the State of Israel and non-citizen bodies are maintained in a way that is

---

136 We discuss these issues further in chapter 8.

clearly nondiscriminatory in both their process and in the effect they have on the lives of citizens.

We do not imagine that resolving these issues will be easy. The more that progress is made toward meeting them, however, the more Israel will become a "normal" state among the other democratic states of the world, rather than a special case. (We recall that the normalization of the status of the Jewish people among the peoples of the world was an important part of the dream of many early Zionists.)

In addition, the more that Israel can meet the claims of those of its citizens who are ethnic Palestinians, the more effectively these Palestinian Israelis will be able to act as a genuine bridge between Israel's Hebrew-speaking majority and its Arabic-speaking neighbors throughout the Middle East. Indeed, we suggest that Jewish Israelis might discover that the talents of the Palestinian Israelis are a resource of real value to the state. Never before in history has there been such a large community of non-Jews who are fluent or near-fluent in Hebrew! As the claims of the Palestinian Israelis start to be met, the cooperation between Arabs and Jews inside Israel can become a model for Jewish-Arab cooperation elsewhere as well.

Part Three

Toward A Just Resolution

[8]
Rethinking Negotiations

[T]he time has come for the Jews to take into account the Arab factor as the most important facing us. If we have a just cause, so have they. If promises were made to us, so were they to the Arabs. If we love the land and have a historical connection with it, so too the Arabs ... If we too wish to live in this living space, we must live with the Arabs, try to make peace with them. I do not know if this is possible. But this is a task worthy of Jews.
—Judah Magnes, university president, Jerusalem, 1939

[T]he Israelis have to make up their minds! They can give us our rights either individually, inside Israel, or collectively, in a Palestinian state. But to carry on living on top of us as they currently do? That is impossible.
—Sari Nuseibeh, university president, Jerusalem, 2002

For some decades now, the people dominating the diplomacy on the Palestinian Israeli conflict have argued that key issues aspects of it—primarily Jerusalem, refugees, borders, and the future of the settlers—are so sensitive and complex that they cannot be discussed immediately but should be deferred to a later round of "final-status" negotiations that would take place only after some confidence has been built through the implementation of a preliminary "transitional" agreement or set of such agreements. That was the approach adopted in 1978, in the (aborted) Palestinian portion of the Camp David Accords concluded between Israel and Egypt. It was, as noted in chapter 4 above, the approach adopted in the 1993 Oslo Accords. Most recently, the same approach was used in the seemingly ill-starred Roadmap for Peace published by U.S. President George W. Bush in May 2003. Each of these attempted negotiations was designed to start out with a transitional, "confidence-building" phase during which the final outcome was still, by design, left open-ended. And in each, negotiations on the final outcome would not even begin until later, many months into implementation of the transitional phase or phases.

For our part, we cannot help but note that this approach seems to have had many weaknesses and indeed, that every one of these peacemaking efforts up until now has led nowhere.[137] One particular weakness has been that, in the absence of a clearly defined and mutually acceptable end-point, any problems in implementation that have occurred along the way—as can happen during any process of peacemaking—have become magnified, since people on each side have tended to interpret each setback, however small, as evidence of massive bad faith on the part of the other party, and then, too frequently, to over-react swiftly and badly.

In addition, given that Israel has been the status-quo power and the Palestinians the claimants on that power, the failure to address the final-status issues successfully or in a timely fashion has been a factor that time after time has decreased the confidence of Palestinians in the intentions of the Israelis and of the (principally U.S.) sponsors of the negotiations. The fact that, during all those aborted "transitional phases" from 1979 on, the Israeli governments in power continued to build more settlements in the occupied territories only served to aggravate these Palestinian fears even further.

We therefore strongly urge that the strategy of postponing negotiation of the final-status issues be reconsidered. And we invite the Israelis and Palestinians, along with the diplomats of the major world powers and concerned citizens everywhere, to engage in a visionary attempt not just to secure a temporary disengagement but to *start delineating the final shape of a sustainable long-term relationship between Israelis and Palestinians*. Once a satisfactory shape to that final-status relationship can be agreed upon, we suggest that—as in the Israel-Egypt peace diplomacy, or that in South Africa, or in numerous other successful negotiations around the world—implementation of this final outcome could be phased in a way that could truly build confidence because those interim steps would be directed toward a known and agreed-upon end.

Beyond that, whether the negotiators tackle the final-status issues earlier (as we hope) or later, once they agree to do so we consider that they will face an immediate choice that needs to be made regarding the shape of the final outcome: would it be better to continue to work toward an outcome in which there are two independent states between the Mediterranean Sea and the Jordan River, or to direct their efforts instead toward an outcome involving only one state there? As was noted in chapter 4 above,

---

137 Though perhaps there is still time left for the Roadmap to succeed?

nearly all the diplomacy of recent years has been based on the supposition of an outcome in which two independent states—one Israeli and one Palestinian—would live peacefully side-by-side in this area. Until now, in its consideration of how different aspects of the conflict between Palestinians and Israelis might be resolved, this report has generally mirrored that assumption. We recall, too, that one of the very first international voices that argued in the post-1967 period that the Palestinians should be allowed to exercise their right to self-determination in the West Bank and Gaza (and thus, to establish a Palestinian state there) was that of the Quakers who authored the 1970 report *Search for Peace in the Middle East*.

Now, however, based on what we saw on the ground in Palestine/Israel in 2002, 32 years after the publication of that report, and based on what we have learned from our many discussions with Israelis, Palestinians, and each other, we have started to entertain some serious doubts as to whether there can still be an Israeli withdrawal from the occupied territories that is sufficient to provide the Palestinians with the basis for a viable independent state. So we suggest that at this point, precisely because of the high degree of demographic mixing brought about by Israel's settlement project, resolution of the final-status issues might be as easy (or as hard) to negotiate and the overall outcome as ultimately beneficial to the parties if a unitary, bi-national state is adopted as the model for the end-point, as would be the case by continuing to use the two-state model that has dominated the diplomacy of the past 20-30 years.

The question of the viability of the future Palestinian state is crucial, if the long-term interests of both peoples are to be assured through the implementation of a two-state model. It is not enough to merely grant a political entity the formal title of a "state": the territorial and political dimensions of this state's long-term viability have also to be assured. One instructive precedent in this regard is the case of the Bantustans that were created by South Africa's apartheid regime in the 1970s. South Africa accorded each Bantustan the title of an independent "state," but in reality the Bantustans were designed to be and to remain hopelessly dependent on the exclusively 'White' government then ruling in Pretoria.[138]

---

138 When discussing apartheid-era South Africa we have used terms like 'Black', 'White', and 'non-White' to refer to groups that were so identified by the government policies of that era.

One element of that dependency was that no Bantustan was ever accorded anything like a viable territorial/resource base, and another was that Pretoria retained control over key aspects of foreign and security policy, including the movement of people and goods across Bantustan borders. Not one of the Bantustans was ever able to provide a decent livelihood for, or satisfy the other legitimate aspirations of, the members of the ethnic group in whose interest it had supposedly been created. This was not surprising, since Pretoria never made any serious effort to give the residents of these territories any representative say in the design of "their" Bantustans.

Pursuit of the Bantustan policy inflicted extremely grave harms on the Black South Africans and failed to bring to any of the country's people, including its White citizens, the stability and social peace that they sought. Small wonder, then, that when the country's previously disfranchised non-White citizens received full political rights in 1994, the whole Bantustan experiment was abruptly terminated and the territories of those former "states" were reabsorbed into a unitary Republic of South Africa.

The example of South Africa's ill-fated Bantustans convinces us that in Israel/Palestine, as in South Africa, a unitary but intentionally multi-ethnic (in this case, bi-national) outcome would be preferable to the creation of a highly dependent, non-viable Palestinian state. Can a non-dependent, viable Palestinian state still be salvaged from the present situation? We cannot tell. Nor do we feel able to state with any certainty at this point that the outcome in Palestine/Israel should be a two-state, or a one-state, outcome. (Indeed, that is not a choice that we feel is ours to make, since it is rightly the responsibility of the Palestinians and Israelis themselves.) What we are clear about, however, is that whether the outcome is built on the one-state or two-state model, it must be negotiated and constructed in ways that satisfy the basic principles we outlined in chapter 1.

In the rest of this chapter, we will be exploring some of the issues involved in making this choice between a two-state outcome and its one-state alternative.

The Long Debate over the Final Outcome

The two-state model for the governance of the territory of Mandate-era Palestine was enshrined most authoritatively in the

U.N.'s partition resolution of 1947 and has, as noted, been the dominant approach in most of the diplomacy of recent decades. However, throughout the past 60 years a number of other approaches—including different variants of a single-state approach—have also been proposed by both Palestinians and Israelis, and there has always been some level of debate over what kind of model for coexistence would indeed bring both peoples the best chance for peace and national well-being.

Back in the 1940s, Judah Magnes, the first president of the Hebrew University of Jerusalem, and his friend and colleague the influential Jewish philosopher Martin Buber were both active advocates of the establishment of a unitary but bi-national state in the whole of Mandate Palestine. (Buber made numerous, highly valued contributions to the development of Hebrew education in Israel. His philosophy also explored the spiritual value of seeking active encounters with the "Other," a philosophical vision articulated most eloquently in his classic work *I and Thou*. When he died in 1965, the Israeli government accorded him the honor of a state funeral in Jerusalem—and one of the groups that placed a wreath on his grave during that solemn state occasion was the Israeli Arab Students' Organization.[139])

Back in the mid-1940s, the one-state approach was also espoused by the Labor Zionist "Mapam" party in the Jewish community. But David Ben Gurion and other leaders of the "Mapai" party argued against it and opted instead for the creation of an exclusively, or nearly exclusively, Jewish state in whatever portion of Mandate Palestine they could bring under their control. It was on the basis of this latter approach that the leaders of the Zionist movement in Palestine accepted the 1947 partition plan, and proceeded to establish Israel in an area that, comprising 78 percent of the land of Mandate Palestine, ended up being considerably larger than that accorded to the Jewish State in the partition plan. David Ben Gurion, the head of Mapai, became Israel's first prime minister.

Twenty years later, in the late 1960s—after the far-flung Palestinians had started to recover from their 1948 defeat and their subsequent scattering and exile—the PLO adopted a program that called for the establishment of a single "secular demo-

---

139 *The New Encyclopedia Britannica*, 15th ed. (Chicago etc: 1989), vol. 2, p. 590.

cratic state" in the whole of Mandate Palestine. PLO leaders explained at the time that Jewish residents of this area whose presence dated back to before "the Zionist invasion" could stay as full citizens of the proposed state. It was assumed, and sometimes stated, that all the rest would have to leave. This proposal therefore failed to win any serious number of adherents from the Jewish-Israeli community. (The PLO's leaders also notably failed to spell out how the specific language, religious, and other concerns of those few Jewish residents allowed to stay in "Palestine" would be met within the formula they proposed.)

In 1974, the PLO modified its stance, saying it was now prepared to accept the establishment of a "Palestinian national authority" within any part of historic Palestine that could be "liberated" from Israeli control. It was on the basis of this new formula that the PLO pursued the diplomatic campaign of the three decades that followed. Along the way, PLO decisions started to speak more clearly about the aimed-for entity being an independent Palestinian state, rather than just an ill-defined national authority; and PLO leaders started to talk openly of establishing this state alongside an Israel that would return to its pre-1967 borders, rather than replacing Israel.[140]

Even after the PLO's leaders had started to say clearly that their goal was the establishment of a Palestinian state alongside Israel rather than in the place of it, many Jewish Israelis continued to express fears that this state would just be a springboard from which the Palestinians might subsequently seek to take over all of Israel as well. (People who expressed such fears displayed little confidence that Israel could resist this later campaign—or that, in negotiating the terms of a two-state settlement, Israel could insist on the inclusion of measures to forestall the possibility of it ever being launched.) The PLO's leaders tried to assuage those Israeli concerns. Their efforts culminated in the formal recognition of the State of Israel expressed by PLO Chairman Yasser Arafat in a letter he wrote to Israeli Prime Minister Yitzhak Rabin as part of the Oslo Accords of September 1993. In the letter Arafat stated explic-

---

140 Other models, in addition to those involving the establishment of one state or two states west of the Jordan River, have also been discussed. These include a two-way confederation between a Palestinian state and Jordan and a three-way confederation among Israel, Palestine, and Jordan. Confederations are, however, based on the prior independent existence of their member states.

itly that, "The PLO recognizes the right of the State of Israel to exist in peace and security." Rabin wrote to Arafat at that same time that, "in light of the PLO commitments included in your letter, the Government of Israel has decided to recognize the PLO as the representative of the Palestinian people and commence negotiations with the PLO within the Middle East peace process."[141] It was on the basis of this bedrock of reciprocal recognition that the diplomacy of the post-Oslo years proceeded.

By the time we were in Israel/Palestine, however, nearly all the expectations that people in both communities had earlier entertained that the post-Oslo diplomacy might lead in a timely way to a sustainable two-state outcome had long since dissipated. A number of the Palestinians with whom we spoke warned clearly that if the Israeli government remained strongly intent on its pursuit of the settlement project, and on the concomitant destruction of the territorial base that any viable Palestinian state would need, then the Palestinians could—and perhaps should—change their focus from demanding the creation of an independent Palestinian state alongside Israel to demanding equal political rights for Palestinians within the whole of the area that is presently under Israeli control.

Sari Nuseibeh is a philosopher, and the president of the Palestinian Al-Quds (Jerusalem) University. When we met with him, he was also the head of the PLO's bureau for Jerusalem affairs (though as noted in chapter 5, he was later relieved of that post). "If the time comes when there are so many problems with so many settlers not wanting to move out of the occupied territories, I don't mind saying we don't want an independent state any more," he told us.

> At any time, if it becomes impossible for us to have a state, then I would ask to become an Israeli citizen and to have equal political rights inside Israel. Israelis should fear this. If the settlers want to stay where they are, then I'm in favor of a one-state solution. But if there's a two-state solution, then the settlers should all leave our state—in return for us saying that none of our refugees would return to inside Israel.[142]

---

141 The texts of both letters can be found at <http://www.brookings.edu/press/appendix/appen_p.htm>.

142 Nuseibeh's words here may seem to imply an equivalence between the situation of the settlers and that of the refugees. Many people have voiced strong objections to this equivalence.

Realistically, a one-state solution is the only way. But the Israelis have to make up their minds! They can give us our rights either individually, inside Israel, or collectively, in a Palestinian state. But to carry on living on top of us as they currently do? That is impossible.

When we were in the West Bank town of Dura with writer and analyst Khaled Amayreh, he told us he already thought that a two-state solution was "no longer viable." "There are 138 settlements," Amayreh said. "No Israeli government is going to pull them all out. Any government that tried to remove them would bring about a Jewish internal civil war. The only solution is a single, bi-national, secular state." He said he would be prepared to see many of the settlers stay where they are: "I'm against uprooting all the settlers from the occupied territories. If Hebron is so dear to the hearts of Jewish settlers, who am I to say they should not live there? But we should have reciprocity! If Khaled Amayreh wants to go and live on the coast, inside 1948 Israel, he should be allowed to do that, too." Standing in Amayreh's garden after our discussion, we looked down over some lower hills, and right across Israel to see the afternoon sun glinting off the Mediterranean Sea.

A number of the other Palestinians whom we met also seemed to be openly weighing the advantages and disadvantages of a one- or a two-state solution. (In Umm el-Fahm, inside Israel, secular political leader Raja Aghbariyeh had told us, "Now we seek a uni-fied, democratic secular state. It seems the best solution. It is our dream... ") The willingness of a broad range of Palestinians to dis-cuss the switch from a two-state goal to a one-state goal seemed to gather increasing momentum in the months after our visit.[143]

Among Jewish Israelis, however, there has seemed until recently to be far less readiness to entertain the idea of a one-state outcome, since most Jewish Israelis have judged that this formula is not compatible with the strong attachment they feel to the idea of keeping Israel as an exclusively, or almost exclusively, Jewish state. When we met Yossi Alpher in Tel Aviv's Jaffee Center for Strategic Studies, he asserted forcefully that, "Jewish Israelis are agreed that the reason for the existence of the State of Israel is for it to be a democratic *Jewish* state. Otherwise, why would we have

---

143 In July 2002, Sari Nuseibeh seemed to be giving the two-state approach one fur-ther chance when he worked with the Jewish Israeli political figure Ami Ayalon to unveil and then gather popular support for a "Statement of Principles" that openly called for "two states for two peoples"; see chapter 10.

it?" (Alpher was the one who compared the peace negotiations with the Palestinians with the process of a "messy divorce." It was his colleague Shai Feldman who argued strongly that the divorce in question needed to be "total.") Another Jewish Israeli strategic analyst, Efraim Karsh, has warned ominously that the one-state proposal, "seek[s] Palestinian domination over a country built on Israel's ruins," and "seeks to subvert Israel in one fell swoop by flooding it, not only with millions of Palestinian refugees and their descendants but also with the 2.5-million-strong Palestinian population of the West Bank and Gaza... [T]he creation of such a 'binational state' would be tantamount to Israel's immediate destruction."[144] Even Jewish Israelis considerably to the left of these three have sometimes seemed aghast at the idea of the Palestinians starting to demand a one-state solution. "Anything but a two-state solution would lead to the worst kind of one-state solution," warned Naomi Chazan of the staunchly pro-peace Meretz Party when we met her.

More recently, however, there have been intriguing signs of a new debate on this topic opening up among significant members of the Israeli peace camp. For example, Meron Benvenisti is an Israeli-born, 70-year-old stalwart of the "Zionist left" who for a while was Deputy Mayor of Jerusalem. (He has been described as a former "right-hand man" to the late Teddy Kollek, the man who as longtime Israeli mayor of the city did as much as anyone to implant Jewish settlers in occupied East Jerusalem.) In August 2003, Benvenisti wrote an essay in which he said he thought that his previous support for a two-state outcome had been based on an incorrect analysis. Now, he wrote, it was clear to him that:

> We will never reach a point at which one group will truly renounce the right of return and the other group will truly abandon its longing for Beit El.[145] We will never reach a situation in which the Arabs in Israel forgo their demand for their own collective rights.

> The conclusion is that the seemingly rational solution of two states for two nations can't work here. The model of a division into two nation-states is inapplicable. It doesn't reflect the depth of the conflict and doesn't sit with the scale of the entanglement that exists in large parts of the country...

---

144 Efraim Karsh, "A Trojan Horse?," part of the section, "The Case for Binationalism" published in *Boston Review*, vol. 26, no. 6 (Dec. 2001/Jan. 2002), p.14.

145 Beit El (Hebrew for "the House of God") is a place near Ramallah, in the West Bank, that is of religious significance to many Jews. It houses a growing Israeli settlement plus a key regional headquarters for the Israeli occupation forces.

In the past year, then, I reached the conclusion that there is no choice but to think in new terms. There is no choice but to think about western Palestine [Eretz Yisrael, or the land of Israel] as one geopolitical unit.[146]

Just as the South African rulers understood, at a certain point, that there was no choice but to dismantle their regime, so the Israeli establishment has to understand that it is not capable of imposing its hegemonic conceptions on 3.5 million Palestinians in the West Bank and Gaza and 1.2 million Palestinians who are citizens of Israel. What we have to do is try to reach a situation of personal and collective equality within the framework of one overall regime throughout the country...

[I]n the end we are going to be a Jewish minority here. And the problems that your children and my grandchildren are going to have to cope with are the same ones that de Klerk faced in South Africa. The paradigm, therefore, is the binational one. That's the direction. That's the conceptual universe we have to get used to.[147]

Benvenisti's essay was accompanied by a second one, separately written by another former (though more reluctant) supporter of the two-state solution called Haim Hanegbi. Hanegbi came to exactly the same conclusion as Benvenisti. Both men are veteran Israeli political activists. Writing at a time when the major initiative being undertaken by his national government was the construction of the massive fence/wall intended to separate Israelis physically from their Palestinian neighbors, Hanegbi wrote:

In essence, the binational principle is the deepest antithesis of the wall. The purpose of the wall is to separate, to isolate, to imprison the Palestinians in pens. But the wall imprisons the Israelis, too. It turns Israel into a ghetto. The wall is the great despairing solution of the Jewish-Zionist society. It is the last desperate act of those who cannot confront the Palestinian issue...

In general, we have to shift to a binational mode of thinking. Maybe in the end we have to create a new, binational Israel, just as a new, multiracial South Africa was created.

There will be no other choice, anyway. The attempt to achieve Jewish sovereignty that is fenced in and insular has to be abandoned. We will have to come to terms with the fact that we will live here as a minority: a Jewish minority that will no longer be squeezed between Hadera and Gedera, but will be able to settle in Nablus and Baghdad and

---

146 In this context, "western Palestine" seems clearly to refer to the area of Mandate Palestine. The clarifications in the text are likely from his English translator.

147 Meron Benvenisti's essay presented in Ari Shavit, "Cry, the beloved two-state solution" in *Ha'aretz*, 6 Aug. 2003. Available at <http://www.haaretz.com/hasen/objects/pages/PrintArticleEn.jhtml?itemNo=326313>.

Damascus, too—and take part in the democratization of the Middle East. That will be able to live and die here, to establish mixed cities and mixed neighborhoods and mixed families. But for that to happen, the mad dream of sovereignty will have to be given up...[148]

Significantly, in both these thoughtful essays, the writers express real affection and nostalgia for the Palestinian Arab neighbors whom they had known as they grew up in the mixed Jerusalem of the 1930s and early 1940s. (A similar nostalgia for the inter-communal links that existed before 1948 can also frequently be heard from older-generation Palestinians, such as educator Samia Khoury, whom we met at Sabeel's headquarters in Jerusalem.) In addition, both Benvenisti and Hanegbi movingly expressed the horror they felt when they reflected on what happened to their former Palestinian neighbors in 1947-48.

The publication of the essays by Benvenisti and Hanegbi indicated that 55 years after 1948 the thinking of at least some Jewish Israeli intellectuals was coming back full circle to the creative concepts and ideals advocated in the Jerusalem of their youth by Judah Magnes and Martin Buber. It also initiated a new debate on this important topic within the Jewish Israeli community. Later in August 2003, the debate was joined by Avraham Burg, a Knesset member who had been Speaker of the Knesset until earlier in the year, and a former chairman of the Jewish Agency. Burg challenged the arguments Benvenisti and Hanegbi had made, writing:

Here is what the prime minister should say to the people: ...

Do you want the greater Land of Israel? No problem. Abandon democracy. Let's institute an efficient system of racial separation here, with prison camps and detention villages. Qalqilya Ghetto and Gulag Jenin.

Do you want a Jewish majority? No problem. Either put the Arabs on railway cars, buses, camels, and donkeys and expel them en masse — or separate ourselves from them absolutely, without tricks and gimmicks. There is no middle path. We must remove all the settlements — all of them — and draw an internationally recognized border between the Jewish national home and the Palestinian national home. The Jewish Law of Return will apply only within our national home, and their right of return will apply only within the borders of the Palestinian state.

Do you want democracy? No problem. Either abandon the greater Land of Israel, to the last settlement and outpost, or give full citizenship and voting rights to everyone, including Arabs. The result, of course, will be

---

148 Haim Hanegbi's essay in Shavit, op. cit., is available at the same URL but <...itemNo=326324>.

that those who did not want a Palestinian state alongside us will have one in our midst, via the ballot box.

That's what the prime minister should say to the people. He should present the choices forthrightly: Jewish racialism or democracy. Settlements or hope for both peoples. False visions of barbed wire, roadblocks and suicide bombers, or a recognized international border between two states and a shared capital in Jerusalem...

Israel's friends abroad — Jewish and non-Jewish alike, presidents and prime ministers, rabbis and lay people — should choose as well. They must reach out and help Israel to navigate the road map toward our national destiny as a light unto the nations and a society of peace, justice and equality.[149]

The movement for a two-state outcome received a further boost in October 2003 when two veterans of the Taba negotiations of early 2001—Yossi Beilin, a former minister of the Israeli government, and Yasser Abed Rabboo, a former minister of the Palestinian Authority—jointly unveiled a new peace plan known as the "Geneva Accord." Not surprisingly, the new plan echoed many aspects of the skeletal agreement that the two sides had reached at Taba, but it added a considerable mass of new detail. P.A. leader Yasser Arafat had quietly supported the "unofficial" dialogue project that led to the new accord, while Ariel Sharon rejected the whole project and the accord in fierce terms. For his part, Beilin commented that the fact the project's participants had been able to agree on such a wide-ranging document put the lie to Sharon's claim that there was "no one to talk to" on the other side.

It was unclear what further progress the dialogue project that resulted in the accord could make so long as the Israeli participants in it continued to lack any official negotiating mandate. And even this promising endeavor—like Taba before it—seemed at odds with some of the principles we set forth earlier in our report, especially with regard to the rights of refugees and the future of Israeli settlements, notably those in and around Jerusalem. Nevertheless, once Israel's leadership should prove ready to move toward serious pursuit of peace, then the Geneva Accord would provide another helpful building-block that could considerably speed up negotiations toward a viable two-state outcome.

---

149 Avraham Burg, "A failed Israeli society collapses while its leaders remain silent," translated by J.J. Goldberg in *Forward* (New York), 29 August 2003; accessible at <www.forward.com/issues/2003/03.08.29/oped3.html>. It was not clear whether, when he urged the removal of "all the settlements," he was including in that designation the settlements in and around Jerusalem, or not.

"Final-Status" Issues in a One- or Two-State Model

In chapters 4 through 6 above, we explored how the various portions of the traditional final-status agenda might most helpfully be approached within a two-state paradigm. We noted that once the authoritative national-level negotiations on the final-status issues did belatedly get underway in late 2000 and early 2001, the negotiators were able—on all these supposedly very difficult issues—to significantly narrow the gaps between them. Along the way, they were able to "unpack" many previously intractable aspects of these agenda items and come up with creative and potentially workable approaches to them that might still, in the right circumstances, provide the basis for reaching a viable two-state solution.

In the present section, however, we will compare the kinds of proposals presented in those earlier chapters with some preliminary ideas on how these same final-status issues might be resolved in the context of a one-state paradigm.

Let us start (as we suggest the negotiators might profitably do) with the issue of Jerusalem. If a two-state model is used, numerous tricky questions regarding Jerusalem will require ingenious—and always momentous—answers. Within such a model should there be, essentially, a redivision of the city between the Palestinian and Israeli states? Would this redivision be effected through the construction of a solid fence with checkpoints, or would the city somehow be kept "open" for free movement around all of it by citizens of both states? How would this new line of separation be drawn?

Alternatively, if some separate special status is accorded to Jerusalem, as mandated in the U.N.'s 1947 partition plan, how would that work out in practice? How could the rights of the city's actual Israeli and Palestinian residents be assured? And how about the claims that non-Jerusalemites in both national communities have to Jerusalem as their national capital? Could those claims be met within a *corpus separatum* model?

With or without a *corpus separatum* for Jerusalem, how could free access to the city's many holy sites, and the thorny issue of control over them, be resolved?

The answers to each one of these questions is of intense concern, remember, not just to all Israelis and all Palestinians, but also to literally billions of Christians, Muslims, and Jews around the world. What effect would it have on these believers if, instead, authoritative Palestinian and Israeli national leaders stood up together and simply declared, "In line with all that is best in our religious and national traditions, we would like to tell you that we have decided to share this Holy City so that it can stay as a lively, livable city that will be the capital of the new, single state we have decided to build together?"

Under such a model, Jerusalem's situation as a city could, within a very short period of time, become normalized and considerably improved. No longer would housing and access to services within it be strictly segregated along national lines. No longer would one-third of the city's residents be trapped, essentially voiceless, in filthy ghettoes. No longer would hundreds of thousands of the city's indigenous sons and daughters be prevented from returning to the city of their birth. No longer would every slight tussle between the city's religious authorities threaten to launch a broad Jewish-Arab conflict with possibly worldwide consequences. No longer would millions of Palestinian Muslims and Christians be denied free access to sites very holy to their religion. Jerusalem could become—like Cape Town, or Brussels, or scores of other cities around the world—a vivacious city that is the pride of its polyglot residents, a center of the arts and culture, and a peaceful magnet for visitors from all around the world.

Then, if the Israelis and Palestinians discover they can find a way to share this most beloved and most hotly-contested of cities, what could stop them from finding a decent, democratic formula that would allow them to share the rest of the land they contest, as well?[150]

Next, consider the question of the settlements and their residents. We saw in chapter 4 that participants in the January 2001 negotiation in Taba made great progress toward reaching an agreement that involved making adjustments in the Green Line to enable 80 percent of the settlers living in the West Bank outside of Jerusalem to be included in the "final-status" territory of Israel. Despite the progress made at Taba, the negotiators there were still unable to reach an agreement. Nonetheless, the kind of outcome

---

150 Alternatively, as noted in chapter 5 above, a shared Jerusalem could be an important linchpin for the success of a two-state solution.

that they were working toward there seemed to us to be problematic in a number of ways and to raise a whole series of new and difficult questions. For example, the proposed annexations of land to Israel—in various parts of the West Bank including, massively, in and around Jerusalem—would leave many Palestinian communities cut off from each other, while allowing lines of communication between the annexed settlement blocs and Israel that look very vulnerable and no or few lines of communication among the settlement blocs themselves.

In addition, if the land of the West Bank and Gaza, which already comprises only 22 percent of the land of Mandate Palestine, is further reduced to allow for these annexations, what does that mean for the ability of the Palestinian state to absorb all those Palestinian refugees who might want to return to it? Then again, how acceptable is the idea of summarily swapping an area of present-day Israeli like the Triangle in and around Umm el-Fahm for those settlement blocs? Should such a land-swap even be considered unless there is a provision for, say, a referendum on this issue among all the area's residents? Would those residents carry the rights they have as Israeli citizens with them, or would they be forced to give them up?

Finally, there is the question of the 20 percent of the settlers who would still live east of any such proposed final boundary: What options would they be offered? Could we not expect that many of them would mount massive resistance to being faced with a choice between being uprooted from their home communities and staying where they are under Palestinian sovereignty?

We might ask, too, whether in a negotiation more equitably structured than that at Taba, the Palestinian side might be able to win a resolution on the settlements issue that seems more in line with the apparent requirement of international law that the settlements should simply be abandoned (as France's former colonial properties in Algeria were abandoned, or as colonizing populations in many other places around the world were also forced to give up their ill-gotten gains.)

An outcome based strictly on the requirements of international law might satisfy Palestinian claims for justice, but it would likely be very hard to "sell" to the Israeli public. It would moreover leave the settlers themselves in a position of having to give up homes that in some cases they have lived in for 30 years. Under a two-state solution, a more compassionate approach to the issue of the settlers might allow some portion of them to stay in their homes, provided they accepted Palestinian sovereignty and were willing to compensate their Palestinian neighbors for lands earlier confiscated to build the settlements. Some Palestinian negotiators have expressed openness to discussing such ideas, but our encounters during our trip indicated that very few Palestinians or settlers were at that point disposed to entertain such a solution.

Thus, if one remains within the optic of a two-state formula, the question of what to do with the settlers raises a host of tricky questions. In the context of a one-state outcome, however, this issue might be easier to resolve. Since we are taking as a given that the one state in question would be a normal (though intentionally binational) democracy, then all of its housing stock and other real estate east and west of the present Green Line would be open for residence, purchase, or rental by any citizen of the state on a quite non-discriminatory basis. And it goes without saying that within any such democracy loans to support home-building or home-purchase would also be available either on a totally non-discriminatory basis or on the basis of a reparative affirmative-action policy. So the present settlers could stay where they are once the issue of compensation has been addressed. But the housing stock in the settlements, like that in all of the unitary state, would be opened to purchase or rental by all citizens.

The main group whose interests would need special attention within this formula would be those Palestinians whose lands and properties have been expropriated to make way for the settlements and the network of settler-only roads and other facilities. Some of these Palestinians—for example, those whose lands have been summarily fenced off for "security" reasons or as so-called "nature reserves"—might fairly easily be able to regain control of previously expropriated real property. Others would not be able to. These latter Palestinians could be compensated for their loss by a mechanism similar to that which would be introduced in order to compensate Palestinians displaced in 1948 for properties they had been separated from inside present-day Israel that for whatever reason they could not regain possession of under the new peace agreement.

Finally, consider the question of those Palestinian refugees themselves. At Taba, the two parties started discussing an approach to this issue in which only very few of the refugees would be allowed to "return" to Israel. If they persisted in seeking return rather than resettlement, then most of the refugees would, according to the formula discussed at Taba, have had to accept a "return" either to some part of the West Bank or Gaza—parts of historic Palestine which were not, for the vast majority of them, their homeplaces—or, possibly, to that portion of presently Israeli land to be included in a future land swap. But the absorptive capacity of the West Bank is already very limited (and would be even more limited, if huge portions of its land and its prime housing stock are summarily annexed to Israel); and Gaza and the Triangle areas are both severely overcrowded. So within the context of a two-state solution, not many refugees could actually be offered a "return" to Palestine on terms that would give them a chance of making a decent livelihood. This would perpetuate the injustice meted out to the refugees for many decades now. It would also constitute a continuing cause of political vulnerability for the peace settlement.

Within the context of a one-state solution, however, a "return" on decent terms could be offered by the unitary state to a very much larger number of refugees since this state would by definition have control over the large land reserves inside Israel that are now held by the Israel Lands Authority (ILA), for the nearly exclusive benefit of "the Jewish people." If any fully democratic one-state approach is adopted, then those land reserves would have to come under the control of a state-affiliated body that is answerable to all the state's citizens rather than to a supranational body such as the ILA which putatively represents the interests of a global ethno-religious community.

If a one-state model is adopted, then the outcome that would likely result would in essence be a broad political bargain between the two nations regarding access to, and control over, land. The settlers would get to stay where they are; and a greater number of Palestinian refugees would get to return to the homeland—and to return closer, moreover, to their ancestral homeplaces—than would be able to undertake such a return under a two-state solution.

We have referred a little already, in the context of both Jerusalem and the settlements, to the complexity that the border issue assumes in the context of a two-state outcome. In the case of a one-state outcome, it becomes a non-issue. That is, if the goal is to create a one-state outcome, then the main border that needs to be dealt with is not the physical border between the two states but the mental border that exists in the heads of people on both sides of the national divide: that is, their reluctance to accept members of the "other" group as bearers of rights that are fully equal to those that they claim for themselves, and rights-bearers, moreover, alongside whom it is possible to think of living in harmony and equality.

Psychological Barriers to a One-State Approach

We do not want to underestimate the size of the psychological barrier faced—on both sides of the national divide—by any proposal to work toward the establishment of a unitary binational state. Nonetheless, the existing situation of deep and seemingly endless conflict is so unbearable for people in both communities that there is a real chance that bold visions that were previously swept aside as "too idealistic" or simply "unworkable" might now receive serious consideration.

What are these psychological barriers?

First of all, we have to recognize that each of these national communities perceives itself as a threatened group that must remain vigilant and alert to potential dangers if it is to have a chance of protecting its ever-fragile existence. For example, many Jewish Israelis also see themselves as a minority population that is embattled and shunned in the Middle East and worldwide. The history of the suffering of the Jewish people in their successive diasporas (and especially, the memory of the Holocaust) is still very vivid in the minds of many Jewish Israelis, who see Israel as a haven in which they can feel that the term "never again" has real meaning for them and their descendants. For their part, the Palestinians might be part of the majority "Arab" community throughout the broader Middle East, and be perceived that way by most Israelis. But most of them see themselves as a distinct minority within the land of Mandate Palestine, which they consider their ancestral homeland; and they see the presence of their people in the homeland as under great threat from Israeli expansionism. Many Palestinians also see themselves as shunned and subjected to discrimination by most of the Arab countries.

Understandably, therefore, many Palestinians have felt a deep desire to have a state of their own that can be their haven against the intrusions and harms inflicted by a hostile world.

We recognize that for many people in both these national communities, the idea of sharing political space with members of this particular "other" community might be a very hard one to accept. For many Palestinians, it has been extremely hard to see the Zionists' success in establishing a flourishing, Hebrew-speaking national community in a land that prior to 1948 hosted only a much smaller and more polyglot Jewish community. As has sometimes been the case in other colonized countries, members of the indigenous population have often responded to the arrival of the newcomers by avoiding contact with the colonizing people as much as possible and shunning them and their ways.

For many Jewish Israelis, simple human recognition of the Palestinians has seemed equally problematic. Many of the early Zionist organizers promised their followers that they would be taking them to "a land without a people," that would be a fit home for the "people without a land." And many Zionists have undoubtedly been people of high idealism, for whom the recognition that the land was not in fact unpopulated would have been hard to absorb. In addition, the linguistic, cultural, and historical links between the Palestinians and other Arabs has frequently made it seem to Jewish Israelis as if the Palestinians are just an advance bridgehead for a potentially threatening Arab "horde." There are many parallels here with the situation of apartheid-era Afrikaaners in South Africa, who justified their actions against their country's indigenous Black population on the basis that the struggle the country's Blacks were waging for equal rights was somehow connected to a mysterious and deadly "total onslaught" being planned against South Africa by Black nationalist leaders from throughout sub-Saharan Africa.

From some points of view, the "messy divorce," two-state option between Palestinians and Israelis may seem easier to many people in both communities than any unitary option, even an explicitly binational one.

For our part, we do not see the idea of a unitary binational outcome as a ploy whose intent is to scare Jewish Israelis into going along with a relatively generous version of the two-state outcome.

The unitary binational formula has numerous merits on its own account, as Judah Magnes and Martin Buber, and other Jewish leaders recognized 45 years ago. We suggest that if determined and sensitive efforts are made to start envisioning the benefits and possibilities of such a formula and actively to seek out lessons from the experience of other peoples who have successfully created intentionally multinational democracies elsewhere, then those efforts can start to gain success.

Criteria for a Just Settlement

In evaluating the foreseeable consequences of any proposed one- or two-state outcome, we suggest it would be helpful to return to the principles we enunciated at the end of chapter 1:

Ending the occupation: This very basic requirement means that no outcome that involves Israelis continuing to exercise control, Bantustan-style, over a Palestinian political entity can be judged acceptable (and neither would it prove sustainable). Of course, should the power imbalance ever be reversed, no solution involving Palestinian control over the Jewish Israelis would be acceptable, either.

Human Equality: This principle indicates clearly that, whether the outcome contains one state or two, within whatever entity results each individual citizen should have full and equal political rights. Such a state or states should have all the attributes of a democracy, including freedom of religious belief and the separation of state bodies from religious bodies. If there are two states, it further indicates that each of these states should have equal standing in the community of nations and equal powers of sovereignty, such as control over its natural resources, borders, and security affairs.

The principle of human equality might seem hard to satisfy within a two-state model since even with a total Israeli withdrawal to the pre-1967 line some 7.9 million Palestinians (or 6.8 million, if we set aside those Palestinians who are Israeli citizens) would be expected to satisfy their national aspirations in just 22 percent of the land of Mandate Palestine, while 6.2 million Israelis would exercise theirs within the remaining 78 percent. Luckily, access to land is not the only determinant of national well-being, and compensatory allocations of other factors could help to equalize the sit-

188

uation between the two peoples.[151] Evidently, though, within the context of any long-term settlement (or even without one), international financial aid should be distributed in a way that reduces rather than exacerbates the disparities between the economic levels enjoyed by the two peoples.

The principle of human equality would seem a relatively straightforward one to satisfy through a one-state formula. However, we realize that no state is culturally "neutral," and therefore that the cultural nature of the one state in question would be a very important issue. We heard both Israelis and Palestinians articulate their strong desire to be able to express their national and cultural self-realization within and through the state of which they are citizens. We therefore believe that any unitary political formula should also embody a significant, though not territorially based, degree of autonomy at the cultural level.[152] Many basic human rights, including rights in the spheres of language and other attributes of culture, cannot be exercised by persons living as individuals but must be exercised in the context of the communities that sustain them. We therefore consider that the principle of human equality itself leads to the conclusion that any unitary outcome should be one that is affirmatively committed to the principle that the Hebrew-speaking people of this state and its Arabic-speaking people can alike realize their cultural and community aspirations within it. In other words, though other forms of a unitary state are conceivable, the only kind of a one-state outcome that would seem to us to meet the "human equality" criterion would be one that is intentionally binational and bilingual, and bi- or multicultural.[153]

There are many helpful precedents around the world where people of different language groups and radically different cultures act together politically within the context of unitary democratic state that is multinational and multicultural. South Africa represents a particularly exciting example: it is a single democrat-

---

151 We would like, however, to restate our firm opposition to any allegedly "two-state" proposal that involves any radical truncation of the area given the Palestinian state.

152 This was the position espoused by the early Cultural Zionist philosopher Ahad Ha'am.

153 Each national community already includes a number of different "cultures," or at least subcultures. We would not want to see that diversity quashed in the context of any rigid pursuit of biculturalism.

ic country with eleven official languages, scores of different religious groups, and an active commitment to promoting linguistic diversity and the survival of indigenous languages.[154] Article 29 (2) of South Africa's 1994 Constitution states that "Everyone has the right to receive education in the official language or languages of their choice in public educational institutions where that education is reasonably practicable"; throughout the country, official notices are routinely published in a broad bouquet of the national languages. Belgium and Canada also provide worthwhile examples of states committed to creating a bicultural or multicultural society, though in Belgium (and, to a certain extent, in Canada) the constitutional provisions regarding language have a defined territorial dimension to them.

Equal rights and equal voice for all: Under a two-state formula, all Palestinians with the exception of those who are citizens of Israel should be expected to exercise their citizenship within the Palestinian state, and all Israeli citizens (whether Jewish or non-Jewish) to exercise theirs within Israel. In a one-state formula, each Palestinian and each Israeli should be seen as having an equal *prima facie* claim on the land and resources of Israel/Palestine, and an equal right to participate in its governance. Evidently, within either formula, a large-scale initial adjustment would be needed in order to deal with the Palestinians' remaining claims from the past against Israel, and to put an end to them.[155] This initial adjustment could also help to level the socio-economic playing field on which the members of the two nations engage with each other. (It should be noted, though, that many diaspora Palestinians have done well economically during their years of exile, so the economic encounter between the two peoples would by no means be a simple confrontation between "rich" Israelis and "poor" Palestinians.)

Within the context of a one-state formula, it would be necessary, but quite easy and straightforward, to enact constitutional provisions that would prevent any majoritarian domination of the

---

154 Considerable interesting information about South Africa's language and other cultural policies can be accessed at <http://www.cyberserv.co.za/users/~jako/lang/>.

155 It would also be helpful if property claims that the Mizrachi Israelis have against the Arab governments, and that many Arab nationals have against Israel, could be resolved in a simultaneous but separate process, since these claims are not directly a part of the Israeli-Palestinian relationship.

political system. Such provisions could be applied in a democratic way in the unitary state of Israel/Palestine, as they already have been for many years in many other countries of the world. The Hebrew-speaking Israeli community would still be robustly in existence in, and enjoying the fruits of, its national homeland. But it would no longer be exercising exclusionary dominion there over the remnants of another people; instead, it would be living in respectful coexistence with the robust Palestinian community also living in and enjoying the fruits of its national homeland.

Regarding how the Palestinians and Israelis would get from the "here" of the present difficult situation to the "there" of either a one-state or a two-state outcome, the principle of "equal rights and equal voice for all direct stakeholders" is also, as noted in chapter 6 and elsewhere, very important. We merely repeat here that we see no justification at all for the continued exclusion of diaspora Palestinians from taking a proportionate part in determining the future of their country. They are direct stakeholders in the situation in their homeland and a way must be found for their voice, experience, claims, and wisdom to be proportionately represented in all deliberations over the final outcome.[156]

Nonviolence: We affirm the Quaker tradition that stresses the intimate connection between ends and means. Therefore, we suggest that not only is the attainment of a peaceable situation in Israel/Palestine the goal, but in addition, the use of respectful, nonviolent means of persuasion is by far the most effective way to reach this goal. It is on this basis, and on the basis of our belief in human equality, that we urge all those concerned with the situation in Palestine/Israel—both direct stakeholders and other parties—to do everything they can to foster a climate of equality and mutual respect between Israelis and Palestinians in which these two peoples can calmly, without the use or threat of coercion by any party, decide firstly whether they want to build their future relationship within the context of two states or one, and secondly, how to attain their chosen goal.

---

156 One friend asked whether this means that diaspora Jews should also be given a proportionate voice in these deliberations. We note, however, that diaspora Jews have nearly all been given an opportunity to express their identification with Israel by making *aliya* (immigrating to Israel and gaining Israeli citizenship), and many of them have done so. Diaspora Palestinians have not been given an opportunity to return to their homeland, and many or most of them still suffer the vulnerability of statelessness. We therefore do not see the two situations as comparable.

The principle of nonviolence should also inform the security/military policies of the resulting state or states. We recognize that each of these peoples has suffered greatly at the hands of the other; but it is our expectation that if the peace negotiations between them are held in a spirit of human equality, mutual respect, and reciprocity, a good deal of the currently strong climate of mistrust between them can be dissipated. In any case, whether a one-state or a two-state outcome is the target, any peace talks will need to include a strong focus on measures that can reciprocally build confidence between the parties in the security sphere along the way, as well as long-term safeguards—perhaps supplemented by security guarantees from outside powers—against the possibility that either party might retreat from its commitments.

In some senses, the negotiation for a unitary, binational state outcome may seem harder at the outset than that for a two-state settlement, since it would require that civil society on both sides of the national divide grapple with tough issues of redefining national goals and clarifying national priorities while simultaneously starting to grant members of the "other" nation a true recognition of their equal humanity and future equality of status as co-citizens of the future state. So if it is to be successful this kind of negotiation might well require the building of greater trust along the way than would the crafting of a two-state outcome. But that trust would be a continuing source of strength in the relationship between the two peoples once implementation begins.

In the context of a one-state scenario, the security aspects of the relationship between the two groups would also have to undergo a radical re-evaluation along the way, since the goal would be the establishment of only a single military apparatus, under a single, unified national command. For Jewish Israelis this redefinition of the nature of the state to which they belong would have considerable effects on the kind of security apparatus with which they would want the new state to be endowed. As in South Africa, the move toward a unitary, fully democratic state could be expected to lead to a large-scale reduction of the country's military establishment.

We realize too that, in addition to the harm each of these two nations has suffered from the other, each has also suffered at the hands of other neighbors over the past decades. In Israel, its people's memories of those past sufferings and the perception of its policy-makers that many of those external threats still exist have led to heavy investment in maintaining a military apparatus much larger and more expensive than anything that would be warranted if Israel faced "only" the threat that they perceive comes from the Palestinians. Reaching a respectful, viable peace agreement with the Palestinians will not eliminate all those external threats to Israel, but it will reduce many of them. In particular, we already know that in the context of a viable two-state outcome, if the Palestinian state is established within all the Palestinian lands occupied by Israel in 1967, and if Israel also withdraws fully from Syria's still-occupied Golan, then the Arab states have promised that they will build normal, peaceful relations with Israel. If, as we certainly hope, that promise is fulfilled, this new regional web of relationships would radically reduce the "strategic" threat that Israel claims it faces from various other, non-Palestinian, Arab parties.

We therefore judge that, whether progress toward a truly sustainable Palestinian Israeli peace is pursued within a one-state or a two-state context, this pursuit will bring with it the prospect of a large-scale reduction of Israel's military establishment, as well as of the much smaller security apparatus maintained by the Palestinians. These two peoples can then redirect a considerable portion of what they currently spend on military/security items into much more productive and peace-enhancing enterprises.

[9]

International Involvement

Peace is a never-ending process, the work of many decisions
by many people in many countries....
It cannot be forced on the smallest nation or enforced by the largest.
—*Oscar Arias Sánchez, Nobel peace laureate, 1987*

For decades now, the situation in Israel/Palestine has been a matter of intense concern to millions of people and scores of governments all around the world. This is the case for a complex mixture of strategic, religious, and emotional reasons. And if intense international concern with the situation in Israel/Palestine is a given, so too is a high level of actual international involvement at the military, diplomatic, and economic levels. Arab nations, European nations, Russia, Japan, and others have all manifested their close concern for the situation there in different ways. In the past quarter century, however, no country outside Palestine/Israel has been more deeply involved with the situation there than the U.S., and this involvement has made a number of crucial contributions, in particular, to the ability of successive Israeli governments to continue to pursue their settlement project in the occupied West Bank and Gaza.

In this chapter we will therefore first describe the impact of U.S. involvement. Then we will hear the views of some Palestinians, some Israelis, and some of their Arab neighbors. Finally, we will explore some of the ways that concerned citizens from around the world can respond constructively to the multiple tragedies of developments in Israel/Palestine.

U.S. Involvement

As we traveled throughout the Israeli-occupied West Bank and Gaza Strip, we saw direct evidence of the considerable de facto help that the U.S. government has given to Israel in its pursuit and defense of the settlement project there. We traveled on high-speed bypass roads, from which Palestinians are barred, built with the blessing of the U.S. government. We saw many of the massive, U.S.-made armored bulldozers that IDF engineers had recently used to demolish Palestinian homes, or to dig the trenches or build the earthen barricades that isolated Palestinian towns and villages from neighboring communities. Much of the cost of the settlement project was made possible by the very large amounts of aid that the U.S. has given to Israel continuously since 1967. When we visited Karnei Shomron, we learned that a U.S. corporation, the American Greeting Card company, has a manufacturing plant there. Karnei Shomron's Sondra Baras, like many other settlers in the occupied territories, is allowed to retain her U.S. citizenship while living in the West Bank under the protection of the Israeli military and with all the rights and privileges of an Israeli citizen.

As noted previously, Israel's entire settlement project—in East Jerusalem, the rest of the West Bank, the Gaza Strip, and Syria's Golan—is in direct contravention of Article 49 of the Fourth Geneva Convention and other basic provisions of international humanitarian law. Indeed, Article 147 of the Fourth Geneva Convention also spells out explicitly that, in the context of a military occupation, "extensive destruction and appropriation of [the indigenous residents'] property, not justified by military necessity and carried out unlawfully and wantonly" actually constitutes a "grave breach" of the Convention—that is, a war crime whose perpetrators are (under Article 146) liable to criminal prosecution by any state party to the Geneva Conventions.[157]

Throughout the first thirteen years of the occupation, the U.S. government had remained part of the broad international consensus that judged that Israel's settlement project was fundamentally illegal. In March 1980, for example, the U.S. joined other members of the U.N. Security Council in adopting resolution 465, which restated the Council's long-standing judgment that, "[All] measures taken by Israel to change the physical character, demographic composition, institutional structure or status of the Palestinian and other Arab territories occupied since 1967, including Jerusalem, or any part thereof, have no legal validity and that

---

157   Several of Israel's other practices in the West Bank and Gaza also constitute "grave breaches" under Article 147.

Israel's policy and practices of settling parts of its population and new immigrants in those territories constitute a flagrant violation of the Fourth Geneva Convention."[158]

But in early 1981, the U.S. position changed. That was the year Ronald Reagan became president. Soon after his inauguration, Reagan stated that though his administration still considered the settlements "obstacles to peace," henceforth the U.S. no longer judged them to be illegal. There followed a long string of U.S. vetoes of Security Council resolutions that sought to restate, essentially, the judgments expressed in Resolution 465. Those vetoes effectively silenced the Security Council on the question of settlements. Resolution 465 still stood on the books as formal U.N. policy—along with scores of other unheeded resolutions denouncing Israel's policies in the various Arab territories it occupied. But the repeated U.S. vetoes on the settlements issue gave crucial political protection throughout the 1980s and 1990s to those who wanted the settlement project to succeed.

Throughout those same two decades, the U.S. was cementing its position as the principal outside broker of peace diplomacy between Israelis and Arabs, including between Israelis and Palestinians. Palestinian leaders always felt that the U.S. was distinctly biased in favor of Israel. They accepted Washington's role, however, because they saw no realistic alternative—and also because they believed that if they could only convince the U.S. of the legitimacy of the Palestinians' claims, the United States would then pressure Israel to respond positively to Palestinian demands. Palestinian leader Yasser Arafat in particular was convinced that the U.S. role as Israel's chief supporter meant that only with U.S. acquiescence could the Palestinians achieve their political goals: he stated repeatedly that "the U.S. holds the key to Israel."[159] Thus, under presidents from Jimmy Carter through George W. Bush, the U.S. continued to monopolize the peacemaking on this issue of great global concern.

---

158 The text of the resolution is available at <http://domino.un.org/UNISPAL.nsf/db942872b9eae454852560f6005a76fb/5aa254a1c8f8b1cb852560e50075d7d5!OpenDocument>. The resolution called on the government and people of Israel to dismantle existing settlements and to cease constructing or planning any new ones. It also requested other states "not to provide Israel with any assistance to be used specifically in connection with settlements in the occupied territories."

159 See, for example, *Time*, 11 Nov., 1974.

At the beginning of the 1990s, the U.S. made a notably constructive, though regrettably short-lived, contribution to this diplomacy. In March 1991, after a U.S.-led invasion successfully reversed Iraq's occupation (and attempted annexation) of Kuwait, U.S. President George H.W. Bush told a specially convened joint session of Congress, "We must do all that we can to close the gap between Israel and the Arab states and between Israelis and Palestinians." He spelled out that "A comprehensive peace must be grounded in United Nations Security Council resolutions 242 and 338 and the principle of territory for peace. ... The time has come to put an end to Arab-Israeli conflict."[160]

At the end of October 1991, Bush and Soviet President Mikhail Gorbachev convened a historic peace conference in Madrid that brought together Israel's Prime Minister Yitzhak Shamir, the foreign ministers of Syria, Lebanon, and Jordan (none of which had made peace with Israel at that point), and a high-ranking Palestinian group that participated as part of a "joint Jordanian-Palestinian delegation." After the momentous opening of that conference, the Bush administration moved the subsequent rounds of Arab-Israeli diplomacy to two different types of fora. There were bilateral negotiating groups between Israel and each of the Arab delegations and multilateral groups that addressed regional issues like security, water, regional economic development, and refugees.[161] The most successful of the bilateral negotiations was the one conducted between Israel and Jordan after that track was split off from the Israeli-Palestinian track in 1993. In October 1994, amid much fanfare, the leaders of Jordan and Israel signed a full final peace agreement between their countries.

By the time our group made its journey to Palestine/Israel, the broader regional environment within which the Israelis and Palestinians were dealing with each other had changed considerably from that encountered by the Quaker fact-finders who visited in 1968 and in 1979. By 2002, Israel had peace treaties of proven durability with two of the neighboring Arab states, Egypt and Jordan. The peace treaty with Egypt, the Arab world's most pop-

---

160 This portion of Bush's speech is available at <http://www.brookings.edu/dybdoc-root/press/appendix/appen_l.htm>.

161 For the Palestinian refugees, the part of the refugee discussion that most mattered was their long-standing (and distinctly bilateral) claim against Israel; little progress was made on the issue in this multilateral process.

ulous state, had survived since 1979. That with Jordan, which shares a lengthy land border with Israel and contains many residents and citizens of Palestinian background, had lasted since 1994. In addition, on the Syrian front, a ceasefire negotiated between Israel and Syria in 1974 had also proved durable for nearly thirty years.

In the Palestinian Israeli sphere, the U.S. continued to be the predominant outside sponsor of this portion of the diplomacy throughout the 1990s. But in late 1992, when the Israeli and Palestinian leaderships started to explore the possibility of conducting a bilateral peace negotiation separate from the cumbersome Israeli-Jordanian-Palestinian negotiation mandated by the Madrid conference, they did so using the good offices of the government of Norway. That exploration led to the conclusion of the historic Oslo Accords in September 1993. But even before the accords were signed, the negotiators had all reached agreement on the judgment that they would need to reengage the close commitment of the U.S. government in subsequent rounds of their peace diplomacy if it was to have any chance to succeed. Thus, despite their name, the Oslo Accords were signed in September 1993 on the White House lawn.[162] From then on, the "Oslo" process became a U.S.-dominated venture.

By 2002, it was clear that the grand experiment of Oslo had failed. Some weeks before our visit to Israel-Palestine, the administration of President George W. Bush had taken the constructive step of convening a "Quartet" mechanism that brought the U.N., the E.U., and Russia into a joint peacemaking effort with the U.S. in the Middle East. Quartet diplomats consulted closely with officials in Israel, the P.A., and elsewhere, and in the fall of 2002 they drafted a plan called a "performance-based roadmap to a permanent two-state solution to the Israeli-Palestinian conflict." The Roadmap's text was not formally published until April 30, 2003 (though its terms had become common knowledge some months earlier). It established a timetable for such steps as: reforming the Palestinian leadership; Israel's dismantlement of some of the settlement "outposts" that even the Israeli government itself judged to be illegal; the establishment of a Palestinian state within "provisional" borders; a broader freeze on Israeli settlement activity; and the negotiation of an (undetermined) final peace agreement.

162 Two members of our working party were present at this ceremony.

According to the Roadmap, each of the parties—the Israelis, the Palestinians, and the international community—should undertake the tasks assigned to it in parallel with the performance of their respective tasks by the other parties.[163]

The Roadmap had a number of weaknesses. Like Oslo, it failed to spell out a convincing and detailed description of the final outcome, but instead prescribed a multi-year transition period that would lead to an undetermined outcome. Under the Roadmap, moreover, negotiation of final-status issues would not even begin until the third of the three transitional stages prescribed. Where the Oslo Accords had allowed the return of at least some diaspora Palestinians to the homeland, the Roadmap now kept all the diaspora Palestinians in their state of exile from their homeland, disfranchised, and without a voice throughout the process of transition. It did not specify any consequences that either Israelis or Palestinians would face if they failed to comply with the Roadmap's plan of actions. The Quartet members did not commit themselves to any particular borders for the Palestinian state that they envisaged—or even for the "provisional" state with which the Palestinians were to be content until 2005 or sometime thereafter, though White House officials did spell out that the (eventual) Palestinian state should enjoy "contiguity" of territory.

These were all evident weaknesses in the Roadmap's approach. Nevertheless, the Roadmap did perhaps have the potential of acting as a useful diplomatic vehicle through which the Bush administration could reengage in Palestinian-Israeli peacemaking, and engage the energies and input of other, non-U.S. sponsors into the process, if he should determine that that was what he wanted to do. (His trajectory in launching the Roadmap recalled that of his father 12 years earlier, in that he reengaged in this diplomacy in the immediate aftermath of a U.S. military victory over Iraq.)

As we noted in chapter 4, as part of the political/diplomatic activity conducted around the Roadmap, in March 2003 the PLC approved the establishment of a new post of Palestinian prime minister, and Mahmoud Abbas took up the job. In May 2003, just a few weeks after the U.S. forces' military victory against the

---

163 The text of the Road Map is available at
<http://www.state.gov/r/pa/prs/ps/2003/20062pf.htm>.

Saddam Hussein regime in Iraq, intense diplomatic activity by U.S. and other Quartet diplomats succeeded in winning approval of the Roadmap from both the Israeli and Palestinian leaderships. (The Palestinian government expressed unconditional approval. The Israeli government attached fourteen reservations to its approval of the plan.[164]) Acting on the basis of these expressions of approval, Bush attended a historic summit meeting in early June in Aqaba, Jordan, along with Abbas, Sharon, and Jordan's King Abdullah. At a media event after the summit, Abbas said, "Our goal is two states, Israel and Palestine, living side by side in peace and security." Sharon said, "It is in Israel's interest not to govern the Palestinians, but for the Palestinians to govern themselves in their own state. A democratic Palestinian state fully at peace with Israel will promote the long-term security and well-being of Israel as a Jewish state."[165] However, the initial momentum that the success of this summit seemed to provide for the peacemaking did not last very long. Significantly, too, the confident predictions that had been voiced by some supporters of the U.S.-U.K. invasion of Iraq, to the effect that toppling Saddam Hussein's regime would make peace in the Palestinian-Israeli conflict easier to achieve, proved to be totally unfounded. By the end of summer 2003, the Israeli government and Palestinian militants were once again locked into their ongoing cycle of killings.

We have given special effort to trying to discern clearly the role that people who share our concern from around the world should play. What can be done to support the efforts of the peace-and-justice movements within Palestinian and Israeli society? Can we help to transform U.S. government policy into one that truly helps to build a hope-filled reconciliation in the Holy Land? Can we help other forces in global society, including the U.N., governments other than the U.S. government, and international civil society, to make a real contribution to building peace in this vital region?

Before we explore these questions, let us report what some of the most concerned pro-peace activists from inside the conflicted communities told us on this score, during our visit.

---

164 The text of these reservations can be accessed at <http://electronicintifada.net/referencelibrary/keydocuments/doc_page104.shtml>.

165 The text of all the public statements made at the Aqaba summit can be found at <http://usinfo.state.gov/regional/nea/potus/texts2003/030604bush.htm>.

Pleas from the Conflict Zone

In Gaza, Palestinian human rights advocate Raji Sourani described the many differences that he and other members of the global human rights movement see between a strictly international-law-based approach to issues like settlements and the rights of the Palestinian refugees, and the approach the U.S. sought to implement during the 1990s. "Our position is that the Fourth Geneva Convention applies in the occupied territories, and so does all the body of international law regarding the inherent right of refugees to return to their home," Sourani told us. He noted that the International Committee of the Red Cross, which is responsible for implementing the Geneva Conventions, had recently restated its judgment that the Fourth Geneva Convention still applies to all the occupied territories. But, he said, "The U.S. legal advisors deny and ignore the applicability of the Fourth Geneva Convention. The U.S. just says, 'Put all these issues about land, settlements, and the refugees back to the direct negotiations between the parties.'" His comment on that advice was that it amounted to putting a sumo wrestler and a small child in a room together with instructions to "sort out your differences between yourselves."

Sourani's many years of work as a human rights advocate had gotten him into considerable trouble with both the Israeli authorities and also—during its time in existence in Gaza in the 1990s—with the P.A. For a while in the mid-1990s, he recalled, the leaders of the P.A. were so heavily invested in the Oslo process that they even opposed the efforts of local and international human rights workers to win support for the international law position on such issues as settlements, human rights, and international standards for due process.

We asked Sourani what strategy might be pursued now, given that the Oslo process seemed definitely to have failed. "The United States could still pursue an ethical, law-based policy," he said. But he warned that if it did not do so, "no one should expect the Palestinians to be 'good victims.'"

In Jerusalem, Naim Ateek of the Sabeel Center stressed that help for the Palestinians could in theory come from a number of different sources—though he sounded notably pessimistic about the U.N., saying simply "It cannot do what it should." Of the

Europeans, he said, "They could help, though they do tend to bow to the Americans. ... The Arab countries could give us more backing in the diplomacy, though they won't or can't do so. The Palestinians see a series of closed doors! However, there are two doors that could open for us: in the United States, and in Israel itself."

The U.S., Ateek stressed,

> could change the situation completely, if it chose to. But we have great frustration on that score, since the U.S. seems silent and complicit regarding Israel's policies. Do we see any chance for a real policy change? Not in the U.S. Congress, that seems clear. And meanwhile, President Bush just seems totally focused on 'chasing terrorists.'

> We see an 'axis' in the U.S.A. that prevents a change in policy: it consists of the Christian Zionists,[166] the Jewish lobby, and the right-wing Republicans. Their combined forces are formidable. Between them, they work to block any serious help coming to the Palestinians, and any real pursuit of truth and justice in this arena.

Regarding Israel, he said, "We do not know how or when change will happen there. But we think it's more likely to happen in Israel than in the U.S.A."

From the Israeli portion of the pro-peace camp, meanwhile, Naomi Chazan was forthright in her discussion with us regarding the need for international intervention. She had told us that, in her view, the ultimate objective was clear ("some combination of the Clinton proposal, what was discussed at Taba, and the Saudi plan"), but that what had been lacking since the beginning of 2001 was "a diplomatic channel that will help us get there." She said she judged that international intervention was urgently needed at four different levels. First, the deployment of international forces on the ground was "essential—because all the current friction comes from the proximity of the two sides." Second, she saw the convening of an international conference as an essential step in

---

166 Christian Zionists are people who believe that the "ingathering of the Jews" into Israel is an important precursor to the Second Coming of Christ, and therefore something to be actively encouraged. For many Christian Zionists, their position is based on a literal reading of the Book of Revelation, including portions that indicate that after the ingathering of the Jews is complete most people who are not Christian believers will perish in an event called the "Rapture," and the only Jews to survive will be those who have been converted to Christianity by that event. The support that Christian Zionists have shown for Israel's settlement project in the West Bank has been a source of concern to many Jewish people in Israel and elsewhere, as well as to many Christians.

restarting the diplomacy. Third, an international monitoring and supervisory force would be needed to implement any peace plan. Fourth, she said, "We may even need to return to the idea of an international mandate over the West Bank and Gaza." As recent, successful examples of such a mandate she cited the U.N. mandate over Namibia in 1989-90 and the U.N.'s more recent transitional regime in East Timor.[167]

Views from the Region

In addition to traveling to Israel and Palestine, we all spent a few days in Jordan, and smaller groups of us visited Egypt, Lebanon, and Syria. All these countries have been intimately involved with "the Palestine problem" since its beginning. All were involved in one or more wars against Israel from 1948 on— though as noted above, Egypt and Jordan have now been at peace with Israel for many years. All have hosted substantial numbers of Palestinian refugees. (In Jordan's case, the number of citizens of refugee origin exceeds that of Jordanians of indigenous, "East Bank" origin.) The attitudes of the citizens and leaders of these countries are an important factor in any peacemaking effort. During our sojourns in those countries, many people were generous with the time they gave to meeting us and explaining their point of view. Here, we will recount just a few highlights of what we heard, in the hope of sketching out some significant dimensions of the broader regional environment within which the Palestinians and Israelis deal with each other.

In Egypt, Foreign Minister Ahmed Maher el-Sayed described his country's policy, based on the long-standing ties it has with both Palestinians and Israelis, as being "to push for ... mutual comprehension, to work for peace. We believe that the voice of moderation exists on both sides." He said that for a long time the U.S. had claimed that it was the only outside power entitled to sponsor Israeli-Palestinian peacemaking:

> And of course, they have been biased towards the Israelis. But we are passing through a period when things are changing. The U.S. has realized that despite its attachment to Israel, there is another side to the story, and the sense of fairness, that I believe is one of the characteristics

---

167 Chazan was speaking many months before the question arose of what role the U.N. should play in Iraq.

of the Americans, is now trying to emerge; and there is also a realization that all the interests of the West are threatened. The Israelis will not disappear and the Palestinians will not disappear—therefore it is essential to have a modus vivendi.

The Egyptian minister zeroed in on the importance of what he called "the moral aspect of the conflict." "Accepting the 'other' is important," he said. "Minds need to be dealt with as well as the material situation—to show that even when people have conflicts of interest they can still accommodate each other. Sometimes in the heat of conflict they forget that human beings are involved. They don't see people as individuals, people just like themselves." He advised Quakers that our role could be, "To remind both sides [of those truths]. And the way to do that is to work to make an agreement that allows people to live together. The Qur'an says that if you kill one man, you kill all men—the sanctity of human life. We should all encourage courageous people on both sides to speak out. Actually, at the end of the day, the Israelis and Palestinians are very much alike!"

In Jordan, we had a poignant meeting with Kamel Abu Jaber, the president of the country's Higher Media Council. Back in 1991, Abu Jaber had been Jordan's foreign minister: it was he who headed the joint Jordanian-Palestinian delegation at the Madrid peace conference. He talked eloquently about how the hopes of peace and well-being that were raised at the time of that conference had subsequently been smashed, and the intense anguish that process of disillusionment had caused him. "In my own speech at Madrid, I said that my own 'dream of peace' was that every Jordanian child could have at least a glass of milk in the morning," he said. "But Israel has stolen this energy for peace, this dream."

He said that at that point (2002) he was far less hopeful about the future than he had been in 1991, or at the time of the signing of the Oslo Accords in 1993. "I'm pessimistic because Israel is moving to the extreme right. ... Now, Sharon has wrecked Oslo and is against a Palestinian state. ... And the U.S. has moved to the extreme right, too."

He told us he had few hopes from U.S. diplomacy, though he took pains to point out that his criticism of current U.S. policy was not part of any broader anti-Americanism. "I am the product of American education—even American Quaker education," he said. He recalled fondly the American Quaker, John Sutton, who had established a school in Amman in 1928 called the Bishop's School, where Abu Jaber had been a student just one class ahead of the late King Hussein.

Abu Jaber spoke about the concern with which he and other Jordanians had heard well-placed Israeli political figures advocate the option of "transferring" Palestinians out of the occupied territories and even, possibly, out of Israel itself. "As though the Palestinians were bugs and cockroaches! They talk about putting them in the Jordanian desert or in Iraq." He said that any further expulsion of Palestinians to Jordan would place an unbearable burden on Jordan:

> We have already borne such a large share of responsibility for the refugees, more than anyone else. … The main constraint is water. Even here, in this middle-class neighborhood, we only get water once every two weeks, in tanker trucks like the one you saw in the street. Some people only get it once a month. And it's getting worse … Of course we are afraid of what Sharon will do. He says Jordan *is* Palestine.

In both Syria and Lebanon, we met with religious as well as secular leaders. In Syria, we were graciously received by the patriarch of the Syrian Orthodox Church and the Director of Abu Nour Islamic Foundation, among other religious leaders. The patriarch, Zakka Iwas, is just one of a number of heads of eastern churches headquartered in Syria. He received us in the spacious new church complex that the denomination was building on government-donated land north of Damascus.

"Naturally we side with the Arabs," he told us. "This is an Arab country. And our church has institutions in Palestine—in Jerusalem and Bethlehem. We pray for peace! But the mechanism for reaching it—we leave that to the politicians." He told us, "When President Bush referred to Ariel Sharon as 'a man of peace,' that was a travesty." Gesturing toward a gilded icon of Jesus hanging on the wall, he said, "That is a man of peace! There's no way you can compare Sharon to him."

Iwas' church has 2,000-year-old roots in Syria. Its liturgical language is Syriac, a version of Aramaic, the language that Jesus of Nazareth most likely spoke. Iwas told us the church has good relations with the Muslims who make up around 85 percent of Syria's population. But like a number of other church leaders we met with while we were in the Middle East he warned explicitly that these inter-religious links could be threatened if local Muslims perceived

U.S. government actions as being aimed against Muslims as such. He expressed appreciation for Arab leaders—including those in Syria and Iraq—who had declared that no anti-Christian actions would be tolerated inside their countries. "Luckily in Syria we have a long friendship between Muslims and Christians—and even with the Jews when they were still here," he said.

In Lebanon, our members spoke with representatives of many of the religious denominations and religion-linked groups that are part of the country's complex social mosaic. One Lebanese intellectual we met was Naif Krayyim, the Chairman of the Al-Manar television station, which is owned by the predominantly Shiite Muslim Hezbollah ("Party of God"). Hezbollah was founded in late 1982, in response to the large-scale invasion and occupation of Lebanon that Ariel Sharon—then Israel's defense minister—had launched some months earlier. Hezbollah started as a resistance movement, with its first goal being to liberate all of Lebanon from Israel's occupation. But it also became a broad social movement and a political party that, when we visited in 2002, had eight seats in the Lebanese parliament.

Hezbollah used many different tactics in its struggle to liberate Lebanon from Israel's military occupation. These included armed attacks (some, but not all of them, against civilians) and broad, very effective social organizing. In May 2000 it achieved its goal. Eighteen years after Sharon sent the IDF into Lebanon another Israeli government ordered a unilateral withdrawal from the country, with no political strings attached. Hezbollah supporters (and many other Arabs) judged that that outcome vindicated their use of armed resistance.[168]

Our sub-group had an extended and open discussion with Krayyim about the morality and utility of violence. He maintained that many years of simply waiting for the implementation of U.N. resolutions had not brought satisfaction either to the Palestinians or to the people of Lebanon. "We don't advocate violence willy-nilly," he said. "But the occupation itself is violence, also." Our members described traditional Quaker testimonies that reject the use of violence and coercion, and advocate the use of active non-violence to combat injustice and violence. Krayyim responded by

---

168 By one count, the IDF had been in South Lebanon for 22 years by then, since first establishing a bridgehead position there in March 1978.

focusing on various Qur'anic injunctions to limit aggression to the level used by your enemy and to avoid overreacting. However, he also stressed his view that it is legitimate to defend oneself and to fight against an occupation force.

For many years, the U.S. State Department has placed Hezbollah—and some Palestinian organizations—on its influential list of "Foreign Terrorist Organizations." Because of that designation, the U.S. government has refused to engage in contacts with the organization. For his part, Krayyim insisted that engaging in dialogue is always desirable. "Indeed, it is a requirement. And this is happening ... with all these embassies except the United States— such as with the English, French, Italians, Spanish, etc." He said that Hezbollah also had contacts with Jewish individuals, though not with Israelis, and with non-governmental groups in the U.S.

He expressed sympathy for the situation of the Palestinian refugees still in Lebanon but stressed that the best solution was for the refugees to return to their own country: "They need to go back to that entity. A Palestinian should go back to the place that he left. If he wants to stay here, where he is, then okay—it is his right to ask for citizenship here. But it is also the right of the Lebanese to give the answer to that request that suits them."

He described his ideal vision of the future as having a Middle East that looks like other regions of the world, "especially those enjoying peace and prosperity." He did not speak directly to the issue of whether this peaceful region would include an Israeli state, though he had told us earlier that one of Hezbollah's main objectives was, "to speak to the Jews who came to Palestine without knowing the facts" (that is, without understanding that there had already been an indigenous population living in Palestine before they arrived), and to tell them they would not feel safe until they "go back where you came from and give the Palestinians their rights."

Mobilizing International Energies for Peace

We place great stress on the principle that in any conflict the people who are directly involved in it should be empowered and encouraged to take responsibility for talking with each other and working together to find a reasonable outcome. However, in the context of the Palestinian-Israeli conflict as it had evolved by 2002-2003, it seemed that many people in both societies were still so traumatized by the violence, pain, and despair that they had suffered that they were almost unable to figure out how to use peaceable means to reach the compromise outcome that they felt to be acceptable.

At the same time, many actors elsewhere in the international community also had a large (if still distinctly secondary) stake in the stability of Israel/Palestine; and some of these actors, in addition, bore some responsibility for prolonging key aspects of the conflict, such as the occupation, the settlement project, and the use and encouragement of violence. Therefore we think it is not only appropriate but also necessary that people of goodwill from throughout the international community—along with governments, non-governmental and inter-governmental organizations—should engage actively in helping both Palestinians and Israelis reach the compromises needed to build the peace that the vast majority of people in both societies desire. We propose, moreover, that the four principles we spelled out in chapter 1 provide a useful framework within which to do this.

The *U.S. government* is the outside actor with the greatest direct involvement in the affairs of Israel/Palestine and the greatest ability to influence the actions of the parties there. It is therefore the outside party that has both the greatest responsibility for transforming that situation into one of hope and healthy relationships, and the greatest potential for doing so.

During our visit to Israel/Palestine, we heard peace activists in both the Palestinian and Israeli communities pleading for meaningful engagement from the U.S. (as well as other international actors). Seeking to steer the U.S. government's policy in a pro-peace direction should therefore be a joint project, to be undertaken by close cooperation among pro-peace forces in those communities as well as their allies working within U.S. society. U.S. peace-and-justice activists working on this issue face many challenges. There is a need to overcome the deep reluctance of many U.S. politicians—and other members of the U.S. political elite—to say anything that might be construed as critical of Israel. There is a need to find ways to do this that do not echo or reinforce the voices of anti-Semitism that persist in U.S. society as in many other places around the world. There is a need to understand and explain the roots and nature of violence in both the Palestinian and Israeli communities while making it clear that all such violence is offensive and counterproductive, and much of it quite illegal.

We note that the Christian Zionist community worldwide, but especially within the U.S., gives considerable support to Israel's settlement project, as do conservative elements within the Jewish community. Many Christian Zionists, moreover, espouse a "territorial maximalist" view of the Zionist project, arguing that the whole of the West Bank should be peopled by Jews in order to hasten the Second Coming of Christ.

We, however, continue quietly to affirm that—as Quakers have traditionally said—"There is that of God in everyone." We reject the belief that Jewish Israeli people have a claim to ownership and control of Jerusalem, the rest of the West Bank, and Gaza that supersedes the claims—and even the rights—of other communities that have dwelt in those areas for centuries or even longer. We note that in July 2002, Friends United Meeting, an organization representing Quakers from eight countries including the U.S., issued a minute on Palestine/Israel that stated,

> The belief among some Christians that unquestioning support for [the then-current Israeli policy in the occupied territories] might hasten Christ's Second Coming is doing grievous harm to possibilities for peace, justice, and the application of international law, and has especially impacted the Palestinian Christian community remaining in the area. Christ's purpose is that all might have life and live it more abundantly. We reject as contrary to the Good News a focus on the Second Coming which denies this life to others.

Many other Christian denominations in the U.S., in addition to the Quakers, have also endorsed policy statements on the Palestine-Israel conflict that affirm a belief in human equality as integral to their understanding of Christianity.[169]

We urge all individuals based in the U.S. who are working to support a just and enduring Palestinian-Israeli peace to reach out and engage as many members as possible of all the country's faith communities—including the Jewish and the evangelical Christian communities—in what we are doing. We believe that faith-based peace activists have a special role to play in this effort, since so much of the discourse of the pro-settlement movement in the U.S. has

---

169 The Washington, DC-based organization Churches for Middle East Peace (CMEP) has compiled statements issued by many U.S.-based Christian denominations regarding the Palestinian-Israeli conflict. They can be accessed at <http://www.cmep.org/ Statements/denomstat.htm>. CMEP's compilation of ecumenical and interfaith statements can be seen at <http://www.cmep.org/Statements/ecumenstat.htm>.

been couched in explicitly "religious" terms, whether Christian or Jewish. We need to engage in this discussion on the basis of our own most deeply held principles: in particular, our beliefs in human equality and the totally counter-productive nature of violence.

We note the important role that U.S. citizens, as well as other "internationals" have played by taking a direct part in witnessing, protection, humanitarian or solidarity actions within Palestine/ Israel, and by sharing the insights learned from such experiences after their return to their home countries. We certainly urge all of our readers who may be considering taking part in such actions to follow up on that leading. We suggest, however, that as citizens of a representative democracy, U.S. citizens have a special responsi- bility for the actions of their national government—a government that up until now has given Israel the massive economic, military, and diplomatic support without which the Israeli settlement proj- ect could never have continued as far or as successfully as it has. U.S. citizens therefore have a strong responsibility to work within the U.S. political context to change those policies to policies that foster, rather than impede, the urgent quest for peace and justice.

We are all deeply disquieted that the policies pursued by the U.S. government since 1967 have allowed the rapid expansion of Israel's settlement project, the concomitant repression and strip- ping of the rights of those territories' indigenous people, and its denial of the most basic rights of the Palestinian refugees. Those of us who are U.S. citizens urge our co-citizens to join with us in exploring all the ways in which our government's policy might be corrected. At a national level, AFSC and such groups as the U.S. Campaign to End the Israeli Occupation, Friends of Sabeel/North America, and United for Peace and Justice have many suggestions on actions that congregations and other grassroots organizations can take. In addition, many U.S. Arab and Jewish organizations and leaders advocate policy changes that merit support. For exam- ple, in August 2003 Rabbi Arthur Hertzberg, a past president of the American Jewish Congress and a noted historian of Zionism, published an article stating, "Never has it become more clear that diplomacy alone cannot secure a workable truce between the Israelis and Palestinians.... The most effective way to force a reduction of the violence on both sides is to take punitive eco- nomic measures." He urged the U.S. to take $1 billion of the approximately $4 billion that it supplies annually to Israel's national budget and hold it in escrow, "to help those settlers who would peacefully move back into Israel's pre-1967 borders."[170]

At the local level, there is an urgent need to contact lawmakers to urge them to dissociate themselves from any policy that might perpetuate Israel's settlement project and its pursuit of apartheid-like policies in the occupied territories, and to support instead the kinds of policy that, being based on a deep commitment to human equality, can hold out a beacon of hope and a peaceful future for Israelis and Palestinians alike. There is also a continuing need, in localities and in the media throughout the U.S., to conduct broad campaigns of public education about the terrible human costs of Israel's settlement project and the importance of truly upholding the principle of human equality when considering the rights and interests of all the people of the Holy Land. No entire nation should be demonized or penalized because of the actions of some of its members. This is true for Israelis; it is also true for Palestinians.

In the meantime, all of us—U.S. citizens and citizens of other countries—should exert significant effort to bring the peacemaking potential of non-U.S. parties to bear on the challenge of making peace in the Holy Land. The U.N. is one evident locus of such potential, as are the European Union, the Arab countries, and numerous other governments and non-governmental groups from around the world.

The *United Nations* has been a key participant in Israeli-Palestinian diplomacy since 1947. At many points in the history of the conflict, U.N. mediators have played the leading diplomatic role: from Folke Bernadotte and Ralph Bunche in the 1940s, to Gunnar Jarring in 1970.[171] It created the United

---

170 *The New York Times,* Aug. 27, 2003.

171 Bernadotte was head of the Swedish Red Cross during World War II and in 1945 helped save the lives of some 30,000 survivors of Nazi concentration camps. Later, he was appointed the U.N.'s first mediator on the Israel-Palestine issue. In 1948 he produced two plans to resolve the conflict, but they were rejected by both sides. In September 1948 he was assassinated in Jerusalem. A Swedish government website states "It is now well established that the decision to kill the U.N. mediator was made by the Central Committee of the LEHY [a Jewish extremist organization also known as the Stern Gang], which included Yitzhak Yezernitzky-Shamir." (<http://www.sweden.se/templates/FactSheet____4198.asp#9>, accessed July 3, 2003). In 1991, Shamir was the first Israeli prime minister to sit at a peace negotiation with a representative of the Palestinians.

Nations Relief and Works Agency (UNRWA) to provide relief services to the Palestinian refugees and has maintained a truce supervision organization in the area since 1949. In the mid-1970s, the leading diplomatic role passed from U.N. negotiators to a succession of U.S. negotiators, from Henry Kissinger through Colin Powell, while the U.N. was reduced to a secondary role; but then, in 2002, George W. Bush made an intriguing course-change when he agreed to allow the U.N. (along with the E.U. and Russia) to join the Quartet. Over the year that followed, it still was not clear whether the U.S. was ready to permit any of its partners in the Quartet to have any really decisive input into determining the Quartet's over-all strategy.

We believe that the U.N.'s role should be the central outsider role in Palestinian-Israeli peacemaking. Until today, U.N. resolutions still continue to provide the only basis in international law that can regulate relations among Israel, the Palestinians, and the existing Arab states. If the principles of international law—including the U.N. Charter and all the resolutions adopted by the U.N. Security Council, as well as the parallel provisions of international humanitarian law codified in the Geneva Conventions—continue to be undermined in Israel/Palestine, then it seems clear to us that it may be impossible for the Israelis and Palestinians to find another basis on which to construct a durable peace. In addition, the very concept of international law and international legitimacy would be seriously damaged at a global level. We are convinced, therefore, that the office of the U.N. secretary general should reassume the role it used to play as the leading shepherd of this diplomacy, and the guardian within it of the principles of international legitimacy.

We note that many Israelis, but in particular those of the pro-settlement parties, are resistant to the U.N. being given any larger role in the peacemaking. There are various reasons for that resistance. One is that many Israelis experienced considerable anguish over the 1975 U.N. General Assembly resolution that declared that "Zionism is racism."[172] That resolution was repealed in 1991. More recently, much of the Israeli animus against the U.N. has been directed at the role that UNRWA has allegedly played in the refugee camps in the occupied territories. Some Israelis have gone so far as to accuse UNRWA and the U.N. of complicity in Palestinian terrorism because UNRWA has not prevented refugee camp residents from making or placing bombs. We also heard Israeli accusations that U.N. refugee officials were responsible for anti-Semitic materials in camp school curricula. However, the U.N. has roundly—and to our minds, quite convincingly—refuted all these allegations.

We understand that many Israelis have been disappointed by what they perceive as U.N. failings or partisanship, but we do not feel that the U.N. ought to be sidelined in Middle East peace efforts. Firstly, we believe that many of the accusations that Israelis have made about U.N. partisanship have been exaggerated. Secondly, the U.N. and the broad body of international legitimacy that it represents provide the only basis that the world currently has for the maintenance of ethical relations among states, and among the peoples whose interests are represented by those states. Israel's very "birth certificate" as a member of the modern state system was provided by the U.N.'s partition resolution of 1947. It was that resolution that provided the framework whereby Israel gained its current standing as a state in today's international system of states—a standing that enabled Israel in its early years to offer a refuge, citizenship, and a solid sense of belonging to hundreds of thousands of Jews whose citizenship had been stripped away by the Nazis. Moreover, all the considerable progress that Israel has made in recent decades toward gaining recognition from Arab neighbors of its right to exist has been based upon its U.N.-granted "birth certificate" as a state and not on any histori-

---

172 The term "racism" is understood differently in different parts of the world—as is the concept of race. In the U.S., race is construed predominantly along the lines of skin color; elsewhere, it is construed more along lines of ethnicity. The U.N. spelled out its definition of "racial discrimination" in the 1966 International Convention on the Elimination of All Forms of Racial Discrimination as being: "any distinction, exclusion, restriction, or preference based on race, color, descent, or national or ethnic origin which has the purpose or effect of nullifying or impairing the recognition, enjoyment or exercise, on an equal footing, of human rights and fundamental freedoms in the political, economic, social, cultural or any other field of public life."

cally or biblically based claim that the Jewish people may have asserted to the land of Israel/Palestine.

The partition resolution also provided a birth certificate of equally strong validity for the establishment of a Palestinian Arab state alongside Israel in the land of Mandate Palestine. The Partition resolution therefore embodied an ideal of reciprocity and peaceful coexistence between these two states that remains valuable to this day. The Palestinian leadership's apparent willingness to accept a territory smaller than the Palestinians were originally accorded in 1948 does not negate that principle. We stress that Israel has the U.N. to thank for international recognition of its right to exist, and it will similarly benefit if its final boundaries are negotiated under U.N. auspices and with the U.N.'s blessing.

We believe, therefore, that the U.N. must be urged to resume the principal role in seeking a viable peace settlement in Israel/Palestine (as well as among Israel, Syria, and Lebanon). Other parties can also help push the vital task of peacemaking forward as well.

The *European Union* has a special role by virtue of its close economic connections with both the Israelis and the Palestinians, its generally prominent role in world affairs, and its geographic and cultural proximity to Palestine and Israel. These connections could all be used to help to structure the incentives for peace within the Palestinian and Israeli communities, as well as to advocate more forcefully at the global level for a just and hopeful resolution of this conflict.

The E.U. is Israel's main trading partner, and it gives Israel preferential access to European markets. This access is not a right for Israel but a favor from the E.U., and it brings considerable benefit to Israel's citizens and economy. During the 1990s the E.U. was, in addition, far and away the most generous provider of external aid to the P.A., as the P.A. sought to establish viable Palestinian institutions throughout the areas under its control. In 2002, when Sharon started attacking P.A. installations, his campaign destroyed facilities of many different types—including ministry headquarters, the Palestinian port and airport in Gaza, and Palestinian courthouses and police precincts throughout the occupied territories—that had been providing vital infrastructure and services to the Palestinians, and that had been funded by the E.U. One E.U. survey estimated that the Israeli forces caused around

U.S. $600 million of damage to E.U.-donated facilities during a three-week campaign in April 2002. Some, but not all, E.U. governments urged the E.U. to claim reparations for this damage from Israel.

In many respects, there is much more that the E.U. could be doing to make sure that its economic and diplomatic policies are being effectively used to help strengthen the pro-peace parties in Israel, and to make clear to Israel's government and voters that there will be real costs involved in the continued pursuit of the settlement project and the continued drive against Palestinian institutions.

The *Arab states* should also be expected to continue to make a substantial contribution to the quest for peace. In late March 2002, they took one very constructive step when their leaders unanimously adopted the Beirut Declaration. The declaration had originally been proposed by Saudi Arabia's influential Crown Prince Abdullah. In it, the Arabs expressed their commitment to concluding peace treaties with Israel, establishing normal relations with it, and "provid[ing] security for all the states of the region"— on the condition that Israel undertake a complete withdrawal to the pre-1967 lines, and accept both the establishment of a "sovereign independent Palestinian state" in the areas evacuated and the achievement of "a just solution to the Palestinian refugee problem."[173]

That declaration, and the unanimity of support it won from Arab states, was unprecedented. For the first time, Arab states as varied as Iraq, Libya, Algeria, and the Kingdom of Saudi Arabia were saying that in return for a full Israeli withdrawal from the occupied territories, they would not only end their 54-year state of hostility with Israel, but they would also establish peace treaties and normal relations with it, and also (by strong implication) enter into a series of military/technical arrangements that would help guarantee its security. The steps outlined in the declaration had real potential both to allay Israel's long-standing fears of facing unending rejection and hostility from the Arab

---

173 The text of this declaration has been published as Appendix B of International Crisis Group, *Middle East Endgame I: Getting to a Comprehensive Arab-Israeli Peace Settlement* (Brussels and Washington DC: ICG, July 2002).

states, and to help to integrate Israel more fully into the region of which it is a part.

Immediately after the declaration was issued, however, its significance and the potential for peace that it represented were swamped under the news of Prime Minister Sharon's end-of-March (2002) escalation of his campaign against the Palestinians in the occupied territories. Over the months that followed, the Arab leaders did little actively to pursue the vision of regional peace embodied in the declaration. But toward the end of 2002 several of them—most notably Egyptian President Hosni Mubarak and Jordan's King Abdullah—became key interlocutors as the U.S. and the other members of the Quartet pursued their plans for the Roadmap. Egypt, in particular, played a key role in persuading Yasser Arafat to undertake some of the steps required under the Roadmap such as allowing Mahmoud Abbas to take up the new post of Palestinian prime minister. (Egypt also helped retrain the Palestinian security forces who would be serving under Abbas.)

There remained much more that the Arab states and Arab non-governmental groups could do, however. For example, the Beirut Declaration's formal expression of readiness to establish "normal relations" with Israel could be made much more tangible for Israel's Jewish citizens if they could see that Arab states and leading non-state actors were already prepared to treat Israel's pro-peace activists as valued partners in the quest for a region wide peace. But that was still not happening. Governments and pro-peace non-governmental groups in the Arab countries could do a lot more to build and demonstrate good working relations with members of the Israeli peace camp.

Other governments in addition to those mentioned should also be urged to consider how they can contribute to the search for a sustainable, values-based peace in the Holy Land. For example, South Africa might share lessons about what helped South Africans escape from decades of deeply embedded violence and repression and install democracy. Many Latin American countries could share lessons about what needs to be done as the arbitrariness of military rule is replaced by democratization. Canada and Scandinavian countries could share valuable lessons about peace-keeping and various non-military approaches to investing in peace.

In today's highly inter-connected world, *non-governmental organizations* (NGOs) have an important role to play in educating and mobilizing people in numerous different communities around the world. People cannot work for justice and peace until they know what the injustices and causes of strife and conflict are, and how they can work together to bring about new and better policies. Today, the thousands of different NGOs around the world can play those roles, and they may be just as important as governments in bolstering moves towards peace. For example, in 1997-98 a worldwide coalition of citizen groups and small and mid-sized governments brought into being an international treaty to ban landmines. Today, we can start envisioning a worldwide coalition of citizen groups and governments of all sizes that can help bring about a values-based peace in Palestine/Israel.

The International Campaign to Ban Landmines and the global campaign that in 1998 won a treaty to establish an International Criminal Court (ICC) were, however, conducted in a somewhat different context than the campaign to bring about peace in the Holy Land. In the case of the former campaigns, activists from non-governmental groups and small and mid-sized governments were able to make an "end run" around the opposition of the reluctant but powerful governments of the world by winning their goals through conclusion of an international treaty, which would still exist and have some effectiveness even if powerful nations— such as the U.S.—should choose not to join it. In the case of making peace in Israel/Palestine, by contrast, there is no international treaty that would have any value if it failed to involve Israel, and Israel's principal backer, the U.S. That is why any global citizen campaign for a Palestinian-Israeli peace must seek to work with and through the U.S. and Israel, as well as the U.N. and the Palestinian leadership. Despite this difference, however, many of the same global organizing tactics used by the landmine campaign and the ICC campaign should be actively embraced by citizen activists working for an Israeli-Palestinian peace.

Principles for Global Engagement

In chapter 1, we enunciated a number of priorities and key principles that, we suggested, could provide a sound basis for building a durable Palestinian-Israeli peace. These principles, moreover, are consonant with many of the highest values and aspirations of the international community—especially since 2000-2010 has been officially designated by the U.N. as the Global Decade of Nonviolence. We therefore return to these principles and suggest that they can provide a particularly strong basis for mobilizing energies from around the world into the task of building peace in Israel/Palestine.

Ending the occupation: This must be a top priority, in order to halt the myriad forms of harm that the occupation inflicts on members of both societies (albeit very disproportionately on the Palestinians) and also, to start to "level the playing field" between the two communities as they sit down to negotiate a final peace. It is very hard for—in Raji Sourani's vivid terms—a "sumo wrestler and a small child" to have an equitable, respectful conversation about their future relationship. Various parts of the international community may have a role in helping to form and support an interim, "buffer" administration in Gaza and the West Bank, as the IDF forces that staff the occupation are withdrawn. But the context and agreed direction of all such efforts must be a definitive end to Israel's occupation rule. The sad precedent of Oslo—which seemed to promise an end to occupation but resulted only in its reapplication— must not be repeated.

The principle of human equality: Much of the support that Israel's settlement activities have received from around the world has been based on the distinctly undemocratic notion that people have claims of different worth to the fundamentals of a good life or to the sympathies of others—based solely on the "national" or "religious" group to which they are seen as belonging. Much of the support that Palestinian suicide bombings have received has been based on a similarly invidious notion. We believe that reconnecting with the simple but powerful principle of human equality that has been an underpinning of the U.N. system since its inception can help us to sort through the many conflicting claims made on the land and other resources of Palestine/Israel.

Equal rights and an equal voice for each direct stakeholder, and the primacy of the interests of these persons: This principle flows directly from the preceding one. The question of defining the direct stakeholders, needless to say, is a key one. In chapter 1, we defined the group of people who have a direct stake in the situation in Palestine/Israel as comprising all Israelis (both Jewish and

Palestinian), all Palestinian residents of the occupied territories, and all the Palestinian refugees.

We realize that the proposal to include the Palestinian refugees on this list may be controversial, but we have seen no argument that has convinced us that the exiled Palestinians have done anything that would justify them all, as a group, having their rights curtailed, their claims unaddressed, or their voice silenced. After all, no other refugee group anywhere else in the world has been asked in recent times simply to give up their claims on their homeland! We note that throughout nearly all of the Oslo process of the 1990s, the claims of the Palestinian refugees were not considered at all, and no effort was made to enfranchise or give voice to any refugees other than the small number who returned to the occupied territories with Yasser Arafat in 1994. In chapter 6, we surveyed the conditions and views of the refugees, and urged both that their claims be integrally addressed in any peace negotiations and that ways be found to include their direct representation in the peace talks. While this should be true for all refugees, we urge that particular priority be given to according a meaningful form of inclusion in the Palestinian body politic for those refugees who still remain stateless—in Syria, in Lebanon, and elsewhere.

Nonviolence: On both sides of the national divide in Palestine/Israel, people have invested great efforts in finding force-based ways to impose their views, policies, and—in the occupied territories—their sheer physical domination on others. Violence has taken on many forms throughout this conflict: physical, administrative, economic, and symbolic. None of those mechanisms or structures of violence, however, has brought into being the secure, peaceful environment that Israelis and Palestinians, like all persons, crave and deserve. We believe the time is ripe for a rejection of violence and solutions based on armed force, accompanied by a recognition that only through nonviolent resistance can the respectful, fair, and cooperative relations with others necessary for a lasting peace be built.

An Opening for Nonviolence

Nonviolence takes a sustained discipline and planning.
At this time in our history, we hear a lot of Palestinians,
especially those who were engaged in armed struggle,
serious fighters, saying nonviolence is the way;
teach us, we need to know more about it.
—Jonathan Kuttab, Palestinian lawyer and nonviolence organizer, 2002

There is nothing surprising in a Muslim or a Pathan like me subscribing to the creed of nonviolence. It is not a new creed. It was followed 1400 years ago by the Prophet all the time he was in Mecca ... But we had so far forgotten it that when Gandhiji placed it before us we thought he was sponsoring a novel creed.
— Badshah Khan (the "Gandhi of the Pathans")

While we were in Palestine/Israel we met numerous individuals with long and rich experience in nonviolent organizing and nonviolent activism. It is important for us to restate this fact since during the lengthy period of violence that has engulfed Israelis and Palestinians since September 2000 the nonviolent approach to seeking justice and peace has often seemed to be a distinctly "minority view" in both communities.[174] It did indeed seem undeniably true during our visit—as it has been since then—that in each community there still is a sizeable number of people who actively express support for the use of armed force in order to attain highly valued social goals, and that the Palestinian and Israeli advocates of a nonviolent path have often felt isolated and discouraged.

Nevertheless, we have three solid reasons for stating our continuing faith that a strong and hopeful nonviolent movement may yet reemerge in Israel/Palestine. These are:

1. The fact that in each community, alongside the expressions of support for violence, a clear majority of the people still also

---

174 We wonder to what extent this perception is the result of the focus that most the global media place on acts of violence and their consequences, rather than on the simple grace shown by people helping their families and communities make it through tough times.

repeatedly express their readiness to share the land of Palestine/Israel in some way with the members of the "other" community;

2. The years-long experience of the second *intifada,* and the many acts of violence organized and committed during it by members of both communities, showed clearly to us—as it seemed to be showing with increasing clarity to many Israelis and Palestinians—that no amount of additional violence could actually bring to either community the well-being and sense of security that its members continued to crave; and

3. There already exist (as noted above) many individuals in both Palestine and Israel with rich histories of nonviolent organizing; and the networks of organizations that these people have continued to sustain provide a strong foundation on which the revitalized nonviolent movement of the future can be built.

The issue of violence and nonviolence in Israel and Palestine is a complicated one. Since the history of these two peoples' long experience in this regard may not be much known to our readers, we have decided to include this chapter. We thought it would be helpful to start by revisiting the question of the role that violence has played in the thinking of each national community, and examining some statements from people on each side of the line who support the use of violence and who explain clearly what political goal it is that they see the violence as realizing. We shall quickly recount the history of nonviolence in Israel/Palestine in the past 20 years, describe some encounters we had with a number of experienced local nonviolence activists, and sketch out some perspectives on nonviolence. Finally, we shall make some suggestions of actions that people who are not directly involved in the conflict might consider taking, that would help to support and strengthen the work of the nonviolence activists working within the region.

Violence: To What End?

For both Israelis and Palestinians the dominant national discourse has often been one in which, precisely because of the need both peoples have felt to escape from a troubling legacy of past weakness, ideas and representations of weapons have a notable popular potency. Guns, armies, and fighting men have been given a particular role in the venture of nation-building, or nation-reconstitution—by both national leaderships. From this point of view, adoption of the tools of violence can be seen as often having a strongly expressive function, expressing the much-appreciated fact of escape from a time of past weakness, or the possibility of escape from continuing weakness. Some months after our trip, one of our group members wrote:

> We must address respectfully the perspective of a humiliated and almost helpless people who turn to or support violence as a means of regaining their self-respect and self-determination; as an attempt to protect their families and friends; as a protest and a refusal to go on passively accepting the endless bludgeoning without letting their oppressors know that they cannot continue without suffering consequences.

Some of the acts of violence committed in Israel and Palestine over recent years have, we do not doubt, been committed in pursuit of this expressive function. Others have been committed out of blind rage, nihilistic despair, a highly personal desire for revenge, or other barely political motivations. But most of the violence there has been both political and instrumental. It has been the kind of violence that seeks to realize the laudable political end of securing or increasing the well-being of the national community, but to do so by exerting physical control and "pacification" over another population, or terrorizing those others into submission, or forcing their relocation, or "breaking" their will in some other way.

We heard this instrumental view of violence expressed most forcefully by Sondra Baras, the community activist in Karnei Shomron whose views we described in chapter 2. "We should act fiercely against those who harbor terrorists," Baras told us. "We should surround their homes and neighborhoods, search house-to-house. If necessary, we should bomb whole neighborhoods. The IDF takes casualties now, because they are too careful... We need a very tough, harsh attitude. We need to make them suffer so much that they quit! .... Only massive force, firmly applied, will quell them. We can do no less. Otherwise we will be attacked." Evidently, she was urging the use of violence as a means somehow to modify the *behavior* of the Palestinians suspected of harboring terrorists.

We did not meet IDF Chief of Staff Moshe Ya'alon. But the interview he gave to *Ha'aretz* in August 2002 (that we described briefly in chapter 4) revealed a lot about what this authoritative leader of Israel's military saw as the reasoning behind Israel's use of force against the Palestinians. Significantly, in that whole lengthy interview, which was conducted in Hebrew with an Israeli journalist, Ya'alon did not once mention the idea that the intention of Israel's military actions against the Palestinians was the interdiction, pre-emption, or direct prevention of Palestinian acts of violence against Israelis, though these are the reasons Israeli leaders routinely give to foreign audiences for the IDF's proactive operations in the occupied territories. Nor did Ya'alon describe the Israeli army's use of violence as aiming directly at modifying any other aspects of the Palestinians' behavior. Instead—like masters in the world of judo to whom he referred in the interview, and also (paradoxically) like many of the smartest practitioners of non-violence—he stressed that the main aim of the forceful acts undertaken by the IDF was to change the *mindset* of the opponent.

As we noted in chapter 4, Ya'alon described the contest with the Palestinians as an "existential" one for Israel. When asked how he defined victory in the confrontation with the Palestinians, he replied that it was, "the very deep internalization by the Palestinians that terrorism and violence will not defeat us, will not make us fold... If that [lesson] is not burned into the Palestinian and Arab consciousness, there will be no end to their demands of us."[175] He added,

> The key point here is the staying power of the Israeli society. That is the most important factor that is being put to the test at this time and will continue to be put to the test in the near future. That is what the campaign is about. When the Palestinians initiated the [second *intifada*], their evaluation was that Israel would not be able to withstand even a few dozen casualties. They were surprised... But if they see cracks and a chance of [Israel's] disintegration, a prospect of Israeli capitulation, that achievement will be erased.

Because of this latter fear, he said, Israel should under no circumstances undertake any withdrawals at all, however small or tactically advantageous they might be to Israel, until after the Palestinians had completely ended their violence.

Fourteen months later, Ya'alon had apparently changed his mind on some of these issues. After a briefing he held with Israeli journalists at the end of October 2003, Ya'alon was quoted as hav-

---

175 Ari Shavit, "The enemy within," in *Ha'aretz*, Aug. 29, 2002. Hebrew-language specialists have told us that the word used here for "burn" also carries the connotations of "sear" or "brand."

ing told them that Israel had made a mistake by maintaining such a tough regime on the Palestinians of the occupied areas. "It increases hatred for Israel and strengthens the terror organizations," he reportedly said. "There is no hope, no expectations for the Palestinians in the Gaza Strip, nor in Bethlehem and Jericho... In our tactical decisions, we are operating contrary to our strategic interest." In line with this analysis, he had reportedly urged the easing of the controls imposed on Palestinians.[176]

Such an admission, coming from the IDF's topmost commander, was intriguing and possibly very significant. Back in August 2002, however, Ya'alon was still making clear that, in Israel's confrontation with the Palestinians, he saw it as engaged in a complex battle of wills, one with implications far beyond the confines of Israel/Palestine:

> After the Six-Day War, we succeeded in burning into the regional consciousness the fact that it is impossible to destroy Israel by military means... However, since our first withdrawals from Lebanon after Operation Peace for Galilee [Israel's 1982 invasion of Lebanon], that accomplishment was increasingly eroded. For nearly 20 years, the feeling developed in the Middle East that even though the Israeli army is strong, the unwillingness of the Israeli society to make sacrifices is creating a strategic Achilles' heel.

On the Palestinian side, we did not meet with anyone of the command stature of Ya'alon. However, as recounted in chapter 6, those of us who went to Damascus had an intriguing discussion with a person who expressed support for the actions of the Palestinian suicide bombers—or, as he called them, "martyrdom fighters." That was Ahmed Berqawi, one of the Palestinian professors we met at Damascus University.

Berqawi accused Israel of having rejected all the peace plans the Palestinians had presented them with. "The ending of the occupation? It's refused! The return of the refugees? It's refused! They reject everything. ... There is no hope, no solution now in view—unless Jewish society itself, inside Israel, changes its views."

We asked how this change might be brought about.

"Well, there is no end in view right now," he said. "But it

---

176 Moshe Ya'alon, quoted by Nahum Barnea in *Yediot Aharonot*, Oct. 29, 2003. At the time, Barnea referred to his source merely as a "senior military official," but the fact that it was Ya'alon emerged later that day. See Molly Moore, "Top Israeli officer says tactics are backfiring," *The Washington Post*, Oct. 31, 2003, p. A1.

remains true that no one can prevail by military force—on either side... The Palestinians cannot declare a war on Israel and hope to win, but they can continue struggling for their rights."

He said he favored an outcome "built on the political basis of coexistence—one in which we share the land in equality. Not by separation or occupation. Neither side should oppress the other. This outcome offers the best future for Israel." And in order to bring it about, he judged that the actions of the "martyrdom fighters" was slowly proving to be effective.

"Every person loves life!" he said. "But the martyrdom fighters have come to their decision to make these actions after they have faced such deep brutality from Israel and the loss of all hope. Plus, the religious believers among them see death as a passage to a better life. It is Israel's conduct that brings on the phenomenon of the Palestinian bombers! Israel deprives us of our land, builds settlements, and denies us all our rights." However, he did state quite explicitly that the Palestinian "martyrdom fighters" should go after Israeli military targets rather than civilians.

He remained convinced that once the conflict had been resolved, "Palestinians and Israelis can be friends, can live together." He noted that many Palestinian activists had good relations with peace activists in Israel. Such Israelis, he said, "respect us. Plus, we both reject Sharon and the racism of the Israeli government. We seek to strengthen the alliance with the peace groups. If such views gain ground in Israel, it would remove the need for the martyrdom bombers."

We suggested that, on the contrary, the bombers' actions weakened the peace forces in Israel.

"But they keep the focus on the root causes of the conflict!" he countered. "Only by addressing those causes can we bring an end to the bombings. It's just like in South Lebanon. There, the Israelis could not prevail by force. In the end, after suffering so many casualties, they decided to pull out."

Later, he indicated that he, like Moshe Ya'alon, judged the conflict to be at its core, a battle of wills.

> We need to make the Israelis know that the Palestinians will persist in our struggle. That there is no military 'answer' to their problems. That no purely military 'victory' is possible. The Israelis must come to see this real-

ity and therefore to give up their reliance on force. After all, the Palestinians are not asking for much. Just for life, and a Palestinian state.

He also seemed to confirm the judgment expressed by Ya'alon, that the successive withdrawals that Israel effected from Lebanon under the pressure of Hezbollah's operations there had raised hopes in other Arab communities that Israel's behavior could be modified through the application of violence. There were other similarities between the views expressed by these two thoughtful, articulate men, as well. As Ya'alon did in his interview, Berqawi stressed the fact that, while no "victory" in this battle was imminently in sight for his side, still, he saw evidence that the forceful strategy he advocated was starting to bear fruit. We venture to guess that Berqawi might also—as Ya'alon did, just two months later—describe himself as both a "liberal" and a "humanist."

Where the views that Berqawi shared with us differed significantly from what Ya'alon said in the interview was that while Berqawi expressed his support for a future of coexistence and equality with the Israelis, Ya'alon did not say anything clear in the interview about the long-term relationship he sought with the Palestinians.[177] In Berqawi's view (which we do not share) the use of violent means to change the mindset of Israelis would not seriously complicate the subsequent establishment of cordial relations.

Roots of Palestinian Nonviolence

There is much in the heritage of Palestinians that has always emphasized the seeking of alternatives to violence. The well-known Islamic and Arab practice of *sulha* is a traditional form of community mediation of disputes, providing a centuries-old alternative to feuding and the pursuit of campaigns of revenge. Then in the twentieth century, the Palestinians adopted many practices of nonviolent community organization in their resistance to the colonial regime that Britain maintained over their country from 1922 through 1948, and to the arrival of the Jewish immigrants who came to the country under the auspices of Britain's rule. These practices involved strikes, demonstrations, the delivery of petitions, sit-down protests, and the maintenance of informal, community-level, networks that aimed to bolster Palestinian self-sufficiency.

---

177 Ya'alon may have addressed this issue in public, but we have not found any reference to such utterances.

Resistance to British rule came to a head with the "Arab Revolt" of 1936-39 which spread throughout nearly all of Mandate Palestine. Numerous Palestinian organizers showed great creativity and courage during that revolt, which started out with what has been called "the longest nonviolent commercial strike in history." Increasingly, though, as the revolt continued, tactics of nonviolence gave way to armed struggle; in the end, the British were able to break the revolt, killing or jailing many of its leaders and outlawing a broad range of Palestinian community organizations. That defeat left the Palestinian community significantly weakened when, in the 1940s, it found itself faced with a new and more tenacious threat from the new waves of Zionist immigrants fleeing the wreckage of Hitler's Europe. The legacy of the 1930s revolt provided an essential background to the *nakba* the Palestinians suffered in 1948.

In the years after the Palestinians of the West Bank and Gaza came under Israeli occupation in 1967, they started to develop and enact a deeply-held philosophy of quiet resistance to that rule that was called in Arabic *sumoud* (steadfastness). The cardinal goal of *sumoud* was for these Palestinians to stay on their land. *Sumoud* involved trying to hang onto whatever institutions of Palestinian self-governance and self-organization they could, while also building new Palestinian institutions, with the development and growth of the Palestinian universities being a very visible example of this latter effort. Throughout the late 1960s and the 1970s there were also many systematic efforts to build community-based organizations like women's committees, labor unions, and professional associations.[178] From this point of view, *sumoud* involved many of the elements of *swaraj*, which was Gandhi's famed concept of self-governance.

Sumoud involved, on occasion, making non-trivial concessions to the power of the occupying force—as, for example, when administrators of the growing universities had to work with the occupation authorities to get the endless "permits" required by the authorities if the administrators were to implement their growth plans. *Sumoud* seemed, on the surface, to be quietist from the perspective of overt politics. But deeper down, it was "political" at the

---

178 A good description of these developments can be found in Joost R. Hiltermann, *Behind the Intifada: labor and women's movements in the occupied territories* (Princeton, N.J. : Princeton University Press, 1991).

level where it really counts—in terms of building the robustness of community institutions, along with the self-confidence of community members.

For many years after 1967, the Palestinians of Gaza and the West Bank continued to hope that their liberation from military occupation could be brought about by outside actors. But after the IDF defeated the PLO's military forces in Lebanon in 1982, the activists in the West Bank and Gaza who had had many years' experience of organizing for *sumoud* started to realize that there was little point in waiting for liberation to come from elsewhere: they would have to try to take their future into their own hands. Five years later, in December 1987, the entire Palestinian population of the occupied territories—including East Jerusalem—used its already rich experience of organizing for *sumoud* and entered a major new phase in their encounter with the Israelis: the more confrontational phase of *intifada*, which in Arabic means "shaking off."

What followed were primarily the classic techniques of nonviolent activism: boycotts, tax refusal, silent vigils, non-cooperation, civil disobedience, parades, strikes, fasts, and other forms of protest. Underground organizers linked in a shadowy body called the Unified National Leadership of the Uprising (UNLU) issued periodic leaflets giving instructions for territories-wide actions. For example, on the ninth day of each month, there was a total strike, to mark the events that had started the *intifada*. The fully mobilized population followed UNLU's instructions enthusiastically. There were some compromises with nonviolence, including fairly extensive throwing of stones against (mainly) Israeli troops, and some assaults with Molotov cocktails. But for the most part the first *intifada* was an attempt to carry out a campaign of nonviolence in the Gandhian tradition, drawing from a vision articulated by community leaders like Jad Isaac and Ghassan Andoni (whom we met with in, respectively, Bethlehem and Beit Sahour), and by Mubarak Awad, a native of Jerusalem.[179]

A vivid example of the ingenuity of Palestinian nonviolent resistance in this period was their manner of displaying their

---

179 Awad's right to reside in his native city had been withdrawn by Israel some years before. He had U.S. citizenship, however, and in the early 1980s he used his U.S. passport to return to Jerusalem to set up the Palestinian Center for Nonviolence. His activities attracted little attention from the Israeli authorities until the *intifada* started, at which point they promptly deported him on the grounds that his visa had expired.

national colors. One of the thousands of outrageous regulations that the Israeli military authorities had imposed on the Palestinians outlawed any public display of the Palestinian national flag. During the *intifada*, however, residents of remote Palestinian villages would defiantly tie the black, red, white, and green flag to the top of their minarets; residents of refugee camps would toss makeshift flags attached to small counterweights over the many utility lines that criss-crossed their alleys; townsfolk would come out at night and proudly paint it on their walls. Nearly every time, Israeli troops or squads of border police squads would go in to try either to remove the offending emblem themselves or, as part of their continuing battle of wills with the populace, force the Palestinians living nearest to those subversive patches of color to erase them themselves. Palestinian artists—who had always been drawn to the use of this particular color combination—stepped up their use of it in their paintings. Women of all ages stepped up the wearing of the national colors in their dress.

In late 1989, the U.S. nonviolence theorist Gene Sharp wrote in the *Journal of Palestine Studies* that he judged that up until then the *intifada* had been "85 percent" nonviolent. He wrote that the two-year-old *intifada* had achieved a considerable measure of success as a nonviolent movement, but he urged Palestinians to give up throwing stones and Molotovs and become "fully nonviolent."[180]

One of the notable centers for Palestinian nonviolent organizing has for many years been the West Bank town of Beit Sahour, near Bethlehem. Beit Sahour is regarded by Christians as the site of the "Shepherds' Field" in which the angel announced Jesus' birth to local herdsmen. Early in the first *intifada*, after Israel's then-defense minister Yitzhak Rabin called on Israeli soldiers to "break the bones" of Palestinian protesters, the people of Beit Sahour invited Jewish Israelis who had supported their efforts into their homes in an act of friendship called "Break Bread, Not Bones." They also captured world attention with a courageous tax-resistance campaign called "No Taxation Without Representation." The Israeli authorities retaliated very harshly against the tax resisters. They confiscated machines used in cottage industries, trade goods, and household furnishings from families judged to be delinquent in paying their taxes.

---

180 Gene Sharp, "The Intifadah and Nonviolent Struggle" in *Journal of Palestine Studies*, vol. XIX, no.1 (Autumn 1989), pp. 3-13.

For six years, 1987-93, the Israeli authorities— who deployed one of the world's most technologically sophisticated and best-funded armies—were unable to break the back of the *intifada*. The Palestinians built on the dense network of community-based organizations that they had created since the late 1960s to sustain an organizing structure throughout the territories that openly defied Israel and survived all the many ruses and force-based counter-measures that the Israeli military deployed against it. Traditional class lines broke down as Palestinian city women kicked off their high heels to dig victory gardens alongside peasants. Residents of refugee camps in the West Bank, on hearing of a particular crisis in Gaza, would pool their resources and send relief supplies to their fellow refugees there. When the Israeli military authorities shut the Palestinian schools, locally-based popular committees launched networks to organize classes in people's homes. When the authorities tried to cut off food supplies, agricultural committees multiplied their efforts to organize community-wide cultivation programs. In Beit Sahour, Jad Isaac, one of the organizers of the tax-resistance campaign, established a seed-distribution network to support the planting efforts. When we talked with him, he recalled that he had once been arrested and detained for six months. His crime? Selling seeds.

Shunning the Israeli-controlled courts, the Palestinians made widespread use of the traditional Arab conflict-resolution mechanism, *sulha*, to address a range of internal civil and political disputes. Use of this inclusive, reconciliation-based approach to resolving internal conflicts further strengthened the community.

There were Medical Relief Committees that organized community-based health services in remote areas. There were Women's Committees that helped Palestinian women work together to survive the terrible rigors imposed on their families and to break down traditional gender discrimination that existed in Palestinian society. There were Agricultural Relief Committees that organized actions such as Jad Isaac's seed-distribution network and supported agricultural and "Victory garden" ventures throughout all the Palestinian areas. Groups like the Palestinian Human Rights Information Center, Al-Haq (Law in the Service of Man), the Mandela Institute for Political Prisoners, the Gaza-based Palestinian Center for Human Rights, the Palestinian Center for Rapprochement, and Sabeel all supported the communities involved in the *intifada* in different ways. The activities undertaken by all these organizations led to the Madrid conference and the Oslo Accords, since the Israeli government came to realize that the Palestinians in "the territories" were proving to be ungovernable by refusing to accept passively their status of being permanently under occupation.

In addition, many of the organizations named above participated in joint actions alongside Israeli and international counterpart groups. These joint actions were a particular feature of the first *intifada*.[181] In both the Israeli and Palestinian communities, participation in them posed a deep challenge to previously prevalent norms that refused to grant recognition to members of the "other" nation as co-equal members of the human family.

Roots of Israeli Nonviolence

By the time the first *intifada* broke out in 1987, the Israeli peace movement already had its own impressive history. In the development of the State of Israel, there have always been a number of Jewish Israelis who worked for understanding and trust between Arabs and Jews. Though their numbers have often not been large, these women and men have carried a lot of moral weight with their Jewish neighbors. Most Israeli nonviolent activists have not been absolute pacifists. (People like Nathan Chofshi, Amos Gvirtz, Joseph Abileah, and a handful of others were notable exceptions to this rule.) In the deeply challenging days of the 1930s, people like Martin Buber argued against Mahatma Gandhi that nonviolence would not have worked against Hitler in Nazi Germany. But inside Mandate Palestine in that same exact period, Buber—along with Hebrew University President Judah Magnes—was active in groups like Brit Shalom and the Ihud that were working for Jewish-Arab coexistence there. Indeed, Buber and Magnes testified before the United Nations Special Committee on Palestine (UNSCOP) in favor of the creation of a binational state in which Arabs and Jews could live in peace as equal partners.

All those early "pioneers" of the Jewish/Israeli peace movement left a rich legacy of activism in favor of coexistence to the many Israeli peace groups that have functioned throughout the long period of Israeli occupation of the West Bank and Gaza.

---

181 In 1989 one of our IQWP members, a U.S. citizen, took part in a campaign to form a human chain around the walls of the Old City of Jerusalem. That nonviolent action was met with water cannons and beatings by the Israeli police.

These latter groups have worked in solidarity with Palestinian organizations, and have also organized broad-scale lobbying actions on their own government. As one thinks about the present despair in the Israeli peace camp, it is good to remember the many Israeli peace groups, such as Yesh Gvul, the "Twenty-first Year," Women in Black, Peace Now, Oz ve Shalom, East for Peace, the Committee Against the War in Lebanon, and others that have since 1967 mounted numerous nonviolent, grassroots campaigns aiming at a future peaceful coexistence between Israelis and Palestinians.

Peace Now and the other Israeli peace groups had their finest hour in 1982, when they led the movement of Israelis who opposed their government's push into Lebanon. In September 1982, after the IDF commanders in Beirut colluded with Lebanese militiamen who killed hundreds of unarmed Palestinians in the Sabra and Shatila refugee camps, Peace Now and its partners organized demonstrations that brought hundreds of thousands of Jewish Israelis out onto the streets to express their strong protest at the role their army had played. Those protests helped persuade Prime Minister Menachem Begin to comply speedily with a U.S. request that the IDF withdraw from Beirut and its environs. Ariel Sharon, who led the invasion, was removed from his position as defense minister, and his decisions were the subject of a high-level commission that eventually judged that he bore indirect responsibility for the massacres, and recommended that he never again hold public office in Israel. Peace Now and a number of partner groups kept up the pressure on the government to effect further withdrawals from Lebanon.

By the time the first *intifada* started in 1987 these groups already had a lot of organizing experience and a lot of strategic clarity in their view of the role of the Israel's military. They also had a rich experience of having organized joint actions with Palestinian counterparts. Some notable joint Israeli-Palestinian campaigns were the "Campaign for Abu Ali Shaheen" (1984), the Ramya Committee for Solidarity (1991-92), the "Committee in Solidarity with Bir Zeit University (1980-82), Women and Peace (1991-92), the Committee Against the Iron Fist (1988), and the Committee Against Expulsions (1993).[182] Perhaps the best-known of these joint actions involved one led by Mubarak Awad and

---

182 For more information on these actions see Maxine Nunn, *Creative Resistance: Anecdotes of Nonviolent Action by Israeli-Based Groups* (Jerusalem: Alternative Information Center, 1993).

Jonathan Kuttab in the West Bank village of Qatana in 1986: on that occasion international volunteers, Palestinians, and Israeli members of the International Fellowship of Reconciliation worked together to replace olive trees that had previously been uprooted by the Israeli authorities and taken to be planted along the boulevard leading to the Martin Luther King, Jr., Memorial in Jerusalem! That action was captured on film, and became part of the documentary *Courage Along the Divide*.

The spirit that had motivated all those earlier joint actions for peace has been kept alive in present-day organizations like Bat Shalom, Ta'ayush, Rabbis for Human Rights, the Israeli-Palestinian Center for Research and Information (IPCRI), the Israeli Committee Against House Demolitions (ICAHD), Physicians for Human Rights-Israel, the Coalition of Women for a Just Peace, and Gush Shalom. On a parallel track, the spirit behind such earlier Israeli military refusal organizations as Yesh Gvul has been kept alive by groups like New Profile, "Courage to Refuse," the Shministim of high-school-aged draft resisters, and the group of Israeli Air Force reserve pilots who in September 2003 declared their conscience-based objection to participating in airborne extra-judicial killings of Palestinian suspects. In addition, a range of Israeli human rights organizations like B'tselem have—as we have noted throughout this report—continued to shine a light of conscience on developments in the West Bank and Gaza.

Results of the First Intifada

Despite the significant skills and experience that members of the Palestinian resistance movement and their supporters among the Israeli peace movement demonstrated during the first *intifada*, they did not achieve the result they both desired: the ending of the occupation. What happened? This question is an important one that requires considerable additional study. We can surmise, however, that the reasons for the intifada's failure to "shake off" the occupation included the following:

• The Israeli governments of both Prime Ministers Yitzhak Shamir and Yitzhak Rabin undertook repeated, broad campaigns of forceful repression and collective punishment involving massive violations of human rights, in their attempts to suppress the *intifada*. And they found a generally understanding ear from the U.S. government, whose aid flows to Israel were even increased during these years. Those campaigns, sustained over six years, finally started to take their toll.

- When Saddam Hussein fired a number of conventionally-tipped missiles into Israel and threatened to "burn" it in 1991, many, but by no means all, Palestinians expressed support for Hussein's actions and bombast. Nearly all Jewish Israelis felt terrified and deeply threatened by Hussein's belligerency. Many people in the Israeli peace movement were horrified by the Palestinian reaction to it and drastically reduced their pro-peace activism as a result.

- Though the *intifada* was predominantly a nonviolent movement, the activists and organizers of nonviolence failed adequately to develop and promulgate an entire and convincing philosophy for their approach. They failed to develop an organizational infrastructure strong enough to sustain nonviolent successes. The international community and key peace groups in Israel also failed to give the Palestinian nonviolence activists all the support they could have given. Meanwhile, there were many in the Palestinian underground resistance movement who had a very well-developed philosophy of "righteous" or "redemptive" violence. These included militants of the secular-nationalist movement, as well as organizers in the new, Islamist-activist organizations—Hamas and Islamic Jihad—that were born during the early months of the *intifada*. As the *intifada* dragged on into its fourth and fifth years with no respite in sight, the Palestinians' use of physical violence mounted—both against the Israelis and to try to resolve differences of opinion inside Palestinian society. National unity started to erode, as national exhaustion set in.

- The activists and leaders of the *intifada* had all along resisted the urgings of Israeli and U.S. government officials that they negotiate their own future themselves, without involving the exiled PLO. "Only the PLO can represent us," they stated repeatedly. In 1993, they got what they had asked for: Israel did finally conclude the Oslo Accords directly with the PLO. Once Arafat and his colleagues "returned" to the occupied territories, however, they proved to be a hugely damaging disappointment for the people there. Long used to the secretive, authoritarian ways of an exile-based underground, Arafat almost immediately felt threatened by the network of community organizations he found in Gaza and the West Bank. As Raji Sourani reminded us in Gaza, Arafat then set about working to dismantle the very community-based organizations whose grassroots activism had brought him back to his homeland.

Palestinians Debate Nonviolence, 1993-2003

In the years following the adoption of the Oslo Accords, it became clear to many of the organizers and theorists of the Palestinian nonviolent movement that the Oslo process, and the performance of the PLO leadership after it returned to the occupied territories as part of that process, fell far short of their expectations.

Jonathan Kuttab is one such theorist/organizer. (In addition to his work as a lawyer, Kuttab had helped to found a number of non-violence-based institutions including the Mandela Institute for Political Prisoners.) "We gained many things with the nonviolent activism we used during the first *intifada*," Kuttab told us when we met with him in Jerusalem.

> It was that activism that brought about Oslo! But afterwards, we mismanaged the political process. I stress that all must bear responsibility for this: We blew this chance. What happened was that through and after Oslo the forces of evil and violence took away all our slogans. They hoodwinked everyone in seeming to be for liberation. But actually what they sought was power, domination, racism. They should be put on trial for that!

> Who am I talking about? Successive Israeli governments, and the U.S. government, and the Arab regimes, and the top elites of the Palestinian Authority. All of them. They all disrupted and derailed the peace process.

> Essentially, at Oslo, the Israelis co-opted the top Palestinians—and the rest of us did not insist on full internal democracy. We accepted being manipulated by the P.A., under the slogan of 'Don't embarrass Arafat!' But where was transparency, accountability?

He said that he and many others had, in the early years after Oslo, agreed to make compromises on matters of principle that in hindsight he judged should not have been made. For a while after Oslo, Kuttab himself worked with the P.A., heading the Palestinian legal team at one of the negotiations that had flowed from the Oslo agreement. "We all went along on this ride," he told us somberly in 2002.

For example, on the question of settlements. We had always previously stuck to the international-law position that the settlements were simply illegal. But then at Oslo, both sides agreed that this issue would be settled through 'direct negotiations'. But such negotiations leave international law and international legitimacy outside the room! There are no rules. The lion and the lamb are in the room alone...

The Oslo track was bound to fail. But where was the peace and justice community? It had been lulled to be quiet. How could this negotiation succeed without law and justice? ... Oslo could not make such an imbalance come out 'even'. The Palestinians who went to the [post-Oslo] talks moved away from the popular movement, and from the people. The Palestinian 'leaders' had their own goals and interests—and popular accountability would get in the way of that.

The intense disappointment that Kuttab expressed in the "fruits" of Oslo was a judgment that we also heard from every other Palestinian with whom we talked. (Nearly all our Jewish-Israeli interlocutors expressed strong disappointment in Oslo, too. But many of them adduced very different reasons for this: for them, Oslo failed to bring the domestic peace and tranquillity that they had thought it promised.) On the Palestinian side, the disillusionment with Oslo had a direct bearing on the violence-nonviolence debate, since the conclusion of the Oslo Accords was widely, and probably correctly, seen as one of the main achievements of the nonviolent resistance that had been so widely used during the first *intifada*. And the Palestinians who had been most vocal in criticizing the theorists and organizers of nonviolence during the first *intifada* were among those who, in and since September 1993, were most critical of the Oslo Accords.

It is also worth recalling that back in December 1992, Israeli Prime Minister Yitzhak Rabin had tried to expel more than 400 accused leaders of the Palestinian Islamic organizations to Lebanon. That move evoked many of the Palestinians' deepest fears of a repeat of the mass relocation and scattering that their people had suffered in 1948, and provoked an uproar throughout the Arab world. Before long, U.S. President George H.W. Bush insisted that Rabin agree to a timetable for the return of the expellees.[183] But for a number of months in early 1993, the

---

183 This expulsion was, of course, a clear infringement of the Fourth Geneva Convention. However, the fact that even that dramatic escalation failed to win for Israel the intended goal of damping down the *intifada*—indeed, it had just the opposite effect—likely helped persuade Rabin to try the different strategy of supporting talks with the PLO, instead.

expellees stayed camping under canvas on a hillside in South Lebanon, awaiting implementation of that agreement, and while there many of them reportedly took part in what some commentators called "Hezbollah University." When they returned home they brought with them many new skills—in mass community organizing and in guerrilla warfare.

By early 1996, the Palestinians' disappointment in Oslo was starting to be intense. Far from bringing the improved living conditions Palestinians had desperately hoped for, in many parts of the occupied territories conditions became progressively harsher during the mid-1990s, as we noted earlier. Meanwhile, the Palestinians saw Israel continuing to expand its settlements, and even starting to link the settlements together with the new settler-only road network.

In late February of 1996, organizers from the Muslim militant groups Hamas and Islamic Jihad launched a new offensive, sending suicide bombers into civilian areas of West Jerusalem and Tel Aviv in killing operations that took the lives of 55 Israelis. Though individual Palestinians, or small groups, had carried out suicide operations against Israeli civilians before then, the 1996 campaign marked the clear adoption of this tactic for the first time by significant Palestinian militant organizations. Those operations may have helped members of Jihad and Hamas to "express" something they felt they needed to express. But they also helped Likud's Binyamin Netanyahu to win the election held in Israel ten weeks later. Despite that outcome, however, the leaders of Jihad, Hamas, and some of the militant secular nationalist organizations in Palestinian society evidently judged that the tactic of using suicide/killing operations was one that would be worth repeating in the future.

Many factors, therefore, combined to ensure that when the second *intifada* broke out in September 2000 the conditions for nonviolent organizing were very different from those during the first *intifada*. These factors included: the near-unanimous Palestinian disappointment in Oslo, and frequently therefore, by association, in the nonviolent tactics that had brought Oslo into being; the enhanced level of organization of Palestinian militant groups; and the presence in Gaza and the West Bank of substantial numbers of weapons brought in originally for use by the P.A.'s police force.

There was another important difference, too. In May 2000, 18 years after Defense Minister Ariel Sharon took Israel's troops deep into Lebanon, Prime Minister Ehud Barak undertook the last (or near-last) stage of Israel's multi-staged withdrawal from Lebanon. That withdrawal was undertaken because of the intense weariness of Jewish Israelis with the steady attrition Israeli troops had suffered at Hezbollah's hands for the preceding 18 years. The withdrawal was unilateral and unconditional. Israel had "won" from Lebanon few of the objectives Sharon had sought when he launched the invasion 18 years before.[184]

When we met with Jonathan Kuttab, he told us about the potency inside Palestinian society of what he called, "the Hezbollah argument." He characterized it thus: "The outcome of the Hezbollah attacks in Lebanon 'proved' that the Israelis paid attention to violence, and could be induced to withdraw from occupied territories if the occupation could be made too costly."

Kuttab pointed out that there were deep flaws in this argument. He noted that beside the moral objections to it, there were also practical ones. Crucially, in his view, the "Hezbollah argument" failed to take into account the distinction for most Israelis between Lebanon, where they have no strong territorial claims, and the West Bank and Gaza, which many of them consider part of the historic "Land of Israel."

Many proponents of a "Hezbollah-style" strategy in the Palestinian national movement have, anyway, overlooked the fact that an important factor in Hezbollah's success was its ability to build vast, interlinked mass organizations inside Lebanon's Shi'ite community, and to reach out with smart political overtures to a range of other groups throughout the country. It was those political and organizing skills that, crucially, allowed Hezbollah to withstand the many defeats that Israel's powerful military inflicted on it, again and again, on the battlefield.[185]

Meanwhile, hawkish thinkers inside Israel were also—as we saw from Chief of Staff Ya'alon—deploying their own "Hezbollah

---

184 He had, of course, won what he had sought from the Palestinians in Lebanon, namely the dispersal of the PLO's leadership from there. But beyond that goal, he also sought to use the 1982 invasion to install a pro-Israeli government in Beirut. And that, he notably failed to do.

185 An account of Hezbollah's political work can be found in Amal Saad-Ghorayeb, *Hizbu'llah: Politics and Religion* (London and Sterling, VA: Pluto Press, 2002).

argument." Their version of it agrees with the Palestinian version that Hezbollah's violence against Israeli troops in Lebanon was significantly linked to Israel's withdrawal. But many Israelis (including Ariel Sharon) argued all along that it had been a major mistake for Israel to withdraw from Lebanon under the pressure of Hezbollah's attacks, because that withdrawal weakened Israel's "general deterrence"; and therefore, that this mistake should under no circumstances be repeated in the Palestinian territories. Palestinian suicide bombings played into the hands of the Israeli proponents of the "Hezbollah argument" since it hardened Israeli attitudes toward Palestinians and encouraged the talk of transfer, separation, walls, etc., as Israelis witnessed the scenes of terrible carnage brought about by these suicide bombings.

When we visited Beit Sahour in 2002, we heard a sober assessment of the then-current state of the Palestinian nonviolence movement from Ghassan Andoni, executive director of the Palestinian Center for Rapprochement Between People (PCR) "Palestinians are obsessed to keep the 'resistance' going," he told us:

> They react badly when we say, 'Not with guns!' We want to find a way of resistance that does not rely on violence.
>
> Some take pride in 'hurting Israel'. It makes them feel good. So the attacks, the bombers: they are generally seen as endorsed by the public.
>
> Also, everyone wants an end soon. They want it now! Violence might pretend to offer them that. But we know that building Palestinian independence is a long-term project. We must not lose patience.

Andoni talked about the role that international solidarity actions had started to play. His organization was then hosting some of the activists from the International Solidarity Movement (ISM) who had recently started working in the occupied territories, and had trained some of the ISM activists in both Beit Sahour and Jerusalem. "Thousands of people from around the world have told us they are ready to come and do this work," Andoni told us. "But Israel is not letting most of them in." He said he had seen a positive Palestinian response to the work of both PCR and ISM: "But we do not yet see mass demonstrations and mass curfew-breakings of the kind we would like to achieve... Our goal is to have masses of Palestinians come to demonstrations and other actions. But it is seen as so dangerous to do so these days. That's why we need the ISM and other internationals to help to provide us with cover, and with media coverage."

"Palestinian society must be organized further in order to reach the mass base," he told us. "Our education system has been at fault. Our mentality does not see and honor the full range of nonviolent techniques." He voiced a few words of veiled criticism of the militant Islamic activists:

> Some people now seem to be more committed to Islam than to Palestine, as such. It's a challenge for us to keep our priority on our national goals. We need a much better education system, to clarify this... We seek to create positive attitudes. Our commitment is to the goal of having the full society pursuing our national independence. Bombers can hurt the Israelis, perhaps—but only an organized people can win our independence! So we're seeking to draw more and more young Palestinians into this work.

He stressed that this remained a long-term task and admitted that at that point,

> Palestinians seem to have lost confidence in themselves, and their sense of community. We need to build all this, and to have a coherent movement. But we've lost all sense of trust... We must share the risks, in public actions, and not be abandoned or betrayed. There is so much corruption and self-aggrandizement evident. We need a mass nonviolent movement to strengthen Palestinian society.

> I cannot promise that it will succeed on its own. But I doubt we can get to independence without it.

Andoni told us that PCR's nonviolent approach was not endorsed by the P.A. or by the Palestinian political factions, though some factions had asked for training in nonviolent techniques to explore their use as part of their struggle.

PCR had recently, he said, had to cancel one big nonviolent action it had been hoping to stage along with counterparts from inside Israel: creating a human chain all the way from Nablus in the north of the West Bank, to Gaza. With prospects for that action dashed, they were still hoping to stage a reenactment of the smaller, 1989 human chain around the Old City of Jerusalem, which he invited us to join. But that plan, too, was later cancelled because of the huge logistical obstacles erected by the authorities and the small number of people—from both communities—ready to commit themselves to taking part. (Over the year that followed our visit, the number of joint Palestinian-Israeli nonviolent actions that took place started modestly to increase.)

Further Directions for Nonviolence

In both Israel and Palestine, we witnessed a great deal of despair. We heard notes of despair expressed even by seasoned activists in the nonviolence movement. There is an urgent need to bolster that spirit of hopefulness without which these extremely courageous individuals will find it hard to continue their work.

There are, fortunately, a number of causes for some optimism. Firstly, it is important to note that even during the second *intifada* there have been many occasions on which courageous Palestinian advocates of nonviolence have mounted significant, mass-based nonviolent challenges to the reality of the IDF's power. In Nablus, there have been cases of mass curfew-breaking. In and around Ramallah, actions have been organized to dismantle checkpoints and undertake the "normal" activity of moving from one town to the next. (The avoidance of checkpoints by using rutted back-paths is already a near-daily occurrence in the occupied territories; mass defiance of the very idea of checkpoints has been more rare.) On nearly all of these occasions, however, either public support for the mass action petered out, or youths started throwing stones and the discipline of nonviolence broke down. Too often, the advocates of violence—from both sides of "the Wall"—have ended up winning the day.

One longer-lived peace initiative was launched by Al-Quds University head Sari Nuseibeh soon after we visited him. Nuseibeh had drafted a "Statement of Principles" jointly with Ami Ayalon, a pro-peace Jewish-Israeli man who was a retired head of one of Israel's much-feared security organizations, the Shin Bet. (Such changes of heart have not been unusual in Israel's history—which is itself another cause for optimism. In November 2003 Ayalon joined with three other former Shin Bet heads to state publicly their shared condemnation of the policies of the Sharon-led government as disastrous for the future of Israel.)

The Nuseibeh-Ayalon statement, which was first released on 27 July 2002, was a simple declaration of six short paragraphs. It called for "Two states for two peoples," with their borders to be only slightly modified from those prior to the 1967 war; Jerusalem would be an "open city"; and Palestinian refugees would have the right to "return" only to the Palestinian state, not to Israel.[186] The

---

186 Text available at <http://www.mifkad.org.il/eng/PrinciplesAgreement.asp>.

statement met with much criticism from inside both national communities. For example, many Palestinians were deeply upset by the apparent denial of the "right of return" for Palestinian refugees to ancestral homes inside Israel and by territorial arrangements that would, they feared, leave in place many Israeli settlements in East Jerusalem and other parts of the West Bank. And of course, neither Nuseibeh nor Ayalon had any official negotiating mandate. Yet their statement was notable because of the campaign that continued around it long after July 2002: its supporters kept up a steady, low-level effort to collect signatures for it from people in both communities. By November 2003, they had reportedly won more than 100,000 signatures from Israelis, and 60,000 from Palestinians.

Another sustained campaign with profound potential to bolster the move toward sustainable long-term peace was the "Palestinian National Initiative," a pro-democracy movement that was launched in Ramallah in June 2002 by three veterans of the national independence movement: Gaza physician Haidar Abdel-Shafei, West Bank physician Mustafa Barghouti, and Jerusalem engineer Ibrahim Dakkak. The Initiative's founding statement called for "the establishment of a national emergency leadership, the immediate implementation of democratic elections at all levels of the political system, and reform of political, administrative, and other institutional structures in order to meet the needs of the Palestinian people." The statement argued that these steps were needed if the Palestinians were to attain their national rights and a durable, just peace.[187]

The Initiative's leaders organized a number of grassroots actions like demonstrations against the Separation Wall that Israel was building inside the West Bank, or campaigns against Israel's lengthy detention of Palestinians without bringing them to trial. In some of these actions it worked with Israeli or international counterpart groups. Meanwhile, it also kept up its campaign for democratic accountability within the P.A. and all other Palestinian institutions.

---

187 Information from <www.palestinemonitor.org/Other%20Updates/palestinian_national_initiative.htm>. The Initiative has its own website, with an English-language section accessible at: <www.almubadara.org/en>. The Palestinian-American scholar-activist Edward Said was a strong supporter of the Initiative until his death in September 2003.

An additional cause for optimism lies in the continuing creativity and capacity for reflection shown by the nonviolent activists in both communities. We have already written much in these pages about some of these individuals. Another of them—whom we were not able to meet on our trip—is Iyad Sarraj, the executive director of the Gaza Community Mental Health Program. In May 2003 he wrote very perceptively that, "There are many lessons learned from the past two years. One is that violence can only breed violence. The suicide bombers of this *intifada* are the children of the first *intifada*—people who witnessed a great deal of trauma as children. As they grew up, their own identity merged with the national identity of humiliation and defeat, so they are avenging that defeat at both the personal and national levels."

In an attempt to help bring this repeating cycle of violence to an end, Sarraj issued a powerful invitation for Palestinians and others to join together to struggle for an ultimate political outcome that would be, in his words, "just, fair, and viable":

> Enlightened Jews, Palestinians, and friends of peace and justice everywhere should rise above the ocean of hatred and division and be united in their struggle to achieve their noble goals. Unfortunately, Palestinians and Arabs have failed to build alliances with Jews, many of whom object to the occupation of Palestinian land. There has been little attempt by Arab politicians and intellectuals to understand the Israeli 'enemy.' Furthermore, any attempt at the extension of understanding and reconciliation has been targeted as the work of a fifth column. In the meantime, Israel has engulfed itself in a shell of paranoia and fear.[188]

The suggestion by Sarraj that Jews, Palestinians, and friends of peace and justice everywhere should work together for their goals is particularly potent, expressed as it is by a person forced to deal on a daily basis with the damaging effects of the Israeli occupation on his own life, his own family, and the community that his organization serves. It is also a suggestion that is in line with the tradition of universalist bridge-building that is embedded in the best of the worldwide experience of nonviolent activism. When Mahatma Gandhi was leading the Indians' struggle for independence from the British, he was clear that the ultimate relationship he strove for with the British was one of friendship. When Desmond Tutu was deeply engaged in the struggle of Black South Africans for politi-

---

188 Common Ground News Service, transmission of May 16, 2003. Text available from Search for Common Ground, 1601 Connecticut Ave NW, # 200, Washington DC, 2009, or from <www.sfcg.org>.

cal rights, he wrote friendly letters to the apartheid government's prime minister John Vorster, inquiring about the health of his family and seeking to build a relationship within which he could persuade Vorster to do the right thing by all the country's citizens.

Gandhi and Tutu—like numerous other leaders in the worldwide nonviolence movement—well understood that nonviolence is not just a smart "tactic" that currently weak peoples can choose to adopt or ignore at will. Nonviolent engagement is a spiritual venture, and one that has a unique power to transform both human relationships and the people involved in them. If pursued with wisdom, compassion, and authenticity it can open a chink of understanding in the heart of a current opponent, opening up the possibility that he may indeed be tomorrow's negotiating partner, ally, or even friend. As the veteran Norwegian theorist of nonviolence Johan Galtung wrote in a small 1989 book about nonviolence in Israel/Palestine, "The whole theory of nonviolence is based on the idea of Self recognizing the human being in the Other, appealing to that human being not only for [com]passion with one's own plight, but also for self-interest in a better future, to be enjoyed together."[189]

The whole history of the Palestinian-Israeli conflict since the 1930s has shown that when nonviolence is adopted merely as a tactic, rather than embraced as an entire philosophical and spiritual vision, then whenever setbacks occur in this struggle for justice—as they inevitably do, somewhere along the way—many individuals will turn to other tactics, principally the tactics of violence. Moreover, if the "playing-field" on which the parties engage is the field of violence, then the side that has the deadliest means of violence at its disposal will win. What Gandhi, Tutu, Martin Luther King, Jr., and other great philosophers of nonviolence understood, however, is that if nonviolence is embraced as an entire and transformative worldview, then its proponents can explain and transcend setbacks while remaining true to their radical, transformative goal. For this to start happening in Israel/Palestine, it will probably require that nonviolence activists from both communities commit both to some version of a deep philosophical-spiritual vision of nonviolence and to engagement in those kinds of transformative actions that flow from such a vision.

---

189 Johan Galtung, *Nonviolence and Israel/Palestine* (Honolulu: University of Hawaii Institute for Peace, 1989), p.14.

This principled nonviolence is what most Quakers embrace as a logical extension of our belief that "there is that of God in every person." It is what Bishop Tutu of South Africa describes as "*ubuntu*," an African word embodying the meaning that "we are human in as much as we recognize the equal humanity of others."

Since the mid-1980s, numerous peoples around the world have overthrown undemocratic regimes or won their independence using active nonviolence: the Philippines, Haiti, Chile, South Korea, Poland, Hungary, East Germany, Czechoslovakia, Bulgaria, Latvia, Lithuania, Estonia, Slovenia, Albania, South Africa, Serbia, and Macedonia are all good cases of this. One could add a dozen examples from the breakup of the Soviet Union. Both Israel and Palestine compare favorably to several of these countries in factors that are helpful to the cause of nonviolence, including levels of education; the presence of a variety of civil institutions in society through which people can make connections; the vitality of their mass media; a fairly clearly established sense of national identity on both sides; and their numerous connections with the outside world.

The harsh controls that Israel has imposed on the Palestinians of the occupied territories have undoubtedly hindered the Palestinians' ability to organize active nonviolence; but even in this respect the Palestinians have some advantages over some of their predecessors in nonviolent struggle. Israel is, in some ways, a very suitable "target" for nonviolent action. It is a relatively open society, with a press that, in our experience, is readier to address the realities of the occupation than most of the mainstream media in the U.S. Israelis are marked almost as much by their ideals for their country as they are by their ethnic and religious identity. This creates a valuable opportunity for nonviolent activists to highlight the dissonance between Israel's stated ideals and the reality of what Israel is doing in the occupied territories. Israel is, physically, extremely close to the victims of its occupation: few Israelis live more than a few miles away from the roadblocks, razor-wire, and constant humiliations of the Palestinians' daily existence in the occupied territories. Oftentimes, they live very close indeed to the Palestinians. In both Hebron and East Jerusalem we saw settlers living in the upper stories of buildings whose lower floors were occupied by Palestinians. Very few of the 20th century examples of successful active nonviolence that we cited involved groups in such intimate proximity as Israelis and Palestinians. In Palestine/Israel, in addition, the two communities carry burdens of historic suffering that have many, many parallels with each other. Though in the midst of pain and suffering it may be hard to see these parallels, once recognized they can provide a powerful basis for continuing joint action for justice and peace.

We therefore agree with those on the scene who are convinced that active nonviolence offers the most promising path toward a just and sustainable resolution of the Israeli-Palestinian conflict. Assertive, creative Palestinian nonviolence has immense potential to stir world opinion. And if a commitment to nonviolence is sustained systematically over a period of time, and in the face of even harsh and violent Israeli counter-measures, it can impose mounting cognitive dissonance on the Israeli public, highlighting as it would the contradictions between Israeli ideals of justice and democracy and the reality of Israeli occupation of Palestinian lands.

It would be hoped, too, that this experience could lead, in both communities, to the next step of finding one's own experience reflected in the experience of the other. As the Jewish theologian Marc Ellis wrote in 1987,

> The torture of the death of Palestinian children calls us to a theology which recognizes empowerment as a necessary and flawed journey toward liberation... Today, the Palestinian people ask the fundamental question relating to Jewish empowerment: Can the Jewish people in Israel, indeed Jews around the world, be liberated without the liberation of the Palestinian people? Once having understood the question posed by the Palestinian people the occupation can no longer continue.[190]

For his part, Johan Galtung is especially good in addressing the question of the imbalance of power by insisting that the nonviolent actions of the oppressed alone cannot produce a victory. What is needed, Galtung argues, is nonviolent action from within the oppressor community that is supported by nonviolent actions of those outside the situation:

> It is not obvious that nonviolence against an oppressor is primarily the task of those who are oppressed. They certainly have not only the right but also in a sense a duty to resist. But if their resistance is an invitation to even more brutal oppression the question can be legitimately be asked. What are the alternatives? One answer, very well known, is violent

---

190 Marc H. Ellis, *Towards a Jewish Theology of Liberation* (Maryknoll, NY: Orbis Books, 1987), p.132.

instead of nonviolent resistance from below. That answer is unsatisfactory to the believer in nonviolence. Hence, a much better answer is the one that I am leading up to in this chapter: nonviolence, to destroy the oppressive structure, but by others than the victims themselves; *for* them, on *behalf of* them, partly also *of* them, but not primarily *by* them.[191]

It was clearly our experience that nonviolent cooperation between the Israeli, Palestinian, and international communities will be required if peace is to be achieved and sustained. We are moreover convinced that such cooperation is possible. We conclude this section with three very inspiring examples from Jewish Israeli peace activists of the kinds of action that they have been pursuing.

Yitzhak Frankenthal is chairman of the Bereaved Families Forum, an organization of Israelis and Palestinians he founded after his 19-year-old son, Arik, was killed by Hamas militants in 1994. He writes about his son's killing with painstaking clarity:

It is unethical to kill innocent Israeli or Palestinian women and children. It is also unethical to control another nation and to lead it to lose its humanness...

We lost sight of our ethics long before the suicide bombings. The breaking point was when we started to control another nation. My son Arik was born into a democracy with a chance for a decent, settled life. Arik's killer was born into an appalling occupation, into an ethical chaos. Had I myself been born into the political and ethical chaos that is the Palestinians' daily reality, I would certainly have tried to kill and hurt the occupier; had I not, I would have betrayed my essence as a free man. My son Arik was murdered when he was a soldier by Palestinian fighters who believed in the ethical basis of their struggle against the occupation. My son Arik was not murdered because he was Jewish but because he is part of the nation that occupies the territory of another.

Frankenthal has put these values into action. The Bereaved Families Forum provides mutual support to families from throughout Palestine/Israel who have lost children to political violence. The three principles adopted by the group are "preferring the ways of peace and negotiation as a means of achieving the legitimate goals of the Israeli and Palestinian people; favoring the dignity of a person, his/her freedom, well-being, safety and welfare over any other value (mostly over territorial values); striving for reconciliation and lasting peace between the Israeli and Palestinian people."[192]

---

191 Johan Galtung, *Nonviolence and Israel/Palestine*, p.20.

192 More information about the Bereaved Families Forum and Yitzhak Frankenthal is available at <http://www.theparentscircle.com/parents/about.asp>.

The second example is a description by Gila Svirsky of a peace vigil held in Tel Aviv in late May 2003, to mark the near-completion of the 36th year of Israel's occupation of the West Bank and Gaza.

The speakers alternated—Jews and Palestinians from Israel, two Palestinian women from the territories, and one woman representing the internationals who risk their lives in an effort to intervene nonviolently. Dalit Baum, feminist Jewish activist, opened by showing the connections among all the forms of violence—occupation, poverty, brutality against women—through their common roots. Suher abu-Uksa Daoud, a Palestinian writer doing her doctorate at Hebrew University, spoke of how her own life moved from anger to peace activism. Yali Hashash, a feminist defender of Mizrachi rights among Jews, challenged us to examine our commitment to justice, and pay a solidarity visit to the protest encampment of impoverished Israelis in Tel Aviv...

A particularly moving letter written by Cindy Corrie, the mother of Rachel—the American peace activist who was killed by a bulldozer as she tried to prevent the demolition of a Palestinian home—was read out loud and said, in part: 'There have been times when I have been quiet because I felt there were others who knew more. But I am no longer intimidated by experts and critics. After all, my daughter had the courage to stand in front of a bulldozer.' Shulamit Aloni, former Israeli cabinet minister and outspoken defender of justice and equality, was eloquent in demanding an end to the bloodshed and the dawn of an era of peace...

Zahira Kamal, senior official in the Palestinian Authority, and committed all her life to peace, women, and workers, declared 'I believe in the power of women. Women are grounded in their awareness of the sanctity of all human beings...I believe we can work together for ending the occupation and that we can live in peace together.' Rauda Murkus, Palestinian from Israel, closed with an aching and touching poem...

As the situation in the territories gets worse; as witnesses are barred from the scenes of violence; as political rhetoric raises expectations and then retracts them; our hopes still lie with the duet of the people, the lament caressed by quiet clapping, the Palestinians and Israelis who have kept their faith, who still reach out to each other inside the pain and wait—and work together—for the lament to end.[193]

For her part, Israeli linguist and peace activist Tanya Reinhart commented favorably in one of her recent books on the Palestinian thinker Edward Said's view that, "The Palestinian struggle... must be based on the understanding that the Jewish people are here to

---

193 Communication by e-mail from Gila Svirsky, 30 May, 2003.

stay. The struggle must strive towards a settlement that will enable coexistence based on human dignity, a settlement that will capture the imagination of the world." She added,

> On the Israeli side, on March 20, 2001, 140 academics published an ad in three Palestinian newspapers that said: 'we extend our arms to you in solidarity with your just cause...and wish to cooperate with you in opposing the IDF's brutal policy of siege, closure and curfews.' In the spirit of Mandela and Said they too believe that this cooperation 'may serve as a precedent-setting example for future relations between the two communities in this country, our shared country.'

> On March 2001, in the village of Rantis near Tul Karem I watched, bewildered, as approximately two hundred Israelis—youth along with old veterans—demolished with their bare hands the stone and earth barricade erected by the IDF—just one of the dozens of events of this kind that have taken place since the current round of Israeli oppression began. The people knew that as soon as they left, IDF bulldozers would return to reconstruct the barricade. Still they looked happy. Because they knew that they, too, will be there again. They will be there for the only future worth living—a future based on basic human values.[194]

Suggestions for Actions by Concerned Outsiders

We do not presume to tell nonviolent activists in either the Israeli or Palestinian community what they should do. We do, however, feel able to suggest some directions that people in other places might consider taking to support the nonviolent organizations inside those two communities, as indicated in the following paragraphs.

SELF-EDUCATION

All of us need to learn a lot more about the rich and complex history of nonviolence in the Palestinian-Israeli context, and about the debates between advocates of nonviolence and advocates of violence that continue inside each community. (We also need to continually educate ourselves about the roles our own governments play in the area.) Most of the organizations mentioned in this chapter—or elsewhere in the report—have good websites, and many of them have printed publications that are very informative. In addition, there are numerous English language articles and a growing list of books on this topic. We have tried to indicate in Appendix D which of these resources might be most helpful.

---

194 Tanya Rhinehart, *Israel/Palestine: How to End the War of 1948* (New York: Seven Stories Press, 2002), pp. 234-35.

Aiding Palestinian and Israeli Nonviolent Organizations

When we asked Ghassan Andoni how we could help the Palestinian Center for Rapprochement, his response seemed modest:

> We need resources, funds. But not a lot. For example, we need to buy prepaid phonecards, in order to stay in touch with each other. During the siege at the Church of the Nativity in Bethlehem,[195] when we were supporting the ISM people who were in there, we were using 30-35 phone cards a day! Then, we need to create a media center here. We often have specific requests and needs…

> I stress that we have no paid staff. All are volunteers. But the internationals who come to work with us need to have their living expenses covered. Perhaps we could link to churches or Quaker meetings or other groups?

Many of the Israeli and Palestinian nonviolence organizations post specific requests on their websites or in their publications. We urge readers to do what they can to respond.

Building Long-term Partnerships

Andoni's suggestion of "linking" with faith-based or other support groups internationally seems to us an excellent one that can strengthen the work of everyone involved. An important aspect of any such partnership would be for the internationals to provide consistent and loving support for the women and men involved in the work of the local group in a way that helps these courageous people to bear the hardships of their situation while reducing the sense of isolation and despair that can on occasion beset them.

Such a partnership might also involve making a solid commitment, on a long-term basis, to funding, technical support, fundraising support, or the provision of other needed resources. It might grow to the point where some members of the international group might volunteer to go to Palestine/Israel and work for and with the on-site organization. Another possible way to support the people in these organizations might be to provide a "respite ministry" that provides a safe and supportive environment away from tensions of the homeland where they can collect their thoughts, restore their energies, and engage in some brainstorming and experience-sharing with members of the partnering group.

---

195 During "Operation Defensive Shield" in spring 2002, the IDF reoccupied Bethlehem. A few dozen Palestinian militants sought sanctuary in the Church of the Nativity, around which the IDF then threw a tight siege. Some ISM activists slipped into the church compound, bringing humanitarian supplies for the people inside.

Bearing Witness

All of us, because we had the huge privilege and challenge of being part of the IQWP, feel under the weight of a leading to bear witness about what we saw and experienced on our journey. (This publication is part of that effort.) We know that many other "internationals" who have had similar experiences of traveling around Israel/Palestine, or who have had the privilege of working with nonviolence organizations there, have similarly found ways to spread their witness as widely as possible; and we urge the continuation of such efforts.

This might involve something as simple as inviting friends over for dessert so you can tell them what you saw, or convening a small group of interested persons from your congregation or other civic group; or it might involve becoming passionately engaged in a large-scale attempt to sway your national government; or, anything in between. All such efforts are good! We would suggest, however, that a good portion of all these messages might usefully focus on the role of the nonviolence organizations in Israel and Palestine. All of us can help to magnify their voices in the global discourse.

If you have not had the opportunity to visit Palestine/Israel yet—or even if you have—you can always help to spread the testimony of other witnesses.

Missions to Palestine and Israel by International Nonviolence Organizations

We know of a number of international groups that do activist work in Palestine/Israel based on an intentionally nonviolent philosophy. A few of these are listed below.

The most experienced such group is the *Christian Peacemaker Teams (CPT)*. It started out as a ministry of the historic "peace churches" (Church of the Brethren, Mennonites, and Quakers) and continues to embody a specifically gospel-based, pacifist approach to its work. CPT has maintained a full-time presence of four to six team members in downtown Hebron since 1995. On its very informative website, CPT explains that: "Hebron typifies a condition in which one party has most of the power and the other has little. Until both parties have hope for a fair relationship that begins at the negotiating table the conflict appears unresolvable.

CPT workers try to emphasize or encourage nonviolent methods for redress and get in the way of violence when they can."[196]

While the CPT sees its role in Hebron as primarily a ministry of presence, the *Ecumenical Accompaniment Program in Palestine and Israel (EAPPI)*, a younger organization, bases its work on the more mobile approach of "accompaniment." EAPPI's website explains that it "is an initiative of the World Council of Churches. . . Its mission is to accompany churches in Israel and the Occupied Palestinian Territories (OPT) in their nonviolent actions and concerted advocacy efforts to end the occupation and support a just peace in the Middle East."[197]

The International Solidarity Movement (ISM), which was mentioned above by Ghassan Andoni, is a secular group organized along loose "affinity-group" lines. It describes itself as a "Palestinian-led movement of Palestinian and International activists working to raise awareness of the struggle for Palestinian freedom and an end to Israeli occupation. We utilize nonviolent, direct-action methods of resistance to confront and challenge illegal Israeli occupation forces and policies. As enshrined in international law and U.N. resolutions, we recognize the Palestinian right to resist Israeli violence and occupation via legitimate armed struggle. However, we believe that nonviolence can be a powerful weapon in fighting oppression and we are committed to the principles of nonviolent resistance."[198]

We have also heard with interest about a proposal that the U.S.-based Quaker organization *Friends Peace Teams (FPT)* might establish a presence in or around the Friends Schools in Ramallah in order to develop the ability of Friends worldwide to contribute to nonviolence work in Palestine and Israel.[199]

---

196 <http://www.cpt.org/publications/history.php>, accessed on July 15, 2003.

197 <http://www.wcc-coe.org/wcc/what/international/palestine/eap.html>, accessed July 15, 2003.

198 <http://www.palsolidarity.org/about/aboutISM.htm>, accessed July 15, 2003.

199 We have little news at this point about the progress of this proposal. A visit to the FPT website is probably the easiest way to find out about its status: <www.friendspeaceteams.org>.

Supporting the Vision of Nonviolence in Israel/Palestine

We have noted above the robust state of pro-violence discourse in Israel and Palestine (including both versions of the "Hezbollah argument"), and the disadvantage that some advocates of nonviolence have felt in the field of public opinion. Are there things that thoughtful outsiders can do to help strengthen the nonviolent voice in the internal debates in each community?

We hesitate to suggest we have answers on this, but we also recognize that the advocates and organizers of nonviolence in Israel and Palestine are trying to live and work under horrifying conditions that often leave little mental energy for study and reflection, and also that for most Palestinians access to libraries, seminars, and conferences is simply impossible. There may be more that outsiders not suffering these impediments can do, acting in close conjunction with the local activists, to strengthen their capacity to interpret their work and its guiding vision.

Are there books or other printed materials that they would like to use or to distribute, that outsiders could donate? Is there translation work, into Hebrew or Arabic, that they would find useful? Are there experiences of nonviolence movements elsewhere in the world that they would like to learn more about? Are there conferences elsewhere in the world that they want to attend, but for which they have trouble finding either the travel costs or the necessary permissions (from Israel or the host country)? Are there other such areas in which outsiders might help?

We believe it is especially important to stress in the Palestine/Israel context that nonviolence is not a specifically Christian doctrine, but part of the spiritual heritage of all humanity. Are there, therefore, specific intellectual tasks like restoring the heritage of Muslim thinkers of nonviolence like Jalal al-Din Rumi or (more recently) Badshah Khan, or their Jewish counterparts like Martin Buber or Abraham Heschel, that could help Palestinian and Israeli nonviolence organizers to undertake more effective faith-based outreach to Muslims and Jews?

[11]
Conclusion and Executive Summary: Moving Beyond Silence

Common folk ... if they devote themselves to resolute insistence on goodwill
in place of force ... can do something to build a better, peaceful world.
The future hope of peace lies with such personal sacrificial service.
To this ideal humble persons everywhere may contribute.
—*Henry J. Cadbury, representing AFSC at Nobel Peace Prize ceremony, 1947*

Our lives begin to end the day we become silent about things that matter.
—*Martin Luther King, Jr., Nobel peace laureate, 1964*

The Semitic languages give the world a great gift by making clear that the word they use for "peace"—*salaam* or *shalom* —conveys the sense not just of the absence of conflict, but also, more positively, of the active flourishing of communities and of the individuals who make them up.

We have a vision of Israel/Palestine as a land of peace, and we would like to share it with you. Every Palestinian and every Israeli who wants to live in this land of *shalom/salaam* can find in it a home community in which she or he feels secure and respected. This land of peace supports Israelis and Palestinians in conducting lives that are quite free from any legal or administrative obstacles to the pursuit of the normal endeavors of individuals or families. It offers every Palestinian and every Israeli such prerequisites of a decent life as a general atmosphere of public security, the securing of all basic human freedoms, the right to participate as a full and equal citizen in a project of accountable democratic governance, and the opportunity to participate in a vibrant national culture well-rooted in the land he or she loves.

This is our vision, and we are convinced that it is realizable. Indeed, there are at least two (and perhaps more) very different ways in which it could be brought into being. It could come about according to the formula of two fundamentally equal nation-states living side by side in the area between the Jordan River and the Mediterranean Sea. Alternatively, it could come through the establishment of a single binational state in the whole of that area.

Whichever of these models the Palestinians and Israelis should choose, however, it can succeed at bringing the *salaam/shalom* that the vast majority of them crave only if it is founded on a profound respect for human equality. This respect for equality could be expressed by ensuring the equal sovereignty of the two independent states living side by side, or it could be expressed through ensuring the civic equality of all Palestinian and Jewish citizens within a single state.

In contrast to these two manifestations of the principle of human equality, we consider that any form of institutionalized discrimination that is based on perceived racial, ethnic, or religious categories is quite unacceptable. We recall that in November 1973, the U.N. General Assembly declared that apartheid was a "crime against humanity," and "declare[d] criminal those organizations, institutions, and individuals committing the crime of apartheid." Any apartheid-like situation in Israel/Palestine should be judged by these same criteria.

In addition to being morally distasteful, such institutionalized discrimination will always, in Palestine/Israel as elsewhere, sow the seeds of destruction of any political order that is built upon it. A people that bases its own concept of "security" on the destruction of its neighbors' sense of security is building a false citadel whose walls will most certainly crumble.

* * *

There are a number of other actions currently being taken or proposed by different actors from the Israeli and Palestinian communities that are—like any suggestion of creating an apartheid-like order—intolerable to the conscience of humanity. Such actions are also, in our view, clearly doomed to prolong the conflict between Israelis and Palestinians and thus to rebound against the longer-term interests of members of both national groups. It is important to identify and list these actions. They include the following:

- First, Israel's settlement project in the occupied territories is a violation of the Fourth Geneva Convention and a war crime under the 2002 Rome Statute of the International Criminal Court. The settlement project is a colonial system, based on deep-seated discrimination against the territory's indigenous people. All further pursuit of, and investment in, this illegal and discriminatory project must be ended immediately.

- Second, Israel's 36-year military occupation of the Gaza Strip and the West Bank long ago became an intolerable abuse of a situation that, in international law, was only ever envisaged as a transitional one. Israel has not used the powers of occupation to conclude a peace agreement and transfer power to a local government in the occupied areas, but instead has abused its power as occupier to pursue its colonial settlement project there. The occupation has hardened into a terrifying authoritarian system of governance over three million Palestinians and must be ended immediately.

- Third, the use by some influential nonstate actors within the Palestinian community of tactics that deliberately apply lethal violence to civilians is intolerable and must be ended immediately.

- Fourth, Israel's refusal for nearly all of the past 55 years to engage in serious, good-faith negotiations about the claims of the Palestinian refugees has left those four million-plus men and women exiled, dispossessed, scattered, and with little hope of imminent redress. The Palestinian refugees cannot continue to be marginalized and treated as somehow less deserving of rights than others of God's children.

- Fifth, all acts of deliberate, extrajudicial killing by either Israelis or Palestinians are intolerable, regardless of whether or not the perpetrator is a government agent and regardless of what allegations there may be against the persons killed. If allegations of grave misdoing exist, then the only acceptable place in which they can be tested and the accused individuals sentenced is a publicly accountable court of law.

- Sixth, more generally, any attempt to use the attributes of physical power including the power to intimidate or terrorize, or de facto control over land, resources, and borders, in order to impose inequities in either the design or outcome of negotiations is unacceptable.

It is worth remembering that these kinds of action are all *choices* that are made by individuals inside and outside of governments, as well as—in some cases—by the voters who bring governments to power. There is nothing foreordained or mechanically "structural" about such choices. They are choices that are made by men and women: men and women, moreover, who in most cases are honestly pursuing what they consider to be the best interests of the community to which they belong. But such choices are all profoundly unethical, as well as essentially counter-productive in that they fail to bring about the increased community well-being that is their stated goal. We therefore urge the citizens and governing powers in these communities to reconsider and reverse their support for all policies that depend on treating members of the "other" community as somehow less human, or somehow less deserving of basic, God-given rights, than themselves.

* * *

In writing this report, we have tried to share not only as much as possible of what we felt and learned about the situation of Israelis and Palestinians in these troubled times, but also our sense of the complexity and interconnectedness of the different ways in which these two national groups relate to each other.

We started out by recounting our many rich experiences in the Gaza Strip and the West Bank, and our many encounters with the Palestinians of those areas and with Jewish Israelis both in the occupied territories and inside Israel. From the Israelis with whom we met, we heard of the multiple harms and pain that their community has suffered as a result of the repeated terror bombings to which some Palestinian non-governmental groups have subjected them, and their intense frustration that the Palestinian Authority seemed unable or perhaps unwilling to control those groups. From several of our Jewish-Israeli interlocutors we heard expressions of more generalized fears: a sense that the hostility that the Israelis faced from Palestinians was vividly reawakening memories of the centuries of anti-Semitism that the Jewish people had faced during their own years in diaspora from their homeland; a sense that the hostility they faced from the Palestinians was just the tip of a vast wave of hostility directed toward Israel from nearly all the Arab and Islamic worlds; and, notably, a strong sense of fear that Jewish Israelis risked losing their majority status by any large-scale return of the Palestinian refugees.

From the Palestinians we talked with in the occupied territories, we heard strong descriptions of the catastrophe that their society was living through: a catastrophe that with the extended lockdowns, restrictions on their freedom of movement, and other harsh collective punishments imposed since September 2000 had entered a period of particularly acute suffering, but a catastrophe that had previously been many years in the making. From nearly all these Palestinians (as from many Jewish Israelis) we heard a sense of crushing disappointment that the once-welcomed Oslo peace process had resulted in such an unsatisfactory outcome. We heard pain and some reproach that the suffering of the Palestinians seemed to have been forgotten by the world, and in particular by the government of the United States, a body in which the Palestinians had earlier placed so much trust.

In the Palestinian community, we met many individuals who continued with a great sense of commitment (and considerable grace and good humor) to try to ease the burdens that Israel's repressive rule had imposed on their families and their communities, who tried to ensure the survival and spread of humane values in a society riven by pain and flashes of intense anger, and who brainstormed with each other and with us on ways to bring about a stable and hope-filled peace with their neighbors the Israelis.

In the Jewish-Israeli community we likewise met many women and men who were working tirelessly to find ways to put a workable peace process back on track, to reach out to their Palestinian neighbors, and to rebuild the inter-communal ties that had been frayed so badly by the events of the second *intifada*.

We noted that for many of these peace activists, from both national communities, upholding their support for the values of peace and equality often meant posing a strong challenge to their own societies (and facing a strong challenge from) the dominant discourse in a surrounding society where hate-speech often seemed far more prevalent than support for peaceful values. We salute the courage and dedication with which these activists continue their work.

As a special part of our study of the situation in the occupied territories, we paid particular attention *to the situation in Jerusalem,* a city that is at the heart of so much of the conflict between these two peoples and presents its own special challenges.

In Jerusalem, the insertion of large numbers of Jewish-Israeli settlers into the heart of areas of Palestinian population has been more intense than anywhere else in the areas occupied in 1967. Therefore, any "unscrambling" of the demographic omelette, such as would be required under most versions of the two-state solution, would be far harder to devise for East Jerusalem than it would be anywhere else in the occupied territories. Jerusalem, moreover, is not simply "just another city" contested between two groups of its residents. It is a city of profound importance to both national groups, as well as to billions of adherents of the three Abrahamic faiths around the world.

If Jerusalem can be looked at for a moment in terms simply of good municipal governance, then it is evident that the kinds of institutionalized discrimination that the city's Palestinian residents have suffered for more than 36 years at the hands of their Jewish-Israeli governors cannot be tolerated by people around the world who have struggled to end discrimination in housing or provision of municipal services against people who are Jewish, black, or belong to other politically marginalized minorities. If it is looked at as Yerushalayim/Al Quds, a city holy to so many and bearing the weight of so much religious and national longing, then the tragedy of what it has become today challenges all of us to work harder to imagine what it might—with goodwill—become tomorrow.

We were also able to visit with *Palestinians living in exile* in near-by countries, and we heard vivid testimonies of their 55-plus years of displacement, dispossession, and scattering. From all the refugee Palestinians we met with, both inside and outside the occupied territories, we heard much frustration that their rights had for so long been almost completely ignored. From some, we heard a degree of resigned acceptance that they might not in the end be able to return to the ancestral properties that they and their families had fled or been forced from so long ago. But we also heard a burning insistence that their claims on history, on Israel, and on an often hostile world needed to be listened to seriously. We judge this insistence to be quite legitimate. The Palestinian refugees have the same rights as any other group of people; they have a claim on the land and other resources of Palestine/Israel that cannot be ignored, marginalized, or annulled; and they have ties to that part of the world, and to the rest of the Palestinian people, that cannot summarily be severed. They are stakeholders in the situation in Israel/Palestine just as much as is any Jewish or Palestinian person who currently resides there.

Later in our visit, we had the opportunity to meet with *Palestinians who are citizens of Israel*, and to learn about their situation and the state of relations between Israel's Jewish and Palestinian citizens. In many respects, the situation of these Palestinians is like that of any politically marginalized minority group inside an otherwise mainly democratic society. We heard about the struggles they have waged against institutional discrimination in many areas of their life and about some of the partial successes they have won in the approaches they have made to the Israeli courts for redress.

So long as the broader Israeli-Palestinian conflict continues unresolved, the Palestinian Israelis will be facing the additional burdens that the conflict places upon them. They have close family ties with many of the Palestinians who became refugees in 1948— whether these refugees ended up living in Syria, Lebanon, Jordan, or the occupied territories. In the years after 1967, the Palestinian Israelis were able to resume their close acquaintance with their compatriots (and often, family members) living in the occupied territories. Most of the Palestinian citizens of Israel feel themselves to be very Palestinian, and this strong sentiment often tugs hard against their desire to do as well as they can by their families by acting within Israel's ethnocratic society and politics. We have suggested that in a time of broader peace, the Palestinian Israelis could be in a special position to build bridges between members of the two societies that they know so well. So long as there is no such peace, it is unlikely that the Palestinian Israelis can know much peace at home.

What did become clear from the fact that we were able to visit with Palestinians living in their diaspora and with Palestinians who are citizens of Israel as well as with Palestinians in the West Bank and Gaza was that though the circumstances of all these Palestinians may be very different, they have nonetheless retained dense networks of personal, familial, and political connections with each other. It was also clear that the political challenges faced by Palestinians in all these different circumstances are equally intimately bound up with each other. For very, very few of these Palestinians has the fact of their lengthy fragmentation broken the strong ties they feel to the rest of their national community or to its homeland.

* * *

The two groups of visits we made with Palestinians in the diaspora communities and inside Israel strengthened our understanding of the situation of the Palestinian people as a whole at the dawn of the third millennium, CE. But the first motivation that had led us to visit the region was our concern at the serious wave of Palestinian-Israeli violence that had engulfed the occupied territories since September 2000. Subsequent to our trip, as we reflected on our experiences in Gaza and the West Bank and further deliberated with each other about what we had seen and heard, it became clear to us (as indicated in chapter 4 above) that the Palestinians of the occupied territories and the Jewish citizens of Israel were locked into *two overlapping processes of violence,* with each of these processes seeming frequently to feed off the other.

On the one hand, there was the fairly visible "cycle" of violence, a process wherein egregious and often newsworthy violence undertaken by one side would inflict pain and suffering on members of the other community, and this pain and suffering would then be used to "justify" either a tit-for-tat reaction or—quite frequently—a highly escalatory response. (In late summer 2003, the typical nature of these acts was, on the Israeli side, extrajudicial killings of Palestinian militants, and on the Palestinian side, suicide bombings against targets inside Israel.) Often, it was quite hard to tell who had "started" any particular round of this cyclical violence. During the second *intifada,* a number of truces or temporary de-escalations were arranged. Sometimes the Israeli side broke these truces. Sometimes the Palestinian side did.

Though we describe this process as cyclical, we want to emphasize once again here its deeply asymmetrical nature. On the Israeli side, the vast majority of killings of Palestinians were carried out by members of organized security forces under the control of Israel's elected government, while only a relative handful were perpetrated by extra-governmental groups or individuals. Many of the killings by government forces were quite deliberate. For example, the Israeli human rights group B'tselem has compiled a list of 110 acts of deliberate, extra-judicial killing that were carried out by Israeli forces between November 2000 and June 2003. (The list also contains information on other, non-targeted individuals who were killed during these operations.)

On the Palestinian side, by contrast, very nearly all the acts that killed Israelis were carried out by nonstate actors, and very nearly all of them were denounced by the Palestinians' elected national leadership. Yasser Arafat could perhaps have done more to incapacitate the groups advocating and carrying out acts of violence—though it is hard to see how he could have done this after his own security infrastructure had been incapacitated by the Israeli attacks against it in spring 2002. We know of no evidence, however, that he or anyone else in the P.A. leadership ever ordered any killings of Israelis.

Another aspect of the asymmetry: Israel's powerful and well-funded security forces command means of killing that are more lethal, more numerous, and much easier to deploy than anything that any Palestinians have access to. In addition, nearly every single violent action undertaken by the Israeli security forces against the Palestinians has received the explicit or tacit approval of the most powerful government in the world: the United States. These factors helped to account for the fact that around three times as many Palestinians as Israelis lost their lives in the first three years of the second *intifada.*

To note these asymmetries is not to diminish for one moment the pain felt by an Israeli parent whose child has been killed by a suicide bomber, or the more generalized sense of fear and abandonment that the whole phenomenon of suicide bombings engendered in most of Israeli society. We do, however, need to remember that the pain of a Palestinian parent whose child is killed as, for example, "collateral damage" in an Israeli assassination operation is no less deep, no less real, than that of her Israeli neighbor; and the Palestinians have also suffered from a generalized sense of fear and abandonment as a result of the suffering that the Israeli government has inflicted on them.

As we noted in chapter 4, however, we also discerned that behind the more visible cycle of violence is a second, parallel process of violence in which proponents of Israel's settlement-building project have continued to expand their control over Palestinian land and resources in the occupied territories and to implant additional Jewish settlers into the settlements, while the Palestinians have done what they could to resist this process of colonial expansion. Here again, the process has been highly asymmetrical, since Israel's settlement project has enjoyed nearly full backing from Israel's powerful government and has been condoned by the U.S. government, while the Palestinians have had pitifully few national-level means to coordinate any effective resistance against this institutionalized colonial violence.

We should note that there have often been strong interactions between the "cyclical" and colonial processes of violence. For example, in the years that followed Ariel Sharon's election as Israel's prime minister in early 2001, the people in the settler movement were quite confident that they had strong support within the national government. This government then often exploited the security fears of Israelis living inside the green line—including many who hold a generally pro-peace position—in order to "justify" such actions as maintaining lengthy lockdowns and tight movement controls on the Palestinians of the occupied territories, expanding the boundaries of the settlements, or building the very harmful security "wall" that snakes through the West Bank. The effect (and sometimes, quite possibly, also the intention) of such actions has been to increase the area of the land over which the settlements have direct control, to decrease the amount of land in which Palestinians can hope to make a livelihood, and radically to undermine the Palestinians' ability to organize a defense of their ancestral lands.

Despite the many interactions between the two processes of violence that we have identified, we nonetheless consider it important to restate that we see both these different processes underway since our attitude toward each of them is significantly different. When we consider the visible cycle of violence, our overwhelming reaction is one of grief for the quite avoidable suffering that has been inflicted, and deep sympathy for all who have had their lives blighted by all these hateful acts. We stand foursquare against all acts of killing and all acts that deliberately inflict suffering on others. We stand, as the Israeli peace-and-justice activist Jeff Halper has clearly expressed it, "on the side of humanity."

We note, moreover, that this whole maelstrom of deadly violence and suffering that has continued in Palestine/Israel since September 2000 has done nothing to change the essential fact that there are still around six million Israelis (of whom one million are of Palestinian ethnicity) and three million non-Israeli Palestinians all living in the land of Israel/Palestine, and a further four million Palestinians living outside it but maintaining their claim on it—and it is clear to us that, basically, none of these population groups is going to melt away. One day, sooner or later, these thirteen million men and women will have to find a way to co-exist. The maelstrom of visible, deadly violence has not changed that fact. The challenge of finding a workable means of coexistence remains.

The situation was all the more tragic, since even while public support for the undertaking of acts of violence remained quite high in each community, still, as Gila Svirsky and others stressed to us, a clear majority of people on each side of the line continued to voice support for an outcome based on just about the same territorial compromise.

Regarding the other, deeper process of violence, the clash between the colonial project and its resisters, we cannot, however, stand neutral. Here, we judge that we must stand firmly against the colonial project, which constitutes a large-scale process of coercive "taking" of land and resources to which the colonizers have no valid claim. We say this in full knowledge that many participants in our group are members of communities that in the past participated in or were the beneficiaries of projects of colonial land-taking (though others of us have, by contrast, been the direct victims of such projects). This knowledge humbles us and causes us to continue to explore how those past harms might be repaired. It does not, however, encourage us to turn a blind eye when we see other projects of colonial taking being pursued in the present day. We stand firm with our adherence to the principle of human equality, and therefore to the idea that the rights of all peoples should be equally respected.

If devout Jewish people want to visit sacred sites in the West Bank or elsewhere for religious purposes they can always seek to do so in peace and with the consent of the people of who dwell in those areas, and their attempt to do so should surely be supported. If they want to live near such sites, that request should certainly, in an ideal world, receive sympathetic consideration from the duly constituted authorities that govern those areas. By contrast, the settlers' claim that they have a God-given right not just to live in the West Bank and Gaza but also to exert their own direct control over most or all of this land is quite a different matter. This claim can in no way cancel out the right of the indigenous people of these lands to exercise their own sovereign control over them, or the rights of millions of Palestinian exiles who seek a return to their homeland. The Spirit within which we strive to dwell is not one that picks out any one group of people to stand above the rest, but one who urges recognition and respect for all our fellow humans. The Inner Light that illumines our lives and our being is not one that permits us to sanction anyone's use of force-backed coercion to impose their will on others, or the establishment of institutions that systematically discriminate between people on grounds of ethnicity or manner of worship. This Light is one that endows us with a radical commitment to human equality, human connectedness, and the building of compassionate reciprocity in human relationships. It challenges us to exercise empathy with our fellow humans, and call directly to that of God in each of them.

When we say, therefore, that we stand firmly against the Israeli settlement project, does this mean that we support the use of any and all means to combat it? No, it does not. What we saw during our time in Israel/Palestine convinced us more firmly than ever before not only that mass civilian nonviolent organizing continues to be the most effective route to ending the occupation and building a fair and sustainable peace but also that this is by far the most ethical and farsighted way to proceed.

Many Palestinians claim that under international law they have a "right" to engage in armed resistance against military occupation. This may be so (though no law gives them permission to launch lethal attacks against civilians). But just because someone has an abstract "right" to do something, that does not mean that is always the smart or the ethically sound thing to do. We believe that in the circumstances that the Palestinians face, the adoption of a strong transformative strategy that seeks, through persuasion, to enroll a large section of the Jewish-Israeli community in a joint campaign for a just and peaceful order stands a far better chance of success than any strategy that seeks, through violence, to "scare" Israelis into doing the Palestinians' bidding. What we saw and heard while in Israel/Palestine convinced us that a violence-based Palestinian campaign will only drive Jewish Israelis further and further behind their barricades of fear and thus perpetuate the suffering of *both peoples* for more generations to come. A campaign based on persuasion and nonviolent direct action, by contrast, can help melt those barricades of Israeli fear and thus hasten the coming of a just order, while it also helps to combat the scourge of violence-based thinking that has permeated both societies so deeply and that will, if unchecked, prove a longlasting impediment to the flourishing of both peoples.

* * *

We, the members of the International Quaker Working Party, have been on a very long journey together—not just when we traveled together in the Middle East, but also as we labored together over many subsequent months reflecting on what we had seen and how best to make sense of it in this report. At the end of the day, what emerged for us was that though the various conflicts in the Middle East are frequently considered to involve states, potentially hostile governments, and large arsenals of threatening weapons, here in Israel/Palestine the central issue is not one of military security, traditionally defined, but rather, a straightforward question of how and when two groups of people can find a way to co-exist, and the cause of justice be served. The "story-line" of this report, as of our experience in the region, has been an intensely human one; and when the Palestinians and Israelis do finally find an escape from their present tragic vortex of violence and hostility it will be because women and men like those you met in these pages will have led the way.

We invite you, our readers, to join us in considering what you might do to help them.

In these pages we have presented numerous suggestions of the types of actions you might consider taking and the types of organization you might consider working with. There are more suggestions along these lines in the Appendices. We have not, however, presented any detailed formula for how we think the Palestinian-Israeli dispute should be resolved. As noted earlier, this is partly because most of us do not live there and therefore we are hesitant to tell our Israeli and Palestinian friends what they should do. It is also partly due to our own uncertainty as to whether aiming for a two-state or a one-state outcome would be the best path to take.

What we did present was our own, well-considered list of the basic principles according to which we believe any peacemaking venture should be judged. We hope that readers find this list a helpful tool with which they can make their own judgments in the months and years ahead—especially since these months and years will likely be ones of much significance and quite possibly much political movement, for the Palestinians and Israelis.

Will that political movement be in the direction we would like to see, of justice, peace, and reconciliation? Partly, that is up to those of us who live outside the area of the conflict: What can we do to support the work of the peace activists in Israel and Palestine? What can we do to organize in support of a just peace in our meetings, our congregations, our communities? What can we do to build relationships with other like-minded people, to publicize the work of Palestinian and Israeli peace activists, or to steer our national governments into wiser and more peace-oriented paths?

"The call to love and justice," as we noted at the beginning of this report, "is a joyous call to resistance and transformation." We urge you to consider whether, on this issue and at this time, it is also a call to action.

* * *

> *[W]e are not satisfied, and we will not be satisfied until justice rolls down like waters and righteousness like a mighty stream.*
> —Dr. Martin Luther King, Jr., August 1963

Appendices

Appendix A
Participants in the Quaker Middle East Working Party
June 11—July 1, 2002

(Organizational affiliations are listed here for identification purposes only.)

Kathy Bergen (Canada) National coordinator of the AFSC Middle East Peacebuilding Program; formerly director of the Geneva-based ICCP Office (the UN-initiated International Coordinating Committee for NGO's on the Question of Palestine); co-editor of *Justice and the Intifada* and numerous articles on Israel-Palestine.

Tony Bing (U.S.A.) Former Director of Peace and Global Studies at Earlham College, Richmond, Indiana; clerk of the National Peacebuilding Unit committee of the American Friends Service Committee; co-clerk of the International Quaker Working Party.

Max Carter (U.S.A.) Professor at Guilford College, Greensboro, North Carolina; long active in Middle East affairs with Friends United Meeting, Richmond, Indiana; organizer of projects in cooperation with the Friends Schools, Ramallah, and Ramallah Friends Meeting.

Helena Cobban (U.S.A.) Global affairs columnist for The Christian Science Monitor (Boston, MA) and *Al-Hayat* (London); author of four books on the Middle East and a volume based on interviews with Nobel Peace laureates, *The Moral Architecture of World Peace;* a member of Charlottesville (Virginia) Monthly Meeting.

Jim Fine (U.S.A.) Clerk of the AFSC National Middle East Peacebuilding Committee; former Quaker International Affairs Representative for the Middle East; former co-director of Quaker Legal Aid and Information Center in East Jerusalem; advisor for the Office of International Programs at University of Pennsylvania; co-clerk of the International Quaker Working Party.

Deborah Gerner (U.S.A.) Professor of political science at the University of Kansas; also, a visiting professor at the American University in Cairo and at Birzeit University (West Bank); editor of *Understanding the Contemporary Middle East;* author of *One Land, Two Peoples: The Conflict over Palestine* and numerous Middle East articles and book chapters; a member of Oread Friends Meeting (Lawrence, Kansas).

Stevie Krayer (U.K.) Poet living in rural Wales with a long-standing concern for racial justice; member of the Quaker Life Outreach Committee of Britain Yearly Meeting; came to Friends in 1990 from a secular Jewish background.

Jim Matlack (U.S.A.) Director of the Washington Office of the American Friends Service Committee, 1983-2003; formerly a professor at Cornell University and the University of Massachusetts; participated as AFSC representative in seven previous trips to the Middle East.

Richard McCutcheon (Canada) Has held positions as MCC/AFSC Field Representative to Iraq, Assistant Professor of Conflict Resolution Studies and International Development Studies at Menno Simons College, and research associate on the Health of Children in War Zones Project at McMaster University; a member of Hamilton (Ontario) Monthly Meeting and Clerk of Canadian Yearly Meeting.

Mmereko Emily Mnisi (South Africa) Adult educator and researcher for the South Africa Department of Education and the South African Federation for Mental Health; representative of the Friends World Committee for Consultation (FWCC) at the 2002 World Conference Against Racism; and Africa Section representative of the FWCC.

Ron Mock (U.S.A.) Director for Peace Learning and associate professor of Political Science and Peace Studies at George Fox College, Newberg, Oregon; author of studies in conflict resolution and nonviolent witness.

Hilda Silverman (U.S.A.) A long-time activist with Jewish peace/justice groups; member, Cambridge (MA) Peace Commission and Holocaust Commemoration Committee; member of the National Middle East Peacebuilding Committee of the American Friends Service Committee.

Gwendolyn Zoharah Simmons (U.S.A.) Assistant professor of religion at a U.S. university; specialist on Islam, Women in Islam and the contemporary impact of the *Shari'ah* (Islamic Law) on Women; formerly (in the 1960s) a civil rights activist with the Student Nonviolent Coordinating Committee (SNCC); then, for 23 years, a staff member of the AFSC.

Jean Zaru (Palestine) Presiding clerk of Ramallah Friends Meeting, Palestine; former member of the Central Committee of the World Council of Churches (WCC) and of the WCC's Working Group on Interfaith Dialogue; involved locally and internationally for more than two decades in interfaith dialogue and advocacy on human rights and the situation in the Middle East; founding member of Sabeel (Jerusalem) and Vice-President of its Board of Directors.

Appendix B

Alphabetical list of most of those with whom we met, June 12-July 2, 2002; and a brief itinerary

Abdel-Atty, Badr, Cabinet of the Foreign Minister, Cairo, Egypt

Abdel-Hadi, Mahdi, Director, Palestinian Academic Society For Study of International Affairs (PASSIA), Jerusalem

Abul-Ardat, Fathi, member of Political Committee, Ein el-Hilweh Camp, Lebanon

Abu Ali, Hassan, member of Political Committee, Ein el-Hilweh Camp, Lebanon

Abu Hadid, Khalil, Director of International Organizations, Foreign Ministry, Syria

Abu Jabr, Kamel, Pres., Jordanian Higher Media Council, former Foreign Minister, Jordan

Abul-Ainayn, Sultan (Abu Riyad), PLO official, Rashidiyeh Camp, Lebanon

Abu Majdi, Fuad Charkawi, member of Popular Committee, Ein el-Hilweh Camp, Lebanon

Abu Tawahina, Ahmed, staff psychologist, Gaza Community Mental Health Center, Palestine

AbuZayd, Karen Konig, Deputy Commissioner-General of UNRWA in Gaza. Palestine

Aghazarian, Albert, Director of Public Relations, Bir Zeit University, Palestine

Aghbariyeh, Raja, General Secretary, Abna' al Balad Movement, Umm el-Fahm, Israel

Aghbariyeh, Suleiman, Mayor of Umm el-Fahm, Israel

Al-Adawi, Salah (Abu Yusef), leader, Workers Union, Ein el-Hilweh Camp, Lebanon

Alpher, Joseph (Yossi), former Director, Jaffee Center, Tel Aviv, Israel

Amayreh, Khaled, journalist and researcher, Dura, Palestine

Andoni, Ghassan, Director, Rapprochement, Beit Sahour, Palestine

Asadi, Mahmoud, member of Political Committee, Ein el-Hilweh Camp, Lebanon

Ateek, Naim, Director, Sabeel, Jerusalem

Avnery, Rachel and Uri, leaders in Gush Shalom, Tel Aviv, Israel

Bak, Shaher, Minister of State for Foreign Affairs, Jordan

Bakhit, Marouf, Coordinator for Peace Issues, Foreign Ministry, Jordan

Baras, Sondra, organizer, Christian Friends of Israeli Communities, Karne Shomron, West Bank

Beit-Halahmi, Benjamin, Professor of Psychology, Haifa University, Israel

Berqawi, Ahmed, Professor of Philosophy, Damascus University, Syria

Berri, Nabih, Speaker of Parliament, Lebanon

Bin Talal, Hassan, Former Crown Prince, Jordan

Bishara, Azmi, Member of Knesset from Nazareth, Israel

Bishara, Rana, Palestinian Non-governmental Organizations Network, Nazareth, Israel

Bishara, Suhad, staff attorney, Adalah, Haifa, Israel

Bodine, Ann, Political Officer, U.S. Embassy, Lebanon

Bolling, Landrum, Senior Advisor, Mercy Corps; former President of Earlham College, Richmond, Indiana, U.S.

Chazan, Naomi, Deputy Speaker of Knesset, Israel

Dajani, Omar, Regional Affairs Officer, U.N. Special Coordinator's Office (UNSCO), Gaza, Palestine

Fayoumi, Moukhtar, National Center for Middle East Studies, Cairo, Egypt

Feldman, Shai, Director, Jaffee Center for Strategic Studies, Tel Aviv, Israel

Ghali, Mona, AFSC Field Coordinator, Gaza, Palestine

Golan, Gadi, Head of Religious Affairs Bureau, Ministry of Foreign Affairs, Israel

Hamarneh, Mustafa, Director, Center for Strategic Studies, University of Jordan

Hamidi, Ibrahim, Bureau Chief for Al-Hayat, Damascus, Syria

Hammami, Sheikh Jamil, Co-leader, Inter-Faith Dialogues project, PASSIA, Jerusalem

Hammoud, Sanaa, program officer, Ittijah, Haifa, Israel

Hiller, Ruth, founder, New Profile, anti-militarism activist, Tel Aviv, Israel

Ibrahim, Sa'ad ed-Dine, Professor, American University of Cairo, Egypt

Isaac, Jad, Director, Applied Research Institute, Jerusalem (ARIJ), Bethlehem, Palestine

Iwas, Zakka, Syrian Orthodox Patriarch of Antioch and all the East

Jibril, Amneh, General Union of Palestinian Women, Ein el-Hilweh Camp, Lebanon

Jumblatt, Walid, Leader of Popular Socialist Party, Lebanon

Kabbani, Sheikh Rashid, Sunni Grand Mufti, Lebanon

Kamphoefner, Kathy, member of Christian Peacemaker Team, Hebron, Palestine

Kasmieh, Khairia, Chair of History Dept., Damascus University, Syria

Keating, Michael, Director for Aid and Socio-Economic Affairs, UNSCO, Gaza, Palestine

Keller, Adam, leader, Gush Shalom, Tel Aviv, Israel

Khadr, Dunia, General Union of Palestinian Women, Ein el-Hilweh Camp, Lebanon

Khalil, Khalid, Association for Progress and Development in Galilee, Ittijah, Haifa, Israel

Khoury, Mahat Farah, former office director, Middle East Council of Churches (MECC), Damascus, Syria

Khoury, Samia, educator and board member, Sabeel, Jerusalem

Kippels, Craig, representative, Lutheran World Federation, Jerusalem

Kodmani, Bassma, Program Officer, Ford Foundation, Cairo, Egypt

Krayyim, Nayef, Al-Manar Radio station, Beirut, Lebanon

Kuftaro, Salah, Director, Abu Nour Islamic Foundation, Damascus, Syria

Kuttab, Beth, UNRWA Regional Director for Relief and Social Services, Amman, Jordan

Kuttab, Jonathan, Palestinian lawyer and human rights activist, Jerusalem

Lee, William, Director of UNRWA Operations in Jordan

Letlaka, Karabo, First Secretary, Embassy of South Africa, Egypt

Makhoul, Ameer, Director of Ittijah, Haifa, Israel

Ma'oz, Moshe, professor, Director of Truman Institute, Hebrew University, Jerusalem

Mawla, Saoud, professor, Lebanese University, Beirut, Lebanon

Nabulsi, Afif, Chief Shi'ite Cleric in South Lebanon

Neu, Pat, aid administrator, Jerusalem

Neu, Thomas, field director, American NearEast Refugee Aid (ANERA), Jerusalem

Nounou, Hussam, staff member, Community Mental Health Center, Gaza, Palestine

Nuseibeh, Sari, President, Al-Quds University, Jerusalem

Perkins, Jackie, First Secretary, Embassy of U.K., Egypt

Rahmeh, Kananah, General Union of Palestinian Women, Ein el-Hilweh Camp, Lebanon

Reinhart, Tanya, peace activist and professor, Tel Aviv University, Israel

Rempel, Terry, BADIL, Bethlehem, Palestine

Rosenberg, Reena, staff attorney, Adalah, Haifa, Israel

Sahhar, George, board member, Sabeel, Jerusalem

Sahyouni, Salim, President, MECC, Beirut, Lebanon

Said-Ali, Abdel-Monem, Director, Al-Ahram Center for Political and Strategic Studies, Egypt

Sayed, Ahmed Maher, Minister of Foreign Affairs, Egypt

Sfeir, Boutros, Maronite Patriarch, Lebanon

Shafa'i, Ghadir, staff attorney, Association for Arab Youth, Ittijah, Haifa, Israel

Shueibi, Imad Fawzi, professor, government advisor, Syria

Sourani, Raji, Director, Palestinian Center for Human Rights, Gaza, Palestine

South, Colin, Principal, Friends Schools of Ramallah, Palestine

South, Kathy, Friendly presence, Friends Schools of Ramallah, Palestine

Svirsky, Gila, leader, Women in Black and Bat Shalom, Jerusalem

(al-)Wahidi, Atta, vice-chair, camp committee, Bakaa refugee camp, Jordan

Warschawsky, Michael, co-founder, Alternative Information Center, Jerusalem

Weaver, Alain, Mennonite Central Committee, Jerusalem

Yacco, Samir, Protestant Evangelical Pastor, Damascus, Syria

Yazigi, Hisham, Deputy General Manager, Syria Shell Petroleum, Syria

Zilversmidt, Beate, leader, Gush Shalom, Tel Aviv, Israel

BRIEF ITINERARY OF QWP

June 12-14	Amman, Jordan
June 14-18	sub-groups visit Egypt, Syria and Lebanon
June 18	Amman, Jordan
June 19-30	Israel and Palestine: visits to Jerusalem, Hebron, Dura, Tel Aviv, Gaza City, Haifa, Umm el-Fahm, Karnei Shomron, Bethlehem and Beit Sahour, and bus tours around various parts of West Bank and Gaza

Appendix C
International Quaker Working Party on the Israel-Palestine Conflict

Epistle to Friends Jerusalem, 30 June 2002

The International Quaker Working Party on the Israel-Palestine Conflict is composed of members of the Religious Society of Friends (Quakers) along with Jewish and Muslim members who have traveled together to Israel, the occupied Palestinian territories, Jordan, Syria, Lebanon, and Egypt from 11 to 30 June 2002. We set out on this journey under a strong concern for the breakdown of the Israeli-Palestinian peace process, the rise in the level of violence, and the suffering being experienced by both peoples.

After having traveled in Arab countries for one week, and in Israel and the occupied Palestinian territories for nearly two weeks, our concern is even more urgent. We have heard much about the current suffering and seen it at close quarters. We witnessed a young Palestinian man being kicked during interrogation on the street by Israeli soldiers. We heard an Israeli friend describe her grief when visiting a colleague whose mother and daughter were killed in a recent suicide bombing. We witnessed Palestinians being humiliated at roadblocks. We saw areas of the West Bank where every village was cut off from its neighbors by Israeli army barricades across all access roads. We saw the effects of systematic legal and budgetary discrimination against the 18 percent of Israeli citizens who are Palestinian. We heard the distress of an Israeli mother whose children faced the call to military service. We heard an Israeli settler describe the painful impact of lethal attacks against members of her community. We heard the despair of Palestinian refugees in Lebanon, Syria, and Jordan, whose hopes for an end to their 54-year-old exile have once again been dashed. We witnessed many signs of the heavy burdens and dislocations that the current state of tension places on Israel's social fabric and economy. We heard about, and saw indications of, an impending humanitarian disaster in the occupied Palestinian areas.

Our own plans were significantly affected by Israel's closures and other administrative actions. Our travel and appointment schedules had to be altered or canceled repeatedly. We were unable to enter Ramallah, which was under curfew, to be with Quakers who live there. We felt this frustration and pain very directly through the experience of our Palestinian Quaker colleague, Jean Zaru, who was not permitted to travel with us much of the time, and had great difficulty in reaching her Ramallah home due to Israeli blockades and curfews.

Despite the widespread tension and hardship, everywhere we went people from a variety of backgrounds, positions, and political persuasions received us with warm hospitality and candor. We experienced time and again a deep generosity of spirit, which is alive and well, if under severe threat, amongst the people caught up in this conflict.

This generosity of spirit coexists, however, with a great deal of fear in both societies. Many Israelis fear for the continued existence of their Jewish state. Palestinians increasingly express fear of a new *nakba* (catastrophe), like the 1948 flight and expulsion of 700,000 Palestinians from their homes in areas that became Israel.

From our experiences and the in-depth discussions we had with scores of organizations and individuals, we believe that Israelis and Palestinians are now locked into an escalating, highly destructive cycle of repression and violence. Behind this cycle, however, we discern the existence of a deliberate project that seeks to dispossess the Palestinians from their land. This project is not new, but its advocates are acting with greater boldness now. They use force to implement it and they use the occurrence of Palestinian violence to justify it. We have seen new fences built in the West Bank that expand the land controlled by Israeli settlements to the very edge of Palestinian villages. We have seen dispossessed Palestinians, removed by the Israeli army from their ancestral grazing grounds and forced to live adjacent to a Jerusalem municipal garbage dump. In the Gaza Strip, we saw an Israeli bulldozer overturning Palestinian crops alongside a Jewish settlement near Beit Lahia; the bulldozer was guarded by an Israeli tank perched on a nearby hill.

Throughout our travels we saw evidence that the present Israeli government is intensifying policies that strangle the Palestinians' economy and destroy their physical and social infrastructure in the West Bank and Gaza. These policies have already brought many communities in these areas to the brink of a major humanitarian disaster. In the Israeli-controlled portion of Hebron, for example, we saw evidence of a dying community in the deserted markets, vandalized shops and abandoned homes. The Hebron reality demonstrates the effects of policies that some Israelis hope will persuade Palestinians voluntarily to leave their homeland. We are concerned that such policies leave Palestinians extremely vulnerable to further pressures, or even to the possibility of mass expulsion from the land in which they have been deeply rooted for generations.

We have been disturbed to find that within Israel the option of "transfer"—that is, the ethnic cleansing of large numbers of Palestinians from the occupied territories, or even of Palestinian citizens from inside Israel itself—is now discussed openly by politicians, intellectuals, religious leaders, and many other segments of society. As a Quaker working party, we condemn this idea and any other proposal that fails to respect the equal worth of all of God's children.

In the same spirit, we oppose the use of violence to resolve human conflicts. We grieve for each precious life lost or shattered. We mourn especially the civilians—Israeli and Palestinian—who have been killed and we condemn without reservation the acts of violence that have struck them down in the course of their daily lives. We recognize the grievous harm done to societies who come to rely upon the use of force to solve their problems, as well as the damage done to those they attempt to coerce. As many persons in the region have concluded, there is no solution to this conflict through violence.

We issue an urgent appeal to everyone inside and outside the Quaker community to raise awareness of this deepening crisis and to work for a broad range of mechanisms to ensure the protection and rehabilitation of threatened Palestinian communities. Such mechanisms should include the deployment of a protective force sanctioned by the United Nations drawing on the precedent of East Timor. In addition we urge the dramatic expansion of citizen and faith-based protective activities, such as accompanying Palestinians, riding Israeli buses, monitoring settlement activity, reporting human rights abuses, and cooperating with Israeli and Palestinian nonviolent peacemakers and justice advocates. We are convinced that these measures will serve to reduce the threat of violence to both Israelis and Palestinians.

We affirm the need, once international protection is in place, for reform and transparency in Palestinian political and economic institutions. Such reform cannot be fully implemented while the Israeli occupation remains in place. Meaningful elections are impossible when civil institutions are in ruins and people cannot move beyond their homes or neighborhoods. Economic revival cannot occur if people and institutions are under constant threat of destruction. The trust necessary for effective negotiations cannot develop at gun-point.

Beyond the urgent issue of protection, we believe that concerted international action is still needed in two areas. **We call for all necessary steps to bring about a speedy end of the Israeli occupation of the West Bank and Gaza.** We base this call on a fresh awareness that the Israeli occupation of these areas, which has continued for 35 years, is devastating for Palestinian society and deeply harmful to the moral fabric and long-term security of Israel. As part of the process of ending occupation, we call for effective actions to end all international support for Israel's continuing expansion of exclusive Jewish settlements and related infrastructure, including construction within the settlements' current zoning and planning areas.

The other objective which requires urgent international response is to secure a final status agreement between Israelis and Palestinians based on all relevant U.N. resolutions and international law. We believe this agreement must take into account not only the final status of the West Bank, including East Jerusalem, and Gaza, but also the legitimate claims of Palestinian refugees wherever situated; the yearning for dignity and equality that we heard from Palestinians who are Israeli citizens; and the strong desire we heard from Jewish Israelis for a secure existence in the land to which they are deeply attached.

We recognize that this is an ambitious agenda. We do not offer any single formula for how these goals can be achieved, though we shall amplify our analysis and recommendations in a fuller report we plan to issue in the coming months. We share our profound sense of urgency regarding both the humanitarian and the political crisis. Because we believe that there is that of God in everyone, we call on Quakers and others to work energetically and nonviolently for a solution based on the equal worth and dignity of each person, and on the power of love, forgiveness, moral imagination, and generosity of spirit to find a way to resolve even those conflicts that may appear intractable.

Kathy Bergen (Canada)	Tony Bing (U.S.A.)
Max Carter (U.S.A.)	Helena Cobban (U.S.A.)
James Fine (U.S.A.)	Deborah J. Gerner (U.S.A.)
Stevie Krayer (U.K.)	James H. Matlack (U.S.A.)
Richard McCutcheon (Canada)	Mmereko Emily Mnisi (South Africa)
Ron Mock (U.S.A.)	Gwendolyn Zoharah Simmons (U.S.A.)
Hilda Silverman (U.S.A.)	Jean Zaru (Palestine)

Appendix D

History of Friends Work in Palestine and Israel

1868	Friends began to explore work in Palestine (New England Friends, British Friends, and Five Years Meeting, which later became Friends United Meeting).
1889	Friends Girls School is built in Ramallah.
1901	Friends Boys School is built in Ramallah.
	Both schools were turned over to Friends United Meeting (FUM) and partially devolved in 1986.
1948-1950	American Friends Service Committee (AFSC), at the request of the United Nations, provides humanitarian relief for Palestinian refugees.
1949-1962	AFSC Palestinian-Jewish youth work in Israel (Acre Neighborhood Center).
1950-1955	AFSC works in agricultural development in Turan, a northern Palestinian village in Israel.
1948-1950	AFSC begins self-help projects for internally displaced Palestinians in western Galilee.
1960	Friends Service Council (FSC-London) makes available annual grants for bursary assistance to the Friends Schools in Ramallah.
1951-1957	AFSC organizes youth exchanges (workcamps).
1967-1968	AFSC explores possible program options in Israel and Jordan.
1967-1995	AFSC establishes and continues to support Quaker kindergartens in Gaza.

1970   AFSC publishes *Search for Peace in the Middle East,* a study prepared by AFSC and the Canadian Friends Service Committee, acting in association with the Friends Service Council (London), the Friends World Committee for Consultation, and the Friends Peace and International Relations Committee (London).

1972-present   Middle East Quaker International Affairs Representatives (ME-QIAR) maintain a presence in the region, including Israel and Palestine, working on behalf of all Quaker bodies and supervised by AFSC.

1973   AFSC begins the Quaker Legal Aid and Information Center in East Jerusalem (devolved to local board in 1997).

1977-1981   AFSC operates Children with Disabilities Program in Beersheva, Israel.

1982   AFSC publishes *A Compassionate Peace: A Future for the Middle East* (prepared by a Working Party appointed by the AFSC Board of Directors).

1984-1994   Quaker Peace and Service (QPS), former FSC, establishes a position in Jerusalem and sends volunteers to work with Palestinian and Israeli NGOs.

1984-present   AFSC supports Israeli NGOs working on Palestinian-Israeli coexistence among youth and women.

1987   AFSC publishes *Missed Opportunities for Peace.*

1988-1992   AFSC seconds to the Union of Palestine Medical Relief Committees a physical therapist to work in the village of Idna in the West Bank.

1994-present   AFSC Palestine Youth Program in West Bank and Gaza.

1998-2000   QPS sends staff to work at the Friends Schools in Ramallah.

2002   Quaker Peace and Social Witness (QPSW), former QPS, sends observers to Palestine to witness the situation of Palestinians living under Israeli military occupation.

2002-present   AFSC supports the Refusenik and Conscientious Objector movements in Israel.

              AFSC responds to requests from Palestinian NGOs to support and assist in training for non-violent resistance and direct action.

2003-present   AFSC appoints Quaker International Affairs Representatives (QIARs) for Jerusalem.

2003-present   Observer Project of QPSW becomes the Ecumenical Accompaniers Project for Palestine and Israel (EAPPI).

Appendix E

Principles for a Just and Lasting Peace Between Palestinians and Israelis
American Friends Service Committee
October 28, 1999

Because of the many political, economic, and social changes that have taken place since the 1989 revision of A Compassionate Peace, *the AFSC has felt the need to update and reaffirm its policy regarding the long-standing Israeli-Palestinian conflict. We believe that an articulated position based upon historic AFSC principles might offer some ways to reshape the peace discourse and allow it to move forward.*

From its beginnings in 1917, the American Friends Service Committee has sought to repair the destruction caused by war and violence by relieving and healing its victims. The AFSC has sought to respond to suffering whether it is caused by direct human actions or by oppressive structures that human beings have created. When peacebuilding through humanitarian aid has led the AFSC to enter the political arena, the AFSC, in its support for peacemaking, has sought reconciliation between antagonists, endeavoring to help create the conditions of genuine peace that are based upon the preservation of basic human rights and the restoration of justice. In its role as peacemaker as well as peacebuilder, the AFSC has operated from a nonviolent ethic of care that acknowledges and embraces the humanity on all sides of those in conflict.

The AFSC has approached its work from a spirit of love, but an equally strong motivation for its work has been its commitment to truth. Indeed, only after there is truth can we begin the task of serving justice as well as love. Only after parties in conflict can believe in the possibilities of justice can there be hope for reconciliation. The AFSC believes that in speaking truth, in struggling for justice, and in exhibiting compassion, the organization may help reshape the ways human beings speak about and think about peace and how they act upon those words and thoughts.

The AFSC's long experience in the Middle East, reaching back to the end of World War II, convinces us that looking at issues of war and peace from an ethical and religious perspective can be useful and timely. The AFSC believes that focusing on the precious humanity of those in conflict with one another will open new ways for considering how peace might be achieved and sustained. The Middle East policy of the United States and most of the rest of the Western world, as well as the policy of the Israelis and Palestinians, has for too long accepted the myth that only violence and the threat of violence can produce stability and create peace. The reality is that violence has not brought peace, and the threat of violence has only exacerbated the conflicts.

By definition, the peace for which the AFSC is working will be not merely the absence of war, but the presence of justice—justice between nations, and within nations as well. Because we are worried that not all involved parties are on the road to a peace sustained by justice, we welcome this opportunity to explain our position on some of the most contentious elements in this conflict, including some that have not been addressed at all in the aftermath of Oslo. As we state our position, we hope to make clear that it is informed by a concern for truth and justice, and is shaped by compassion and care.

Components of a Just Peace
1. Self-determination

Self-determination has been a leading principle in the breakup of colonial empires and in the creation of independent states in the Twentieth Century. The truth is that Israelis have already exercised their right to national self-determination and now have their own state. The Palestinians continue to be denied that right. In accordance with its ethical and religious beliefs and with international law, the AFSC has consistently upheld peoples' rights to self-determination. Specifically, the AFSC affirms the right of both Israelis and Palestinians to live as sovereign peoples in their own homeland, a right that encompasses the possibility of choosing two separate states. We acknowledge that other options such as bi-national state and confederation are being discussed. Ultimately it will be up to both parties to determine national boundaries, but the AFSC believes that the starting point for discussion should be those borders reflected in United Nations resolutions 242 and 338, substantially the borders that were in place before the war of June 1967. Since the issue here is of one land and two peoples, no one's right to self-determination should be exercised at the expense of someone else's. Consideration of this issue should address, in a timely way, the repatriation of refugees. Any settlement of boundaries must be based upon respect for the rule of law and for the right of both peoples to determine their own future. Both parties should be guided by an ethic of reciprocity: what holds true for one side in a conflict should hold true for the other as well. This ethic will help address the very real power imbalance that currently exists between Israelis and Palestinians, an imbalance that works against mutually acceptable and just agreements.

2. Rights

The same principles of reciprocity present in self-determination must also extend to the discussion of human rights, which provide the foundation to any building of peace. Human rights include the freedom to practice one's

religion, the freedom of assembly, free speech, free press, the right to education and adequate nutrition, and civil rights for all people, regardless of race,
religion, gender, sexual orientation, political orientation, nationality, or ethnicity. Rights of minorities within the Israeli state and within a future
Palestinian state must be safeguarded. Other important rights include the
right to legal representation, a fair trial, and protection against discrimination in employment, housing, education, and health care. The AFSC also
affirms the right to freedom of movement within borders and freedom from
collective punishment, because these rights often have been denied. These
rights ought to be secured not only at the end of the peace process, but also
to inform the process itself. The AFSC has long contended that means determine ends. Therefore just ends can be accomplished only through just means.

3. Economic Justice and Natural Resources

All parties need to take action to ensure equitable access to resources such as
land and water. Fair taxation and distribution of resources are critical elements to establish and maintain peace, not only between Israelis and
Palestinians, but also within each separate society. It is important that people,
goods, and services be able to move freely in the region. People should have
the right to build and live anywhere, but not as a result of unwarranted land
confiscation and illegal settlements. Mobility for trade, employment, education,
and residence is critical to establishing and sustaining peace. These issues can
be addressed before, during, and after any political solution to the conflict.

4. Governance

The AFSC supports the rights of both Palestinians and Israelis to choose
their forms of governance. We affirm our support for a democratic process
that is accountable to all its people as the surest means of achieving sustainable and just political structures.

5. Security

The foundations of security are to be found in trust, respect, and mutual
recognition of the humanity and past and present sufferings of both parties.
Security is contingent upon the achievement of self-determination and the
promotion and protection of basic human rights. Such security does not currently exist. While it is tempting to suppose that only military strength can
achieve and guarantee security, the AFSC has maintained that military might
only increases fear and distrust and exacerbates the power differences that
already exist between conflicting parties. Consequently, the AFSC supports
substantial reduction of armaments to all states in the Middle East, because
the availability of arms contributes to the prevalence of violence and causes
the use or threat of violence to be the first resort to settle any personal, com-
munal, or national dispute.

6. Status of Jerusalem and Settlements in Gaza and on the West Bank

Since the 1967 war, unilateral Israeli settlement in Jerusalem and on the West Bank and Gaza has been one of the great obstacles to the peace process. The AFSC believes that the building of settlements in the occupied territories, including in the city of Jerusalem, violates Israel's obligations as an occupying power under the terms of the Fourth Geneva Convention. Compensation or restitution to those who have lost their homes and lands by illegal means are topics that must be and have not yet been addressed. Consistent with AFSC's belief that Israel and Palestine is a land for two peoples, Jerusalem must be regarded as a city that can be united but also can be shared by both peoples. Since the status of Jerusalem continues to be a very great obstacle to peace at the present time, the AFSC believes that no party in the conflict should alter the reality on the ground in a unilateral way, as Israel has done with its settlement policy. The AFSC also affirms its support for open access to the city for Palestinians, as well as Israelis, as a religious, political, socio-economic, and residential center, even before the final status of Jerusalem has been determined.

7. Responsibilities of the International Community

It is in the national interest of all countries that there be peace in the Middle East. Countries within the United Nations have already given support for an eventual two-state solution based upon U.N. Resolution 242. All countries, but especially the United States, should affirm the principles of self-determination in accordance with human rights and international law, and should support the control and reduction of arms into the area and the expansion of economic, non-military aid. Aid should be linked to programs that build democratic infrastructures, secure human rights, and preserve human dignity. The AFSC believes that the world community's goal should be disarmament in the whole region of the Middle East and elsewhere and the implementation of the nuclear non-proliferation treaty.

Conclusion

The road to peace needs to be carefully re-constructed and followed. Violence and the threat of violence often appear to be short-cuts to reaching the goal. However, as A. J. Muste observed, they are short cuts that become blind alleys. The surest road to peace is the path of empathy, where self interest can give way to shared interest, where separateness can give way to reconciliation, where domination can give way to justice. Helping to build that road and joining with Israelis and Palestinians who choose to walk it, are tasks to which the AFSC continues to dedicate itself.

Appendix F

Minute

To Friends United Meeting Triennial Session From Interest Group on the Middle East July 14, 2002

Members of the Religious Society of Friends (Quakers) representing 29 yearly meetings from eight countries meeting in Triennial Sessions of Friends United Meeting in Nairobi, Kenya, are conscious of the absence of our Palestinian Quaker brothers and sisters. Owing to the Israeli/Palestinian conflict, they have not been able to join us in our rich fellowship in the Spirit.

As we have experienced the loss of their presence we are reminded of the devastating impact of the conflict on all people in Israel and the Occupied Palestinian Territories and wish to extend our deepest concern and desire for peace.

We are tempted to feel helpless in the face of the complexities of the situation but know that we can reach out in Christian love to ALL people in the region.

The belief among some Christians that unquestioning support for current Israeli policies might hasten Christ's Second Coming is doing grievous harm to possibilities for peace, justice, and the application of international law, and has especially impacted the Palestinian Christian community remaining in the area. Christ's purpose is that all might have life and live it more abundantly. We reject as contrary to the Good News a focus on the Second Coming which denies this life to others.

We call on member meetings and churches in FUM to demonstrate in a tangible way their love, accompaniment, and concern. One way to do this is to pray for individual Christian congregations and write to them in expression of our solidarity and support.

We recommend that FUM, in consultation with Christian communions in Israel and the Occupied Palestinian Territories, provide contact information for Friends. We ask FUM to implement a plan to send teams and continue to work with other Christian bodies, the Christian Peacemaker Teams, and the World Council of Churches, to find ways together to work for peace, justice, and reconciliation.

Appendix G

Yearly Meeting 2003
Religious Society of Friends in Britain

Minute 14: 'And what does the Lord require of you?'
—a reflection on the situation in Israel/Palestine

In a deeply gathered meeting we have explored together our response to the situation in Israel/Palestine, hearing from Friends whose sense of witness has taken them in person to this troubled land. Concentration on the inhumanity of the situation does not guide us towards what we can do. The good acts of both Israelis and Palestinians are sparks of light in a suffocating ocean of darkness. The evil acts of both Israelis and Palestinians are inexcusable. Yet, there is no evil act, however terrible, which makes one human being less human than the next.

We must seek to understand why people do these things. The inhumanity of the situation springs from a shadow which exists in our own hearts. We have acknowledged that because of our Jewish and Christian heritage we are not outsiders but participants in this conflict who are called to be with those who say "that injury, that pain, I will not pass on to another" however difficult it may be to act in this way.

Let us now continue to pray for all the people of Israel/Palestine and for ourselves.

And what does the Lord require of you, but to do justly, and to love mercy, and to walk humbly with your God? (Micah 6:8).

Appendix H

Palestine-Israel Timeline

1516–1918	Ottoman (Turkish) Empire controls most of the Middle East.
1880s	Beginning of Arab movement for independence from the Ottoman Empire.
1881–1903	Russian pogroms against Jews; first wave *(aliyah)* of Jewish immigration to Palestine; Dreyfus affair in France reflects widespread European anti-Semitism.
1896-1897	Publication of Theodor Herzl's *The State of the Jews* sets the stage for political Zionism; first Zionist Congress meets at Basel, Switzerland, discusses establishment of a Jewish state.
1904–1928	Second and third *aliyot* (predominantly Soviet and Polish Jews) reflect a socialist-political form of Zionism.
1914–1918	World War I; Britain makes conflicting commitments regarding future of Palestine in the Hussein-McMahon correspondence (1915-1916), Sykes-Picot Agreement (1916), and Balfour Declaration (1917); end of the Ottoman Empire.
1919-1923	U.S.-sponsored King-Crane Commission tells Paris Peace Conference of Arab desires for independence; Newly created League of Nations ignores King-Crane and gives Britain mandatory control of Palestine.
1924-1928	Fourth *aliyah* includes fewer socialists, more middle-class eastern European and Soviet Jews.
1929	Western Wall riots between Palestinians and Zionists; Palestinians kill dozens of Jews from Hebron's historic Jewish community, survivors evacuate town.
1933-1935	Hitler comes to power in Germany; Germany's Nuremberg Laws formalize discrimination against Jews; fifth *aliyah* peaks as Jews escape from Germany and German-controlled areas.
1936–1939	Arab Revolt in Palestine; Britain crushes rebellion, expels or executes its leaders; ever-increasing persecution of Jews in Germany .

1937   British Peel Commission report recommends partition of Palestine into Jewish and Arab areas, angering the majority Palestinian Arab population.

1939   British MacDonald White Paper recommends restrictions on Jewish immigration and land purchases; calls for establishment within ten years of independent, binational state in Palestine, angering Jews who comprise 31 percent of Palestine's inhabitants.

1939-1945   World War II in Europe; Holocaust: Nazi regime responsible for death of approximately six million Jews (the *Shoah*) and millions of homosexuals, Roma, Slavs, and other "undesirables."

1945   U.N. established; World War II ends, leaving 100,000 eastern and central European Jews in "displaced persons" camps.

1946   Anglo-American Commission of Inquiry recommends U.N. trusteeship over Palestine; Palestinian and Jewish violence against British and each other; Jewish Holocaust survivors begin to flee to Palestine through clandestine land and sea routes.

1947   Britain requests that the U.N. deal with the question of Palestine; U.N. General Assembly Resolution 181 calls for Palestine to be divided into a Jewish state (57% of Palestine), an Arab state (43% of Palestine), and an internationally controlled *corpus separatum* for Bethlehem and Jerusalem.

1948   Civil war in Palestine; Britain ends its mandate, Israel declares independence, Arab states declare war against Israel; Israel gains control of 77% of British Mandatory Palestine, including some areas designated for Palestinian Arab state; Jordan and Egypt hold the West Bank and the Gaza Strip respectively, Jerusalem divided; 600,000-900,000 Palestinians displaced before, during, and after the fighting are not allowed to return; U.N. General Assembly Resolution 194 supports right of Palestinian refugees to regain their homes if they so desire or to receive compensation if they choose not to return.

1948–1958   Large-scale Jewish immigration to Israel from Europe, North Africa, and Asia.

1950   Israeli Law of Return and Absentee Property Law enacted; extensive confiscation of Arab property.

1956-1957   Suez War begins when Israel, supported by Britain and France, attacks Egypt; Israel conquers, later withdraws from, Sinai and Gaza Strip.

1964	Egypt and other Arab states establish Palestine Liberation Organization (PLO)
1965	Fateh (founded in 1959 by Yasser Arafat and others) conducts first guerrilla action against Israel..
1867	June (Six Day) War begins when Israel attacks Egypt, claiming it is acting preemptively; Israel occupies West Bank, Gaza Strip, Egyptian Sinai, and Syrian Golan Heights, expands Jerusalem boundaries and extends Israeli law over East Jerusalem; U.N. Security Council Resolution 242 calls for withdrawal of Israeli troops from territories newly occupied.
1968–1970	Israel begins to establish Jewish settlements in newly occupied territories; PLO adopts goal of a democratic secular state in all of Mandate Palestine; Arafat named chairman of PLO; War of Attrition between Israel and Egypt, Israel and Syria.
1970	Civil war between Jordanian army and Palestinians following airplane hijackings by a Palestinian guerilla group; PLO expelled from Jordan, moves to Lebanon.
1973	October (Yom Kippur/Ramadan) War begins when Egypt seeks to regain by force Egyptian land that Israel captured in 1967; U.N. Security Council Resolution 338 calls for cease-fire and comprehensive peace conference; oil embargo by Arab petroleum exporting countries.
1974	Arab League declares PLO the sole legitimate representative of Palestinian people; Arafat addresses United Nations which grants PLO observer status in 1975.
1975	U.S. promises Israel it will not to talk officially with PLO until, *inter alia*, PLO accepts U.N. Resolutions 242 and 338.
1976	Pro-PLO candidates sweep Palestinian municipal elections in the West Bank.
1977	Likud wins Israeli elections, Menachem Begin becomes prime minister; Egyptian President Anwar Sadat visits Jerusalem and addresses the Israeli Knesset; negotiations begin between Israel and Egypt.
1978	Temporary Israeli invasion of southern Lebanon; Begin, Sadat, and U.S. President Jimmy Carter sign the Camp David Accords.
1979	Begin and Sadat sign Israeli-Egyptian Peace Treaty in Washington, D.C.
1980	Israel's Basic Law on Jerusalem annexes East Jerusalem; U.N. Security Council condemns action.

1981	Israel attacks Iraqi nuclear reactor; U.S. sponsors cease-fire between Israel and the PLO that lasts until June 1982; Israel annexes Syria's Golan region.
1982	Israeli invasion of Lebanon; PLO evacuated from Beirut to Tunisia; massacre at Sabra and Shatilla refugee camps near Beirut; 400,000 Israelis demonstrate, call for investigation of Israel's role in massacre.
1985	Israel withdraws from most of Lebanon, leaving an Israeli-allied Lebanese force in control of the southern areas; Israel bombs Tunisian headquarters of the PLO.
1987-1993	Predominantly nonviolent (demonstrations, strikes) Palestinian *intifada*.
1988	Jordanian disengagement from West Bank; emergence of Hamas; declaration of the State of Palestine at the Palestine National Council meeting in Algiers; Arafat condemns terrorism, accepts U.N, Security Council resolutions 242 and 338, and recognizes the State of Israel; U.S. opens direct discussions with PLO.
1989	U.S. State Department publishes highly critical report on Israeli human rights practices; massive international peace demonstration in Jerusalem.
1990	Israeli coalition government collapses over proposed negotiations with Palestinians; influx of Jews from former Soviet Union to Israel begins; Yitzhak Shamir forms a narrow, right-wing government headed by Likud; U.S. suspends dialogue with PLO; Iraq invades Kuwait.
1991	U.S.-led coalition defeats Iraq; international Arab-Israeli peace conference in Madrid includes Palestinians in joint Jordanian-Palestinian delegation.
1992	Ongoing bilateral and multilateral peace talks; Labor party wins Israeli elections, Yitzhak Rabin becomes prime minister; Bush administration attempts to limit Israeli settlement by delaying U.S. loan guarantees.
1993	Israel drastically restricts Palestinian movement between Occupied Palestinian Territories (except East Jerusalem) and Israel; Israel and the PLO sign Declaration of Principles (the "Oslo Accords") on interim self-government arrangements.
1994	Massacre of Palestinians praying in Hebron mosque by Israeli settler; Cairo Agreement on implementation of the Oslo Accords; Arafat establishes Palestinian Authority headquarters in Gaza; Israel and Jordan sign peace treaty.

1995	Oslo II Accords establish three types of control in the West Bank (Area A: direct Palestinian control, Area B: Palestinian civilian control and Israeli security control, Area C: Israeli control); Rabin assassinated in Tel Aviv by Jewish Israeli male.
1996	First Palestinian elections for president and parliament result in Arafat victory; Palestinian suicide bombings in Jerusalem and Tel Aviv; Israeli "Grapes of Wrath" operation against Lebanon; Binyamin Netanyahu elected Israeli prime minister.
1997	Hebron Protocol divides West Bank city of Hebron into Israeli and Palestinian areas; Israel begins building Har Homa settlement between East Jerusalem and Bethlehem.
1998	Wye River Memorandum; PLO renounces anti-Israel clauses in PLO charter.
1999	Ehud Barak elected Israeli prime minister; Sharm el Sheik memorandum.
2000	Clinton-led Camp David II summit and negotiations end in failure; new Palestinian uprising *(al-Aqsa intifada)* begins, sparked by Ariel Sharon's visit to el-Haram el-Sharif/Temple Mount.
2001	Taba negotiations fail; Palestinian hard-liners continue suicide bombings against Israeli military and civilians; Israeli forces increase "targeted killings" (assassinations) of Palestinians and armed incursions into Palestinian-controlled areas; Sharon elected Israeli prime minister; U.S. Mitchell Report calls for immediate cease-fire and complete freeze on building of Jewish settlements in the West Bank and Gaza Strip.
2002	Palestinian suicide bombings and Israeli "targeted killings" continue; Israel forcefully reoccupies nearly all Palestinian areas evacuated as part of Oslo process; Arafat under house arrest in Ramallah; Arab League endorses plan to recognize Israel in exchange for end of occupation; Israel begins construction of "security fence" (The Wall) within the West Bank, confiscating additional Palestinian lands; "The Quartet" (U.S., U.N., Britain, European Union) proposes Roadmap to Peace.
2003	Palestinian suicide bombings and Israeli "targeted killings" continue; U.S.-led war against Iraq overthrows Saddam Hussein; Mahmoud Abbas (Abu Mazen) chosen as Palestinian prime minister; Israel completes first stage of "The Wall"; Abu Mazen resigns, replaced by Ahmed Qrei'a (Abu Ala'); Israel bombs alleged guerilla training camp in Syria.

Appendix I

History of the Israeli-Palestinian Conflict

By Deborah J. Gerner

INTRODUCTION

The Palestinian issue remains one of the most significant and difficult dilemmas facing the international community. The ongoing conflict between Israelis and Palestinians—a struggle over land and political control—is the result of a search for national identity and self-determination by two ethnonationalist groups in the context of nineteenth-century European imperialism, twentieth-century decolonization, and evolving international understandings of statehood and nationalism. Israeli-Palestinian hostility has directly or indirectly spawned half a dozen regional wars in the past five decades, threatened Western access to critical petroleum resources, provided a justification for increased militarization throughout the region, and led to civilian deaths as a result of terrorism by both state and nonstate actors. The United States, the Soviet Union/Russia, the European states (particularly Great Britain), and the Arab countries have all attempted to manipulate or control the Israeli-Palestinian conflict in order to enhance their own perceived national interests. The United Nations has also been involved. It has passed numerous resolutions and has sent peacekeeping forces to patrol the Egyptian, Syrian, and Lebanese borders with Israel, but it has been kept out of an active mediation role. Overall, the policies of actors external to the conflict have frequently exacerbated rather than re-duced tensions between the principal participants.

HISTORICAL BACKGROUND

At the start of the twentieth century, the Ottoman Empire ruled much of the Arab world, including Palestine, the area now referred to as Israel, the West Bank of the Jordan River, and the Gaza Strip. With the Allied victory in World War I, Palestine came under the control of the British, who made contradictory promises to French, Arab, and European Zionist leaders about how—and by whom—the area was to be governed. In a series of letters exchanged in 1915 and 1916, Sharif Hussein, head of the Hashemite. family and governor of Mecca, and Sir Henry McMahon, the British high commissioner of Egypt, discussed the terms under which the Arabs would assist the British war effort by revolting against their Ottoman rulers. Britain promised that, in exchange for this support, the Arabs would receive independence after the war ended. At the same time, European Zionists (Jewish nationalists) felt that the 1917 Balfour Declaration, which called for a "Jewish national home in Palestine," provided international sanction for Jewish political aspirations to be fulfilled in the same small territory. In addition, Britain had signed a secret agreement with France specifying how these two countries would divide control over the Arab parts of the Ottoman Empire once the latter had been defeated.

Not surprisingly, these irreconcilable commitments led to tensions within Palestine between the Jewish and Palestinian communities. In 1922 about 88 percent of the population of Palestine was Arab (Muslim, Christian, or Druze). The Jewish community included a small group of long-time residents (living mostly in Hebron, Safad, Tiberias, and Jerusalem), older immigrants who had fled persecution in Russia in the late 1800s, and more recent immigrants (particularly Zionists from Central Europe). The number of recent immigrants increased dramatically in size following Adolf Hitler's rise to power in Germany, leading Palestinians to fear that a Jewish homeland would indeed be created—at Palestinian expense. Between 1936 and 1939, Palestinians engaged in a massive revolt against British rule. Initially the rebellion was nonviolent; however, after a British commission recommended splitting Palestine, the revolt flared again in a much more violent form. The commission's proposal was widely rejected and was not implemented. Instead, Britain issued a new, equally problematic, policy that limited Jewish immigration and land purchases.

In the aftermath of World War II and the near destruction of European Jewry, on November 29, 1947, the United Nations General Assembly voted in favor of Resolution 181, which called for the creation of two states—one Jewish, one Arab—within a partitioned Palestine as soon as the British mandate ended in May 1948. The plan gave the proposed Jewish state 56 percent of the territory, including most of the fertile coastal area, although at this joint the Jewish community owned only 6 to 8 percent of the total land and made up about a third of the population. Jerusalem and Bethlehem were designated as international zones. Fighting between Palestinian and Jewish inhabitants began almost immediately after the United Nations announced its vote. Although small in number, the Zionist military forces were well-trained, well-armed, and well-organized; the Palestinians were not. By the time Britain withdrew and Israel declared independence, Zionist troops had conquered most of the areas allocated to Israel as well as some additional lands intended for the Palestinians. The surrounding Arab countries, which had territorial aspirations of their own and no interest in allowing a Palestinian state to come into existence, intervened militarily and took over those parts of Palestine not occupied by Israel. When armistice agreements were finally signed in 1949, Israel held 77 percent of Palestine, Egypt controlled the Gaza Strip, and Jordan claimed sovereignty over East Jerusalem and the hilly West Bank. The name "Palestine" was wiped off the political map of the world.

Only about 150,000 Palestinians remained in what became Israel. A second, much larger, group of Palestinians—over 700,000 people by most accounts—who had fled the fighting found themselves refugees at the end of the war. Forbidden to return to their homes in Israel, many remained in refugee camps in the West Bank, the Gaza Strip, and nearby Arab countries; others traveled to the Gulf, Europe, or the United States in search of work. Finally, a significant number of Palestinians who were living in the West Bank and Gaza Strip before the war remained there and came under Jordanian or Egyptian rule.

The Palestinian *nakba* (catastrophe), with its massive dislocation, dispossession, and economic deprivation, stunned Palestinians and created an immediate and profound crisis for the Palestinian nation. Until the mid-1960s, most Palestinians within Israel were ruled under strict military regulations, many first imposed during the years of British rule. They had to obtain permission to travel in or out of their immediate area, faced restrictions on their economic activities, and were subject to arrest or even expulsion for political reasons. Egypt and Jordan pressured Palestinians in the West Bank and the Gaza Strip not to challenge the status quo or engage in acts of resistance against Israel. Demoralized and without effective political or military direction (since Britain had expelled most Palestinian leaders in the late 1930s as part of the suppression of the Arab revolt), the Palestinian community entered into a period of political quietude that lasted well into the 1960s.

Less than 20 years after *al nakba,* during the June 1967 Six-Day War, Israel conquered the rest of the former mandate of Palestine as well the Egyptian Sinai (since returned to Egypt) and the Syrian Golan Heights. In the aftermath, Palestinians faced further dislocation and economic hardship as well as renewed shock and disappointment in the failures of the Arab military forces. Whereas the Palestinians had been completely disheartened by the events of 1948 and to a large extent withdrew from political activities, this time their response was one of active resistance, born out of the conviction that none of the Arab states could be relied upon to help. In Gaza, women and men engaged in an insurrection that began in 1968 and lasted for three years. In the West Bank, charitable organizations provided an organizational structure through which Palestinians could undertake resistance activities. Outside the borders of mandatory Palestine, nationalist guerrilla groups took over the Palestine Liberation Organization (PLO), which was established by the Arab states in 1964, and in 1969 elected Yasir Arafat chairman.

The mid-1970s, after the October War of 1973, was a period of increased international awareness of and support for the Palestinian national movement and for the PLO specifically. In October 1974, at the Arab League conference held in Rabat, Morocco, the Arab states acknowledged the PLO as the "sole legitimate representative of the Palestinian people." The next month, PLO leader Yasir Arafat was invited to address the members of the United Nations; after his speech, the United Nations granted the PLO observer status within the organization. Despite these political victories, the Palestinians still lacked the ability to determine their own destiny rather than serving as pawns in the political games of the superpowers and the Arab countries. This was made brutally clear when Egypt and Israel signed the

Camp David Accords in 1978 and followed this with a peace treaty the next year, despite the failure of the accords to resolve any aspect of the Israeli—Palestinian conflict. The message was reinforced when Israel invaded Lebanon in 1982 to eliminate the PLO's political and military infrastructure in that country (where the PLO had relocated after being expelled from Jordan in 1970).

The outbreak in December 1987 of the Palestinian *intifada* (uprising) marked the beginning of a community-wide mobilization against the lengthy Israeli occupation. Strikes, demonstrations, tax resistance, boycotts of Israeli products, and other acts of civil disobedience were co-ordinated through locally based popular committees. Palestinian resistance activities also included stone throwing and the creation of barricades to hinder the movement of Israeli forces. Massive Israeli arrests of Palestinians (over 100,000 by the end of 1993), the "administration detention" of more than 18,000 suspected activists for periods of six months to several years, deportations, curfews and closures, and the sealing or destruction of hundreds of homes affected virtually the entire population. In addition, more than 300 Palestinians and 11 Israelis were killed in the first year of the *intifada;* by the end of the *intifada,* Palestinian deaths numbered over 1,000. *

On July 31, 1988, Jordan renounced its claim to the West Bank, creating new political opportunities for the Palestinians, and in November 1988 the Palestine National Council met and declared the independence of the State of Palestine. The following month, Arafat, in addressing the United Nations General Assembly, committed the PLO to "a comprehensive settlement among the parties concerned in the Arab-Israeli conflict, including the state of Palestine and Israel and other neighbors within the framework of . . . Resolutions 242 and 338."** Arafat's explicit and very public declaration was an irrevocable act that changed forever the framework of the conflict and set the stage for the U.S.-sponsored Madrid Conference, the Oslo Agreement, and subsequent Israeli—Palestinian negotiations aimed at resolving the conflict.

THE CONFLICT

The core issues dividing the Israeli and Palestinian ethnonational communities have remained relatively constant over the years. They include the following:

- Borders: specific, fixed, agreed-upon boundaries for Israel and for the Arab states in the region, including whatever form of Palestinian state or political entity is created

- Status of Jerusalem

- Settlers and settlements: the political, civil, and national status of approximately 400,000 Jewish Israelis currently living on occupied land within the West Bank (including East Jerusalem) and the Gaza Strip

- Refugees and the right of return: the political, civil, and national status of Palestinians currently living outside the borders of the historic Palestine

- Compensation for Palestinians and Israelis who were forced to leave their homes and property as a direct result of the Israeli-Palestinian conflict

- Natural resources: the allocation of resources such as water among the region's peoples

- Assurance of mutual security for all states and all peoples in the region

- Political, civil, and national status of Palestinians currently living within Israel

- Economic viability of all the states in the region

- Role of the international community in supervising a negotiated settlement.

Each of these points reflects a significant and controversial aspect of Israeli-Palestinian relations that must be addressed before their conflict can be fully resolved.

MANAGEMENT OF THE CONFLICT

Throughout the twentieth century, various efforts were made to arbitrate the dispute between Palestinians and Israelis. The United Nations was heavily involved in the years following its vote to partition Palestine. It created the United Nations Relief and Works Agency to take responsibility for Palestinian refugees, sent mediators to the region throughout the 1940s, 1950s, and 1960s, and passed dozens of General Assembly and Security Council resolutions calling for cease-fires, condemning aggressive actions by each of the parties, and suggesting approaches for conflict resolution.

In recent decades, the United States has attempted to take a leading role in managing the conflict and has worked to exclude the United Nations from participation. The close relationship between Israel and the United States has hampered the ability of the United States to serve as a neutral mediator, however. Furthermore, for 13 years, the United States refused to acknowledge or deal officially with the PLO because of a promise the United States made to Israel in 1975:

> *The United States will continue to adhere to its present policy with respect to the Palestine Liberation Organization [PLO], whereby it will not recognize or negotiate with the Palestine Liberation Organization so long as the Palestine Liberation Organization does not recognize Israel's right to exist and does not accept Security Council Resolutions 242 and 338.****

The two UN Security Council resolutions referred to—242 and 338—marked the end of the June 1967 and October 1973 Arab-Israeli wars, respectively. Palestinians maintained these resolutions were an inadequate basis for negotiation because, among other issues, they did not address Palestinian demands for self-determination, referring instead only to a "settlement of the refugee problem." Later, in 1984, Congress wrote the 1975 pledge into law and added that the PLO had to renounce the use of terrorism *before* there would be any formal diplomatic discussions between the two parties. In the absence of relations with the PLO, the United States was forced to rely on other Arab states to represent Palestinian interests; a task these countries did poorly and without enthusiasm. After Arafat's conciliatory statements in December 1988, the United States opened direct contacts with the PLO.

The inability of the United States and the international community to resolve the Palestinian situation became a problem for the United States when Iraq overran Kuwait in August 1990. There were urgent calls for Iraq to withdraw, and the United States immediately began to put together a coalition to reverse the invasion. Palestinians were livid, asking why the Iraqi occupation was instantly condemned while Israel's occupation of Palestinian lands was ignored and, in the case of the United States, implicitly supported through U.S. economic and military assistance to Israel. In order to build a broad coalition against Iraq—one that included a number of Arab states— the United States committed itself to addressing the Israeli-Palestinian conflict once the war ended. Throughout the spring and summer of 1991, the United States undertook a series of meetings with Arab and Israeli leaders that culminated in a regional peace conference, cosponsored by the United States and the former Soviet Union, in Madrid, Spain.

Over the next two years, the Madrid negotiations, now moved to Washington, D.C., dragged on with a series of bilateral and multilateral meetings that accomplished little. A U.S. commitment to Israel guaranteed that the United Nations would have no role in the process. Unexpectedly, at the end of August 1993, the Israeli government and the PLO announced they had been meeting secretly in Norway and had reached an interim agreement for Palestinian self-government. The Declaration of Principles (DoP), signed in September, outlined a process for transforming the nature of the Israeli occupation but left numerous issues unresolved, including the status of Jerusalem, the right of return for Palestinian refugees, the disposition of Israeli settlements, security arrangements, and final borders between Israel and a Palestinian state.

Under the DoP, Israel was to relinquish day-to-day civil authority over parts of the Gaza Strip and West Bank to a newly created Palestinian National Authority headed by Arafat, who returned to Gaza in 1994. Ultimate power, however, remained with Israel, which exercised its control by sealing off the Palestinian-governed areas from the rest of the Occupied Territories and from Israel *for* extended periods of time, an action that devastated a Palestinian economy already weakened by years of occupation. In addition, Israel continued to confiscate land and to build settlements and roads that served to separate Palestinian cities, towns, and villages from each other, exacerbating the fragmentation of the West Bank and Gaza.

Subsequent agreements in 1994 (Cairo Agreement), 1995 (Oslo II), 1998 (Wye River I), and 1999 (Wye River II) failed to address the fundamental weaknesses of the DoP. The 314 pages of the Oslo II agreement, for instance, extended Palestinian civilian jurisdiction over major population areas, specified the form that Palestinian elections for a legislative council and president would take, and set May 4, 1996, as the deadline to begin final status negotiations that would deal with outstanding issues. It did not, however, indicate the consequences of a failure to meet the May deadline. Nor did Oslo II contain provisions to halt the creation of new "facts on the ground" that would influence the final form of any eventual agreement. The Wye I agreement, which took nineteen months to achieve in part due to the assassination of Israeli Prime Minister Yitzhak Rabin by a Jewish Israeli, simply rearticulated how Israel and the Palestinians were to carry out what they had already agreed to in Oslo II and were supposed to have finished more than a year earlier: interim steps toward a final status agreement. Wye River II set a new target date of September 10, 2000, for a permanent peace agreement.

With Palestinian-Israeli negotiations stalled and the final status talks not yet begun, U.S. President Bill Clinton called a summit at Camp David in July 2000. After two weeks of tense discussion, the conference ended without a deal, and by late September—following a provocative visit by Israeli Likud Party leader Ariel Sharon to the Noble Sanctuary/Temple Mount site—a second Palestinian *intifada* had begun. The massive and widespread violence rapidly dwarfed what had been seen during the first uprising. The Israel Defense Force killed alleged Palestinian militants, regularly shelled Palestinian police stations and other government buildings, and bulldozed Palestinian houses and crops, creating barren swaths of land. Israel also tightened its control around the Palestinian population enclaves and sent tanks and troops into areas that previously had been turned over to Palestinian control. Palestinian suicide bombings inside Israel and attacks on Israeli settlements reflected the increased level of violence. The U.S. "Mitchell Report"—released on April 30, 2001—called for a halt to the violence, a complete end to Israeli settlement expansion, and a return to what it called the "normal" conditions that existed before September 27, 2000. It had no impact. By late September 2001, more than 600 Palestinians and 170 Israelis had been killed. Few outside the region noticed the first anniversary of the uprising, however. Two weeks earlier, on September 11, 2001, nineteen men hijacked four commercial planes leaving New York City and Boston and crashed them into the World Trade Center, the Pentagon Building in Washington, D.C., and a field in Pennsylvania, killing about 3,000 people from dozens of countries. As the United States and its allies prepared for a war on terrorism, management of the Israeli-Palestinian conflict no longer seems to be a priority, even as the ground situation in the Middle East steadily deteriorated to the point where it became necessary in the spring of 2002 to dispatch Secretary of State Colin Powell to a region shattered by almost daily Palestinian bombings and Israeli military reprisals, in a forlorn effort to paste together a new peace.

SIGNIFICANCE

Strife between Israeli Jews and Palestinian Muslims, Christians, and Druze has now lasted more than a century. It is an archetypal example of a protracted, ethno-national conflict. None of the problems created by Britain's irreconcilable World War I promises, the partition of Palestine in 1948, and Israel's conquest of the West Bank and Gaza Strip in 1967 are close to resolution. Despite its military superiority and support from the world's most powerful country, Israel has failed to crush Palestinian nationalism. Nor have the Palestinians succeeded in advancing their cause significantly, despite political support from other states in the region and the vast majority of United Nations member countries. There is a stalemate: neither can defeat the other, yet the terms under which each is willing to end their conflict are unacceptable to the other side.

The importance of this area—the Holy Land—to Judaism, Christianity, and Islam guarantees that, until the conflict is resolved, it will continue to occupy a position of importance internationally far beyond what would be expected given the small territory, resources, and population involved. Furthermore, the failure of the United States to resolve this ongoing dispute challenges its stature and credibility as a world leader. While international law could provide guidance regarding the shape a permanent resolution might take, it is frequently ignored—a situation unlikely to change as long as the United States maintains its dominant position in negotiations. The conflict over Palestine is a dangerous situation that shows little evidence of being resolved in the near future.

NOTES

* The data on Palestinian human rights violations come from the Palestine Human Rights Information Center (Chicago and Jerusalem).

** "Yasser Arafat, Speech at U.N. General Assembly, Geneva, General Assembly 13 December 1988," *Le Monde Diplomatique,* online at <mondediple.com/focus/mideast/a2292>.

*** U.S. Congress, House Subcommittee on Europe and the Middle East, *The Search for Peace in the Middle East: Documents and Statements, 1967—1979.* Prepared by the Foreign Affairs and National Defense Division, Congressional Research Service, Library of Congress (Washington, D.C.: U.S. Government Printing Office, 1979), 15.

Appendix J
Some Key United Nations Resolutions

The U.N. itself maintains an extensive on-line database of resolutions, reports, and other documentation. Its URL is <domino.un.org/UNIS-PAL.NSF?OpenDatabase>. The database contains materials from within the U.N. system, from national governments, and from some NGOs. Another good source for documents relating to post-1967 peacemaking efforts is maintained by the Brookings Institution at: <www.brookings.edu/press/appendix/peace_process.htm>.

What follow are excerpts from the texts of four key U.N. resolutions:

- General Assembly resolution 181 of 1947, mandating the partition of Palestine (along with an excerpt from the U.N.'s Partition Plan itself),

- General Assembly resolution 194 of 1948, dealing with Jerusalem and the rights of Palestinian refugees,

- Security Council resolution 242 of 1967, passed some months after the Arab-Israeli war of that year, and

- Security Council resolution 338 of 1973, passed after the Arab-Israeli war of that year.

U.N. General Assembly Resolution 181 of 29 November 1947. Future government of Palestine ('Partition Plan') A

The General Assembly,

Having met in special session at the request of the mandatory Power to constitute and instruct a special committee to prepare for the consideration of the question of the future government of Palestine at the second regular session;

Having constituted a Special Committee and instructed it to investigate all questions and issues relevant to the problem of Palestine, and to prepare proposals for the solution of the problem, and

Having received and examined the report of the Special Committee (document A/364) including a number of unanimous recommendations and a plan of partition with economic union approved by the majority of the Special Committee,

Considers that the present situation in Palestine is one which is likely to impair the general welfare and friendly relations among nations;

Takes note of the declaration by the mandatory Power that it plans to complete its evacuation of Palestine by 1 August 1948;

Recommends to the United Kingdom, as the mandatory Power for Palestine, and to all other Members of the United Nations the adoption and implementation, with regard to the future government of Palestine, of the Plan of Partition with Economic Union set out below;

...

Calls upon the inhabitants of Palestine to take such steps as may be necessary on their part to put this plan into effect;

Appeals to all Governments and all peoples to refrain from taking action which might hamper or delay the carrying out of these recommendations

...

PLAN OF PARTITION WITH ECONOMIC UNION
PART I
Future constitution and government of Palestine
A. TERMINATION OF MANDATE, PARTITION AND INDEPENDENCE

1. The Mandate for Palestine shall terminate as soon as possible but in any case not later than 1 August 1948.

2. The armed forces of the mandatory Power shall be progressively withdrawn from Palestine, the withdrawal to be completed as soon as possible but in any case not later than 1 August 1948.

The mandatory Power shall advise the Commission, as far in advance as possible, of its intention to terminate the Mandate and to evacuate each area.

The mandatory Power shall use its best endeavors to ensure [that] an area situated in the territory of the Jewish State, including a seaport and hinterland adequate to provide facilities for a substantial immigration, shall be evacuated at the earliest possible date and in any event not later than 1 February 1948.

3. Independent Arab and Jewish States and the Special International Regime for the City of Jerusalem, set forth in part III of this plan, shall come into existence in Palestine two months after the evacuation of the armed forces of the mandatory Power has been completed but in any case not later than 1 October 1948. The boundaries of the Arab State, the Jewish State, and the City of Jerusalem shall be as described in parts II and III below.

4. The period between the adoption by the General Assembly of its recommendation on the question of Palestine and the establishment of the independence of the Arab and Jewish States shall be a transitional period.

U.N. General Assembly Resolution 194 of 11 December 1948. Palestine—Progress Report of the United Nations Mediator (on Jerusalem and the rights of the refugees)

The General Assembly,

Having considered further the situation in Palestine,

1. *Expresses* its deep appreciation of the progress achieved through the good offices of the late United Nations Mediator in promoting a peaceful adjustment of the future situation of Palestine, for which cause he sacrificed his life; and

Extends its thanks to the Acting Mediator and his staff for their continued efforts and devotion to duty in Palestine;

2. *Establishes* a Conciliation Commission consisting of three States members of the United Nations which shall have the following functions...

...

8. *Resolves* that, in view of its association with three world religions, the Jerusalem area, including the present municipality of Jerusalem plus the surrounding villages and towns, the most eastern of which shall be Abu Dis; the most southern, Bethlehem; the most western, Ein Karim (including also the built-up area of Motsa); and the most northern, Shu'fat, should be accorded special and separate treatment from the rest of Palestine and should be placed under effective United Nations control;

Requests the Security Council to take further steps to ensure the demilitarization of Jerusalem at the earliest possible date;

Instructs the Conciliation Commission to present to the fourth regular session of the General Assembly detailed proposals for a permanent international regime for the Jerusalem area which will provide for the maximum local autonomy for distinctive groups consistent with the special international status of the Jerusalem area;

The Conciliation Commission is authorized to appoint a United Nations representative, who shall co-operate with the local authorities with respect to the interim administration of the Jerusalem area;

9. *Resolves* that, pending agreement on more detailed arrangements among the Governments and authorities concerned, the freest possible access to Jerusalem by road, rail or air should be accorded to all inhabitants of Palestine;

Instructs the Conciliation Commission to report immediately to the Security Council, for appropriate action by that organ, any attempt by any party to impede such access;

...

11. *Resolves* that the refugees wishing to return to their homes and live at peace with their neighbours should be permitted to do so at the earliest practicable date, and that compensation should be paid for the property of those choosing not to return and for loss of or damage to property which, under principles of international law or in equity, should be made good by the Governments or authorities responsible;

Instructs the Conciliation Commission to facilitate the repatriation, resettlement and economic and social rehabilitation of the refugees and the payment of compensation, and to maintain close relations with the Director of the United Nations Relief for Palestine Refugees and, through him, with the appropriate organs and agencies of the United Nations;

...

14. *Calls upon* all Governments and authorities concerned to co-operate with the Conciliation Commission and to take all possible steps to assist in the implementation of the present resolution;

15. *Requests* the Secretary-General to provide the necessary staff and facilities and to make appropriate arrangements to provide the necessary funds required in carrying out the terms of the present resolution.

U.N. Security Council Resolution 242 of 22 November 1967.

The Security Council,

Expressing its continuing concern with the grave situation in the Middle East,

Emphasizing the inadmissibility of the acquisition of territory by war and the need to work for a just and lasting peace in which every State in the area can live in security,

Emphasizing further that all Member States in their acceptance of the Charter of the United Nations have undertaken a commitment to act in accordance with Article 2 of the Charter,

1. *Affirms* that the fulfilment of Charter principles requires the establishment of a just and lasting peace in the Middle East which should include the application of both the following principles:

(i) Withdrawal of Israel armed forces from territories occupied in the recent conflict;

(ii) Termination of all claims or states of belligerency and respect for and acknowledgment of the sovereignty, territorial integrity and political independence of every State in the area and their right to live in peace within secure and recognized boundaries free from threats or acts of force;

2. *Affirms further* the necessity

(a) For guaranteeing freedom of navigation through international waterways in the area;

(b) For achieving a just settlement of the refugee problem;

(c) For guaranteeing the territorial inviolability and political independence of every State in the area, through measures including the establishment of demilitarized zones;

3. *Requests* the Secretary-General to designate a Special Representative to proceed to the Middle East to establish and maintain contacts with the States concerned in order to promote agreement and assist efforts to achieve a peaceful and accepted settlement in accordance with the provisions and principles in this resolution;

4. *Requests* the Secretary-General to report to the Security Council on the progress of the efforts of the Special Representative as soon as possible.

Adopted unanimously.

U.N. Security Council Resolution 338 of 22 October 1973.

The Security Council

1. *Calls upon* all parties to the present fighting to cease all firing and terminate all military activity immediately, no later than 12 hours after the moment of the adoption of this decision, in the positions they now occupy;

2. *Calls upon* the parties concerned to start immediately after the cease-fire the implementation of Security Council resolution 242 (1967) in all of its parts;

3. *Decides* that, immediately and concurrently with the cease-fire, negotiations shall start between the parties concerned under appropriate auspices aimed at establishing a just and durable peace in the Middle East.

Adopted ... by 14 votes to none.
One member (China) did not participate in the voting.

Appendix K
Suggested Readings

This is a selection of books that many of us have found valuable in understanding both the tensions between Israelis and Palestinians and a variety of nonviolent approaches to resolving this conflict and others. That we found a book useful does not necessary mean that we agree with all or even most of what it says, but rather that we believe it expresses a perspective that needs to be heard and considered. The categories into which we have placed these books are imprecise. Many works could fit easily in more than one place (e.g., Israeli and Palestinian peacemaking efforts, Palestinian citizens of Israel) so we encourage you to look through the entire list if you are interested in a particular topic.

Nonviolence/Peacemaking/Negotiations

Ackerman, Peter, and Christopher Krueger. *Strategic Nonviolent Conflict: The Dynamics of People Power in the Twentieth Century.* Westport, Conn.: Praeger, 1994.

American Friends Service Committee. *Search for Peace in the Middle East.* New York: Fawcett Publications, 1970.

Bar-On, Mordechai. *In Pursuit of Peace: A History of the Israeli Peace Movement.* Washington, D.C.: U.S. Institute of Peace, 1996.

Bing, Anthony. *Israeli Pacifist: The Life of Joseph Abileah.* Syracuse, NY: Syracuse University Press, 1990.

Bondurant, Joan V. *Conquest of Violence: The Gandhian Philosophy of Conflict.* Princeton: Princeton University Press, 1958.

Burge, Gary. *Who are God's People in the Middle East?* Grand Rapids, Mich.: Zondervan, 1993.

Cobban, Helena. *The Moral Architecture of World Peace: Nobel Laureates Discuss our Global Future.* Charlottesville: University of Virginia Press, 2000.

Easwaran, Eknath. *Nonviolent Soldier of Islam: Badshah Khan, A Man to Match His Mountains,* 2d ed. Tomales, Calif.: Nilgiri Press, 1999.

Enderlin, Charles. *Shattered Dreams: The Failure of the Peace Process in the Middle East, 1995-2002.* Translated by Susan Fairfield. New York: Other Press, 2003.

Fisk, Larry and John Schellenberg, eds. *Patterns of Conflict, Paths to Peace.* Peterborough, Ont.: Broadview Press, 2000.

Galtung, Johan. *Nonviolence and Israel/Palestine.* Honolulu: University of Hawaii Institute for Peace, 1989.

Gandhi, M. K. *Non-Violent Resistance.* New York: Schocken Books, 1951.

Gish, Arthur G. *Hebron Journal: Stories of Nonviolent Peacemaking.* Scottdale, Penn. and Waterloo, Ont.: Herald Press, 2001.

Gregg, Richard B. *The Power of Nonviolence,* 2d ed. New York: Schocken Books, 1935; reprint, Nyack, NY: Fellowship Publications, 1959.

Hedges, Chris. *War is a Force That Gives Us Meaning.* New York: PublicAffairs/Perseus Books, 2003.

Herr, Robert, and Judy Zimmerman Herr, eds. *Transforming Violence: Linking Local and Global Peacemaking.* Scottdale, Penn. and Waterloo, Ontario: Herald Press, 1998.

Holmes, Robert, ed. *Nonviolence in Theory and Practice.* Prospect Heights, Ill.: Waveland Press, 1990.

International Crisis Group. *Middle East Endgame I: Getting to a Comprehensive Arab-Israeli Peace Settlement.* Amman, Washington, and Brussels: ICG, 2002.

International Crisis Group. *Middle East Endgame II: How a Comprehensive Israeli-Palestinian Peace Would Look.* Amman, Washington, and Brussels: ICG, 2002.

Kaminer, Reuven. *The Politics of Protest: The Israeli Peace Movement and the Palestinian Intifada.* Brighton, UK: Sussex Academic Press, 1995.

Lampen, John, ed. *No Alternative? Nonviolent Responses to Repressive Regimes.* York, UK: William Sessions, 2000.

Lederach, John Paul. *Building Peace: Sustainable Reconciliation in Divided Societies.* Washington, D.C.: U.S. Institute of Peace Press, 1997.

Lederach, John Paul. *The Journey Toward Reconciliation.* Scottdale, Penn. and Waterloo, Ont.: Herald Press, 1999.

Lerner, Michael. *Healing Israel/Palestine: A Path to Peace and Reconciliation.* Berkeley, Calif.: North Atlantic Books, 2003.

MacQueen, Graeme, ed. *Unarmed Forces: Nonviolent Action in Central America and the Middle East.* Toronto: Science for Peace/Samuel Stevens, 1992.

Merton, Thomas. *The Nonviolent Alternative.* New York: Farrar, Strauss & Giroux, 1970.

Mendelsohn, Everett. *A Compassionate Peace: A Future for Israel, Palestine, and the Middle East,* rev. ed. New York: Farrar, Straus & Giroux, 1982, 1989.

Niyonzima, David, and Lon Fendall. *Unlocking Horns: Forgiveness and Reconciliation in Burundi.* Newberg, Org.: Barclay Press, 2001.

Nunn, Maxine. *Creative Resistance: Anecdotes of Nonviolent Action by Israeli-Based Groups.* Jerusalem: Alternative Information Center, 1993.

Rantisi, Audeh, with Ralph Beebe. *Blessed are the Peacemakers: A Palestinian Christian in the Occupied West Bank.* Grand Rapids, Michigan: Zondervan Books, 1990.

Reinhart, Tanya. *Israel/Palestine: How to End the War of 1948.* New York: Seven Stories Press, 2002.

Ruether, Rosemary Radford, and Marc Ellis, eds. *Beyond Occupation: American Jewish, Christian, and Palestinian Voices for Peace.* Boston: Beacon Press, 1995.

Saunders, Harold H. *The Other Walls: The Arab-Israeli Peace Process in a Global Perspective,* rev. ed. Princeton: Princeton University Press, 1991.

Savir, Uri. *The Process: 1,100 Days That Changed the Middle East.* New York: Random House, 1998.

Solomonow, Allan, ed. *Roots of Jewish Nonviolence.* Nyack, NY: Jewish Peace Fellowship/Fellowship of Reconciliation, 1985.

Wagner, Don. *Anxious for Armageddon: A Call to Partnership for Middle Eastern and Western Christians.* Scottdale, Penn. and Waterloo, Ont: Herald Press, 1995.

Wallach, John and Janet Wallach, *Still Small Voices.* New York: Citadel Press, 1990.

Whitlock, Katherine. *In a Time of Broken Bones: A Call to Dialogue on Hate Violence and the Limitations of Hate Crimes Legislation.* Philadelphia: American Friends Service Committee, 2001.

Wink, Walter. *Engaging the Powers: Discernment and Resistance in a World of Domination.* Minneapolis: Fortress Press, 1992.

Wink, Walter, ed. *Peace is the Way: Writings on Nonviolence from the Fellowship of Reconciliation.* Maryknoll, New York: Orbis Books, 2000.

Woolman, John. *The Journal and Major Essays of John Woolman,* edited by Phillips P. Moulton. Richmond, Ind.: Friends United Press, 1971.

Israeli-Palestinian Relations

Abdo, Nahla, and Ronit Lentin, eds. *Women and the Politics of Military Confrontation: Palestinian and Israeli Gendered Narratives of Dislocation.* New York: Berghahn Books, 2002.

Armstrong, Karen. *Jerusalem: One City, Three Faiths.* New York: A. A. Knopf, 1996; reprint, New York: Ballantine Books, 1997.

Beinin, Joel, and Lisa Hajjar. *Palestine, Israel and the Arab-Israeli Conflict: A Primer.* Washington, D.C.: Middle East Research and Information Project, 2001.

B'Tselem. *A Policy of Discrimination: Land Expropriation, Planning, and Building in East Jerusalem.* Jerusalem: B'Tselem, 1995.

Benvenisti, Meron. *Sacred Landscape: The Buried History of the Holy Land since 1948.* Translated by Maxine Kaufman-Lacusta. Berkeley: University of California Press, 2000.

Chapman, Colin. *Whose Promised Land?* 2d ed. Batavia, Ill: Lion, 1992.

Cheshin, Amir, Bill Hutman, and Avi Melamed. *Separate and Unequal: The Inside Story of Israeli Rule in East Jerusalem.* Cambridge, Mass.: Harvard University Press, 1999.

Dumper, Michael. *The Politics of Jerusalem since 1967.* New York: Columbia University Press, 1997.

Eliav, Arie Lova. *Land of the Heart: Israelis, Arabs, the Territories, and a Vision of the Future.* Philadelphia: Jewish Publication Society of America, 1974.

Fernea, Elizabeth and Evelyn Hocking, eds. *Israelis and Palestinians: The Struggle for Peace.* Austin: University of Texas Press, 1992.

Gerner, Deborah J. *One Land, Two Peoples: The Conflict over Palestine,* 2d ed. Boulder, Colo.: Westview Press, 1994.

Gerner, Deborah J., and Jillian Schwedler, eds. *Understanding the Contemporary Middle East,* 2d ed. Boulder, Colo.: Lynne Rienner, 2004.

Hirst, David. *The Gun and the Olive Branch: The Roots of Violence in the Middle East,* 2d ed. New York: Thunder's Mouth Press, 2003.

Hourani, Albert. *A History of Arab Peoples.* Cambridge, Mass.: Harvard University Press, 1991.

Human Rights Watch. *Second Class: Discrimination against Palestinian Arab Children in Israel's Schools.* New York: Human Rights Watch, 2001.

Israeli, Raphael. *Jerusalem Divided: The Armistice Regime 1947-1967.* London: Frank Cass, 2002.

The Jaffee Center Study Group. *The West Bank and Gaza: Israel's Options for Peace*. Tel Aviv: Tel Aviv University, 1989.

The Jaffee Center Study Group. *Israel, the West Bank and Gaza: Toward a Solution*. Tel Aviv: Tel Aviv University, 1989.

Laqueur, Walter, and Barry Rubin, eds. *The Israel-Arab Reader: A Documentary History of the Middle East Conflict*, 6th ed. New York: Penguin Books, 2001.

Lesch, Ann M., and Dan Tschirgi. *Origins and Development of the Arab-Israeli Conflict*. Westport, Conn.: Greenwood Press, 1998.

Morris, Benny. *The Birth of the Palestinian Refugee Problem, 1947-1949*. Cambridge: Cambridge University Press, 1987.

Morris, Benny. *Righteous Victims: A History of the Zionist-Arab Conflict, 1881-1999*. New York: Knopf, 1999.

Pappé, Ilan. *The Making of the Arab-Israeli Conflict, 1947-1951*. New York: I. B. Tauris, 1992.

Pappé, Ilan, ed. *The Israel/Palestine Question*. New York: Routledge, 1999.

Reich, Bernard, ed. *Arab-Israeli Conflict and Conciliation: A Documentary History*. Westport, Conn.: Greenwood Press, 1995.

Romann, Michael, and Alex Weingrod. *Living Together Separately: Arabs and Jews in Contemporary Jerusalem*. Princeton: Princeton University Press, 1991.

Ruether, Rosemary Radford, and Herman J. *The Wrath of Jonah: The Crisis of Religious Nationalism and Israeli-Palestinian Conflict*. New York: HarperCollins, 1985; 2d ed. Minneapolis, Minn.: Fortress Press, 2002.

Said, Edward. *The Question of Palestine*. New York: Vintage, 1980.

Said, Edward. *The End of the Peace Process: Oslo and After.* New York: Pantheon, 2000.

Sharoni, Simona. *Gender and the Israeli-Palestinian Conflict: The Politics of Women's Resistance*. Syracuse: Syracuse University Press, 1995.

Shlaim, Avi. *The Iron Wall: Israel and the Arab World*, New York: W. W. Norton, 2000.

Tessler, Mark. 1994. *A History of the Israeli-Palestinian Conflict*. Bloomington: Indiana University Press, 1994.

Ucko, Hans. *The Spiritual Significance of Jerusalem for Jews, Christians, and Muslims*. Geneva: World Council of Churches, 1994.

Wasserstein, Bernard. *Divided Jerusalem: The Struggle for the Holy City*. New York: Yale Nota Bene, 2002.

Israel/Jewish Israelis/Judaism

Asher, Arian. *The Second Republic: Politics in Israel*. Chatham, NJ: Chatham House Publishers, 1997.

Avishai, Bernard. *The Tragedy of Zionism: Revolution and Democracy in the Land of Israel*. New York: Farrar, Strauss Giroux. 1985.

Beilin, Yossi. *Israel: A Concise Political History*. New York: St. Martin's Press, 1992.

Beit-Hallahmi, Benyamin. *Original Sins: Reflections on the History of Zionism and Israel*. Concord, Mass.: Pluto Press, 1992; reprint, New York: Olive Branch Press, 1993.

Carey, Roane, and Jonathan Shainin. The Other Israel: Voices of Refusal and Dissent. New York: The New Press, 2002.

Ellis, Marc. *Toward a Jewish Theology of Liberation: The Uprising and the Future*, 2d ed. Maryknoll, NY: Orbis Books, 1989.

Ellis, Marc. *Israel and Palestine Out of the Ashes: The Search for Jewish Identity in the Twenty-First Century*. London: Pluto Press, 2002.

Evron, Boas. *Jewish State or Israeli Nation?* Bloomington: Indiana University Press, 1995.

Flapan, Simha. *The Birth of Israel: Myths and Realities*. New York: Pantheon, 1987.

Friedman, Robert. *Zealots for Zion: Inside Israel's West Bank Settlement Movement*. New York: Random House, 1992.

Grossman, David. *Death as a Way of Life: Israel Ten Years After Oslo*. Translated by Haim Watzman. New York: Farrar, Straus & Giroux, 2003.

Hazony, Yoram. *The Jewish State: The Struggle for Israel's Soul*. New York: Basic Books, 2000.

Horovitz, David. *A Little Too Close to God: The Thrills and Panic of a Life in Israel*. New York: A. A. Knopf, 2000.

Kushner, Tony, and Alisa Solomon, eds. *Wrestling with Zion: Progressive Jewish-American Responses to the Israeli-Palestinian Conflict*. New York: Grove Publishing, 2003.

Lustick, Ian. *For the Land and the Lord: Jewish Fundamentalism in Israel*. New York: Council on Foreign Relations, 1988.

March, W. Eugene. *Israel and the Politics of Land: A Theological Case Study*. Louisville, Ky.: Westminster/John Knox Press 1994.

Masalha, Nur. *Expulsion of the Palestinians: The Concept of 'Transfer' in Zionist Political Thought, 1982-1948.* Washington, D.C.: Institute for Palestine Studies, 1992.

Oz, Amos. *In the Land of Israel.* Translated by Maurie Goldberg-Bartura. London: Hogarth Press, 1983; reprint, New York: Vintage Books, 1984.

Sacher, Howard M. *A History of Israel: From the Rise of Zionism to Our Time,* 2d ed., New York: Knopf, 1996.

Sacher, Howard M. ed. *The Rise of Israel: A Documentary Record from the Nineteenth Century to 1948.* New York: Garland Publishing, 1987.

Schiff, Ze'ev, and Ehud Ya'ari. *Israel's Lebanon War.* Translated by Ina Friedman. New York: Simon and Schuster, 1984.

Segev, Tom. *1949: The First Israelis.* New York: Free Press, 1986.

Shimoni, Gideon. *The Zionist Ideology.* Hanover: Brandeis University Press, 1995.

Shindler, Colin. *The Land Beyond Promise: Israel, Likud, and the Zionist Dream.* London: I. B. Tauris, 2002.

Sternhell, Zeev. *The Founding Myths of Israel: Nationalism, Socialism, and the Making of the Jewish State.* Translated by David Maisel. Princeton: Princeton University Press, 1998.

Stone, I. F. *Underground to Palestine and Reflections Thirty Years Later.* London: Hutchison of London, 1978.

Torstrick, Rebecca L. *The Limits of Coexistence: Identity Politics in Israel.* Ann Arbor: University of Michigan Press, 2000.

Vital, David. *Zionism: The Origins of Zionism.* Oxford, England: Clarendon Press, 1975.

Vital, David. *Zionism: The Formative Years.* Oxford, England: Clarendon Press, 1982.

Palestine/Palestinians

Abu-Amr, Ziad. *Islamic Fundamentalism in the West Bank and Gaza: Muslim Brotherhood and Islamic Jihad.* Bloomington: Indiana University Press, 1994.

Abu-Lughod, Ibrahim, ed. *The Transformation of Palestine.* Evanston, Ill.: Northwestern University Press, 1971; reprint, 1987.

Aruri, Naseer, ed. *Palestinian Refugees: The Right of Return.* London: Pluto Press, 2001.

Ashrawi, Hanan. *This Side of Peace: A Personal Account.* New York: Simon and Schuster, 1995.

Ateek, Naim. *Justice and Only Justice: A Palestinian Theology of Liberation.* Maryknoll, NY: Orbis Books, 1989.

Ateek, Naim, and Michael Prior, eds. *Holy Land, Hollow Justice: God, Justice, and the Palestinians.* London: Melisende, 1999.

Barghouti, Mourid. *I Saw Ramallah.* Translated by Ahdaf Soueif. New York: Anchor Books, 2003.

Brynen, Rex. *A Very Political Economy: Peacebuilding and Foreign Aid in the West Bank and Gaza.* Washington, D.C.: U.S. Institute of Peace, 2000.

Chacour, Elias. *Blood Brothers.* Grand Rapids, Mich.: Chosen, 1984.

Chacour, Elias. *We Belong to the Land.* San Francisco: Harper Collins, 1990.

Cobban, Helena. *The Palestinian Liberation Organization: People, Power, and Politics,* Cambridge: Cambridge University Press, 1984.

Cragg, Kenneth. *The Arab Christian: A History in the Middle East.* Louisville, Ky.: Westminster, 1991.

Farsoun, Samih K., with Christina E. Zacharia. *Palestine and the Palestinians.* Boulder, Colo.: Westview Press, 1997.

Ghanem, As'ad. *The Palestinian-Arab Minority in Israel, 1948-2000.* New York: State University of New York Press, 2001.

Gorkin, Michael. *Days of Honey, Days of Onion: The Story of a Palestinian Family in Israel.* Berkeley: University of California Press, 1993.

Hass, Amira. *Drinking the Sea at Gaza: Days and Nights in a Land Under Siege,* Translated by Elana Wesley and Maxine Kaufman-Lacusta. New York: Metropolitan Books, 1999.

Hass, Amira. *Reporting from Ramallah: An Israeli Journalist in an Occupied Land.* Translated by Rachel Leah Jones. Los Angeles: Semiotexte, 2003.

Hiltermann, Joost R. *Behind The Intifada: Labor and Women's Movements in the Occupied Territories.* Princeton, N.J.: Princeton University Press, 1991.

Jabbour, Hala Deeb. *A Woman of Nazareth.* New York: Olive Branch Press, 1988.

Lynd, Staughton, Sam Bahour, and Alice Lynd, eds. *Homeland: Oral Histories of Palestine and Palestinians.* New York: Olive Branch Press, 1994.

Kanafani, Ghassan. *Palestine's Children: Returning to Haifa and Other Stories.* Translated by Barbara Harlow and Karen E. Riley. Boulder: Lynne Rienner Publishers, 2000.

Khalidi, Rashid. *Palestinian Identity: The Construction of Modern National Consciousness.* New York: Columbia University Press, 1997.

Kimmerling, Baruch, and Joel S. Migdal. *The Palestinian People: A History.* Cambridge, Mass.: Harvard University Press, 2003.

Mattar, Philip, ed. *Encyclopedia of the Palestinians* .New York: Facts on File, 2000.

Pearlman, Wendy. *Occupied Voices: Stories of Everyday Life from the Second Intifada.* New York: Thunder's Mouth Press, 2003.

Raheb, Mitri. *I am a Palestinian Christian.* Translated by Ruth C. L. Gritsch. Minneapolis: Fortress Press, 1995.

Rigby, Andrew. *Living the Intifada.* London: Zed Books, 1991.

Robinson, Glenn E. *Building a Palestinian State: The Incomplete Revolution.* Bloomington: Indiana University Press, 1997.

Rouhana, Nadim N. *Palestinian Citizens in an Ethnic Jewish State: Identities in Conflict.* New Haven, Conn.: Yale University Press, 1997.

Rubenberg, Cheryl A. *The Palestinians: In Search of a Just Peace.* Boulder, Colo.: Lynne Rienner, 2003.

Saad-Ghorayeb, Amal. *Hizbu'llah: Politics and Religion.* London: Pluto Press, 2002.

Sayigh, Rosemary. *Too Many Enemies: The Palestinian Experience in Lebanon.* London: Zed Press, 1994.

Sayigh, Yezid. *Armed Struggle and the Search for State: The Palestinian National Movement, 1949-1993.* Oxford, England: Clarendon Press, 1997.

Sennott, Charles M. *The Body and the Blood: The Middle East's Vanishing Christians and the Possibility for Peace.* New York: PublicAffairs/Perseus Books, 2003.

Usher, Graham. *Palestine in Crisis: The Struggle for Peace and Political Independence after Oslo.* Chicago: Pluto Press, 1995.

U.S. Policy Toward the Conflict

Aruri, Nasser H. *The Obstruction of Peace: The United States, Israel, and the Palestinians.* Monroe, Me.: Common Courage Press, 1995.

Aruri, Naseer H. *Dishonest Broker: The U.S. Role in Israel and Palestine.* Cambridge, Mass.: South End Press, 2003.

Chomsky, Noam. *The Fateful Triangle: The United States, Israel, and the Palestinians.* Boston. South End Press, 1983.

Christison, Kathleen. *Perceptions of Palestine: Their Influence on U.S. Middle East Policy.* Berkeley: University of California Press, 1999.

Findley, Paul. *Deliberate Deceptions: Facing the Facts about the U.S.-Israeli Relationship.* New York: Lawrence Hill Books, 1995.

Lesch, David W., ed. *The Middle East and the United States: A Historical and Political Reassessment.* Boulder, Colo.: Westview Press, 1996.

Neff, Donald. *Fallen Pillars: U.S. Policy towards Palestine and Israel since 1945.* Washington, D.C.: Institute for Palestine Studies, 1995.

Quandt, William B. *Peace Process: American Diplomacy and the Arab-Israeli Conflict Since 1967.* Berkeley: University of California Press, 1993.

Rubenberg, Cheryl. *Israel in American National Interest: A Critical Examination.* Urbana: University of Illinois Press, 1986.

Schoenbaum, David. *The United States and the State of Israel.* Oxford, England: Oxford University Press, 1993.

Slonim, Shlomo. *Jerusalem in America's Foreign Policy, 1947-1997.* London: Kluwer Law International, 1998.

Spiegel, Steven L. *The Other Arab-Israeli Conflict: Making America's Middle East Policy, from Truman to Reagan.* Chicago: University of Chicago Press, 1985.

Suleiman, Michael W., ed. *U.S. Policy on Palestine from Wilson to Clinton.* Normal, Ill.: Association of Arab-American University Graduates, Inc., 1995.

Appendix L

Contact information and web-based resources

This compilation is not an exhaustive list of organizations working on the Israeli-Palestinian issue. However, many of the websites listed provide links to other organizations. We have provided the mailing address, phone number, and fax wherever possible. Most browsers can find a website if you just type in the URL as follows, but some older ones may need you to type "http://" beforehand. Listing a website does not mean endorsement of the contents of the site.

United Nations Websites

UNISPAL – United Nations Information System on the Question of Palestine
domino.un.org/UNISPAL.NSF?OpenDatabase

Fourth Geneva Convention
www.hri.ca/uninfo/treaties/93.shtml

UNRWA – United Nations Relief and Works Agency
www.un.org/unrwa/

UNDP – United Nations Development Program
www.undp.org/

Quaker Organizations

American Friends Service Committee - Middle East Programs
1501 Cherry Street, Philadelphia, PA 19102 U.S.A.
Tel: +1 (215) 241-7000 Fax: +1 (215) 241-7177
www.afsc.org/middleeast/default.htm

Friends Committee on National Legislation
245 Second Street, NE, Washington, DC, 20002-5795 U.S.A.
Tel: (800) 630-1330   Fax: +1 (202) 547-6019
www.fcnl.org/

Friends General Conference
1216 Arch St #2B, Philadelphia, PA 19107 U.S.A.
www.fgcquaker.org/

Friends United Meeting
101 Quaker Hill Drive, Richmond, IN 47374-1980 U.S.A.
Tel: +1 (765) 962-7573 Fax: +1 (765) 966-1293
www.fum.org/

Quaker Peace and Social Witness
Friends House, 173-177 Euston Road, London NW1 2BJ U.K.
Tel: + (44) 207 663-1073 Fax: + (44) 20 7 663-1049
www.quaker.org.uk/peace/about.html

Quaker United Nations Office
777 UN Plaza, New York, NY 10017 U.S.A.
Tel: +1 (212) 682-2745 Fax: +1 (212) 983-0034
www.quno.org/

Quaker United Nations Office
13 Avenue du Mervelet, 1209 Geneva, Switzerland
Tel: +41 (22) 748-48-00   Fax: +41 (22) 748-48-19
e-mail: quno@quno.ch

Israeli Peace and Human Rights Organizations

Bat-Shalom is a feminist center for peace and social justice.
P.O. Box 8083, Jerusalem 91080 Israel
Tel: + (972) 2 563-1477   Fax: + (972) 2 561-7983
www.batshalom.org/

B'Tselem is an information center for human rights in the occupied territories.
8 HaTa'asiya St. (4th Floor), Jerusalem 93420, Israel.
Tel: + (972) 2 6735599   Fax: + (972) 2 6749111
www.btselem.org/

The following organizations support Israeli soldiers who refuse to serve in the occupied territories or those who refuse to serve in the Israeli army altogether:
www.couragetorefuse.org/english/default.asp
www.yesh-gvul.org/english/
www.shministim.org/english/index.htm
www.newprofile.org/

Coalition of Women for Peace in Israel
www.coalitionofwomen4peace.org/

Defense for Children International, Israel promotes the rights of children in Israel and areas under Israeli jurisdiction.
DCI - 2 Yizhak Elhanan Street, Jerusalem, P.O.B 8028, Israel
Tel: + (972) 2–563-3003 Fax: + (972) 2 5631241
www.dci.org.il/home_en.asp

Gush Shalom is a peace organization whose primary goal is to influence Israeli public opinion towards peace and reconciliation with the Palestinian people.
POB 3322, Tel-Aviv 61033, Israel
www.gush-shalom.org/english/index.html

Israeli Committee Against House Demolitions is a network of Israeli NGOs working to end the occupation with a focus on ending the Israeli policy and practice of home demolitions.
P.O Box 2030, Jerusalem 91020 Israel
www.icahd.org/eng/

Peace Now was founded in 1978 by reserve officers of the Israeli Defense Forces.
www.peacenow.org/shalom_achshav.html

Physicians for Human Rights in Israel
52 Golomb St. Tel Aviv 66171 Israel
Tel: + (972) 3 687-3718 Fax: + (972) 3 687-3029
www.phr.org.il/phr/Pages/PhrHomepage.asp

Public Committee Against Torture in Israel
P.O.B. 4634, Jerusalem 91046 Israel
Tel: + (972) 2 642-9825 Fax: + (972) 2 643-2847
www.stoptorture.org.il/

Rabbis for Human Rights gives voice to the Jewish tradition of human rights.
42 Gaza Road, Jerusalem, 92384 Israel
Tel: + (972) 2 568-7731 Fax: + (972) 2 566-2815
www.rhr.israel.net

Organizations of Palestinians inside Israel

Adalah works to protect human rights in general and those of Palestinian citizens of
Israel in particular.
PO Box 510, Shafa'amr, 20200 Israel
Tel: + (972) 4 950-1610   Fax: + (972) 4 950-3140
www.adalah.org/eng/index.php

Arab Association for Human Rights promotes and protects the rights of the Palestinian
minority living in Israel.
HRA - The Arab Association for Human Rights
P.O. Box 215, Nazareth 16101 Israel
Tel: + (972) 4 656-1923   Fax: + (972) 4 656-4934
www.arabhra.org/

Association of Forty works for the official recognition of unrecognized Palestinian villages in
Israel.
Ein Hod, near Nir Etzion, 30808, Israel.
www.assoc40.org/

Galilee Society works to achieve equality in health, environmental, and socio-economic conditions and opportunities for Palestinian citizens in Israel.
P.O. Box 330, Shefa-Amr 20200 Israel
Tel: + (972) 4 986-1171/2 Fax: +(972) 4 986-1173
www.gal-soc.org/

Ittijah is a network of Palestinian non-governmental organizations (NGOs) in Israel.
Union of the Arab Community Based Organizations
P.O.Box 9577, Haifa 31095, Israel
www.ittijah.org/

Palestinian Peace and Human Rights
Organizations in West Bank and Gaza

Al-Haq, the West Bank affiliate of the Geneva-based International Commission of Jurists protects and promotes the principles of human rights and the rule of law.
P.O. Box 1413, Ramallah, West Bank, Palestine
www.alhaq.org/

Al-Mezan Center is based in Jabalia Refugee Camp, Gaza; works for the promotion of human rights in the occupied territories.
P.O.Box: 2714 Main St, Jabalia Camp, Gaza Strip, Palestine
Tel.: + (972) 8 245-3555 Fax: + (972) 8 245-3554
www.mezan.org/

Applied Research Institute of Jerusalem promotes sustainable development in the occupied Palestinian territories and the self-reliance of the Palestinian people through greater control over their natural resources. Their website carries good maps.
ARIJ, P.O.Box 860, Bethlehem, West Bank, Palestine
www.arij.org/

Badil is a community-based organization providing information and analysis on Palestinian refugee issues.
P.O. Box 728, Bethlehem, West Bank, Palestine
www.badil.org/

Birzeit University Guide to Palestinian Websites
www.birzeit.edu/links

Defense for Children International-Palestine promotes the rights of Palestinian children in the West Bank and Gaza.
Al-Bireh/Ramallah Office, Al-Khoulafa' Street, Al-Sartawi Building, Second Floor
Tel: + (972) 2 240-7530   Fax: + (972) 2 240-7018
www.dci-pal.org/

Health Development and Information Policy Institute undertakes policy research and planning regarding the Palestinian health care system.
www.hdip.org/

Holy Land Trust is dedicated to strengthening the lives of children, families, and communities.
P.O. Box 127 Manger Street, Bethlehem, West Bank, Palestine
Tel: + (972) 2 276-5930 Fax: + (972) 2 276-5931
www.holylandtrust.org/

MIFTAH is an institution that fosters the principles of democracy and effective dialogue based on the free exchange of information and ideas.
P.O. Box 38588, Jerusalem 97800 via Israel
Tel: + (972) 2 585-1842 Fax: + (972) 2 583-5184
www.miftah.org/

Palestinian Centre for Human Rights promotes human rights, the rule of law, and democratic principles in the occupied territories; the Gaza affiliate of the Geneva-based International Commission of Jurist and the International Federation for Human Rights.
P.O. Box 1328, Gaza City, Gaza Strip, Palestine
Tel/Fax: + (972) 8 282-4776/5893/3725
www.pchrgaza.org/

Palestinian Centre for Rapprochement Between Peoples, located in Beit Sahour, provides information on the International Solidarity Movement.
P.O. Box 24, Beit Sahour, West Bank, Palestine
www.rapprochement.org/

Palestinian Environmental NGOs Network:
PENGON, P.O.B. 25220, Beit Hanina, East Jerusalem, via Israel
Tel: + (972) 2 676-9460 Fax: + (972) 2 676-8011
www.pengon.org/
www.stopthewall.org/

PINGO is a Palestinian non-governmental network.
P.O. Box 2322, Ramallah, West Bank, Palestine
Tel: + (972) 2 296-3847 Fax: + (972) 2 296-3848
www.pngo.net/

Sabeel is an ecumenical grassroots liberation theology movement among Palestinian Christians.
P.O. Box 49084, East Jerusalem, 91491 via Israel
Tel: + (972) 2 532-7136 Fax: + (972) 2 532-7137
www.sabeel.org/

Wi'am is a grassroots organization that addresses injustices on both sides of the conflict and promotes human rights and peace among all people.
P.O. Box 1039 Bethlehem, West Bank, Palestine
Tel: + (972) 2 277-0513
www.planet.edu/~alaslah/

Joint Israeli-Palestinian Sites

Bitterlemons
www.bitterlemons.org/

Israeli-Palestinian Center for Research and Information
www.ipri.org/index1.html

Neve Shalom — Wahat al-Salam
www.nswas.com/

Parents' Circle/Families Forum includes Palestinian and Israelis families who have lost a family member as a result of the Arab-Israeli conflict.
Israeli-Palestinian Bereaved Families for Peace
Hayasmin 1 St., Ramat-Efal, 52960 Israel
Tel: + (972) 3 535-5089 Fax: + (972) 3 6358367
www.theparentscircle.com/parents/

Ta'ayush
www.taayush.org/

Web-based Alternative Media

Media criticism and links to international press sites.
www.abunimah.org/

Breaking news, fact sheets on human rights, and background documents.
www.alternativenews.org/

Challenge Magazine on line
www.hanitzotz.com/challenge/

Common Dreams
www.commondreams.org/

Electronic Intifada publishes news, commentary, analysis, and reference materials on the Israeli-Palestinian conflict from a Palestinian perspective.
electronicintifada.net/new.shtml

Ha'aretz Israeli English daily on line.
www.haaretzdaily.com/

Jerusalem Media and Communication Center/Palestine Report
www.jmcc.org/

Middle East Research and Information Project
www.merip.org/

Palestine Independent Media Center
www.palestine.indymedia.org/

Palestine Monitor
www.palestinemonitor.org/

Palestine Media Watch
www.palestine-pmc.com/

Tikkun, a monthly journal produced by Rabbi Michael Lerner
www.tikkun.org/

Washington Report on Middle East Affairs
www.washington-report.org

Znet is an American Jewish website of alternative news and analysis.
www.zmag.org/

Governmental Websites

Israeli Government Ministry of Information
www.mfa.gov.il/mfa/home.asp

Palestinian National Authority
www.pna.org/

Israeli Ministry of Information
www.israel.gov.il/eng/min-dat.asp

Palestinian Central Bureau of Statistics
www.pcbs.org/

Organizations Outside Palestine/Israel

Al-Awdah
PRRC, P.O. Box 1172, Orange, CT 06477 U.S.A.
www.al-awda.org/

American-Arab Anti-Discrimination Committee
4201 Connecticut Ave, NW, Washington, D.C. 20008, U.S.A.
Tel: + 1 (202) 244-2990 Fax: + 1 (202) 244-3196
www.adc.org/

American Muslims for Jerusalem
208 G Street, NE, Washington, DC 20002 U.S.A.
Tel: +1 (202) 548-4200 Fax: + 1 (202) 548-4201
www.amjerusalem.org/

Americans for Peace Now
1101 14th Street, NW, 6th Floor, Washington, DC 20005 U.S.A.
Tel: + 1 (202) 728-893 Fax: +1 (202) 728-895
www.peacenow.org/about.html

Amnesty International
www.amnesty.org/

Brit Tzedek V'Shalom
P.O. Box 180175, Chicago, IL 60618-0175 U.S.A.
Tel: + 1 (773) 583-5747 Fax: +1 (773) 583-5772
www.btvshalom.org/

Canadian Friends of Peace Now
1054 Centre Street Suite 312, Thornhill, Ontario L4J 8E5 Canada
Tel: +1(905) 707-5308 Fax: +1(905) 707-5464
www.peacenowcanada.org/

Canadian-Palestinian Educational Exchange
323 Chapel Street, 3rd Level, Ottawa, Ontario, K1N 7Z2 Canada
Tel: +1(613) 236-7825 Fax: +1 (613) 237-5969
www.cepal.ca/

Center for Economic and Social Rights
162 Montague St., 2nd Floor, Brooklyn, NY 11201 U.S.A.
Tel: +1 (718) 237-9145 Fax: +1 (718) 237-9147
www.cesr.org/

Christian Aid – UK
35 Lower Marsh, Waterloo, London, SE1 7RL U.K.
Tel: + 44 (207) 620-4444 Fax: + 44 (207) 620- 0719
www.christian-aid.org.uk/

Christian Peacemaker Teams
Box 6508, Chicago, IL 60680-6508   U.S.A.
Tel: +1 (773) 277-0253 Fax: +1 (773) 277-0291
www.cpt.org/

Churches for Middle East Peace
110 Maryland Ave NE, #311
Washington DC 20002   U.S.A.
Tel: +1 (202) 543-1222 Fax: +1 (202) 543-5025
www.cmep.org/

Council for the Advancement of Arab-British Understanding
1 Gough Square, London EC4A 3DE   U.K.
Tel: + 44 (207) 832-1310 Fax: + 44 (270) 832-1329
www.caabu.org/

Council for American Islamic Relations
453 New Jersey Ave., S.E. Washington, D.C. 20003 U.S.A.
Tel: + 1 (202) 488-8787 Fax: + 1 (202) 488-0833
www.cair-net.org/

European Jews for Justice for Palestinians
EJJP p/a EAJG Postbox 59506
1040 LA Amsterdam, Netherlands
Tel: + 31 (2) 679-5850/664-1687

Evangelicals for Middle East Understanding
P.O. Box 553, Union, WA 98592-0553 U.S.A.
www.emeu.net/

Fellowship of Reconciliation
P.O. Box 271, Nyack, NY 10960 U.S.A.
Tel: +1 (845) 358-4601 Fax: +1 (845) 358-4924
www.forusa.org/

Foundation for Middle East Peace
1761 N St. NW, Washington, D.C. 20036 U.S.A.
tel: +1 (202) 835-3650 fax: +1 (202) 835-3651
www.fmep.org/

Human Rights Watch
1630 Connecticut Avenue, N.W., Suite 500, Washington, DC 20009   U.S.A.
tel: +1 (202) 612-4321 fax: +1 (202) 612-4333
www.hrw.org/

Institute for Palestine Studies
3501 M Street N.W, Washington, D.C. 20007 U.S.A.
tel : +1 (202) 342-3990 fax: +1 (202) 342-3927
www.ipsjps.org/

Institute of Policy Studies
www.ips.org/

International Committee of the Red Cross (has an excellent online library of international humanitarian law documents)
19 avenue de la Paix, CH 1202 Geneva, Switzerland
tel: +41 (22) 734- 6001 fax + 41 (22) 733-2057
www.icrc.org/eng

International Solidarity Movement
www.palsolidarity.org/

Jewish Peace Lobby
8604 Second Avenue, Suite 317, Silver Spring, MD 20910 U.S.A.
www.peacelobby.org/

Jewish Voice for Peace
1611 Telegraph Avenue, Suite 500, Oakland, CA 94612 U.S.A.
Tel: +1 (510) 465-1777 Fax: +1 (510) 465-1616
www.jewishvoiceforpeace.org/

Mennonite Central Committee
21 South 12th St., Akron, PA 17501-0500   U.S.A.
Tel: +1 (717) 859-1151or toll-free 1 (888) 563-4676
www.mcc.org/

Middle East Children's Alliance
901 Parker St., Berkeley, CA 94710   U.S.A.
www.mecaforpeace.org/

Not in My Name
2859 Central St., Evanston IL U.S.A.
Tel: (312) 409-4845
www.nimn.org/

Palestinian American Research Center
www.parcenter.org/

Palestinian Welfare Association
P.O. Box 6269 CH-1211 Geneva 6, Switzerland

Refuser Solidarity Network
P.O. Box 53474, Washington DC 20009-9474 U.S.A.
Tel: +1 (202) 232-1100
www.refusersolidarity.net/default.asp

US Campaign to End the Israeli Occupation
P.O. Box 59256, Philadelphia, PA 19102-5926 U.S.A.
www.endtheoccupation.org/

Visions of Peace with Justice in Israel/Palestine
P.O. Box 400479, Cambridge, MA 02140 U.S.A.
Tel : +1 (617) 984-0532
www.vopj.org/

World Council of Churches
PO Box 2100, 150 route de Ferney,
CH-1211 Geneva 2, Switzerland
Tel.: + 41 (22) 791-6111 Fax: + 41 (22) 791-0361
www.wcc-coe.org/

Women in Black (U.S.)
P.O. Box 20554, New York, NY 10021 U.S.A.
www.womeninback.net